GoodBEERGuide
WEST
COAST
USA

BEN McFARLAND
TOM SANDHAM

BOOKS

Published by the Campaign for Real Ale Ltd.
230 Hatfield Road
St Albans
Hertfordshire AL1 4LW

www.camra.org.uk/books

ISBN 978-1-85249-244-1

A CIP catalogue record for this book is available from
the British Library

Printed and bound in the United Kingdom at
the University Press, Cambridge

Managing Editor: Simon Hall
Project Editors: Ione Brown; Leon Gray (Aquithie
    Editorial Ltd); Debbie Williams
Editorial Assistance: Emma Haines; Katie Hunt
Design/Typography: Dale Tomlinson
Typefaces: FB Amplitude and Mercury Text
Maps: John Plumer (JP Map Graphics Ltd)
Picture Research: Sarah Airey (Nadine Bazar)
Senior Marketing Manager: Georgina Rudman

PICTURE CREDITS

The Publisher would like to
thank all those who have kindly
given their permission for it to
reproduce their photography in
this guide. Specific thanks go to:

Ben McFarland & Tom Sandham

Vanessa Courtier: 40; Larry
Geddis: 148, 156; Getty Images:
Todd Gipstein 6; Peter Marbach:
t198, 205; REX Features: CSU
Archives/Everett Collection 8,
Charles Sykes 11; San Diego
Convention & Visitors Bureau:
48, 50, 51, 52, 53; San Francisco
Convention & Visitors Bureau:
Phil Coblentz 102, 105, t&b106;
Speakeasy Brewery: 107; Travel
Alaska: Robin Hood 266; Yard
House: 21, 71

Contents

Introduction

American beer

"American cities now offer a diversity of beer styles far greater than that to be found in any single European country."

MICHAEL JACKSON, *the late and great 'Beer Hunter'*

If your initial reaction to a Good Beer Guide about America is "that's a daft idea" then you're probably not alone. The prevailing perception of American beer is hardly favourable. It's been the butt of unenlightened British beer drinkers' jokes for years. "Why is American beer served cold? So you can tell it from urine," is one such gag. "People who drink American beer don't like the taste of beer, they just like to pee a lot," is another. And then there's an even ruder one involving canoodling in a canoe that we couldn't possibly repeat. Google it if you must.

Brewtopia

All very humorous, that's for sure, but the 'funnies' have got it completely wrong. American beer doesn't begin with Bud and end with Miller. If you thought US beer was flavourless fizz, then – oh boy – have we got brews for you. Straight off the bat, let's get one thing straight: America makes some of the world's greatest beers and supplements them with a wider selection of imports than anywhere else you'll find.

Fun, fanatical, cutting edge, joyful, often outrageous and bridled in envelope-pushing zeal, America is beervana, it's brewtopia, it's beer-drinking heaven. In recent times, the gates of mass-marketed mediocrity have been stormed by hordes of joyful microbrewers who have transformed America from a laughing stock to the most adventurous beer-making nation on the planet.

Starting out with a clean brewing slate in the Seventies and born with the desire to be different, the American craft brewing brotherhood has thrown caution to the wind and passionately replicated European beer styles with a glint in its eye. The difference being that, of course, the American versions have been blown up into beers that are bigger, brasher, bolder – and unashamedly so. Some say they're too big, but that's like criticising Brazil for playing football with too much flair.

No other nation can compete with the sheer eclecticism of American ale: smoke-flavoured beers; herb and spice infused brews; American-style Hefeweizens; wood and barrel-aged beers; burly barley wines; pre-Prohibition lagers, honey beers and experimental ales brewed with pomegranate, coriander, beetroot and Kaffir lime leaves represent just a drop in America's bucket of brewing creativity.

Word of these beers is rippling across the Pond. In the UK, American craft beer is the next big thing in the rapidly expanding boutique beer market, with more and more Stateside suds taking on European ales in their own backyard.

The joy of American craft beer is an extraordinarily well-kept secret and one that this guide gleefully aims to let you in on. So come, whether hophead or beer beginner, slip between these covers, slide yourself onto the bar stool of enlightenment, fill your glass and come with us on an entertaining saunter through the beer-drinking wonderland that is the West Coast of America.

Why the West Coast?

Wherever you are in America, locally produced craft beer is never far away, with more than 1,500 breweries and brewpubs nationwide. Of course good ale is by no means exclusive to the West Coast, but that's our focus – not just because we like the sun and

Mickey Mouse, but also because it's the birthplace of American craft beer. Lest we forget, California, Oregon and Washington were the founding fathers of the microbrewing revolution and these states continue to lead the way.

The West Coast is the King Prawn on American beer's BBQ. The cities of Portland, Seattle and San Francisco are well-established beer towns, San Diego is the new kid on the brewing block and Los Angeles has some well-hidden gems.

Las Vegas, Alaska and Hawaii also feature. Whether they're 'West Coast' is up for debate but they're popular places to visit and all three hail the ale with plenty of zest and passion.

What is a craft brewer?

Craft brewer is a curve-ball label. Sadly, a little old man who lives in a shoe, tenderly dropping hops, one-by-one, into a cauldron of beer is far too romantic a vision. Instead, states the US Brewers Association, a craft brewer must be 'small, independent and traditional' – three nebulous terms that demand explanation.

Small means a craft brewer mustn't produce more than two million barrels a year – as always, small in America equals big elsewhere. To be *Independent*, 'less than 25% of the craft brewery must be owned or controlled (or equivalent economic interest) by an alcoholic beverage industry member who is not themselves a craft brewer'. To qualify as *Traditional*, 'a craft brewer must have either an all-malt flagship (the beer that represents the greatest volume among that brewer's brands) or at least 50% of its volume in either all-malt beers or in beers that use adjuncts to enhance rather than lighten flavour'.

Beyond these tight guidelines, however, craft brewing epitomises innovation, localism, distinction, flavour and an overwhelming desire to place a grenade down the underpants of big and bland beer.

What's in the Guide?

GBG West Coast USA is united with other foreign CAMRA beer guides in its eager pursuit and celebration of good beer. However, it is not a comprehensive catalogue of every single craft beer on the left coast and we make no apologies for that. An exhaustive

list of beers would be unfeasible and leave no room for the colour and characters that shape the West Coast's vibrant brewing scene. Instead, we've cherry-picked our favourite beers from each brewery and brewpub, and hope you like them too. In our bar reviews we haven't recommended a specific beer as there's no guarantee it'll be on tap when you get there.

Much like the Good Beer Guides to Belgium, Germany and the Czech Republic, *West Coast USA* is not a guide exclusive to cask beer either. If it were, it would be less a book and more a wafer-thin pamphlet. Cask ale is available in the USA but it's rarer than rocking horse doo-doo and commands a miniscule share of the craft beer market. However, American awareness of cask is growing and if a venue does happen to champion real ale, we have been sure to mention so.

An independent view

This guide is arranged by location. Of course, regional boundaries often blur so we've included a brief overview of each area, explaining our understanding of West Coast geography, history and beer culture.

While we have taken every step to ensure accuracy, there will inevitably be some venues that have changed names, changed hands, relocated or closed altogether. If you're embarking on a long trip to a particular venue, we strongly recommend you call ahead.

All the reviews featured in this guide are based on the experiences and opinions of the writers. All the bars were visited anonymously and the beers paid for. Much to the irritation of our bank managers, no bribe, payment or incentive helped to acquire or sway a write-up. The reviews are based on an array of factors ranging from beer selection and food, location, atmosphere and, predictably, our own personal take on things. Of course, there will be those who disagree with us, but therein lies the beauty of having opinions – if we all had the same ones, life would be jolly dull.

But now it's up to you to experience the beery delights of America's West Coast for yourself...

Cheers

BEN McFARLAND &
TOM SANDHAM

A brief history of the West Coast

THE WEST COAST is a new kid on the block in America. Men wearing loincloth skirts have inhabited the land for 25,000 years, but it is only within the last two centuries that humans have shaped the region that we recognise today. During that time, juvenile seafront metropolises have sprouted training-bra hotspots of international repute like San Diego, Los Angeles, San Francisco, Portland and Seattle, complete with skyscrapers and burgeoning populations. These cities are still separated and banked by gloriously picturesque wide-open spaces as rugged as they were when dinosaurs roamed the land. While the West Coast's short pants still have a few grass stains, the area continues to develop into one of the most vibrant and alluring parts of the world.

Going native

Inquisitive brainiacs who like to dig stuff up inform us that the West Coast has been inhabited since the Ice Age. Since they have unearthed some useful evidence in the form of cave paintings and once buried nick-nacks, we tend to believe them.

The first visitors came across the Bering Strait during the Ice Age when northeast Asia was connected by a convenient land bridge to Alaska. It's pretty chilly up in the northern climes, though, so these settlers high tailed it down south once they realised they could change three layers of bear fur for shark-skin Speedos in California.

When Europeans landed in the 1500s, most of the natives were residing in the warmer reaches. More than a million of them were frolicking around the West Coast, split into various tribes, speaking different languages, killing bears, fishing and generally living off the land.

Financial pressures were probably alien to these people, with little to suggest they were obsessed with material possessions. While territorial skirmishes occasionally broke out, for all intents and purposes it seemed the natives were peaceful people.

Unfortunately, peace-keeping skills weren't a strong point of the European visitors. Settlements that had evolved over millennia were wiped out in a relatively swift 350 years. Most of this conflict would take place in the middle of the continent, as explorers arriving by boat pushed the settlements westwards, only for them to be sandwiched, or 'burger-ed', when American expansion came the other way in the middle of the nineteenth century.

The early birds, 1542–1846

North America's evolution to its present form was largely a European experiment, and the West Coast is no different in this respect. Having conquered Mexico, it was the seafaring Spaniards who were first to land. Southern California was the earliest area for discovery. The Spaniards arrived on the understanding that there was lots of lovely lolly in California. Among the first to chance his arm was Juan Rodriguez Cabrillo in 1542 but, after this initial exploration, progress was slow.

Sir Frances Drake is credited with a landing north of San Francisco in 1579, but it took until the seventeenth century before the likes of navigator Sebastian Vizcaino voyaged as far north as Oregon, mapping and christening as he went. It wasn't until 1769 that the Spaniards started settling with the missionaries.

By this time, all sorts of people were roaming the West Coast, with the English, Russians and French all taking an interest.

So the Spaniards looked to secure the territory by converting the natives to Christianity. But the roll out of missionaries proved as successful as the *Titanic*'s game of iceberg chicken, and European diseases had more of an impact on locals than God.

The Spanish death knell rang when Mexico secured independence in 1821, and their subsequent influx into the same region encouraged the social focus to move from faith to farming. Mexican 'Yeehahs' gradually replaced the 'Amens'. However, the Mexicans would only briefly flex their muscles in this area. Those frisky Americans had more than doubled the population between 1790 and 1820, and as they budged west they brought with them a removal van full of land dispute.

Gold in them thar hills

From the moment of America's discovery in 1492, thousands of settlers had been whizzing across the Atlantic, fleeing from persecution, poverty or other problems. With a mish-mash of travellers firmly in place, the residents sought unity and an identity and fought off the English to establish their own American government.

The east had filled up quicker than Augustus Gloop. With reports from explorers such as Meriwether Lewis and William Clark making it all sound rather exciting, the next obvious step was to push west.

In a bid to alleviate densely populated cities, the government offered land at rock-bottom prices in the middle of the country, and the movement started in earnest as the new America tackled the Frontier. The government made its intentions clear when it took a rumble to the Mexicans in California and Oregon, eventually spanking a few million bucks on a purchase of most of the West Coast.

This acquisition seemed even shrewder when a sharp-eyed chap found a few flecks of yellow metal in the American River of the California Sierra. It was gold, and all of a sudden California became more popular than a $100 bill stuck on Hugh Heffner's front door.

The subsequent 'Gold Rush' brought the most rapid period of change to this part of the world. Those darn seekers of shiny yellow metal couldn't get there quick enough. The commute west became considerably easier

in 1869, when the transcontinental railroad linked east to west, doubling the population in California in little more than ten years. Meanwhile, expansion north up the coast had continued. The strategic purchase of Alaska in 1867 demonstrated the government's desire to move in that direction, and the Gold Rush followed north with the Klondike River, helping to populate cities such as Seattle.

So precious metal and trains meant everything was apparently rosy on the West Coast. As people settled, urban development would continue apace. However, America soon discovered that capitalism has a funny way of biting you on the bum. In 1870, boom became bust. The gold had been gobbled up, and cities such as Seattle, whose entire economy seemed to be based on the stuff, fell to their knees. The situation had become much worse due to the civil war in the east and south, which meant all demands for anything west had faltered.

America is a nation that has always embraced technology, though, and manufacturing started to provide new revenue streams to drag the country out of its mire. As suddenly as boom became bust, the boom started again with the production of raw steel helping gross domestic production triple in the first half of the 1880s. Electric light and power joined coal, oil, steel and railroads as the major industries. As the country looked towards the turn of the century, America was one of the strongest economic forces in the world.

Growing pains

As America heralded the twentieth century, the West Coast was in a 'Schwarzeneggeresque' grip of industrial revolution. Many began to regard the West as best. San Francisco was among the most significant draws for Americans and immigrants alike. Even an earthquake destroying most of the city in 1906 couldn't abate the movement of people there. Los Angeles and San Diego also continued to mature. Farther north, cities such as Portland and Seattle started to recover from the gold bust with booms in town development and shipbuilding.

As Europe fell into the First World War and economies threatened to slide once more, American technological advances came to the rescue once again with Henry Ford's mass production of the motor car. Meanwhile art and culture started to find a place as the 1920s introduced a solid base of writers and musicians who gained international recognition. This cultural explosion gave America the 'Jazz Age' with the first backlash of youth in American history.

For the West Coast this prompted the first stirrings of Hollywood. Motion pictures had been around since the 1860s, but they really began to capture the imagination when the Nestor Company opened Hollywood's first film studio in 1911. Hollywood was in full flow by the 1920s, the inaugural Academy Awards took place in 1928 and the West Coast had unearthed a boom industry that would stick.

The 1920s inexplicably coincided with Prohibition, and artists and dancing revellers alike, always fond of a drink to lubricate a situation, found their greatest muse stolen from them. Bootleggers such as Al Capone quite literally made a killing out of alcohol, but for the average Joe the risk of being caught was too much. By the time the law was repealed in 1933, America was gasping for a drink. Not least because there was another bust at the time – and this one was a biggy.

In 1927, Charles Lindbergh flew a plane across the Atlantic to the delight of his fellow countrymen. Before the aviation industry had a chance to take off, however, the 1929 Wall Street Crash thrust America into the Great Depression. The economic gloom summed up so perfectly by Monterrey resident writer John Steinbeck would last until the conclusion of the Second World War. America was inexorably propelled towards war in 1942 when the Japanese bombed the Hawaiian military base of Pearl Harbor. By the time this exhausting spell of history was done and dusted, America needed another dose of affluence.

Coming of age

The 1950s proved to be the age of the consumer. Americans made up around seven per cent of the world's population but consumed more than 50 per cent of its power. In 1927, Philo Farnsworth invented the world's first working television system. While it was slow to burn, economic revival and the advent of credit cards made TV sets the vogue. The first station arrived on West Coast shores in 1947 in the form of KTLA TV. From then on, nothing could stop a square-eyed revolution that would eventually give us everything from game shows to socio-political commentary (see *Baywatch*).

The goggle box would not yet distract couples from procreation, though, and the 1950s was noted for the remarkable increase in newborns, spawning the 'baby boomer' generation. Nor could it damage Hollywood, with stars such as Cary Grant and Marilyn Monroe becoming international celebrities. Even literature flourished with the Beat generation writers emerging from, or periodically moving to, San Francisco.

Sport seemed to come of age, too. Once the preserve of the East, baseball's National

League moved west with the Brooklyn Dodgers and New York Giants transferring to Los Angeles and San Francisco, respectively. American football, a sport destined for television thanks to the intermittent nature of the game, also gained in popularity. Like baseball, American football had roots dating back almost 100 years, but the 1958 National Football League championship game blew TV viewing records out of the water and cemented the sport in popular culture.

Prosperity and domestic entertainment would fail to gloss over all problems, however, and the 1950s is also referred to as an age of 'anxiety'. Rather than the local shops running out of beer, the paranoia centred on Communism, the upshot of which was a domestic backlash lead by Senator Joseph McCarthy who targeted individuals for 'red crimes'.

On through the decade, Communism's influence on foreign policy saw skirmishes with Cuba, North Korea and North Vietnam, while the relationship with the Soviet Union was frostier than an Eskimo's moustache. On top of this, race relations had flown to the top of the domestic agenda. At the start of the 1960s, America was a sweaty satin-sheeted bed of political intrigue on the cusp of cultural reformation.

In 1963, President John Kennedy was assassinated. In 1964, American ground troops were deployed en masse to South Vietnam. And in 1968, Robert Kennedy and Martin Luther King were both assassinated. This was a fair amount for a country to kop on the chin in a single decade, and the resulting tensions divided generations. Many young people 'dropped out' and opted for life as a hippie. Sex, drugs and rock 'n' roll became the buzzwords as San Francisco became a driver for Western culture with its 1967 'Summer of Love'.

As well as protesting against the war in Vietnam, left-wing activists found a voice on civil rights. As the issues of race discrimination dominated the front pages of the newspapers, the government was forced to reform the country's legislation.

It was a time of social transformation and technological advance, too. In 1969, two Americans took the first steps on the Moon, sending the country into patriotic self-congratulation as it stumbled towards the Seventies.

A conservative approach

Surrounded by all this peace and love, it was only a matter of time before the parents got wise and told everyone to get on with some work. Right from the start of the 1970s, the conservative backlash drop-kicked liberalism out of the ground. It was a mood perfectly embodied by Hollywood in the form of Clint Eastwood's badass cop Dirty Harry, who loved to rough up the 'long hairs'.

It seemed like the country had got out of bed the wrong side. Crime was at a high and the faltering economy was facing a huge war bill and temporary oil shortages. The government had a good old sweat on. The situation was made infinitely worse when President Richard Nixon reminded the world how mendacious politicians can be with the infamous Watergate Scandal.

Hollywood fared well, though, as *The Godfather, Jaws* and *Star Wars* proved big hitters at the box office. Gay rights and disco also prospered in an otherwise thorny decade. Fingers were crossed for a better decade when the Eighties arrived, but the lefties didn't get the start they wanted as another 'Tyson-esque' wallop came in the form of another Republican president and former silver-screen star Ronald Reagan. Although Reagan vowed to continue the Cold War on any front possible, his conservative stretch at least brought with it economic prosperity and wealth became the new domestic focal point.

Health also had a run out, particularly after the AIDS scare. Suddenly, it seemed that everyone there had shoehorned their backsides into day-glo Lycra shorts and laced up shoes with wheels on. The West Coast's laidback lifestyle of surfing and bodybuilding became the envy of the world, and men with such incongruous names as Sylvester Stallone and Arnold Schwarzenegger became household celebrities.

The 1990s arrived with a sigh of relief as the Cold War thawed, but a campaign in Iraq under the first President Bush soon put paid to any conflict respite. And at home, the economy would suffer one more bust before the new millennium.

The dot.com boom arrived with much fanfare, and billions had been invested in Silicon Valley where all the geeks were hanging out. When the arse fell out of the market, investment dropped by 80 per cent, sending the West Coast into spiralling despair and nearby San Francisco, victim of the Gold Rush, once again taking the brunt.

The 2000 celebrations were short-lived then and made more edgy due to a second attempt to depose Saddam Hussein in Iraq and a second President Bush getting his hands dirty in foreign affairs. All this after the 9/11 attacks had brought issues of terrorism to the fore. Life seemed very bleak.

Not that you'd find the average West Coaster lying down. As we enter the tail end of this decade, a predominantly left wing ideology there sees the continued crusade for peace, with residents confident that the economic bust of the dot.com will be boom soon enough. Indeed, the well-seasoned campaigner may even show a slight hint of optimism in the later part of this decade.

Here and now

Past and present foreign policy is often at the forefront of the American debate, but this is hardly the forum for that. What is certain is that there are few places on the planet to have provided the world with so much cultural reference.

Whether it's *Starsky and Hutch*, *Baywatch* or *The O.C.*, the chances are you've experienced the West Coast in some guise on the television. Likewise, any major blockbuster at the cinema is likely to have evolved on the parking lots of Warner Brothers or Universal in LA. Music knows no boundaries. Everything from rock to rap fills the airwaves with plenty between and beyond it, and the old guard of country, blues and jazz are still going strong. There's a culinary twist to dishes from every continent – consider the beef sandwiches known as burgers and chipped potatoes called fries – and the portions are as epic as the movies.

Politically, the West Coast is seen as a Democratic stronghold. While the residents of San Francisco may seem fiercely liberal, there is nothing oppressive about the political viewpoint. The ideologies are maintained with pride, but a good debate with the locals is welcome in most bars.

The economy is strong and rumbles on. There is some degree of caution after so many boom and bust years, however, and one eye is firmly levelled at the emerging economies of countries such as China.

Poverty is apparent on the streets of major cities, and there are some who live without while others prosper. The degrees of separation are far from those of the developing world, and the rags-to-riches 'American Dream' philosophy is alive and well.

As such, there isn't a typical West Coast resident. The ethnic mix is so broad that everyone is welcome to the party. Even the Native Americans, once vilified by the European settlers, seem to have a voice here. The different peoples have all emerged from a region with a short history. In that time, the West Coast has seen more ups and downs than a Hollywood madam's boudoir, more highs and lows than a Disneyland rollercoaster and more stops and starts than a dodgy DeLorean. One thing is for sure... the West Coast is here to stay and it can only become more entertaining with age.

Getting there

THE BEAUTY OF A long haul flight is that in theory you have enough time to get a couple of drinks down you, make advances towards the attractive attendants and become a member of the mile high club. In practice though, you'll possibly have a couple of drinks, watch a few movies and fall asleep.

Either way, your best bet is to get on a plane if you're travelling out this way. The option of a boat obviously exists but you'll have to factor in a week or so for such a jaunt. If you've worked out how to drive here then you're probably the inventor of a flying car and shouldn't be reading this nonsense.

Plane

Virgin Atlantic (www.virgin-atlantic.com), despite its name, has pleasured more customers than Heidi Fleiss and offers flights to Las Vegas, Los Angeles and San Francisco. Direct journeys are available from London Heathrow and London Gatwick (Las Vegas only). Virgin also offers a range of services and prices, with economy proving perfectly adequate. However, we were lucky enough to wheedle ourselves into the business lounge at Gatwick and can report that champagne, full English breakfast and even a haircut are among the pre-flight benefits.

Other carriers will take you from airports around the country including Manchester, Birmingham and Glasgow and include:

United Airlines	www.united.com
British Airways	www.britishairways.com
American Airlines	www.aa.com
KLM	www.klm.com
Northwest Airlines	www.nwa.com
Delta Air Lines	www.delta.com
Air France	www.airfrance.co.uk

Entertainment on long haul flights is crucial. Twelve hours is a long time to spend trying to amuse yourself, trust us, and as some offer better distractions than others it's worth checking what's on offer before you book. Movies are essential.

Economy prices vary – the summer is obviously much more expensive than the winter. The cost ranges from around £350 to Los Angeles in the low season, all the way up to £800 or more for the high. Research is often the key; booking in advance can be a good approach, or gamble on finding a late deal if you're flexible on when you go. Plenty of variety can be found on the information superhighway.

You're obviously going to suffer from jetlag as you cross the time zones. The West Coast is nine hours behind and even the best of us succumb, so prepare to feel odd for a couple of days. Some claim a night flight is a good way of tricking the body but only if you can sleep on the plane. Even then it's debatable; better to make sure you sleep well the night before you travel. And drinking through is not an answer either – it might be good news to hear that alcohol can be three times as strong at altitude, but the hangover will catch up with you quickly. A stuffy plane must be up there as one of the worst places in which to suffer from a headache and nausea.

Boat

A cruise is obviously a very specific type of holiday rather than an alternative form of transport, but if you don't like flying it's an option. You won't get so much precious West Coast beer time taking a tailored trip – they usually last around ten days – but if you are interested then you might want to look at the P&O website: www.pocruises.com. They're not cheap, coming in at around £2,800 in high season, leaving from Southampton to New York.

Being there

Accommodation

In each of the major cities on the West Coast you'll have the option of budget, middle of the road and upmarket accommodation, just as you would in any major city of the world.

Most common is the motel brand, of which there are a host of options. These brands are a bit McDonald's – you know what you're getting in each and it ain't the most satisfying. And some are also franchised so don't imagine one price fits all. But if you find they meet your middle-of-the road requirements then they are just as ubiquitous as the Golden Arches. Because of this you may find late deals and it's always worth negotiating; in many cases a competitor will be five minutes down the road and a little investigation and bartering can knock the price down. We usually managed to pay no more than $70 in the summer months.

We used Best Western as a default choice and they never let us down, otherwise you have Travelodge, Motel 6, Executive Inn & Suites, Ramada... The list goes on and on and in each case we simply turned up the night we wanted a room; even the peak season offered plenty of choice.

However, booking in advance is imperative if you want something specific, boutique or up-market, particularly in the major cities during high season. Off-peak there is usually a chance you can stop somewhere and find a room, but expect to pay double the motel chain prices. For peace of mind we'd recommend sorting your accommodation before you arrive.

Equally the budget options are also very popular – this part of the world attracts European and Antipodean backpackers in equal measure and hostels are very busy throughout the year, so if you want to keep things cheap then you'll need to consider booking before you leave.

That said, we didn't book anything travelling around Washington and Oregon in the summer, so if you're not too fussy where you sleep and are prepared to spend an hour or so looking around, all you require is motivation.

Climate

This varies significantly up and down the West Coast. Las Vegas is the desert, San Diego is next to Mexico and LA rarely feels the cold. In each of these places you can expect a bit of sunshine – shorts and t-shirts are usually the order although for a couple of months in winter you'll need a light jacket and trousers or 'pants' (we always wore pants under our trousers by the way). They did have snow in Las Vegas when we were there in January but this was extraordinary and it still seemed very mild to us.

Due to its location San Francisco has its own weather programme and it's usually dry and sunny but nippy with it so bring a jumper or coat, particularly in the autumn and winter months.

Much of Oregon and Washington shares a similar climate with Europe, although a bit hotter for a bit longer and not quite as cold in parts, but they both suffer from a lot of rain. November to March are the worst months but the others can be changeable so bring an umbrella. Further north it gets a bit colder and if you're planning skiing anywhere then warm clothes are obviously a must.

Travelling around

CAR

If you can get away with not using a car then good luck to you, but as the quintessential 'road trip' experience relies on one, and

pretty much everyone else in this country drives one, it's a big ask.

When you're hiring a car think carefully about your requirements. Petrol or 'gas' is considerably cheaper than in the UK thanks to the exchange rate, but some of the cars available will eat it very quickly – we went from an economical Chrysler Cruiser to a Pontiac V8 and the difference was obvious.

A big car is very useful if you plan to spend a lot of time in it; the roads are often quite busy and everyone else seems to drive something large so if you're in a small, bottom-end economy vehicle it can feel a little intimidating. A 4x4 may seem cumbersome for UK city folks but even in America's most metropolitan zones roads can be freeways and at the very least three lanes of slow-moving traffic. It's a country dedicated to big and the same applies to cars.

If anything goes wrong with your car, most towns have a 'Lube' offering. This inspired plenty of merriment from the authors of this book but the American equivalent of Kwik Fit was actually incredibly helpful when we told them we'd been filling up the oil in our motor with water. Long story.

Returning to the V8 though, it was really quite a quick motor and we were fairly pleased with ourselves when we stretched it out on the open road. That was until we got clobbered by the cops. The fact is that speed limits are incredibly restrictive in the US,

even on roads where you see very little traffic. It's always worth keeping an eye out for the correct limit but it will rarely be above 65mph.

The punishment for speeding is harsh – depending on how much over the limit you are it can be hundreds of dollars – and in some states they'll even threaten to lock you up if you're really flying.

If that's not enough to scare you then simply imagine yourself in the middle of nowhere being questioned by a bored and eager policeman with a gun at his side. And he has his hand on that gun. And you have all your belongings spread out on the road in a desperate bid to find a driving licence that has gone through a washing machine.

Drinking and driving

You'll want to visit some of the brewpubs in this Guide that are in the back of beyond and with that comes the complication of drinking and driving. We were surprised by the number of locals partaking in this ridiculous endeavour, their argument being that the authorities can't be overly punitive – if they were it would seriously knock an economy where the car is king. But these soothsayers were usually inebriated when they fired off this argument and the simple fact is that driving drunk is essentially the same rap in the US as it is in the UK and if you get caught you'll end up in serious bother.

Our advice: drink nothing when driving. If you're stopped and you have booze on the breath you're going to face plenty of grief either way. Fortunately the better brewpubs will let you take away their beers so if it's your turn to drive then pick up a few samples as you go and enjoy them back at the ranch. If you do take sipping samples on site bear in mind that many of these ales are very strong and after a few you can lose track of just how much you've drunk.

Limits vary between states and if you refuse to take a breath test you'll be hauled down the station. So in short: don't do it.

Car rental

A week with a four-door saloon will set you back anywhere between £90 in the low season to as much as £200 at peak times. It's worth checking the small print; some won't mention an additional fee for a second driver, air conditioning is crucial in the south during the summer and unlimited mileage is useful.

Among the providers are:

EasyCar	www.easycar.com
Holiday Autos	www.holidayautos.co.uk
Budget	www.budget.co.uk
Hertz	www.hertz.co.uk
Avis	www.avis.co.uk

OTHER VEHICLES

Some people look for alternative modes of transport, the Winnebago being a popular choice (www.cruiseamerica.org.uk). Bear in mind that apart from fuelling these beasts there are only selected places where you can park. Most of these will offer stunning backdrops and all the facilities required, but you'll have to pay to stay.

Motorbikes are another romantic alternative (www.eaglerider.com). Heading out on the highway with a throbbing chopper between the legs is the dream of many a man and there are plenty of other road users out there who'll salute you as you ride one. Learn the etiquette though – certain gestures are reserved for offence rather than courtesy.

Pushbikes would be a great addition to this section but realistically you'll put them to best use in the beauty spots where hiking and camping are enjoyed. Portland is a very bike-friendly city but even there the traffic is aggressive in parts and it can feel a bit Robin Williams. Hairy.

Taking the train between cities offers more panoramic views and a bit more luxury (www.amtrak.com).

And after all that, if you're pushed for time, internal flights between the major cities are reasonably priced.

SOME USEFUL ROADS

All the major roads are numbered and easy to navigate. The coastline in this part of the world is beautiful so for a start, try and factor in a drive down the Pacific Highway 1. The route from Los Angeles to San Francisco is often regarded as the essential trip. The road along the coast from Washington down to Oregon along the 101 is also stunning.

Inland it's the desert in the south and mountains and forests as you head north.

In the southern parts of California the route from Los Angeles to Las Vegas takes in Death Valley along the 190, a truly staggering mass of barren and rugged land.

Further north the camping in Yosemite National Park is fantastic in the summer, complete with bears, and only a few hours from San Francisco if you pick up the 120 going east.

Take the 395 north from here and you'll hit Lake Tahoe. In the area you'll find some skiing with the occasional brewpub or beer bar.

As well as the stunning coastal route between Oregon and Washington, a trip further north takes in the Puget Sound around Seattle (though ferries are the best way to appreciate the scenery here), with the 5 taking you all the way up to Canada. Coming back, you can head east along the 20 to the North Cascades National Park and then south again on the 97 to pick up the 82 and head through the Yakima hop fields.

Eating

BREAKFAST

The breakfast experience in the US is one of the delights of life and while it's not always healthy, we were determined to start each day with a belter. It's essential you locate the best diner when you get to town, easily done with a quick question directed at a local. Everyone has their opinion but you'll usually be pointed in the right direction.

Eggs were the order of the day for us. They come in every conceivable style, 'over easy' being your basic fried, but the omelettes and Benedict often the choice bets. The beauty of eggs is that they are indeed binding and after a night on the sauce, they prove both tasty and a useful toilet antidote.

Sausage and bacon are not quite what you'd expect from an all-English encounter; sausages more like burgers and bacon usually streaky rather than back. But embrace these modest changes; this is cuisine culture, people.

The coffee keeps on coming as well. It's amazing how much you can neck first thing and it really sets you up for the morning. And of course the pancakes – who could ignore the pancakes? These are a US institution best served with maple syrup.

For those feeling guilty just reading this, freshly-squeezed juices are around in the best of the breakfast diners, and there should be a fruit cup on the menu too. Californians in particular seem conscious of the healthy option, but even here everyone seems to love a hearty start to the day.

If you are out on the road early there are a few restaurant brands that specialise in breakfast but we'd strongly advise you steer clear. It truly isn't worth wasting a breakfast opportunity.

LUNCH

Thanks to the brewpub menu there's always a lot of scope for lunch but if your plan is to eat big at breakfast and then again at dinner, the middle meal of the day might need to be a bit lighter. After all, you'll quickly become a fat bastard if you don't watch yourself.

We recommend a sandwich then, and fortunately the beer and sarnie opportunities are fantastic. In a number of towns you can find a low-key deli, occasionally with vast fridges choc full of beer from around the world. There is nothing that compares in the UK, and there should be.

The choice of sandwich is usually as varied as that of the beer and mostly very fresh. They also have Cheetos, which are a bit like Wotsits.

Among the best is Hollingshead's delicatessen in LA, closely followed by the Hopvine in Seattle.

DINNER

There are staples on the American menu, burgers are obviously one, pizza another. But a bit of hunting around can find plenty of other options, particularly in the major cities and increasingly even the high end restaurants are looking at their beer menus.

In each location we'd advise you try something a bit different. San Diego, being so close to the border, is fantastic for Mexican food. Heading north to LA you can be sure of a fine dining experience – places such as the Hungry Cat around the corner from Hollywood are worth a shout and if you must have a burger then Lucky Devils serves craft brews to accompany some of the very best.

Dinner in San Francisco could easily be Chinese thanks to the incredible range in Chinatown, although the seafood offering is also fantastic – the little restaurant Bar Crudo keeps things interesting with a raw selection.

Portland and Seattle offer incredible range in seafood but also a very artisan approach to cuisine so if you're keen to skip the burgers and pizza keep an eye out for the organic restaurants.

On the highway the options are more challenging and, as with breakfast, the temptation may be to go for something familiar. But, we implore you, at the very least make it to a brewpub if you're in one of the smaller towns – our reviews will alert you to those with more than average cuisine.

Tipping

When you're buying drinks, don't forget to tip. It may seem a bit presumptuous that every server expects a bit extra each time you order a beer, but that's the way the service industry appears to work, so carry plenty of 'ones'. If you run a tab then you can tip at the end, failing that a dollar with each round is reasonably standard practice. This is mainly due to the fact that many in this industry aren't paid well, a structure that at least keeps service standards high.

Around 20% as a tip is generally the going rate although it can vary, but in some bars you'll be well looked after if you're generous so it's always worth making sure the staff are happy with what you're leaving. That said, you don't have to show them the money to get the service in the first place. So if the staff are rude don't feel obliged – you won't be going back anyway.

TVs

As Mike Teavee says in the Tim Burton re-working of *Willy Wonka and the Chocolate Factory*: 'Who wants a beard?' Not entirely relevant, but as someone who is obsessed with television, Mike would certainly have few complaints in US bars. Essentially the TV is a staple and bar managers usually select sport. It's impossible to exaggerate how much it dominates the US bar scene; even in food- or music-led environments there's invariably a set in the corner. We love American sport but in truth we were stunned to find it on screen in some of the bars we visited.

Games

Bar games are great attractions in many US bars. Pool is sometimes free and it will be clear if it is, otherwise it's very cheap. So if you, like us, spent a wasted youth in pubs then you'll be sure to enjoy yourself. If you're on a bar crawl, chances are you'll find a spare table somewhere so don't worry if you need the practice away from prying eyes. Note they have different rules; make sure you ask if you play a native.

But pool is simply one game. Shuffleboard is a great addition to the scene – pushing pucks down a sandy laminated wooden surface has never been more fun. Like heroin, it's highly addictive and can often get in the way of book research.

Computer games, pinball and table football are also a big part of bar life and, while it's not a game, there's usually a juke box to be found in the best dive bars with flashing buttons you can press.

There's also a game called beer pong but ask the locals about that – we're pretty sure it involves irresponsible drinking and we didn't get involved in any of that. In fact the only reason we lost at strip poker is because those girls cheated.

Brewpub brands

The brewpub is a very American animal and has been at the forefront of the micro-brew evolution in the US. The freedom for an indi-

vidual to brew on his own site and immediately gauge customer reaction by serving it at the bar has proved a valuable asset for many.

And in a country that's incredibly brand conscious, the concept was always likely to grab the attention of an entrepreneur keen to make a mark beyond the single local pub. As a result there are now a number of brewpub chains along the West Coast, each trying to replicate the same values and experience.

When it comes to grub, the brewpub menu fast becomes a familiar friend, but if you restrict your eating to the branded names it can also become the over-familiar friend who doesn't understand there are boundaries. Burgers, nachos, pizza, subs, not to mention big salads that ooze dressing (ask for it on the side); the quality is invariably good, the portions fantastic and the service smiling. But if you're away for a couple of weeks the chances are you don't want to sample too much of the same thing.

Likewise, and more importantly, a lot of the beer is going to be uniform. Many of the major brewpub brands hold recipes at a head office, the aim being to replicate the same experience across the board. But one of the reasons there's so much fantastic variety across the US is that brewers experiment, so in principle the branded brewpub doesn't sound overly wise. Fortunately in some of the outlets that brew on site, the team is given a bit more licence to experiment.

Like the food though, it means that if you've tried the beer in Vegas, it could be just the same in San Francisco. As a result we've highlighted some of the better branches of the brewpub chains in our listings and summed up the best of the brand values here.

BJ's Restaurant & Brewhouse
www.bjsbrewhouse.com

As Hugh Grant will no doubt testify, you're never too far away from a BJ in California.

The beginning of the BJ empire, back in 1978, was a rather humble affair: a Chicago-style pizzeria in Santa Ana, California with no house beers. Over the next decade or so, BJ's adopted a slowly, slowly catchee monkey approach to expansion with a few new outlets opening in California.

From 1990 it boomed though and there are now 38 locations in California and around 30 more across the US. In 1996, with just seven Californian restaurants in operation, BJ's began brewing on a 30-barrel brewhouse in Brea, California, and subsequently added brew systems to a number of new and existing restaurants. All of the restaurants serve both BJ's beer and some top-notch guest ales but not all them have breweries. The 11 that do, however, are given free reign to experiment and showboat with seasonal and special offerings (including the odd cask served in strict adherence to CAMRA guidelines) which gives some venues a touch more individual character. The core beer recipes are standard across all the breweries.

BJ's does things big. The restaurants tend to be spacious venues with high ceilings, and the food portions, beer selection, smiles and welcome from the staff are all generously proportioned.

While it's difficult to ignore that BJ's is a corporate chain, we found the upscale beers unswerving in their consistency, well looked after and a tad more adventurous than other brewpub chain efforts we could mention. At the 2007 Great American Beer Festival (GABF), BJ's medalled twice with its Piranha Pale Ale and Nit Wit wheat beer.

Gordon Biersch
www.gordonbiersch.com

Among the best of the brands. The style and décor might be mimicked throughout the branches but the ambience is also always pleasant, the beer often good – and in some cases excellent thanks to certain brewers being given a little more freedom.

Dan Gordon has brewing pedigree and Dean Biersch knows his restaurants, so when they got together in 1987 they were destined to put something interesting together. Their first effort was the Palo Alto site in 1988 which proved so successful they went on to open additional brewery restaurants in California, Hawaii, Nevada and Washington.

Their love is for German beer, so expect beers with Hallertauer hops, two row barley and a special yeast strain imported directly from Germany. These ingredients work together to form staples that include Blonde Bock, Marzen, Pilsner, Hefeweizen and Winter Bock – in most cases all well represented. They even cook and match the beers with the food menu, which is also very tasty.

Among their choice venues is the Vegas GB, a welcome respite from some of the theme-park pubs with actual grown-up experiences including jazz and brunch on a Sunday. And in San Francisco the GB has a brewer with real passion.

To that end you can compare the upmarket venues to something like Pizza Express – you know what you're getting on the menu, the décor largely matches and the food is decent but rarely deviates from the theme. But don't discount them because of this. They are invariably a very safe bet.

Oggi's
www.oggis.com

There are 15 different Oggi's scattered all over SoCal, half a dozen housing their own brewery, and they unite the glorious brewpub triumvirate that is sports, pizza and craft beer.

Much of the beer comes from a 30-barrel microbrewery located on the fringes of San Diego and run by head brewer Rick Smetz. The eight core beers tailor more for the sports fan than the hardened hophead but they've certainly got game.

Oggi's has podiumed several times at the GABF and its best-selling California Blonde is liquid evidence that yellow American beer need not be an experience entirely without character. Yearn for something more challenging? Try the Double IPA which sits for six weeks before being brightened and dry-hopped with 52lbs of Pacific Northwest's finest.

Of the 4,000 barrels Oggi's produces every year, a slice is sold in plastic bottles under the Left Coast Brewing banner at sports stadiums. Oggi's is also the official pizza of the San Diego Chargers and the San Diego Padres.

Ram
www.theram.com
The Ram brand seems to have chosen rather large venues for its projects and as a result they're far from intimate settings, but with the emphasis on sport that's clearly not their concern.

They all offer big menus with big burgers and they're family friendly as well. And while they're located across the country, for West Coast purposes they can be found in Washington and Oregon, the best on our travels proving the Seattle site in the University Village.

The beers have been recognised at the Beer World Cup so are worth checking out; the Cheytown Sweet Stout and Baby Fitzt ESB taking gold a few years back and the Total Disorder Porter earning a bronze more recently. The Buttface Amber is also very good; plenty of malt and sweetness with a bit of hop in there as well.

Rock Bottom
www.rockbottom.com
Despite the name, things really aren't so bad in these venues which tend to tick all the brewpub boxes in their 40 nationwide locations. There is all the wood and brass in the fixtures and fittings to give a corporate sparkle and uniformity, not to mention a standard American feel to the food menu. But much like Gordon Biersch, there is a commitment to good beer, and while trying to replicate the same recipe across this many sites is a challenge, there are a few in the major cities where the brewers are keen and able.

As a result this is another chain that has picked up awards in its time and offerings such as the 33 Strong Ale and Dream Lager have earned a reasonable reputation amongst beer enthusiasts. They tend to appear in the more touristy parts of town and as a result can actually stand out, particularly in San Diego's Gas Lamp District where alternatives like the Irish pubs don't even come close.

Yard House
www.yardhouse.com
Yard House doesn't brew on site but will be a recognisable brand as you travel up and down the coast. Its USP is taps and plenty of them, more than 100 in fact. As is always the case,

Below: spoilt for choice at Yard House

running more than 20 is a challenge so it is questionable whether all the beer is good all the time. And as is also so often the case with anyone who sells the yellow fizz synonymous with Super Bowl, quite a few customers seem to turn to something less crafty. That said, the venues are smart and clean with all the values of a well-funded brand, the food is American brewpub and hearty with it and there really is a good selection of beer.

Beer festivals

West Coast brewers know they've got a great thing in their American beer which is why they seem to celebrate it at every possible opportunity. What's useful about this is that whenever you visit there's a good chance you'll be able to get involved. And hopefully that means enjoying plenty of decent and occasionally very rare beer outdoors in beautiful weather.

It has always been an aim of UK brewers to encourage young and sexy beer drinkers along to festivals and while this is moving in the right direction, the youth movement in America is advanced. College is a big craft beer experience for many US students who love to party with it, so events in the US can often be exceptional fun as well as serious about beer.

Ticket prices for these events vary quite significantly depending on the scale of the festival, and precise dates and fees can be found on the relevant guild websites.

www.sandiegobrewersguild.org
www.washingtonbeer.com
www.oregonbeer.org
www.sfbrewersguild.org
www.brewersassociation.org
www.norcalbrewers.com

Cask Festival, WA
The Cask Festival takes place at the Seattle Centre in March and is held in very high regard by a number of brewers keen to use traditional brewing and dispensing methods for cask-conditioned beer. You'll find more than 50 varieties here.

Washington Brewers Festival, WA
This June shindig has the additional novelty of taking place on Fathers' Day in Kenmore and as a result is a real family affair. As well

as plenty of entertainment for the kids, there's also a brewers keg toss contest and live music, not to mention a huge selection of craft beers.

Winter Beer Festival, WA
Unsurprisingly this Seattle-based festival takes place in November and showcases some of the more hearty brews from the area. Expect to find plenty of strong stuff making it's way out for the 'holiday season'. And we mean strong.

Strange Brewfest, WA
As the name suggests, this Port Townsend festival in January offers up some of the weirder brews and does so with some decent bands and a lot of fun.

Seattle International Brewers Festival, WA
June is a beery time for Seattle folks and this weekend festival invites all-comers to sample more than 100 internationally brewed craft beers including native and European styles.

Oregon Brewers Festival, OR
This Portland event is a must if you're in town in late July. The fact that 60,500 people took part in the 2007 festival indicates that this is a biggie and it celebrates 21 years in 2008.

Holiday Ale Festival, OR
It might be cold, dark and wet but that doesn't stop the Portland crowd from getting outdoors for this four-day festival celebrating the Christmas ales, all under cover and heated of course.

Spring Beer and Wine Fest, OR
Another Portland gig, this time in March and featuring artisan producers from the world of wine, cheese and Northwest craft beer, accompanied by bands and chef seminars.

Strong Ale Festival, CA
In Carlsbad they know all about strong beer and in this December event they celebrate it in style with at least 60 beers over 8%.

Beer World Cup, CA
The location changes but this event, held every other year, tends to take place around April and is fast becoming a strong gauge for the globe's best beers.

San Francisco International Beer Festival, CA
More than 40 brewers come together for one of Northern California's biggest events, taking place in April.

Booneville Beer Fest, CA
A legendary event on the calendar, this one also takes place in April up at the Anderson Valley Brewery and has a Woodstock feel.

Great Alaskan Beer and Barleywine Festival
It's a bit chilly up in Anchorage in January but this event will warm the cockles, and the nutsles for that matter.

Kona Beer Festival
This celebration of beer and food has been running since 1996 and takes place in early March at Kailua Bay on the Big Island of Hawaii.

Great American Beer Festival, Denver
A massive event for the beer fan, this one takes place a bit further afield but remains a must if you're nearby in mid October. The event showcases the very best and is mobbed by mainstream beer heads.

Read all about it
The beer scene is fantastically represented by a number of free magazines and papers you can pick up on your travels. They'll inform you of what's happening in the town or city you've landed in and keep you abreast of any new openings or some of the smaller festivals at local bars.

The *Celebrator* publication is one of the best and has been a mainstay on the craft beer scene for years now. It's a favourite with brewers and consumers alike and packed with interesting stories and information. Editor Tom Dalldorf is a genuine beer enthusiast and wrote the Hawaii chapter of this Guide. Up north the *Northwest Brewing News* also proves a valuable tool with plenty of tips, bar ads and brew maps to keep you occupied and informed.

And if you're on the move with a modem then online resources to log on to include www.beeradvocate.com (complete with its own glossy magazine) and www.ratebeer.com. Both are excellent and will provide additional pointers on beers and beer bars if you need them, particularly any that spring up after this book has been published.

History of beer in America

UNCLE SAM is definitely a beer guy. Check out the red face, glazed eyes and quirky facial hair. Look even closer and you'll see the beer coursing through his veins, drifting deep down into his psyche and percolating through his past. Yes he's definitely a beer guy and, what's more, he always has been.

Beer has played at least a cameo role, if not a star-spangled one, in almost every American tale. George Washington had a weakness for the dark, shimmering charms of porter and even brewed his own at Mount Vernon. The Founding Fathers – they were beer guys, too. Thomas Jefferson scribbled parts of the Declaration of Independence over a couple of pints in the Indian Queen Tavern, Philadelphia. And Benjamin Franklin famously declared:

> "Beer is proof that God loves us
> and wants us to be happy."

Or did he? Historians have credibly questioned the quote's veracity recently but, like George said to Jerry in an episode of *Seinfeld*, "It's not a lie if you believe it."

Beer even induced the early delivery of Europeans onto American soil. When the *Mayflower* landed at Plymouth Rock in November 1620, the ship was several hundred miles north of its intended destination, Virginia. But the Pilgrims decided to stay in frosty Massachusetts. Frankly, they'd had enough of bobbing about with no beer. Spanning two wretched months and nearly 3,000 miles, their journey had been treacherous and miserable. The settlers and the crew were tired and seasick but, most importantly, they were gasping for a beer.

"We could not now take time for further search or consideration…" wrote William Bradford, the Pilgrim's main man, "our victuals being much spent, especially our Beere."

The beer supplies were hardly plentiful back on land, so the early colonists made do with an exotic but immensely elementary elixir brewed by the Native Americans. With no barley available, the Native American brewers used whatever they could find – corn, black birch sap and even pumpkin. It was an acquired taste that settlers had little intention of acquiring. They yearned for their beloved English ale. Soon, breweries were being built throughout the colonies, and English-style ales were lovingly recreated using imported barley, brewers and equipment arriving from Europe.

Drunk by the posh and pauper alike, beer became a vital part of embryonic American society. It was a staple on the dinner table, a social lubricant in the tavern and a significant boost to the economy. Early colonial governments actively encouraged beer production. It served as a valuable export to the neighbouring West Indies and, more importantly, a far less perilous libation than liquor.

Beer wars

Distilled using corn or molasses, liquor was worryingly prevalent and widely consumed in the early eighteenth century. The mass popularity of this moonshine was just one factor restricting the growth of the domestic brewing scene. Breweries remained small concerns that only slaked the thirsts of the immediate neighbourhood. Their top-fermenting ales, so popular at the time, were prone to bacterial infection and resisted travel on rudimentary road networks.

Those pesky Limeys were a further check on domestic growth. The land along the East

Coast did not support barley growth, and the vast majority of settlements were huddled around harbours, so imported beer was big business for the Empire. And the Empire attempted to strike back when domestic brewing – still small beer in comparison – began to nibble away at imports of ale and their associated taxes. In an effort to nip the blossoming brewing scene in the bud, the British flooded the market with cheap ale. Rather than make the colonists merry, however, the Brits' dastardly moustache-twirling move served only to pour fuel on the flames of nationalistic discontent. Buying American beer became a tub-thumping display of patriotism, while British beer became a symbol of imperial oppression.

Beer certainly oiled the Americans during the War of Independence. George Washington insisted troops were rationed with a daily quart of beer which, in lieu of the scarce hops, was infused with twigs of spruce. Sufficiently 'spruced up' for battle, Washington's men opened an almighty can of whoop ass on the Brits and succeeded in their quest to secede the colonies from the Empire.

Growth industry

It is no surprise that homebrewing grew in popularity at the end of the war. Small craft brewing also thrived, and both were actively encouraged by the authorities. A whole gamut of legislature hailed beer as a social virtue. Post the Revolution, tax on beer was curbed (1789) to further encourage commercial brewing and, crucially, undermine the odious influence of liquor. Massachusetts passed an act encouraging the consumption and production of beer while, in the same year, as part of his 'Buy American' policy, George Washington announced that he was only going to drink his beloved porter if it was brewed in America.

By 1810, American brewing was in great shape. Around 132 breweries were producing 185,000 barrels (5.74 million gallons) every year. A growing temperance movement, which continued to advocate beer above liquor, and industrialisation further strengthened the brewer's cause. The wave of German immigration, fleeing turmoil in the fatherland, added another dimension to America's brewing landscape. In a marked departure from top-fermenting ales and porters,

Alt beers and Weissbeers were brewed. With the help of a new strain of yeast, a completely different style of beer swept the beer-drinking nation. It was called lager and, while still amber or brown in hue, its bubbly, bright character tickled the collective fancy. With greater durability than ale and, spurred on by the advent of transparent glassware, lager quickly stole a march on the murky, sediment-laden English-style beers.

Between 1840 and 1848, lager breweries opened in Philadelphia, Cincinnati, Milwaukee, Chicago and Boston. Initially, these breweries served the growing hordes of German-speaking immigrants who supped it, pipe-in-hand, within the refined confines of German-style beer gardens. In 1849, the Adam Schuppert Brewery became the first brewery to open in California, and in San Francisco – home to wide-eyed gold rushers during the 1850s – it was a thirsty business by all accounts. By 1852, the city had more than 352 drinking establishments for a populace of just 36,000. In a matter of years, the population had exploded to 23 million. The number of breweries spiralled to around 430, collectively brewing 750,000 barrels of beer. Many were German-owned and producing lager-bier for local communities.

During this time, some of the big American brewing names such as Pabst and Schlitz first ploughed a furrow on American soil, and in 1852 a man named George Schneider opened a brewery in Missouri. Eventually, this one-man enterprise would become the brewing giant Anheuser-Busch.

By 1860, the brewery count had risen to nearly 1,300. Production had surpassed the one million barrel mark for a population that, by this point, had soared to 31 million.

Beer business unexpectedly boomed during the American Civil War (1861–1865). Breweries positioned near the line of division prospered from increased numbers, while deals were struck with the military to ensure that the troops were nourished, plucky and happy but, well, not *too* happy. Officially, beer rations had stopped but, regarded as a temperate liquid, and even given the thumbs-up by the US Sanitary Commission, lager was seen as a great morale-booster and was rife among the ranks of Union troops.

Almost 1,000 more breweries opened up during the war. Despite Lincoln's decision to levy a wartime tax of $1 on every beer barrel, around 1,000 more breweries fired up their kettles following the end of the hostilities. Beer business was booming, and the number of breweries reached its zenith in 1873 when 4,131 establishments were producing nine million barrels of beer.

Beer had usurped spirits as the nation's favourite alcoholic beverage. Within the beer market, lager had done the same to ale.

Forging ahead

The late nineteenth century was the lager era. Americans turned their backs on the leaden malt-driven ale for lager's recreational refreshment and effervescent allure. The drinking climate in the 1870s could not have been more ready for the arrival of Pilsner, a 'new' lager beer from Bohemia. Pale gold in hue and light in body, strength and taste, Pilsner sparkled delicately on the tongue and charmed the pants off brewer and drinker alike.

Pilsner had been created in the Bohemian town of Pilsen some 30 years earlier. Yet the availability in the West Coast had hitherto been restricted by high price and skepticism among a proud German-American drinking audience loyal to the Bavarian lager style. Word and quaff of this trail-blazing new lager soon spread throughout the land. It is on the shoulders of this gentle golden giant that the vast majority of American lagers now stand.

However, initial efforts to reproduce the style were undermined by the heavy protein character of America's six-row barley. It left all sorts of unsightly debris in the glass, and the new sparkling golden liquid mercilessly highlighted visual imperfections. After no small amount of experimentation, many brewers turned to corn and rice as a stable and sediment-free alternative to barley. While modern-day beer buffs may abhor the use of such adjuncts, the drinkers of late nineteenth century America were really rather excited by the easy-drinking and translucent beer it produced.

That the future for lager in the 1870s was as bright and golden as the beer itself was not merely down to the arrival of Pilsner nor its American cousin, however. Without the emergence of mechanical refrigeration and pasteurisation, advances in bottling or the considerable improvement of the railroads, lager would not have enjoyed quite such a meteoric rise.

Preservation and expansion

Beer was no longer the highly perishable and unstable traveller that it once was. For the first time, and as long as it remained chilled, lager could be dispatched well beyond a brewery's immediate neighborhood. The race to establish a national lager brand had well and truly begun. A handful of well-established German-owned breweries were showing their smaller rivals a clean set of heels. While most breweries were content to remain local, the likes of Pabst, Schlitz and Busch cast their nets wider. They embraced new technology and started to produce some of the finest beers in the world. Enhanced production techniques and increased distribution shrunk America's beer universe and, inevitably, the 1880s was a time of mass consolidation. The smaller breweries struggled financially to meet the consumer demand for bottled beer. Especially as an existing law dictated that separate premises were required for bottling.

Over the next 20 years the big breweries got bigger, forcing their smaller competitors to either shut down or change hands more often than a dog walker on a frosty morning. Many small breweries ended up in the dollar-grabbing mitts of Old World capitalists. By the 1890s, the beer market had polarised into three sections. Hundreds of small and independent breweries remained. Dozens of medium-sized American or British-owned businesses battled for business. And a handful of the big players – Pabst, Anheuser-Busch and Schlitz – just got bigger and bigger. The number of breweries went from more than 4,000 in 1873 to just 1,568 in 1910.

Yet production had mushroomed to more than 50 million barrels. Fewer than half the breweries were now fighting over a market that had grown by almost 600 per cent. As the chase for market share and distribution intensified in the 1890s, breweries began snapping up existing saloons or building their own in which to showcase their wares. Gorgeous and grandiose, these saloons were intended to attract the same kind of genteel family crowd that had been frequenting the serene and refined German-style beer gardens for so many years.

The dawn of the twentieth century

By the beginning of the twentieth century, the number of saloons had doubled from 150,000 to almost 300,000. These premises were principally frequented and often run by the kind of folk you'd rather not introduce to your parents. Saloons became synonymous with ne'er-do-wells, raucous behaviour and the kind of vice about which an upright and decent beer guide would really rather not go into detail.

Indeed, the popularity for saloons soon bred contempt among a growing temperance movement. Having adopted the moral high ground for so long, beer was being widely lambasted as a tipple for tykes, toerags and good-for-nothing trouble makers. Founded in 1893, the Anti-Saloon League (ASL) emerged as one of beer's fiercest opponents. By successfully lobbying the 'dry' politicians, it achieved Prohibition in nine states – mainly in the south and the rural north. This proved a challenge too far for many brewers and, between 1904 and 1914, more than 500 were forced to close their doors.

War and Prohibition

If the emerging Prohibition landed a few telling blows, the First World War was a howitzer-like haymaker that dropped American brewing onto the canvas. The year 1914 was, to put it mildly, hardly a good time to be a German citizen in America. Despite America's initial neutrality, anti-German sentiment was rampant and intense. Mobs were attacking German descendants. They flogged those who spoke German. German shops and houses were daubed in paint. Any product with a Germanic name was vociferously boycotted,which obviously didn't bode well for Germanic breweries such as Busch, Yuengling, Pabst, Miller and Blatz.

To make matters worse, these breweries found themselves on the wrong end of much of the anti-German rhetoric. Prohibitionists jumped on the bandwagon, blaming centuries of beer drinking for Germany's barbaric ways. They accused the brewing and distilling industries of re-routing valuable grain and labour away from the war effort and even harangued members of the Busch family for directly colluding with the enemy.

When Woodrow Wilson limited the alcohol content of beer to 2.75%, it was all too much for a brow-beaten brewing industry. With war hysteria on one side and a vociferous temperance movement on the other, American beer could do little to prevent the inevitable arrival of Prohibition on January 17, 1920.

The Volstead Act stated: 'The manufacture, sale, or transportation of intoxicating liquors within, the importation thereof into, or the exportation thereof from the United States and all territory subject to the jurisdiction thereof for beverage purposes is hereby prohibited.'

This Act crippled a beer industry that faced a rather bleak choice: diversification or downfall. The big brewers initially peddled 'near-beer' – a non-alcoholic beverage made from barley and hops – but the new brew did not gain popularity. Instead people drank rough, ready and illegal 'alley-brew' or surreptitiously brewed their own beer at home.

Anheuser-Busch chanced its arm at root beer, ginger beer, baker's yeast, chocolate and ice cream. Pabst manufactured malt syrup, while the Ulhein brewing family opted for soft drinks. Some brewed beer under the protection of mobsters. Alas, most fell by the wayside and more than 500 breweries – half the national total – closed between 1918 and 1920.

Depression America

However, the 'noble experiment' was to prove rather unsuccessful. Illicit spirits were laying waste to a post-war America in the pocket of organised crime. The stock market crash of 1929 and the subsequent Great Depression that followed did little to support the Prohibitionist argument. In 1932, Franklin D. Roosevelt was elected as president. Almost immediately, Congress proposed the 21st Amendment (legislature proposing the end of Prohibition).

When Prohibition was finally repealed on December 5, 1933, America certainly needed a drink. But after 13 unfortunate years in exile, it was with a whimper rather than a bang that beer returned. Many of the surviving breweries were either in the greedy hands of mobsters or Wall Street opportunists, who were more interested in Greenbacks than quality beer. In the aftermath of Prohibition, the country gripped by the Depression, laws were passed to prevent breweries from owning or leasing saloons.

All of this did little for beer's already jaded reputation. People started to fall out of the habit of drinking. They were driving cars, choosing movie theatres ahead of dreary taverns and, increasingly, staying at home to listen to a new invention – the radio.

Changing fortunes
Another big invention – the beer can in 1935 – was a crucial turning point for American beer. So, too, was the change in legislation that made beer sales out of supermarkets and stores much easier. Focus rapidly shifted away from the nation's hostelries towards people's homes. By 1940, half of all beer sold was in take-home packaging. The Second World War boosted business, too. Brewers with Germanic names were second-generation Americans now, so there was none of the anti-German sentiment seen during the First World War. While the distilleries were put out of action to conserve supplies of alcohol for military use, breweries were busier than ever supplying thirsty troops with beer.

In 1943, the Food Distribution Association decreed that 15% of all brewing production should be ring-fenced for the soldiers. Medium-sized and large-scale brewers jumped at the chance to establish allegiance with millions of appreciative young males. Between 1941 and 1945, American brewing surfed a wave of annual double-digit growth. By 1948, beer sales were riding higher than Hunter S. Thompson on a penny-farthing, with 86.9 million barrels sold and per capita consumption topping 18.5 gallons.

Over the next decade or so, however, this upward curve flattened out as the population grew older and cocktails and fancy spirits became increasingly popular. America was in the throes of a love affair with processed food, frozen food and TV dinners. With its floral hops and sweet malt kick, beer was too darn flavoursome!

With the market shrinking, a Fifties shake out was inevitable, and it was the volume-chasing big brewers that did the shaking. The main players swept through 'Beer Town', nonchalantly putting petrified local breweries out of business. Without canning or bottling plants, multiple breweries and big advertising budgets, the smaller outfits could not compete. Between 1949 and 1958, many of the 400 surviving breweries

shut down or were snapped up by bigger rivals. By 1961, the number had dwindled to 230, of which only 140 were independent. As the battle for brewing dominance switched to the West Coast or, more precisely, the booming state of California, consolidation continued. By 1967, the top four breweries commanded one third of all beer sales, with Anheuser-Busch topping the charts with an impressive 18 million barrels.

In the Sixties, brewers replaced hops and malt with hype and marketing. Brand image took centre stage and, with TVs in nearly every home, fistfuls of dollars were being thrown at advertising. As the struggle for market share intensified, and with imports gaining a small but growing foothold in America, the major brewers also threw their substantial weight behind new products.

The Sixties saw more launches than Cape Canaveral, with breweries unleashing 'lite' beer and ice beer, low-alcohol and no-alcohol beer, 'draft' beer and other such new fangled concepts. But the dynamics of the beer market were changing. People now had more money in their pockets, their horizons had been broadened by foreign travel, they were disillusioned with mainstream brands, intrigued by the emergence of imported beer and becoming increasingly adventurous in their drinking habits.

A bigger concern for the beer industry was the new generation. Beer's traditional lifeblood was seeping away as young people refrained from supping the same soporific suds as their parents. The flower power generation rallied against the war in Vietnam, took drugs, grew their hair, smoked pot and generally tried to 'stick it to the Man'. And the 'Man' didn't come much bigger than a baffled corporate beer industry whose marketing attempts exuded all the cool of a drunken uncle dancing at a wedding. The big brewers were losing touch with their beer-drinking audience. A backlash against the big and bland was snowballing, but the breweries were too busy merging, acquisitioning and shrinking into a ball of insipid, price-driven homogeny to really notice.

New kids on the block
In 1965, a 27-year-old businessman with no knowledge or experience of brewing purchased a filthy fiasco of a brewery in

downtown San Francisco. The likes of Pabst, Schlitz and Anheuser-Busch hardly batted an eyelid. But Frederick 'Fritz' Maytag III, new owner of the Anchor Steam Brewery and heir to the eminent Maytag washing-machine empire, called upon family funds and acute business acumen. In the shape of a counter-cultural beer, Frederick Maytag fired the first shot across the bows of the big boys.

Maytag's beer was different. It was small-batch and brewed with the finest, freshest ingredients. It snubbed hype in favour of history (dating back to 1896) and valued authenticity ahead of advertising. Unwilling and unable to compete on price or the national distribution of the Goliaths, it played on its reputation as a local, loyal 'West Coast' hero.

Maytag's timing and location were immaculate. In the early Seventies, a revolution was starting against the shrink-wrapped, frozen monotony of modern American food and drink. California was leading the charge – proudly flying the flag of epicurean enlightenment and storming the gates of mass-produced mediocrity.

In 1971, the Chez Panisse opened in Berkeley, where legendary chef Alice Walters passionately banged her knife and fork on the table of gastronomic discontent and encouraged the widespread embrace of local, sustainable food. Amid unease over the environmental impact of big business, food scares and general disenchantment with corporate America, the 'local is good' message spread throughout the West Coast. Boutique wineries were cropping up along the Pacific Coast and in the Napa Valley region and beer wasn't that far behind.

In 1976, in the hippy Northern California backwater of Sonoma, Jack McAuliffe, a soldier who fell in love with British ales while stationed in Scotland in the 1960s, set up the first microbrewery since Prohibition. The New Albion Brewery did not last long. But throughout the craft beer community McAuliffe is revered for his visionary derring-do and, more importantly, the derring-don'ts that led to the brewery's demise.

The brewing revolution

McAuliffe and Maytag ignited the fire under the rocking chair of mainstream American beer but it was the homebrewing legislation in 1978 that fanned the flames. Homebrewing accounts for roughly 80% of the craft brewers today. Long before President Carter repealed its ban, a relic from the days of Prohibition, thousands of beer buffs had been furtively brewing in their barns, basements, bathtubs and backyards. As soon as the legal shackles had been removed, 'microbreweries' started to poke their mash-forks into the ass of a beer market screaming out for innovation.

In 1983, Anheuser-Busch, Miller, Heileman, Stroh, Coors, and Pabst owned a staggering, and somewhat stagnant, 92% of beer production. Yet it was the mushrooming craft beer scene that was making all the noise. The volume steadily increased with the advent of the brewpub concept in 1982 (making and serving beer and food on premises was hitherto illegal), which gave craft brewers direct and vital access to the consumer.

By the late 1980s, craft beer was no longer a kooky pastime – it was a bona-fide business idea. The microbrewing revolution was featured on television, it was written about in newspapers and eagerly supported by a rapidly expanding homebrewing community. Over the next five years or so, sales soared and so did the number of craft breweries. By 1994, California laid claim to 84 microbreweries and brewpubs – one more than there had been in all of America for a decade before. Between early 1993 and late 1994, nearly 200 small breweries opened their doors. A year later, the number of micros surpassed 500. Over the next few years, craft breweries continued to open here, there and everywhere.

Unfortunately, the trend could not be sustained. In 1997, there were 1,376 craft breweries producing 5.5 million barrels of beer. Not all of it was good, however, with many new ventures relying on generous bank loans rather than a real passion for brewing.

"There was big growth in the mid 1990s, but the market had become cluttered with people in it more for the money than the beer," said Tom McCormack, chairman of the Californian Small Brewers Association. "For the first time, we began to see people in suits coming to brewing conferences, bankers, lawyers and accountants who didn't share the same passion."

Predictably, a Darwinian shake out ensued. Many feared it to be an ominous death rattle, but it was no more than a necessary growing pain. Pruned of the pinstripes, craft beer picked itself up and dusted itself down. Over the next decade or so, it steadily matured into the most dynamic beer sector not just in America but, arguably, the world.

The stage is set

More than 1,400 breweries now shape a thriving craft beer category, producing well in excess of six million barrels (each containing 31 US gallons) of beer a year. In 2006, in a marked departure from a stagnant mainstream beer market, craft beer sales rose by 11.7%, clocking up retail sales of $4.2 billion. Indeed, craft beer has become the quickest growing segment of the alcoholic beverage industry for the third year running. This double-digit increase follows impressive growth in each of the prior three years (31.5%) and bodes rather well for the future.

This volume and value is underpinned by unprecedented variety. The brewing masters of Europe may have provided instruction and inspiration, but in terms of choice the Americans knock contemporary European brewing into touch. They don't just push the envelope of innovation, they fold it into a paper airplane, attach two Harrier Jump Jet turbines to the wings and launch it into the heavens. Smoke-flavoured beers; herb- and spice-infused brews; American-style Hefeweizens; wood- and barrel-aged beers; big and brash barley wines; pre-Prohibition lagers, honey beers and experimental ales brewed with pomegranate, coriander, beetroot and Kaffir lime leaves represent just a drop in America's bucket of brewing creativity. Uncle Sam has never had it so good...

US beer styles

LIFE IN THE SEVENTIES was so much less demanding for American beer drinkers. They could drink any beer in the world, just as long as it was bland and indistinguishable from the only other one on the bar. Everybody knew where they stood. It was nice and it was simple.

But then in the Eighties, those meddling microbrewers came along and busily set about complicating matters. Long forgotten European beer styles were awoken from their slumbers, entirely new styles were forged and boundaries were merged. Fresh from hedonistic homebrewing adventures, the new wave of eagerly esoteric craft brewers didn't so much rewrite the rulebook as throw it in a mash-tun, chuck in copious amounts of hops, boil it up good and proper, ferment it for god knows how long and mature it in Bourbon oak barrels teeming with unruly yeast.

Driven by derring-do and the kind of cheeky chutzpah that leaves Europeans in a state of bewildered awe, the innovation continued and, today, is thankfully showing little sign of abating. With so many styles, hybrids and twists on tradition, the sheer breadth and depth of choice for beer drinkers is unrivalled.

Yet there are some brewers who play a little fast and loose when it comes to styles. For the uninitiated, this makes choosing a beer in an American bar as baffling an experience as it is tastebud-tingling.

So, in an attempt to clarify the issue, we've called upon the clever clogs at the Brewers Association (BA) to provide the final word on what a beer style should look, taste, smell and feel like. Paraphrased below are the strict competition guidelines used for the annual Great American Beer Festival (GABF) – American craft beer's version of the Oscars. And, for what it's worth, there's also a brief bluffer's shorthand to each beer style and a

West Coast example that we, and not the impartial BA, believe meets the brief.

LAGER

Pilsner (German style)

GABF guidelines: Very light straw or golden in colour and well hopped. Hop bitterness is high. Moderate noble-hop aroma and flavour. Well-attenuated, medium-bodied beer with a malty residual sweetness in aroma and flavour.

Bohemian-style Pilsners, light amber in colour, balance moderate bitterness and noble-type hop aroma. Malty, slightly sweet flavour and medium body. A toasted, biscuit-like, bready malt character.

Bluffer's shorthand: Unfairly lambasted as the last bastion of the scoundrel, Pilsners dragged beer out of the dark ages into the light. Many Pilsners, especially those that use cost-saving adjuncts, are caricatures of a true golden classic.

Try: Trumer Pilsner, *Trumer Brewery, San Francisco*

Pilsner (Pre-Prohibition American style)

GABF guidelines: Straw to deep gold in colour. Hop bitterness, flavour and aroma are medium to high; use of noble-type hops for flavour and aroma is preferred. Up to 25% corn and/or rice in the grist should be used. Malt flavour and aroma are medium.

Bluffer's shorthand: Rice may not please beer buffs today, but for the drinkers of late 19th-century America it was regarded as rather fancy and the easy-drinking, translucent beer it produced was all the rage.

Try: Session, *Full Sail, Hood River, Oregon*

Helles

GABF guidelines: Medium-bodied and malt-emphasised beer with low bitterness. Malt character is reminiscent of freshly- and very lightly-toasted malted barley.

Bluffer's shorthand: Unnerved by the 19th-century success of Pilsner, Munich brewers slaked the European thirst for light beer with a maltier lager armed with a spicy hop kick.

Try: Ninkasi Goddess, *Ninkasi Brewery, Eugene, Oregon*

Oktoberfest

GABF guidelines: Characterised by a medium body and golden, light colour. Sweet maltiness is mild with an equalising balance of clean hop bitterness. Low but notable hop aroma and flavour. American twists are distinguished by a greater hop character.

Bluffer's shorthand: Bavarian beer with a bigger bulge in its lederhosen. If Germans weren't such sensible chaps they'd drink this strong seasonal all year. Their trains, however, would no longer run on time.

Try: Sierra Nevada Octoberfest, *Sierra Nevada Brewing Company, California*

Vienna-style Lager

GABF guidelines: Reddish brown or copper coloured. Medium in body. The beer is characterised by a malty aroma and slight malt sweetness. The aroma and flavour should have a notable degree of toasted and/or slightly roasted character. Clean, crisp hop bitterness.

Bluffer's shorthand: As crisp and sweet as a Super Bowl-winning field goal.

Try: Royal Red Lager, *Triple 7 Restaurant, Las Vegas*

Dunkel

GABF guidelines: Light to dark brown beer with pronounced malty aroma and flavour that dominate over clean, crisp, moderate hop bitterness. Not offering an overly sweet impression, it has a mild balance between malt sweetness, hop bitterness and light to moderate mouthfeel. A classic Dunkel should have a chocolate-like, roast malt, bread-like or biscuit-like aroma that comes from the use of Munich dark malt.

Bluffer's shorthand: Smooth, rich and complex like a tanned and tuxedoed George Clooney. On a sledge.

Try: Firestone Walker Lager, *Firestone Walker, Pasa Robles, California*

Schwarzbier

GABF guidelines: Very dark brown to black beer, mild roasted malt character without the associated bitterness. Not full-bodied but moderate, gently enhancing malt flavour and aroma with low to moderate levels of sweetness. Hop bitterness is low to medium in character.

Bluffer's shorthand: Beneath his dark, mysterious and muscular looks lies a gentle fellow who's not bitter.

Try: Death & Taxes, *Moonlight Brewing, California*

Bock

GABF guidelines: Made with all malt, Bocks are strong, malty, medium- to full-bodied, bottom-fermented beers. Moderate hop bitterness should increase proportionally with strength. Hop flavour should be low and hop aroma should be very low. Bocks can range in colour from deep copper to dark brown. Doppelbocks, full bodied and deep amber to dark brown in colour, are high in alcoholic strength and hop rates increase with strength. Hop bitterness and flavour should be low and hop aroma absent. A stronger version of Doppelbock is strong Eisbock.

Bluffer's shorthand: German Monks once brewed these robust lagers to get through Lent but, thankfully, you can now bock around the clock.

Try: Anchor Bock, *Anchor Brewing, San Francisco, California*

ALES

Golden or Blonde Ale

Straw to golden blonde in colour. A crisp, dry palate, light to medium body and light malt sweetness. Low to medium hop floral aroma should not dominate.

Bluffer's shorthand: Gentlemen prefer blondes. Especially those gents normally devoted to lawnmower lagers. Brusque, gently bitter and very drinkable, it's a powerful weapon in craft brewing's arsenal.

Try: Haymaker Extra Pale Ale, *BridgePort Brewing, Portland, Oregon*

Kölsch

GABF guidelines: Warm fermented and aged at cold temperatures, characterised by a golden to straw colour and a slightly dry, subtly sweet softness on the palate, yet crisp. Low hop flavour and aroma with medium bitterness. Wheat can be used, ale yeast is used for fermentation, though lager yeast is sometimes used in the bottle or final cold conditioning.

Bluffer's shorthand: Originally exclusive to the German city of Cologne, Kölsch's clipped sweetness is being championed by many an artisan ale brewer.

Try: Yellowtail Pale Ale, *Ballast Point Brewing Company, San Diego*

Pale Ale/American Pale Ale/ Strong Pale Ale

GABF guidelines: Classic English pale ales are golden to copper coloured and display earthy, herbal English-variety hop character. Medium to high hop bitterness, flavour and aroma should be evident. This medium-bodied pale ale has low to medium malt flavour and aroma. Low caramel character is possible. American pale ales range from deep golden to copper in colour. The style is characterised by fruity, floral and citrus-like American-variety hop character producing high hop bitterness, flavour and aroma. American pale ales have medium body and low to medium maltiness. Low caramel character is allowable. Fruity-ester flavour and aroma should be moderate to strong.

Bluffer's shorthand: Abandoned by Brits, pale ale was the style that drove the craft beer revolution. Stacked with juicy malt and heightened hop character, pale ales initially blew the doors off light lagers but have since been usurped by 'bigger' pale ale interpretations.

Try: Sierra Nevada Pale Ale, *Sierra Nevada Brewing, California*

India Pale Ale

GABF guidelines: American-style India pale ales have intense hop bitterness, flavour and aroma with medium-high alcohol content, further characterised by fruity, floral and citrus-like American-variety hop character. The use of water with high mineral content results in a crisp, dry beer. This pale gold to deep copper-coloured ale has a full, flowery hop aroma and may have a strong hop flavour (in addition to the hop bitterness). India pale ales possess medium maltiness and body.

Bluffer's shorthand: American IPAs don't normally have to make the sea-faring journey to India but that hasn't stopped brewers making them hoppier than a one-legged man in an arse-kicking competition.

Try: Racer 5, *Bear Republic Brewing Co., Healdsburg, California*

Imperial or Double India Pale Ale

GABF guidelines: Imperial or Double India pale ales have intense hop bitterness, flavour and aroma. Alcohol content is high to very high and notably evident. Colour ranges from deep golden to amber. The style may use any variety of hops. Though the hop character is intense it's balanced with complex alcohol flavours, moderate to high fruity esters and medium to high malt character. Hop character should be fresh and lively and not harsh in quality. The use of large amounts of hops may cause a degree of appropriate hop haze. Imperial or Double India pale ales have medium-high to full body.

Bluffer's shorthand: The hoppiest, most intensely flavoured and high-octane beers in the world. Brimming with hops, hops and more hops, flooding your nostrils with their resinous, herbal fumes; puckering and pickling your tastebuds; leaving your mouth drier than an AA meeting during Prohibition.

Try: Exponential Hoppiness, *Alpine Beer Company, San Diego, California*

American Style Amber/Red Ale

GABF guidelines: American amber/red ales range from light copper to light brown in colour. They are characterised by American variety hops used to produce high hop bitterness, flavour, and medium to high aroma. Amber ales have medium-high to high maltiness with medium to low caramel character. They should
have medium to medium-high
body. The style may have low
levels of fruity ester flavour and
aroma. Imperial or double red
ales have a full body.

Bluffer's shorthand: More than
just a stepping stone for lager
drinkers on the way to the dark
side, Ambers tread a tightrope
between malt sweetness and
hop bitterness. Balance is key.
Try: Red Tail Ale, *Mendocino Brewery, Ukiah, California*

Bitter

GABF guidelines: Ordinary bitter is gold to copper coloured with medium bitterness, light to medium body and low to medium residual malt sweetness. Either English or American hop flavour and aroma character may be evident at the brewer's discretion. Mild carbonation traditionally characterises draft cask versions but in bottled versions a slight increase in carbon dioxide content is acceptable. Special bitter is more robust than ordinary bitter.

Extra special bitter possesses medium to strong hop qualities in aroma, flavour and bitterness. English hop varieties or others that approximate their resulting character are used in this sub-category.
Bluffer's shorthand: Bitter by name but not by nature, the hop hit is a gentle one compared to the extreme IPAs. Inconsistent with the hop culture, beers described with the word 'bitter' tend to struggle.
Try: Younger's Special Bitter, *Rogue, Newport, Oregon*

Scottish Ale

GABF guidelines: Scottish ales are light to medium bodied. Moderate bitterness is perceived but hop flavour or aroma should not be. Despite its lightness, it will have a degree of malty, caramel-like, soft and chewy character. The colour will range from golden amber to deep brown.
Bluffer's shorthand: Scotch ales are to malt what IPA is to hop bitterness but brewers on the West Coast, as is their want, throw them in anyway. The crazy fools.
Try: MacPelican Scottish Style Ale, *Pelican Brewery, Pacific City, Oregon*

Brown Ale

GABF guidelines: American brown ales range from deep copper to brown in colour. Roasted malt caramel-like and chocolate-like characters should be of medium intensity in both flavour and aroma. American brown ales have an evident hop aroma, medium to high hop bitterness, low to medium hop flavour and a medium body.
Bluffer's shorthand: Brawny and tawny, American brown ales have got more nuts than English versions. Often literally.
Try: Hazelnut Brown Nectar, *Rogue Brewery, Newport, Oregon*

Bavarian Style Weizenbier/Weisse

GABF guidelines: The aroma and flavour of a Weissbier with yeast is decidedly fruity and phenolic. The phenolic characteristics are often described as clove or nutmeg-like and can be smoky. These beers are made with at least 50% malted wheat, and hop rates are quite low. Hop flavour and aroma are absent. The colour is very pale to pale amber. Darker versions, known as Dunkel Weizens, are characterised by a sweet maltiness and a chocolate-like character from roasted malt.
Bluffer's shorthand: This is where yeast struts its funky stuff and produces fruit, bubblegum, banana and vanilla flavours. Hefeweizen is unfiltered and cloudy in a cool way. Wedge of lemon optional but probably not.
Try: El Jefe, *Hale's Ales, Seattle, Washington*

Belgian Style White (Wit)/
Belgian Style Wheat

GABF guidelines: Belgian white ales are very pale in colour and brewed using unmalted wheat and malted barley, spiced with coriander and orange peel. Coriander and light orange peel aroma should be perceived. Phenolic spiciness and yeast flavours may be evident at mild levels. These beers are traditionally bottle conditioned and served cloudy. An unfiltered nearly opaque haze should be

part of the appearance. Low hop bitterness and little to no apparent hop flavour.
Bluffer's shorthand: Unlike the Germans, the Belgians – and indeed the Americans – fling herbs and spices into their wheat beer.
Try: Great White, *Lost Coast Brewing, Eureka, Oregon*

Saison
GABF guidelines: Golden to deep amber in colour, Saisons span quite a variety of characters. Generally, they are light to medium in body. Malt aroma is low to medium low. Fruity esters dominate the aroma, while hop character, complex alcohols, herbs, spices and even clove and smoke-like phenolics may or may not be evident in the overall balanced beer. Malt flavour is low but provides foundation for the overall balance. Hop bitterness is moderate to moderately assertive. Herb and/or spice flavours may or may not be evident. Fruitiness from fermentation is generally in character. A balanced small amount of sour or acidic flavours is acceptable. Earthy, cellar like, musty aromas are okay.
Bluffer's shorthand: Very much in season among craft brewers, Saisons are as fruity and spicy as hanky-panky in a hay stack.
Try: Red Barn Ale, *Lost Abbey, San Diego, California*

Belgian Pale Ales
GABF guidelines: Belgian-style pale ales are characterised by low but noticeable hop bitterness, flavour and aroma. Light to medium body and low malt aroma are typical. They are golden to deep amber in colour. Low to medium fruity esters are evident in aroma and flavour. Low levels of phenolic spiciness from yeast by-products may be perceived. Low caramel or toasted malt flavour is okay.
Bluffer's shorthand: A blonde fluffy head like Tintin, spice, sweetness and a feast of yeast.
Try: Redemption, *Russian River, Santa Rosa, California*

Belgian-style Dubbel
GABF guidelines: Medium to full bodied, dark amber to brown-coloured ale. Malty sweetness and nutty, chocolate-like, and mild roast malt aroma – may also have a raisin-like cocoa character. Dubbels are also characterised by low bitterness and no hop flavour. Head retention is dense and mousse like.

Bluffer's shorthand: Strong, complex and mounted proudly on robust malt, it's easy to get into trouble with a Dubbel.
Try: Brother Thelonious, *North Coast, Fort Bragg, California*

Belgian-style Tripel
GABF guidelines: Tripels are often characterised by a complex, sometimes mild, spicy character, but no clove-like phenolic flavour. It may finish sweet, though any sweet finish should be light. The beer is characteristically medium bodied with an equalising hop/malt balance. Traditional Belgian Tripels are often well attenuated. Alcohol strength and flavour should be perceived as evident. Head retention is dense and mousse like.
Bluffer's shorthand: Beware these blonde, baby-faced assassins. Tripels, brewed using three times as much malt, shrewdly hide their strength beneath a comforting blanket of spice, sweetness and a mousse-like head.
Try: Épluche-Culotte, *Midnight Sun Brewing, Anchorage, Alaska*

Porter
GABF guidelines: Porters are mid to dark brown (sometimes with a red tint) in colour. No roast barley or strong burnt/black malt character should be perceived. Low to medium malt sweetness is acceptable along with medium hop bitterness. This is a light to medium bodied beer. Fruity esters are acceptable. Hop flavour and aroma may vary from being negligible to medium in character.
Bluffer's shorthand: Like a bikini-babe chasing Benny Hill, Americans have adopted the neglected English beer-style Porter as their

own. And then made it better and bigger through barrel ageing and smoothing coffee, chocolate and smoked malts.
Try: Alaskan Smoked Porter, *Alaska Brewing Company, Alaska*

Stout

GABF guidelines: Stouts have an initial malt and light caramel flavour profile with a distinctive dry-roasted bitterness in the finish. Dry Stouts achieve a dry-roasted character through the use of roasted barley. The emphasis of coffee-like roasted barley and a moderate degree of roasted malt aromas define the character. Hop aroma and flavour should not be perceived. Dry Stouts have medium/light to medium body. Fruity esters are minimal and overshadowed by malt, high hop bitterness and roasted barley character. Head retention and rich character should be part of the visual character. American-style Stouts should have moderate to high hop bitterness with American citrus-type and/ or resiny hop character. Oatmeal Stouts include oatmeal in their grist, resulting in a pleasant, full flavour and a smooth profile that is rich without being grainy.
Bluffer's shorthand: Begorrah, bejaysus and bejabbers! In terms of hops and toasty roastiness, American Stouts Riverdance all over the traditional, Guinness-inspired perceptions of Stout.
Try: Terminator Stout, *McMenamins, Oregon*

Russian Imperial Stout

GABF guidelines: Dark copper to very dark brown, imperial Stouts typically have high alcohol content. The extremely rich malty flavour (often characterised as toffee-like or caramel-like) and aroma are balanced with medium hopping and high fruity-ester characteristics. Bitterness should be moderate and balanced with sweet malt character.

The bitterness may be higher in the darker versions. Roasted malt astringency is very low or absent. Bitterness should not overwhelm the overall character. Hop aroma can be subtle to moderately floral, citrus or herbal. American-style Imperial Stouts typically have a high alcohol content. Generally characterised as very robust.
Bluffer's shorthand: Opaque, vinous and rich, Imperial Stouts are beer's answer to a top quality port. Sipping sensations with cheese, dessert and a nice puff on a Cuban.
Try: The Abyss, *Deschutes Brewery, Bend, Oregon*

Strong Ale

GABF guidelines: Light amber to mid brown in colour, strong ales are medium to full bodied with a malty sweetness. Hop aroma should be minimal and flavour can vary from none to medium in character intensity. Fruity-ester flavours and aromas can contribute to the character of this ale. Bitterness should be minimal but evident and balanced with malt and/or caramel-like sweetness. Alcohol types can be varied and complex. A rich, often sweet and complex estery character may be evident. This process often softens the perceived bitterness.
Bluffer's shorthand: A strapping sweetness wrapped up in a winter-warming coat of fruit, a touch of spice and rich, juicy malt. Not as potent as barley wine but, still, sip don't swig.
Try: Ritual Dark Ale, *Reaper Ales, San Diego, California*

Barley Wines

GABF guidelines: American-style barley wines range from amber to deep copper-garnet in colour and have a full body and high residual malty sweetness. Complexity of alcohols and fruity-ester characters are often high and counterbalanced by assertive bitterness and extraordinary alcohol content. Hop aroma and flavour are at medium to very high levels. American type hops are often used but not necessary for this style. A caramel and/or toffee aroma and flavour are often part of the character. Chill haze is allowable at cold temperatures.

Bluffer's shorthand: Gorgeous, grandiose ale with huge flavours that ripen and increase in complexity during languid maturation. Dark fruits, citrus notes, chocolate and coffee sharpened by peppery, grassy and floral hop notes.

Try: Firestone 10, *Firestone Walker, Pasa Robles, California*

Cream Ale

GABF guidelines: Mild, pale, light-bodied ale made using a warm fermentation (top or bottom) and cold lagering. Low to very low hop bitterness and flavour. Hop aroma is often absent. Crisp and refreshing, pale malt character predominates with fruity or estery aroma.

Bluffer's shorthand: A beginner's beer. Light, refreshing and crisp. Less is more.

Try: Summer Solstice Cerveza Crema, *Anderson Valley, California*

Fruit Beer

GABF guidelines: Any beers using fruit or fruit extracts as an adjunct in either primary or secondary fermentation, providing obvious (ranging from subtle to intense) yet harmonious fruit qualities. Should not be overpowered by hop character.

Bluffer's shorthand: Fruit beers are fine summer sips and terrific as dessert or aperitif beers. Should be slightly sweet, not overly sickly and use fresh fruit rather than artificial adjuncts.

Try: Watermelon Wheat, *21st Amendment, San Francisco, California*

Herb and Spice Beer

GABF guidelines: Use herbs or spices (derived from roots, seeds, fruits, vegetables, flowers, etc) other than or in addition to hops to create a distinct (ranging from subtle to intense) character, although individual characters of herbs and/or spices used may not always be identifiable. Underhopping often, but not always, allows the spice or herb to contribute to the flavour profile.

Bluffer's shorthand: Before hops were discovered, brewers balanced out malt with herbs

and spices. More than just a nostalgic indulgence, craft brewers are doing the same with some gusto.

Try: Triple White Sage, *Craftsman Brewery, Pasadena, California*

Wood and Barrel Aged Beer

GABF guidelines: Any lager, ale or hybrid beer, either a traditional style or a unique experimental beer that has been aged in a wooden barrel or been in contact with wood. This beer is intentionally aged with the particularly unique character of the wood and/or what has previously been in the barrel.

Old sherry, Bourbon, Scotch, port, wine and other barrels are often used, imparting complexity and uniqueness to the beer. New wood character is often characterised as a complex blend of vanillin and unique wood character. Oak-aged sour beers are born from bacteria and/or 'wild' yeast fermentation which contribute complex esters and result in a dry to very dry beer. They are a marriage of acidity, complex esters and new beer with wood and/or barrel flavours.

Bluffer's shorthand: Go-ahead US brewers are aping wine and whisky making techniques and applying them at the forefront of New World brewing. The beer picks up vanilla, wood, sourness and spiritual wellbeing.

Try: Angel's Share, *Lost Abbey, San Diego, California*

Smoke Beer/Rauchbier

GABF guidelines: Rauchbier should have smoky characters that range from detectable to prevalent in the aroma and flavour. Smoke character is not harshly phenolic but rather very smooth, almost rendering a perception of mild sweetness to this style of beer. This is a medium-bodied, smoke and malt-emphasised beer. This beer should be perceived as having low bitterness and is reminiscent of freshly and very lightly toasted sweet malted barley. There should not be any caramel character. Colour is light straw to golden. Noble-type hop flavour is low but may be perceptible. The aroma should strike a balance between malt, hop and smoke.

Bluffer's shorthand: Smoke, smoke and more smoke. Like drinking through a campfire.

Try: Smoked Black Lager, *Craftsman Brewing, Pasadena, California*

Beer and food

NOTWITHSTANDING the classic American pairing of a cold Coors and a fistful of nachos, beer's relationship with food has tended to be a frosty one – its presence on the dining table or in the kitchen as welcome as a dose of E-coli.

It wasn't too long ago that merely uttering the words 'beer' and 'gastronomy' in the same sentence would have the men in white coats knocking on your door – and we're not talking about inquisitive chefs either.

Yet times have changed – beer has unleashed itself from the straitjacket of misconception and is at last receiving the gastronomic credit it deserves. West Coast micros, brew-pubs, bars and elite eateries are currently hosting more beer and food pairing dinners than they've had hot ones, and beer is being given equal billing to wine.

About time too. Beer, lest we forget, has history firmly on its side. For centuries, it was the grain not the grape that poured supreme in the homes of both the posh and the pauper.

Yet, in recent times, food's traditional relationship with beer has been wrecked by the European eroticism and allure of the grape. Wine's charm offensive has turned the heads of *bon vivants* with smooth candlelit patter and cork-sniffing, glass-swirling refinement. But don't believe the hype peddled by viniculture vultures. Beneath wine's fur coat of sophistication there's a distinct lack of underwear and food is realising the error of its wine ways and rekindling its relationship with cuckolded beer.

Wine may have won the phony battle, but the real war for food's affections takes place on the palate and among one's senses and it is here where beer is truly turning the dining tables.

Beer boasts more than 100 different flavours and styles, thousands of natural aroma compounds and a better finish than most wines. Borne from the hop or roasted malt, the bitterness in beer slices through full-bodied flavours and greasy textures while carbonation, absent from wine, cleanses the palate and renders every subsequent bite as fresh as the first.

Artisan brews, lovingly crafted ales and long and lingering lagers with genuine balance and complexity of flavour are no match for the Chardonnays, Shirazes and even the finest Burgundies of this world when it comes to showing food a good time.

Finding the whole beer and food concept a bit hard to swallow? Then savour oysters with a rich, creamy Stout – a combination that sings hymns going down; sample a sweet Framboise with chocolate torte or foie gras; sip on a full-bodied and herbal rich Bière de Garde with pork or rabbit; or wash down a snappy Weissbier, all coriander and citrus, with grilled fish and a Caesar salad.

Wine may be a wonderful drink in many ways but it doesn't go with everything. Spicy food is a case in point. Beer's flavours stand up strong to the sweetness and spice of ethnic and Tex-Mex cuisine. Shorn of beer's roasted, scorched and caramel flavours, wine simply can't stand the heat of an ethic kitchen.

Nor can it cope with the complexity of the cheeseboard. Cheese is as compatible with wine as it is with chalk. It's an unhappy after-dinner marriage that's crumbling like a Danish Blue. Cheese has unshackled itself from its loveless plonk pretence and done what it's always wanted to: namely sow its wild oatcakes with beer. The bitter nuttiness of barley wine gets on swimmingly well with a rich and creamy Stilton; Dopplebock sidles up to Swiss cheese with a glint in its eye

Left: a light, cloudy wheat beer and goats' cheese is a classic combination

while India Pale Ale mingles magnificently with traditionally-aged cheddars.

The age-old adage of white and red wines matching with their colour-co-ordinated meats doesn't apply to beer. A beer's hue doesn't necessarily dictate its flavour. Golden ale can be strong and powerful while delicate sweetness can flow from the darkest Porter.

Apart from the one that says that ALL beer goes with pizza, there are no rules to beer and food matching, merely loose guidelines. Here are some suggestions for what to eat with your favourite beers.

Made for each other

Pilsner, Kölsch and Light Lager These beers know all about delicate flavours and so won't trample over finely-tuned food: shellfish; Cajun; mildly spicy Indian; smoked meats or fish; tapas; spicy Vietnamese or Thai.

Pale Ale/Bitter A loving and devoted partner to pub grub, pale ales will gild bangers and mash, fish and chips, pizza, pies, pasta (not tomato-based sauces) and a Reuben sandwich with panache.

Indian Pale Ale/Double IPA Think rich. IPAs have the bitterness to cut through fat like a knife through er ... butter. Roasts – especially beef or pork – are a good starting point; curries also suit (and not just because they're from India); chilli con carne; enchilada; spicy sausage and gourmet hamburgers too.

Brown Ale Cajun food, chile, burgers, steak and BBQ ribs.

Trappist/Abbey Ales Dubbel ales (all caramel, chocolate, dark fruit and warming spice) lend themselves heartily to dark meat dishes with fruity sauces such as ribs, steak, game and strongly-smoked fish. Tripel Ales (floral hops, spicy aromatics and fruity flavours) have a foody fetish for herb-crusted dark meats, swanky sausages and foie gras.

Porter/Stout Stout is a dessert beer: terrific with vanilla ice cream, fruit tart, chocolate cake and mousses, pannacotta, cheesecake and plum pudding. It's also excellent with cheese, especially Stilton. Porters make ideal BBQ beers, anything caramelised or chargrilled gives a cheeky wink to the malt sweetness. Let's face it though, with Porter and Stout, nothing beats an oyster.

Fruit Beers Great companions to sweet and savoury dishes. Chocolate dessert is exquisite with Kriek (cherry) beers while Frambozen (raspberry) is simply sublime with foie gras. Strangely, these beers don't complement fruit desserts or dishes. It seems that too much fruit can, after all, be a bad thing.

Witbier & Weissbier Weissbier is food's flexible friend. Light and refreshing enough to complement salads, white meat dishes and pasta dishes, it has the flameproof refreshment to extinguish piquancy too. With Witbier, meanwhile, try to link up citrus flavours in salads, light fish courses or moules mariniere. It may be a cliché but it's a downright tasty one.

Barley Wine & Bock Say cheese. Or say rich dessert, indulgent ice cream and a slice of pecan pie drenched in cream. Please.

Cooking with beer

By Bruce Paton – The Beer Chef

Beer has been in the kitchen for hundreds of years. When cooking with ale there are a few basic principles to remember. On the West Coast one of the more popular styles for consumption is India Pale Ale (IPA). West Coast IPAs are usually highly hopped with a clean, crisp, refreshing, slightly bitter finish. However, your favourite drinking beer may not be your best bet in the kitchen. Highly-hopped beers do not do well in situations where there is a long cooking time or a reduction because when you concentrate bitterness you get a painful experience. Add sugar to the proceedings, however, and the outcome can be delicious.

Beer is great in marinades and brines where you are looking to tenderise or add flavour. I like to use Porters and Stouts for these endeavours because of the roasted flavours the beer imparts on the end product. However I've had great success marinating eggplant with Russian River Damnation, a Belgian-style ale, and grilling it on the barbecue.

Whether you want to cook with it or just drink it, the first thing to do is go out and try some new beers. Then take it from there...

BRUCE PATON *writes a beer and food column for* The Culinarian, *the monthly magazine published by the Culinary Association of the Pacific Coast. His website is* **www.beer-chef.com**.

The Beer Chef

A nationally renowned authority on pairing beer and food, Bruce Paton is the award-winning executive chef at The Cathedral Hill Hotel in San Francisco. Here are his suggestions for dining and cooking with beer.

I have the benefit of living in the San Francisco Bay area which has been a hotbed of brewing creativity for many years. Twelve years ago I was the chef in a restaurant with 30 beers on tap (the proverbial kid in the candy store) and we did a food and beer pairing dinner. One thing led to another and now I am known as 'The Beer Chef'. Pairing food with beer is great fun and to get good at it you have to drink a lot of beer and eat a lot of food. I know that sounds pretty rough but with a certain level of determination you can do it too.

The general rules are very few because all tastes are a little different. Cut, contrast and complement, known as the 'Three Cs', are the basis of any food and beverage pairing. The basic idea is that you want to create more enjoyment for your taste buds by combining the two.

Cut is simply palate cleansing when you eat something that clings to your taste buds, be it chilli pepper, chocolate or fat. You want a beverage that will wash away the flavour so you can enjoy the next bite of your meal as much as the previous one.

The classic example of *Contrast* is the briny flavour of oysters on the half shell with the roasted malt flavours of a Dry Stout. An India Pale Ale is the perfect foil for spicy Asian or Hispanic dishes as well as a slice of prime rib or a well marbled steak.

Complement is my favourite, where the flavour of the food is accentuated by the beer and vice-versa. An Oatmeal Stout paired with a chocolate dessert will enhance both the beer and the food.

Some of my favourite pairings from the past have been cooked up with brewers in the San Francisco area. Watermelon Wheat Beer from the 21st Amendment's Shaun O'Sullivan paired with a smoked salmon salad with heirloom tomatoes, cucumber gelée and scallion crème fraîche. Moylan's Hopsicle (Double IPA) matched with Kurobuta pork, Hawaiian butterfish and sweet potato flan. Russian River's Pliny the Elder (Double IPA) with blue cheese. Salvation Ale (Belgian-style strong Dark Ale) also from Russian River with chilli chocolate mousse. And duck tetrazzini with Anchor Porter from Anchor Brewing.

Dining with beer

Dining with beer can be as simple or as grandiose as you would like it to be. Craft beer comes in a multitude of styles, with each one having several variations. There is a beer to go with whatever you enjoy eating.

If you are already in the habit of enjoying wine with your dinner you have a good head start. Basic beer styles can be broken down in the same manner that wines are. You have lagers and some Belgian-style ales that are similar to white wines, ales that are like red wines and barley wines and other stronger styles that resemble port wine. Glassware is important in the enjoyment of quality craft beer and your wine glasses will stand in just fine for most traditional beer glasses. Even the most expensive craft beer is much cheaper than wine.

Destinations

Southern California

CALIFORNIA is a very big place. Far too big for one chapter. So, we've cut it in half, running a scalpel under the chin of San Francisco.

There's method to our madness. As you travel through the State, locals rarely refer to themselves as Californians without a geographical prefix. There were even a few who proudly spoke of being a 'Central Californian' but, for the sake of simplicity, we're pretending we didn't hear that.

What's more, there's long been talk of officially separating the State. Culturally, it makes a lot of sense as Northern California and Southern California are hardly ideological bedfellows. In the former, the political pendulum swings left while sun-kissed conservatism tends to hold court in the latter – especially Orange County and San Diego.

Talk of division has never got beyond mere talking, however, as it would be economic suicide for all involved. Northern California and Southern California may not get along but with all the money sloshing about in the south (one third of California's population lives in LA County) and most of the natural resources residing in the north, they need each other and a split is highly unlikely.

But we're nothing if not revolutionary mavericks, folks, so we've just gone and pulled them apart like squabbling children. Not least because, aside from a proud dedication to enlightened elbow-bending, the beer scenes in NorCal and SoCal share little in common.

Northern California is where the whole good beer revolution started in the Eighties. San Francisco is as well-renowned for its open-minded beer drinking as its hills, hippies and hedonism while the woodsy wonderland to its north is home to the kind of laid-back liberalism in which craft beer so often flourishes.

While the beer scenes of Southern California may not be as deep-rooted, they're very much energised by the exuberance of youth. In contradiction to its rather rigid Republican image, San Diego is a naughty, mischievous brewing city, and its rogue ways are slowly influencing things up the road in Los Angeles, where beer has traditionally played second fiddle to Botox and beautiful people.

Having somehow remained oblivious to the rest of the West Coast's love affair with craft beer, Angelenos are finally stirring from their Prozac-induced haze and very slowly getting with the programme... girlfriend. The coastal highway, meanwhile, provides a ready-made ale adventure and effortlessly drinks in some superb suds and stunning scenery. Some would say the Central Coast, running roughly from Santa Barbara up to Santa Cruz, is one of the main reasons to visit the Golden State, such is the breath-taking beauty of the place. To top it all off, there's some seriously good breweries and brewpubs in this neck of the woods, making a superb range of hoppy bombs. We know that San Francisco and Los Angeles are the biggest draws for beer lovers, but it's well worth taking some time to explore this part of California, too.

California is a wonderful and seriously weird place that's impossible to summarise, but we hope that by slicing it into two distinct portions, it makes things more manageable. If it doesn't then, well, it's probably worth bearing in mind the words of subversive American author Edward Abbey:

"There is science, logic, reason;
  there is thought verified by experience.
  And then there is California."

Santa Monica is a safe and central seaside city – an ideal base from which to explore the rest of LA.

There's something for everyone in California's third city – fantastic food and superb suds to match.

San Diego

LOCATED AT THE FOOT of California, San Diego is a charming city with bountiful beaches and bays, a salubrious seafront and immaculate streets decked with adobe haciendas, boutique stores and a wealth of restaurants and bars. San Diego seems to be drenched in eternal sunshine, which enhances its aesthetic allure. No other city in America catches more rays, on average, the sun comes out to play more than 300 days a year. Even in June, where hazy episodes of spitting rain and cloud are a bizarre annual phenomenon, the mercury rarely dips below 70°F (21°C). Humidity is mercifully low, the sea breeze ensures that sunny doesn't equal sweaty. The annual rainfall rarely exceeds 10 inches (25 centimetres), with most falling between December and March.

All this sun beats down on more than 70 miles of golden sand and cobalt-coloured coastline. San Diego is paradise for sun worship and ocean sports. There are no shortage of places to surf (with or without a sail/kite), kayak, gawp at sexy, semi-nude strangers and play that game with wooden bats and ball that gets incredibly boring after about ten minutes.

While many are lured to San Diego by the golden orb, it is by no means the city's sole attraction. In addition to the world-famous zoo and SeaWorld (a marine zoo filled with sharks, other fish and the occasional mollusc), San Diego is home to more than 90 museums, one of America's largest urban parks and 7,000 restaurants to suit all budgets. The nightlife is energetic and bustling, and the beer scene is arguably one of the most exciting in all of America. Whether it's for sun, surf, seals or superb sunsets – San Diego is not to be missed.

San Diego history

"San Diego was discovered by the Germans in 1904. They named it San Diego, which of course, in German, means a whale's vagina."
RON BURGUNDY in cult-comedy film *Anchorman* (2004).

Burgundy's quote is historically inaccurate and cited purely for a cheap laugh. Far more reliable sources, such as history books, tell an entirely different story. In fact, San Diego was the birthplace of California. It was discovered in 1542 by Juan Rodriguez Cabrillo, who is regarded as the first European to set foot in California. The Portuguese explorer landed at Ballast Point near the cliffs of Point Loma, less than 9 miles (15 kilometres) north of Downtown San Diego today.

Perhaps discouraged by some moody Native Americans, Cabrillo didn't stay long. After a brief look round, he named it San Miguel and eschewed the whole colonization option in favour of getting back in his boat. Cabrillo sailed farther up the coast to the Oregon border where, unbeknown to him, it rains a lot and where – sadly – he died from a gangrenous splinter wound in 1543. Armed with the benefit of hindsight, one can't help thinking he should have stayed in San Diego.

Cabrillo's loss was the gain of a seafaring Spaniard called Sebastian Vizcaino, who arrived in November 1602. Vizcaino renamed the place San Diego de Alcala. One member of his expedition, Fray Antonio de la Ascensión, conducted the first Christian religious service of record in California. No one knows what he said, but whatever it was it didn't go down well with the natives. After the Mass, they turned up with bows and arrows and threatening faces. Luckily, conflict was avoided through the medium of sign language and Spanish gifts.

Kick back and relax in Balboa Park, one of the largest urban parks in America.

For one reason or another, Vizcaino didn't hang about either. It wasn't until 1709 that Europeans settlers began to call San Diego home. Sixty years later, Father Junipero Serra established the Mission San Diego de Alcala – a primary link in his chain of 21 missions that spread the Christian gospel as far as northern California. In 1774, the Mission San Diego de Alcala relocated elsewhere. The original site became a military garrison with an all-encompassing view of San Diego Bay. Amid growing interest in the New World, the Spanish further reinforced their defenses with the construction of Fort Guirros in 1797. It had a big cannon and everything. In 1821, Mexico won independence from Spain. San Diego then fell under Mexican rule until 1847, when it was captured by America as part of the Mexican-American War.

San Diego witnessed stuttering growth in the second-half of the nineteenth century. Efforts to become the main commercial centre of the West Coast were undermined by earthquakes, droughts, floods and even a hurricane or two. To make matters worse, neighbouring Los Angeles began to steal a march on its southern rival courtesy of a railroad connected directly with the East. When trains finally reached San Diego in 1885, the population exploded. A stampede for land ensued, and investment was rife.

Yet the boom soon went bust. By 1888, the population had shrunk from 40,000 to 16,000.

By the turn of the century, those living in San Diego numbered a modest 17,700. But by 1910, the population had doubled again. Thousands had moved down from San Francisco following the horrific 'Great Earthquake' of 1906.

In 1915, the Marines established a camp at Balboa Park. A year later, the camp played host to a major international exposition that marked San Diego in the national consciousness. Some of the animals from the exposition were quarantined when it closed the following year and opening a zoo seemed like a good option, thus San Diego Zoo was born.

Yet it was the military that shaped the character of San Diego over the following decades. By the start of the Second World War, the city was home to the US Navy's Pacific Command Center, leading military aircraft manufacturers and an Air Command Center that trained 32,000 pilots for the war. Rather brilliantly, this also included the elite 'Top Gun' Flight School. We miss you Goose, we really do.

While San Diego remained – and still remains – one of the largest military complexes in the Western world, the city swapped the uniform for civilian attire at the end of the Cold War in the late Eighties. The city has since diversified into biotechnology, tourism and – with the addition of three University campuses – the world of academia. Established in 1976, the City Center Redevelopment Corporation has overseen the gentrification of huge chunks of the city. The Horton Plaza – a shrine to shopping – was built in 1981, and an impressive revamp of the buzzy Gaslamp District followed as part of a wider transformation of Downtown San Diego. This has converted the area into a glistening district of businesses, boutiques and bayside restaurants, bars and hotels.

For all the sparkly veneer and twinkle-toothed glamour, San Diego is by no means squeaky clean. In recent times, the city has been shaken by scandal and corruption involving some extremely influential city officials. What's more, critics have lambasted the city for its right-wing policy towards Latino immigrants. This has comprehensively debunked San Diego's claim as 'America's Finest City'.

Political tumult aside, San Diego is forever topping those surveys of cities that deliver the best quality of life in America. With a population of more than 1.2 million (2.3 million in the wider San Diego County), it's currently America's seventh-biggest city – and growing. While it may feature further down the list in terms of national importance, there can be fewer finer places in America for cavorting and generally kicking back in the sun.

Today/orientation

San Diego has a reputation for being a little uptight; the finger-wagging conservative cousin to fast-living Los Angeles and bohemian San Francisco. Given the city's military connection and the population of leather-skinned retirees – who flock to the San Diego sun like bees to a honeypot – it's perhaps no surprise that the city's political stance has traditionally been right of centre. Despite San Diego's proximity to the Mexican border, the ethnic mix is far less balanced than in other Californian cities, and the communities to the north and east remain steadfastly conformist.

Don't be fooled, though. Beneath San Diego's fur coat of urbane conservatism, it wears a rather skimpy bikini, with a risqué tattoo and maybe a piercing or two. This is Southern California remember, not southern Arkansas. As the locals will testify, San Diego has chilled out in recent years – it even voted Democrat in the 2004 election. The influx of Latino immigrants, the burgeoning gay community in Hillcrest and the student population have all smoothed over the hard Republican edges. Not to mention San Diego's deep-rooted surf and skate culture, boasting legendary skater Tony Hawk and celebrated surfer Rob Machado as born and bred San Diegans. Down by the city's beaches, the vibe is laid-back verging on horizontal. The only suits being worn have the zips on the back.

For many people, the lure of sand, sun and surf is the main attraction. The three beaches within closest proximity to Downtown San Diego are Ocean Beach, Pacific Beach and Mission Beach. Pacific and Mission aren't the alternative hippy hangouts of the past but, that said, the beachfront bars and restaurants certainly haven't surrendered their cosmopolitan character, and both remain great places to hang out.

Pacific and Mission are linked by a 3-mile boardwalk that buzzes with bikers, inline skaters, runners and skateboarders, all flexing their shapely pectorals and pins. Adjacent to Mission Beach is Belmont Park, featuring the vintage 'Giant Dipper' rollercoaster, a giant indoor swimming pool called 'The Plunge' and all manner of shops, amusement arcades and eateries. Ocean Beach is a far more bohemian beach and boardwalk. Regeneration has slowly,

Belmont Park: home to the 'Giant Dipper'.

although thankfully not entirely, dragged the area out of a funky Seventies time warp.

The slender stretch of sand known as Coronado Beach is within easy access of Downtown, too. The short ferry ride to Coronado is recommended, but you can cross the eponymous bridge. Once there you'll find a charming lamb chop–shaped peninsula of quaint houses, grand mansions, chic boutiques and the ever-so-posh Hotel Coronado, where Marilyn Monroe filmed *Some Like it Hot* with Tony Curtis. Coronado is also home to a massive Naval Air Station. This may explain why all the blokes have similar haircuts.

Just a 45-minute drive from Downtown, Oceanside Beach is home to the 1,942-foot Oceanside Pier – the longest wooden municipal pier on the West Coast of America. There, you'll find the California Surf Museum (www.surfmuseum.org) and, if you're really lucky, you might witness the Annual World Body Surfing Championship held each summer. Surfing competitions, triathlons and speedboat and outrigger races are also very popular.

Back on 'mainland', San Diego boasts a beautiful natural harbor. San Diego Bay doubles up as a buzzy tourist spot and a home-port for the US Navy, a large sportfishing fleet, thousands of pleasure craft and an increasing number of cruise ships. One of the best ways to see San Diego is from the waters of San Diego Bay aboard a harbor tour, a wintertime whale-watching expedition or – if you're feeling flush – a dinner cruise.

If your drinking legs are much stronger than your sea ones, head to the revamped Gaslamp District. Situated south of Broadway, San Diego's main artery, Gaslamp District was once home to drugs, prostitution and general debauchery. This 16-block quarter is now the epicenter of San Diego nightlife and shakes its booty particularly vigorously at weekends. There's a vibrant array of restaurants, bars and pubs, galleries, fancy shops, cute cafes and the odd raucous nightclub.

The predominantly gay district of Hillcrest to the north of the city centre offers a more laid-back, alternative take on San Diegan life. You'll find independent eateries, bohemian coffee bars and plenty of arty shops in which to potter and peruse. Well worth checking out.

Head for the Old Town for a more Hispanic experience. Best explored by foot, Old Town marks the site of the first Spanish settlement on the West Coast and showcases San Diego's Hispanic heritage from 1821–1872, when Mexico gained independence from Spain and took control of the area. The six-block park features 12 acres of Mexican lore presented in shops, restaurants, museums and a theatre. There are also several carefully preserved historic adobe and wooden buildings, including a schoolhouse, blacksmith shops, San Diego's first newspaper office, a stable with carriage collection and even a haunted courthouse.

No visit to San Diego is complete without a stroll through the lush greenness of Balboa Park – one of the largest urban cultural parks in America. Balboa Park is often called the 'Smithsonian of the West' for its concentration of culture. There are 15 museums, eight gardens and the enormous San Diego Zoo – arguably the best in the country. It's even got a Frisbee golf course.

Other tourist attractions include SeaWorld at Mission Bay. SeaWorld does exactly what it says on the tin – a 189-acre marine park with killer whales, manatees, seals, dolphins, sea lions, sea otters, penguins

and a tank that holds more than 6 million gallons of water. Legoland California in Carlsbad is a 30-minute drive north from central San Diego. There you'll find more than 15,000 Lego models constructed using somewhere in the region of 30 million Lego bricks. How do we know that? We counted each and every one of them. Just for you.

Getting around

San Diego is compact and it's easy to get around without a car – useful if you're planning to sink a few crafty beers on your travels. Buses are frequent, cheap and service a vast area; taxis are safe and fairly affordable; the 'Coaster' light rail system ventures as far as Downtown LA; and the San Diego Trolley is a cheap, cheerful and (on the blue line) charming way to see the city. It also sneaks past the Mexican border to Tijuana, where apparently you can get up to all kinds of mischief. San Diego is bike-friendly, too, with miles of designated cycle paths. You can even take your bike onto buses, the Trolley and the ferry to Coronado. But, remember, don't swig and cycle.

Accommodation

LUXURY

Tower23 723 Felspar St., Pacific Beach, CA 92109; **T** 866 869 3723 (866-TOWER23); www.tower23hotel.com
Uber-trendy urban beach resort on Pacific Beach across from Crystal Pier. Tower23 is the brainchild of local entrepreneurs Brett Miller and Robert Watson and designed by Graham Downdes. It's a sleek and luxury boutique hotel located on the boardwalk at the northern tip of Pacific Beach. There are more than 40 stylish rooms, all with ocean

views and patio/balcony, as well as walk-in rain showers, insomnia-busting beds, WiFi throughout and a ludicrously chic seafood restaurant and bar called Jordan (the eponymous basketball star, Michael, wore the number 23). A stunning experience that commands a hefty price tag.

MID-RANGE

La Pensione Hotel 606 W. Date St./India St., CA 92101; **T** 619 236 8000; **F** 619 236 8088; *Toll Free:* 1-800-232-4683
www.lapensionehotel.com
Quirky, renovated Hacienda-style hotel located in 'Little Italy', La Pensione Hotel is within walking distance of Downtown and the right side of town for major attractions such as SeaWorld and San Diego Zoo. As well as 75 simple, charming guest rooms, there are a couple of restaurants, underground parking and some jolly nice staff.

BUDGET

500 West Hotel 500 West Broadway, CA 92101; **T** 619 234 5252; **F** 619 234 5272; **E** generalmanager@500westhotel.com
www.500westhotel.com
Highly recommended
Fun, funky and fantastically good value, 500 West Hotel is a hip, historic hostel-cum-hotel. It enjoys a perfect position just yards from the harbour, Horton Plaza and Gaslamp District. Constructed in 1924, the huge, grandiose building on Broadway was primarily used to house US servicemen during the First and

Second World wars. In 2003, a $9 million renovation transformed it into a European-style hotel with more than 200 simple, stylish rooms finished with a cool, minimalist flourish. Much of the original structure has been maintained, including the lack of en-suite bathrooms. Guests are given a basket to take their toiletries to one of a dozen private yet communal and spotless bathrooms.

For between $49 and 89 a night, this is an absurdly small price to pay for the hotel's central location, WiFi, digital phones, flat-screen TVs, friendly staff and onsite YMCA fitness centre. Highly recommended – even if you're not on a budget!

Beer in San Diego

When it comes to cutting-edge beer, few cities can rival San Diego. But things were different 20 years ago. While San Francisco, Seattle and Portland were brewing up a beer storm in the Eighties and early Nineties, San Diego remain-ed relatively immune to the micro-brewing bug. The city was a brewing wilderness, and the locals were forced to rely on brews produced 'Upstate' rather than their own. It remains a bit of a mystery why this should be the case. Maybe it was just too hot? Or maybe it lacked the left-field liberalism of its northern neighbours? What is certain is that, after years of living in the brewing shadow of its West Coast rivals, San Diego's beer scene came into its own in the mid-Nineties.

The arrival of Stone Brewing Company, Oggi's, Ballast Point Brewing and AleSmith Brewing Company laid out the red carpet on which the likes of Coronado Brewing Company, Green Flash/Reaper Ale Brewing Company and Alpine Brewing now tread. Their beers pour from tap handles all over the county, and they've transformed America's sunniest city into one of America's most vibrant and fast-est-growing brewing metropolises.

You won't want for fine beer in San Diego – it's everywhere. Not content with a dozen maverick microbreweries, a mesmerising array of switched-on tap houses and a smattering of brewpubs, San Diego has even got its very own beer style. Double IPAs (DIPAs) are the signature suds of San Diego. For English drinkers more accustomed to mild-mannered milds and balanced, balmy bitters, a DIPA is a desperately daunting drop. Brimming with more hops than a shovel-load of hops on a frog convention – seriously strong yet strangely seductive – they're devilish, resinous and aggressively bitter liquids that will pickle your palate, torture your taste buds and blister your brain.

Although DIPA wasn't created in San Diego (that honour is bestowed upon Vinnie Cilurzo who unleashed it in 1994 at the now-defunct Blind Pig Brewery in southwest California), hundreds of heady hop monsters run amok in San Diego, outselling other styles in leading beer bars like O'Brien's, Liar's Club and Hamilton's Tavern.

No other city cranks up the IBU (interna-tional bittering units) knob with quite the same wide-eyed passion. Nearly every San Diego's brewer places IPA – either single or double – at the forefront of their burgeoning business. More than ten years on, these ven-tures are now reaching maturity and rightly being drenched in all manner of beer com-petition gongs. Fostered by an industrious San Diego Brewers Guild and QUAFF (the city's award-winning homebrewing club), the close-knit beer community is crammed full of camaraderie. In short, there's plenty in San Diego for the beer-drinking adventurer to get excited about.

That's beer that is!

BREWERS

AleSmith Brewing (1)
9368 Cabot Drive, CA 92126
T 858 549 9888
www.AleSmith.com
Highly recommended

San Diego's finest purveyor of craft beer is arguably AleSmith – an artisan and esoteric brewer inspired by the brewing traditions of Belgium and Britain. Founder Peter Zien is a former homebrewer who turned professional in 1995. He sacrificed a career in law to work his mashfork magic on second-hand dairy equipment in a quirky brewery on the northern fringes of town (he also makes artisan cheese, too). Regularly showered in medals, AleSmiths's all-natural, bottle-conditioned beers are renowned more for their balance than their unabashed bitterness. In addition to its flagship beer – a superb English-style ESB called Anvil (5.5%) – seek out AleSmith's opaque bottles containing Horny Devil (at 11%, a seductive strong Belgian ale infused with coriander seeds) and Wee Heavy (at 10%, a toasty, roasty and typically West Coasty take on a Scotch ale). Fantastic beers.

Brewery tours/Retail hours: Fri, 3pm-5pm; Sat, 1pm-4pm

Recommendation

AleSmith Speedway Stout (12%)
A divine, dark and velvet-textured Imperial stout brewed using copious amounts of coffee beans. Sublime.

Barrel-Aged Speedway Stout (12%)
Rarer than rocking-horse manure, this magnificent matured beer is brewed in small batches and rested in Heaven Hill Bourbon barrels. Fetches up to $200 a pop.

Alpine Brewing Company (2)
2351 Alpine Blvd., Alpine, CA 91091
T 619 445 2337
www.alpinebeerco.com

Situated in the bucolic town of the same name, the Alpine Beer Company is a terrific excuse to venture out of town. The brewery is not big but it's certainly clever producing, as it does, an eclectic range of small-batch beers including the wonderfully-titled Willi Vanilli, a lush, refreshing lager tinged with vanilla. Yet it's the Pure Hoppiness (8%) and Exponential Hoppiness (10.5%), two

Alpine Brewing Company

colossal, classic West Coast IPAs that make the trip truly worthwhile. Stop-by after midday, grab a growler and go camping, and drinking, and get lost in the woods.

Recommendation

Exponential Hoppiness (10.5%)
Ever-doubling doses of American hops infuse this Double IPA with a helluva hoppy, herbal aroma that mellows in the mouth thanks to the late addition of oakchips and measured maturation. Devilishly drinkable.

Ballast Point Brewing Company (3)
10051 Old Grove Rd., Suite B, CA 92131
T 858 695 2739

Owner Jack White has been quietly brewing enduring ales and lagers as a homebrewer since 1992 and as a professional since 1996. In 2005, Ballast Point Brewing Company moved and capacity tripled to meet growing local demand. The beers, named after salt-water game fish, find themselves into numerous tap houses and restaurants. Yellowtail Pale Ale – a West Coast interpretation of a German Kolsch beer – is the biggest seller. The delicious Black Marlin Porter, Wahoo Wheat and Calexico Amber Ale also command a strong local following, while Three Sheets Barley Wine and the infamous Dorado Double IPA are typically San Diegan in their hefty hop character.

Brewery tours: Mon-Fri, 11am-7pm (call ahead)

Recommendation

Yellowtail Pale Ale (4.6%)
Citrus-sweetness on the nose, slightly tangy, with a velvet-gloved hop punch. Extremely drinkable and a welcome respite from the relentless IPA invasion.

Stone Brewing Company (8)

1999 Citracado Parkway, Escondido, CA 92029
T 760 471 4999
www.stonebrew.com
Brewery tours: Mon-Fri, 2pm & 6pm;
Sat, noon, 2pm, 4pm, 6pm;
Sun, 2pm & 4pm
Cost: Free
Duration: 45 minutes

Stone Brewing World Bistro & Gardens
Opening hours: Sun-Thu, 11am-11pm;
Fri & Sat, 11am-2am

In 1996, the Stone Brewing Company burst onto the West Coast brewing scene and defiantly thrust a hot poker into the behind of conventional brewing. Co-founders Greg Koch and Steve Wagner had been working in the LA music industry and shared a love for beer.

GREG: *"The business was going well but I started to fall in love with beer. I was going to breweries, festivals and traveling specifically for beer. I started changing my plans and lifestyle. It was then that I realized I had to either get help or go professional!"*

They chose the latter, moved to San Diego and signed a lease on a new brewery in a nondescript industrial park in the city's northern outskirts. The timing was appalling. In the mid-Nineties, hundreds of craft brewers were hitting the wall – victims of a small beer sector running before it could walk – and plenty of people were sounding the industry's death knell.

GREG: *"We have always been unnaturally optimistic, but we were very concerned that we'd missed the boat. The timing was bad as the distributors were culling a lot of pretty bad beers and drinkers were starting to get tired of experimenting with a lot of unknown brands. But we also felt that there was an untapped opportunity down here. San Diego was a good place to be. Even though it was less-developed than other cities, we sensed a real camaraderie among the brewing community."*

Pizza Port and the Karl Strauss Brewpub had been ploughing a lonesome yet flavoursome furrow, but it was the Stone Brewing Company that really propelled the San Diego beer scene into the thinking drinker's consciousness. Stone re-wrote the rulebook with beers that were colossal in character and even bigger in attitude. A menacing gargoyle adorned its bottles, "warding off modern day evil spirits such as chemical preservatives, additives and adjuncts".

The names of the beers were as defiantly disobedient as the liquid itself. Arrogant Bastard – a 7.2% beast of a beer with an IBU rating so high it's unclassified – epitomises Stone's in-your-face ethos and lives up to it's eyebrow-raising name. Just listen to the words on the back label:

"This is an aggressive beer. You probably won't like it. It is quite doubtful that you have the taste or sophistication to be able to appreciate ale of this quality and depth. We would suggest that you stick to safer and more familiar territory – maybe something with a multi-billion dollar ad campaign aimed at convincing you it's made in a little brewery, or one that implies that their tasteless fizzy yellow beer will give you more sex appeal. Perhaps you think that multi-million dollar ad campaigns make a beer taste better. Perhaps you are mouthing your words as you read this."

Antagonizing drinkers at a time when they're questioning the future of craft brewing may have seemed a rather risky idea but, unlike many of its peers, Stone beers walked the walk as successfully as they talked the talk. Stone's beers were, as the Californian style dictates, exceptionally hoppy. But Stone being Stone, the brewery has taken the coastal character and multiplied it tenfold. Yet, unlike many of its close peers, they're as balanced as they are big and that is why Stone has thrived while others have dived – or even died.

GREG: *"I've no desire for people to just buy our beer once, so I don't want to hoodwink*

In fact, the whole thing looks like it's a design collaboration between Jean Paul Gaultier and Fred Flintstone. The industrial chic of the restaurant and bar is softened by the presence of bamboo, plants and waterfalls. On one side, diners and drinkers are gifted a view of the gleaming brewery, visible through a huge 40-foot window. On the other side, there's a sight of the magnificent gardens. Outside there are tables carved from stone, a bar with three dozen draught taps, waterfalls, trees and even flaming fire torches.

The food makes an equally striking impression. Stone's attitude to food is as opinionated as his attitude toward beer. Don't expect bangers and mash, fish and chips, cutesy crab cakes and other lackluster brewpub food here. And just because the dishes are produced with natural, locally sourced ingredients, it's definitely not all pansy pulses and ethical eating. Sure, freshness and sustainability are placed at the forefront of the food offering but so is the trademark boldness with which Stone made its brewing name.

High-octane highlights include Stone Pale Ale & Garlic Stir-Fried Brussels Sprouts, BBQ Duck Tacos made with Stone Smoked Porter sauce, Stone IPA mash-potatoes and Garlic Cheddar & Stone Ruination IPA Soup. The provocative menu states:

> "If this soup could talk, it would say: 'Not sure? Then have the Sweet Potato soup. Otherwise don't blame me if I'm too strong for you. I am what I am and you have been warned."

Greg makes no apologies for ruffling visitors' feathers.

GREG: *"Stone will not change and will be committed to what we're all about in everything we do. We've got so much grief about our menu from people because people were expecting the usual kind of pub food. But we want our food to reflect our beer. People are always very keen to tell you how badly you've mucked things up, but we wouldn't be where we are today if we listened to the people who we upset. We're very clear about where we stand."*

them into buying something they didn't want. It just irritates people and wastes their time. We don't want to do that. Besides, I have no problem with saving the yellow lager drinkers a couple of bucks."

Having begun as the enfant terrible of American craft beer, Stone Brewing Company has embraced adulthood in recent years and become one of American craft beer's fastest growing success stories. In 2006, Stone unveiled a new $14 million brewery. High up on the hills of Southern California, and just a 30-minute drive from Downtown San Diego, the new brewery is an imposing and impressive testament to Stone's achievement.

The new site is home to more than a dozen towering fermentation tanks, offices for around 200 employees and a jaw-dropping bar, bistro and gardens. The décor epitomizes the Stone identity yet thankfully steers clear of becoming a shrine to Gothic, heavy metal geeks.

[cont. over the page]

[Stone Brewing Company cont.]

In addition to Stone's own selection of beers, the new bistro acts as a showcase for America's more ambitious small breweries. AleSmith, Avery, Ommegang, Dogfish Head and Russian River are all on the list alongside a variety of challenging Belgian beers. In short, if you have even the faintest interest in fine beer or food then a trip to Stone in Escondido is an absolute must.

THE BEERS

Stone Levitation Ale (4.4%)
Who says you need alcohol for flavour? Awesome amber ale that punches well above its modest weight – this is the nearest thing Stone does to a session beer.

Stone Pale Ale (5.4%)
The beer on which the Stone Empire has been built. It's a full-bodied, muscular, copper-coloured Californian interpretation of a classic British beer style. Floral hop character deftly layered on a sweet malt base. At 41 IBUs, it's a very light Stone beer.

Stone Smoked Porter (5.9%)
Chocolate, espresso and slightly singed caramel flavours. Malts smoked over peat also adorn this shimmering ebony-hued beer with a delicious smoky tint reminiscent of Islay whisky.

Stone IPA (6.9%)
This is one hugely hoppy embodiment of the San Diegan IPA style. Dry-hopped for a fortnight and underpinned by a medium malt-sweetness, it's resinous, refreshing and right up your street if you like hoppy beers.

Arrogant Bastard Ale (7.2%)
Another unapologetically hop-heavy beer. Ruddy reddish-brown in colour, herbaceous and pine on the nose and an enormously astringent mouthfeel that dries out the mouth yet, intriguingly, demands revisiting until the bottom of the glass.

Oak-Aged Bastard Ale (7.2%)
Arrogant Bastard but significantly more mellow and sporting a tuxedo. Matured with oak chips, the vanilla and sweet bourbon flavour rounds off the astringent edges of the original. Released in 2004 and available in a funky 3-litre bottle.

Stone Ruination IPA (7.7%)
So-called for the effect it has on your palate. A bigger, brasher or more brazenly bitter beer you'll struggle to find. Hops, hops and more goddamn Centennial and Magnum hops – all fortified by a sweet malt undertone. One is great, two is dangerous.

Double Bastard Ale (10%)
An incredibly robust, exceedingly strong American ale that takes all the malt and hops in Arrogant Bastard and simply doubles them. A beast of a beer released just once a year.

Stone Imperial Russian Stout (10.8%)
Intense, roast character and rich with a lovely texture. Plenty of chocolate, caramel and anise flavours. Darker than your worst nightmares. Annual and limited release.

Stone Old Guardian Barley Wine 95 (11.3%)
A grandiose and vinous bottle-conditioned beer created in 1999 and now brewed to a slightly modified recipe every year. Highly alcoholic, hopped and hankered-after.

Stone Anniversary Ale (various)
An annual release that's abundantly dry-hopped with a different variety each year. At the time of writing, ten have been released. Rare and sought-after by beer boffins.

Stone Vertical Epics (various)
A series of bottle-conditioned Belgian ales destined and designed to be tasted after December 2012. Each edition is released one year, one month and one day after the previous one.

Green Flash Brewing (4)

1430 Vantage Ct., Vista, CA 92081
T 760 597 9012
E info@greenflashbrew.com
www.greenflashbrew.com

Under the re-invigorating stewardship of head brewer Chuck Silva, the 25-barrel brewery has broadened its appeal beyond solid session ales into more adventurous and hop-centric American-style brews. In 2004, Silva rewrote a number of recipes and introduced an imaginative dimension with barley wines, Belgian Trappist beers and, of course, India Pale Ales. Under the ghoulish Reaper Ales banner, even more subversive delights are being brewed. Numerous awards have followed. With plans for brewery expansion afoot Green Flash is – much like the solar-phenomenon it's named after – one to watch.

Brewery tours: Fri, 3pm-7pm; Sat, 11am-3pm (by appointment for the following: tours, tastings, growler fills and keg, case and gift shop purchases)

Recommendation
West Coast IPA (7%)
Deeply pungent resinous hop character balanced out by hints of watermelon and mango.
Belgian Trippel (8.5%)
A bottle conditioned beauty, dry-hopped with Saaz and Styrian Golding hops. Full-bodied, zesty, spicy and with a hint of pear and peach.

Firehouse Brewery (5)

7696 Miramar Rd., CA 92126
T 858 605 1416
E info@firehousebrew.com
www.firehousebrew.com

Not content with rescuing folk from flaming buildings, coaxing cats down from trees and turning the heads of impressionable young ladies, a collection of San Diego firefighters has further served the local community by brewing some merrymaking beer. The Firehouse Brewery was set up as a co-operative by more than 50 San Diego firefighters following 9/11, when 343 of their colleagues perished. A large slice of the profits are used to help the firefighters and their families. An additional percentage goes to local fire departments to help buy safety equipment. Charity is by no means the only reason to drink the beers. Just two are produced at

the 30-barrel brewery, yet distribution has stretched beyond the local neighbourhood to more than 300 outlets throughout California. The American Pale Ale combines the malty allure of Fat Tire with the hop-driven character of Sierra Nevada, while the citrus-laden Hefeweizen is as refreshing as the end scene in *Towering Inferno*.

Brewery tours: Tue-Sat, 9am-5pm
Recommendation
American Pale Ale (5.5%)
Approachable amber ale aimed unashamedly at a mainstream audience who may find hop-centric ales too much.

Lost Abbey Brewing (Port Brewing) (6)
See feature on pages 60-61.

Oceanside Ale Works (7)

3800 Oceanic Dr., Suite #105, Oceanside, CA 92056
T 760 721 4ALE
www.oceansidealeworks.com

A new kid on San Diego's brewing block, Oceanside Ale Works is the brainchild of maths teacher Mark Purceil and local firefighter Scott Thomas. These two homebrewers took their hobby into business in May 2006. The modest-sized manual brewery and tap room is tucked away in a stark business park. It may lack a certain charm, but you can be sure of a warm welcome and a selection of enthusiastically crafted ales. Six beers are kept on tap, with more available to take away in 64-oz growlers or, if you're super keen, kegs. The beers can also be sampled at the nearby 'Ps & Qs' pub on Oceanside Boulevard.

Brewery tours/Tap room: Fri, 3pm-7pm; Sat, noon-4pm (for tours, tastings, growler fills and keg and brewery merchandise)

Recommendation
Buccaneer Blonde Honey Ale (4.2%)
An impressive, well-structured amber nectar with a hefty honey hit. Sweet but not sickly.

Stone Brewing Company (8)
See feature on pages 56-58.

Lost Abbey Brewing (6)

155 Mata Way St. #104, San Marcos, CA 92069
T 760 891 0272
www.lostabbey.com

At Lost Abbey Brewing – the experimental and esoteric arm of Port Brewing – brewmaster Tomme Arthur is inspired principally by the monastic brewing traditions of Belgium. Tomme has passionately crafted beers with a brash West Coast twist and designed to grace the most discerning of dinner tables. The Lost Abbey church is an extremely broad one with an ever-growing congregation. Four beers are issued under the Lost Abbey label year-round: Avant Garde, Lost and Found, Red Barn and Judgment Day. Seasonal and special beers, including Ten Commandments, Cuvée de Tomme and the Angel's Share, are released at various times throughout the year. Barrel ageing, blending and experimentation with various yeast strains are at the forefront of Tomme's crusade. At the sizeable Lost Abbey Brewery in San Marcos – former home to Stone Brewing Company – Tomme's beer can be found languidly maturing for up to 18 months in hundreds of oak barrels which, in their former life, housed anything from wine and brandy to Scotch whisky and bourbon.

For beers such as Cuvée de Tomme – arguably Lost Abbey's most revered brew – sour cherries are thrown into the barrels along with three strains of the infamous *Brettanomyces* yeast. *Brett* (as it's colloquially known) is different to other yeast strains. They say that common yeast strains are like dogs. If trained, treated nicely and well fed, they'll obediently do what their owner says and are easily domesticated. By contrast, Brett is more like an insubordinate cat with an attitude problem. If uninvited and left to run amok in a brewery, Brett can cause havoc with the beer and make it taste rather funny – in an 'Oh Dear!' rather than 'Ha! Ha!' way. Among most brewers, Brett is about as popular as a terrorist, but Tomme has disciplined it like a deftly skilled lion-tamer. At his command, Brett metaphorically jumps through hoops and works with proprietary yeast strains to stunning effect.

Despite being around for just a couple of years, word of Lost Abbey's boundary-pushing beers has already stretched well beyond San Diego and gained a passionate following. Limited production means that Lost Abbey's beers are difficult to find. While they are stocked by a handful of bars and liquor stores in and around San Diego, by far the best way to experience them is by visiting the brewery tap room – Tomme calls it an altar – on a Friday or Saturday. In addition to sampling and buying the principal range, visitors may also have the opportunity to try some limited edition beers available solely at the brewery.

Brewery tours: Brewery tours available during business hours. Call ahead for groups larger than six

Tasting hours: Fri, 4pm-8pm; Sat, noon-5pm

THE BEERS

Red Barn Ale (6.7%)
Ale rooted in the Belgian Farmhouse style akin to the Saison beers of the Dupont brewery. A simple base of barley malt and flaked barley are combined with incredibly flavourful and spicy yeast. Organic ginger, orange peel, black pepper and grains of paradise.

Avant Garde (7%)
Inspired by the Biere de Garde style of northern France, Avant Garde is brewed with long summer days, rocking chairs and porches in mind. An inviting aroma of fresh bread and soft fruits gives way to a beer of great depth.

Lost & Found Abbey Ale (8%)
A deep amber Abbey-style beer brewed from a blend of six malts, sugar and a special raisin puree. Full of yeasty spiciness and a full-on fruit finish.

Veritas Ale (8%)
A unique, one-off limited edition beer made from a blend of oak barrel-aged beers straight out of the world of wine. Smooth notes of red wine, soft French oak, tannins, fruits and cherries.

The Ten Commandments (9%)
Dark Belgian Farmhouse style brewed with raisins, fresh rosemary and honey with a secondary wild yeast added to the brew during bottling. Coffee colours with strong notes of banana and fig.

The Angel's Share (12.5%)
A barley wine that showcases the properties of barrel ageing and maturation with no small amount of panache. It's full-bodied and sweet, with belly-warming alcohol, soft tannins and a finish of vanilla bean and rum.

Tomme Arthur is a key figure on the San Diego beer scene. A native San Diegan, he began brewing at Solana Beach Pizza Port in 1997 and has won many awards. In 2007, Tomme and Lost Abbey was awarded Small Brewing and Brewer of the Year as well as three individual gongs at the Great American Beer Festival (American craft brewing's answer to the Oscars). Currently, Tomme has 15 GABF medals to his name.

Lost Abbey's Ten Commandments

1. The most imaginative beers are our crusade
2. We believe we are all in this together
3. We strive for honesty and integrity in our lives like you
4. Fresh beer is great, aged beer is better
5. Now that you have found us help us spread the message
6. There is good and evil in the world - our beers are good
7. Passion isn't something you can buy at the corner store
8. We believe an inspired life is worth living
9. Life is about choices. The Lost Abbey is a great choice
10. We are not perfect, but no one is

BREWPUBS

Back Street Brewing (9)
15 Main St., Suite #100, Vista, CA 92084
T 760 407 7600

Quick! Someone call an ambiance! This neighbourhood brewpub, located in a strange strip mall, had a less than pulsating vibe during our visit but still served a nice slice or two, and the beer was really rather decent. If you're passing through Vista and heading north out of town on the 78, it's a good spot for lunch. It's paired with the Lamppost Pizza chain.

Recommendation

Chava Lager (5%)
The full-bodied lager was a solid all-rounder and matched the food.

BJ's Brewhouse (10)
8873 Villa La Jolla Dr., La Jolla, CA 92037
T 858 455 0662

Another unremarkable link in the BJ's chain. Attentive service, reassuringly reliable food and decent enough beer, it's a perfectly pleasant experience but, somehow, entirely forgettable, too.

Opening hours: Sun-Thu, 11am-10:30pm; Fri & Sat, 11am-11pm

Recommendation

Tatonka Stout (8.5%)
A forceful, thrusting malt sweetness on the nose followed in hot pursuit by a gaggle of espresso, molasses and – at the back – a touch of chocolate.

BJ's Brewhouse (11)
5500 Grossmont Center Dr., La Mesa, CA 91942
T 619 589 7222

Bigger and better than La Jolla and far livelier. In addition to the house brews, this one stocks a number of bottled Belgians. Grab a table on the patio if you can. A good value, well-run brewpub.

Opening hours: Sun-Thu, 11am-midnight; Fri & Sat, 11am-1am

Callahan's Pub & Brewery (12)
8111 Mira Mesa Blvd., CA 92126
T 858 578 7892

Owned by the same folk as the San Diego Brewing Company, the 'Oirish'-themed

Callahan's has been a stalwart of the San Diego brewing scene since 1989. As well as the SDBC selection of adjunct-free, small batch beers brewed on a three-barrel system, there's a wealth of other draught delights on offer alongside a never-ending list of pan-European pub grub. Fussball and darts are also available. What's with the interrogation-room lighting though?

Opening hours: Mon-Thu, 11am-midnight; Fri & Sat, 11am-1am; Sun, 9:30am-10pm

Coronado Brewing Company (13)

170 Orange Ave., Coronado, CA 92118
T 619 437 4452
www.coronadobrewingcompany.com

Just a few minutes stumble from the ferry terminal, this relaxed, rather ritzy brewpub, sports bar and restaurant serves terrific stonebaked pizzas and great pub grub. But the real draw is the selection of beers brewed on-premise. Its core selection of eight brews is supplemented by a rotating selection of speciality seasonals. According to local beer guys, Coronado has significantly improved consistency and quality in recent times. Most of the

The Coronado: Some like it hop!

locals are sports fans with the odd military uniform knocking about. If gawping at the plasma screens doesn't float your boat, there's a picturesque sun patio where you can watch Coronado's laid-back life unfold. Perfect if you've got an hour to kill before the ferry leaves for San Diego. Fill up a growler and you can take the beer away, too.

Opening hours: daily, from 11am

Recommendation
Coronado Golden (5.4%)
A refreshing foil to the high-octane Idiot. This Pilsner-style golden beer is lightly hopped with Saaz and shines on a hot sunny day, making it ideal after a day on the beach.

Idiot IPA (8.4%)
You don't have to be an idiot to drink this unfiltered beer, but at 8.4% you'll no doubt act like one once you've drunk a few. Brewed with 3lb of hops and eight different hop varieties in each batch, it exudes citrus-flavours and a long, dry, herbal finish.

Gordon Biersch Brewery Restaurant (14)

5010 Mission Center Rd., CA 92108
T 619 688 1120

A reassuringly reliable West Coast outpost of the Gordon Biersch brewpub empire. What it lacks in personality and esoteric brews, it makes up for in slick and smiling service, perfectly drinkable Germanic-style lager beers and good value, wood-fired food in classy surroundings. A good family option. Live music and chalet parking.

Opening hours: Sun-Thu, 11am-1am; Fri & Sat, 11am-2am

Recommendation
Blonde Bock (7%)
A chewy, amber-coloured lager fronted by sweet, malt-driven caramel flavours. A fine all-rounder that copes admirably with the more robust selections on GB's hearty menu.

Karl Strauss Brewing Company (15)

1157 Columbia St., CA 92021
T 619 234 2739
www.karlstrauss.com

Apparently, this is where San Diego beer started. When it opened in 1989, it was San Diego's first new brewery for 50 years. Now approaching its 20th birthday, it's easy to see how Karl Strauss has stayed the distance for so long. While the concept has been usurped by more radical breweries and beer bars, this one has nevertheless maintained an independent personality and steers clear of the polished, impersonal atmosphere that sometimes afflicts other, more-recognised brewpub chains. *The San Diego Tribune* voted it San Diego's best brewpub in 2006.

The beers run the gamut of beer-styles and cater for both the casual drinker and the salivating hophead. There's an impressive food menu with recommended beer pairings, including the ESB with Seared Ahi Burger, Oktoberfest with Beer-Brined Pork Chops and the Stargazer IPA with the extremely spicy En Fuego Jalapeno Burger. Also, on the first Thursday of each month (6pm), there's a firkin party where staff tap and serve a cask of live beer. Karl Strauss, the German-brewer who inspired the beers, sadly passed away in December 2006 aged 93.

Opening hours: Mon-Thu, 11am-11pm; Fri, 11am-midnight; Sat, 11.30am-midnight; Sun, 11.30am-10.30pm

Recommendation
Stargazer IPA (4.9%)
Floral Cascade, Chinook and Centennial hops and tangy grapefruit dominate with a fine balance of juicy malt and a hugely floral aroma. Only 34 IBUs so, unlike most San Diegan IPAs, you may be able to have a second pint.

Karl Strauss Brewing Company (16)
1044 Wall St., La Jolla, CA 92037
T 858 551 2739

Not much in the way of genuine atmosphere but still a good spot to drop in for a decent beer and a burger. Located in the trendy part of San Diego, and popular with a twenty-something crowd.

Opening hours: Sun-Tue, 11.30am-9pm; Wed-Sat, 11.30am-10:30pm

Karl Strauss Brewing Company (17)
9675 Scranton Rd., Sorrento Mesa, CA 92121
T 858 587 2739

Restaurant and U-shaped bar situated in an outdoor mall in a glitzy part of San Diego. Knowledgeable staff, fine-looking clientele and above-average prices. Firkin party on first Thursday of every month at 6:30pm.

Opening hours: Mon-Fri, 11:30am-10pm; Sat, closed; Sun, 10am-2pm

Karl Strauss Brewing Company (18)
5801 Armada Dr., CA 92008
T 760 431 2739

Cosy bar and restaurant located a short drive off Highway 5 in close proximity to the flourishing flower gardens – a popular tourist attraction. Firkin party on first Thursday of every month at 6:30pm.

Opening hours: Sun-Thu, 7am-11pm; Fri & Sat, 7am-midnight

Oggi's Pizza & Brewing Company
E emailus@oggis.com
www.oggis.com

It's been more than 25 years since brothers George and John Hadji first opened the first Oggi's pizza restaurant in Del Mar. What a success they've been! There are now more than 17 Oggi's in California and Arizona, spreading the gospel according to the holy trinity that is sports, pizza and beer. Half a dozen venues have an onsite brewery, while the others source their beer from the Oggi's main brewery in San Clemente – also known as Left Coast Brewing. Their beers can also be discovered in San Diego's various sporting arenas.

Oggi's Pizza & Brewing Company (19)
2245 Fenton Parkway #101, CA 92018
T 619 640 1072

A casual, unpretentious sports bar nestled in the corner of a shopping mall. Good, if unspectacular, pizzas and pasta served alongside a dozen tap-handles serving Oggi's very own brews. Plasma screens show sports inside, and there's a small patio-area outside. Service was friendly, if a little laid-back.

Opening hours: Sun-Thu, 10.45am-10pm; Fri & Sat, 10.45am-midnight

Recommendation
Oggi's Black Magic Stout (6.8%)
A silky, opaque beer brewed with six different malts ventures into imperial/foreign stout territory. Its rich coffee, chocolate and caramel flavours were awarded a silver medal winner at the 2006 Great American Beer Festival (America-style stout category).

Oggi's Pizza & Brewing Company (20)

425 S. Melrose, Vista, CA 92083
T 760 295 3851

Conventional sports-led theme bar serving casual Californian cuisine and what many regard as the best Oggi's beer in town – ask for the one-off speciality brews created within the shiny brew-system behind the bar. Good place to visit on the way to Stone Brewing or Pizza Port or, if you know your shotguns from your swerve balls, take in a game with the locals.

Opening hours: daily, 11am-close

Oggi's Pizza & Brewing Company (21)

10155 Rancho Carmel Drive, CA 92128
T 858 592 7883

Standard and compact brewpub and restaurant with onsite microbrewery and a strong sports slant courtesy of 32 screens.

Opening hours: Mon-Fri, 11am-11pm;
Sat & Sun, 9am-midnight

Pizza Port

www.pizzaport.com

Making pizzas in Solana Beach since 1987, and producing ales and lagers on premise since 1992, Pizza Port was an integral player in San Diego's rise from craft brewing obscurity. Since then, Pizza Port has expanded into three venues – two in San Diego and one in San Clemente. Under the stewardship of Tomme Arthur (among others), it's been honoured with a wealth of brewing awards. All of the Pizza Ports boast their own brewing team. Each is given the freedom to conjure up their own bespoke range of beers. There's a fair bit of crossover, but don't let that stop you visiting all three venues as they're great.

Pizza Port Solana Beach (22)

135 N. Highway 101, Solana Beach, CA 92075
T 858 481 7322

The original Pizza Port is one of the founding fathers of the city's beer culture. If you only have time to go to one Pizza Port, most San Diegans would say go to this one. Not only because it's slightly nearer to the city centre – just a 30-minute drive out to the beach – but also because it's range of gorgeous grog is slightly broader. The multi-styled house selection is bolstered by a whole host of rare

California craft beers, while the pizzas are absolutely delicious, too.

Opening hours: Sun-Thu, 11am-10pm;
Fri & Sat, 11am-midnight

Recommendation

Swamis IPA (7.4%)

Hailed as the 'original' San Diego IPA, Swamis has been brewed here since day one. It's old and bitter. Very bitter!

Pizza Port Carlsbad (23)

571 Carlsbad Village Drive, Carlsbad, CA 92008
T 760 720 7007

With more than a decade under its brewing and dough-flipping belt, this big, bright and busy surf-style bar has skilfully honed the elusive art of great beer and delicious pizzas (the 'Carlsbad' rocks) down to a tee.

In addition to the ever-changing Pizza Port efforts, the beer choice draws in the likes of Stone and Russian River and is served by friendly, laid-back and knowledgeable bartenders. In summer 2007, Pizza Port opened a bottle shop-cum shrine to artisan beers from Europe and America. Every Thursday between 5 and 7pm, there's a gourmet beer and cheese tasting.

Opening hours: Sun-Thu, 11am-10pm;
Fri & Sat, 11am-midnight

Recommendation

Sharkbite Red Ale (5.5%)

Centennial and Cascade hops adorns Pizza Port's feisty flagship ale with a nice slice of spice and sweetness. A reliable right-hand man to almost any of the pizzas on offer.

Rock Bottom Restaurant & Brewery (24)

401 G. Street, CA 92101
T 619 231 7000
www.rockbottom.com

Lively, large brewpub located in the heart of the Gaslamp. This venue attracts trendy whippersnappers, thirsty tourists and shouting sporty-types. The fresh, yet fairly middle-of-the-road, beer is reasonably priced and covers all the usual bases but plays second fiddle to the food and the pursuit of good times. Tournament-sized pool tables and a separate bar can be found upstairs, and there's seating outside – great for people watching. A perfect bar to kick-off a mischief-making mission in the Gaslamp area. Discounts available if you're a member of the Amateur Homebrewers Association.

Opening hours: Sun-Wed, 11.30am-midnight; Thu-Sat, 11.30am-2am

Recommendation

Point Break Pale Ale (5.2%)

Designed unashamedly for the mainstream masses but very drinkable with a faint peppery finish and whack of herbal flavour on the palate.

Rock Bottom Restaurant & Brewery (25)

8980 Villa La Jolla Drive, La Jolla, CA 92037
T 858 450 9277

A less raucous Rock Bottom further north and one block off Highway 5 in the La Jolla district near the university. There's the usual brewpub blend of wood, brass and sparkly waiting staff, while the beer selection is fine but not worth the trip alone. Attracts a strong student following. Pop in if you're in the area.

Opening hours: daily, 11am-close

San Diego Brewing Company (26)

10450 Friars Road Ste. L, CA 92120
T 619 284 2739
www.sandiegobrewing.com

This spacious sports bar and brewpub has been popular with locals since 1993. Don't be fooled by the unglamorous strip-mall location. Once inside, you'll only have eyes for the 50 or so beer taps showcasing European classics and local talent. Co-owner Scott Stamp loves English beer so much he called his son Griffin after London's Fuller's brewery, and the seven-barrel microbrewery brews with a strong English accent. Impressive food menu. Thursday is cask ale night.

Opening hours: Mon-Thu, 11am-midnight; Fri & Sat, 11am-1am: Sun, 10am-10pm

Recommendation

San Diego Hopnotic IPA (7.5%)

Tawny-coloured, dry hopped not once, not twice but three times. Long, strong citrus finish with a touch of marmalade.

San Marcos Brewery & Grill (27)

1080 W. San Marcos Blvd., San Marcos, CA 92078
T 760 471 0050
www.sanmarcosbrewery.com

Long-standing, hacienda-style brewpub and grill north of the city centre. Owner and brewer David Nuley, a genial white-coated boffin that swapped a career in pharmacy for brewing in 1993, is a big fan of CAMRA and English beers. In addition to a core selection of traditional ales, David has also veered off-piste with Belgian beers, delicious honey ale and a refreshing Hefeweizen. Simple no-nonsense décor, friendly and informed staff, outdoors seating, easy parking and within a few minutes drive of Churchill's, Green Flash and Port Brewing. Pop in if you're passing.

Opening hours: Sun-Tue, 11am-10:30pm; Wed & Thu, 11am-11pm; Fri & Sat, 11am-11:30pm

Recommendation

Grabassier Belgian Style Gold (8.4%)

Golden-hued strong Belgian ale with a fantastic frothy white head and a hint of pear drops, banana and cloves. Careful though, it's pretty potent and drinks a lot easier than the ABV suggests.

Taylor's Restaurant & Brewery (28)

721 Grand Ave., Pacific Beach, CA 92109
T 858 270 3596

This beachside boutique brewery and eaterie is very popular among the surfer-dude locals. Homemade hooch in hand, hang out on the rooftop terrace or out on the back deck for some mighty impressive ocean views. The beers are not San Diego's finest but perfectly capable of hitting the spot after a day mucking about in the sun, sea and sand.

Recommendation

Amber Ale

Best of a fatigued bunch that treads gently into lager territory. A refresher but not much else.

BEER BARS

The Aero Club (29)
3365 India St., CA 92101
T 619 297 7211
www.aeroclubbar.com

Dark, Downtown dive bar that's been on the same sketchy-looking street since 1947. Aeronautical workers once sunk brews here after a hard day tinkering around with new-fangled flying machines. While the plane paraphernalia has remained, the clientele now consists of the young and friendly shooting pool and the breeze. The beer list features 20 draught and 20 bottled beers and has been compiled with an unswerving devotion to the left coast craft scene, featuring the likes of AleSmith, Bear Republic and Stone on tap. A strong wine list, too.

Opening hours: daily, 2am-2pm

Cass Street Bar & Grill (30)
4612 Cass St., CA 92109
T 858 270 1320

This bustling beach bar, set back from the Pacific Beach's central drag, is well worth the short diversion. Attracting a slightly older and less self-conscious crowd than the neighbouring student hangouts, there's an audacious beer selection that's reasonably priced and a cubbyhole kitchen serving tasty Mexican and American food (the crab burgers and steak sandwiches are renowned), as well

as two pool tables and shuffleboard. Knuckle-dragging doorman aside, it's a cracking bar and the liveliest in the Pacific Beach area.

Opening hours: Mon-Fri, 10am-2am; Sat & Sun, 9am-2am

Churchill's Pub & Grille (31)
887 W. San Marcos Blvd., San Marcos, CA 92069
T 760 471 8773
www.churchillspub.us
Recommended

There are no hooligans fighting in the (small) car park, no tedious bore at the end of the bar and the clientele's teeth were in fine fettle but, in every other respect, this is a jolly good stab at a traditional British boozer. Owner Ivan Derezin is a passionate proponent of beers from both sides of the Atlantic and boasts one of the most eclectic ranges in San Diego. In addition to some standard British ales and regularly rotating West Coast guest ales, Ivan frequently cracks open a cask of something special – often from the neighboring Stone Brewery. The absurdly extensive bottled beer selection is where he really cuts loose, though. Belgians (Westmalle Dubbel, Cantillon Rose de Gambrinus), Brits (Black Sheep Riggwelter, Wychwood Hobgoblin, Harveistoun Old Engine Oil), Americans (Avery, Ommegang, Allagash), a sole Austrian (Samichlaus) and – don't tell Winston – a whole host of Germans (Aecht Rauchbiers, Franziskaner) feature.

The British pub feel is enhanced by footy on the TV, dartboards, homemade English pub grub (chicken tikka massala and cottage pie) and a red telephone box outside.

Opening hours: Mon, noon-2am; Tue-Sat, 11am-2am; Sun, 11am-midnight

Downtown Johnny Brown's (32)
1220 Third Avenue
T 619 232 8414
www.downtownjohnnybrowns.com

Don't let the neon Coors and Bud signs put you off. There's a handful of top-notch local beer on tap at this sports bar. While it's a little scruffy and the blaring TVs do grate after a while, it's a lively place to sink a pint over a game of pool. There's an outdoor patio if you're not feeling competitive.

Opening hours: daily, 11am-2am

pool tables, table football, shuffleboard, a Playstation or a jukebox spinning Blues and classic rock. On every second Saturday of the month, a local San Diego brewer is showcased with discounted prices, food matching and a speciality or cask beer.

Opening hours: Mon-Fri, 3pm-2am;
Sat & Sun, 1pm-2am

Henry's Pub (35)
614 5th Ave., CA 92101
T 619 238 2389
www.henryspub.com

The guy who served us claimed that martial-arts maestro and lethal Hollywood killing machine-cum-superhero Chuck Norris used to tend the bar here – a man so hard that when he does a press-up, he doesn't lift himself up, he pushes the earth down. Apparently, local legend has it that Chuck Norris' hand is the only hand that could beat a Royal Flush, and when Chuck Norris swam in the ocean he

The Field (33)
544 Fifth Avenue, CA 92101
T 619 232 9840
www.thefield.com

A fairly uninspiring and clichéd Irish Craic-den. You know the kind of thing: Bicycles on the ceiling, signs to Tipperary on the wall and a chap doing a jig and waving his fiddle about. A pedestrian beer selection hardly improves matters while The 'Black & Tan' rivals 'The Irish Car Bomb' in the most insensitively titled drink stakes. References to ruthless British paramilitary units are somewhat hard to swallow especially if, unlike this pub, you're truly Irish.

Opening hours: Mon-Fri, 11am-2am;
Sat & Sun, 9am-2am

Below: Hamilton's Tavern offers a great selection of more than two dozen taps and 150 bottled beers.

Hamilton's Tavern (34)
1521 30th Street, CA 92192
T 619 238 5460
www.hamiltonstavern.com
Highly recommended

A former dive bar transformed into a hop-loving haven located in the historic and leafy South Park District. Offering more than two dozen taps and more than 150 bottled beers, the focus is on Belgian brews, West Coast microbrews and several San Diego local heroes – all at reasonable prices. Tired of elbow bending? Chance your arm at two

didn't get wet, the sea got Chuck Norris-ed. Enough of that nonsense. Henry's Bar may look like yet another Gaslamp party place, and it is, but it also does some killer easy drinking, yet eclectic, beers on draught. And in bottles, too. Don't start any trouble, though, as you never know when Norris may return. Did you know that behind his beard, he doesn't have a chin, he has another fist? No? Well, you've been warned. Regular live music, karaoke and DJs keep the vibe alive all week.

Opening hours: daily

Liar's Club (36)

3844 Mission Blvd., CA 92109
T 858 488 2340
www.liarsclubsd.com
Highly recommended

Located a block away from Mission Beach, the Liar's Club may lack the chic splendour of its surroundings, but there can be no finer place to kickback after a hard day's sunbathing and gnarly six-footers. Manned by what must be the friendliest and most knowledgeable bartenders in San Diego, the bar showcases a wide-ranging selection of local microbrews and the odd Belgian import. But make sure you save room for the fantastic food – the seared Ahi Tuna sandwich is sublime. Every Friday, they open a cask at 6pm, and local beer is just a few dollars a pint. The jukebox rocks, it's teeming with pretty girls and handsome surf dudes and the gentleman's urinal is cheekily decked with old Budweiser and Miller paraphernalia. Go there and don't dilly-dally on the way. It's brilliant.

Opening hours: daily, 11am-midnight

The Live Wire (37)

2103 El Cajon Blvd., CA 92104
T 619 291 7450

The Live Wire is a lively neighborhood music bar hugely popular with twenty-something scensters and a biker crowd. It's renowned for its rotating selection of DJs playing a kaleidoscopic selection of funk, rock and eclectic tunes. There's a retro padded burgundy bar, pool table, pinball, a handful of intimate booths and some classic old-skool video games. There's bounteous beer, too, with two dozen taps dispensing Californian

craft ales – Stone, Russian River, AleSmith, (PBR in tall cans) – and other domestic microbrews. Throw in some super-friendly staff, a heavenly spirit selection and a kick-ass jukebox and, it's fair to say, you've got a mighty fine bar on your hands.

Opening hours: Mon, noon-2am; Tue-Thu & Sat, 8pm-2am; Fri, 5pm-2am; Sun, 8pm-midnight

The Local (Eatery & Drinking Hole) (38)

1065 Fourth Ave., CA 92101
T 619 231 4447
www.thelocalsandiego.com

This is a gnarly surfing bar in the heart of Downtown serving a selection of 'local' beers to an unpretentious, friendly crowd. Sit at the long bar and sip something from Alpine, Green Flash and Ballast Point, or dip into the gut-busting food menu that's freshly prepared and jolly good value – especially the happy hours appetizers. Its 'awesome burgers' are well named, while there are some inventive fish dishes, such as the delicious Blackened Shrimp Burrito and splendid Baja fish tacos. You'll find The Local just round the corner from the more corporate Yardhouse and, we reckon, it's a far finer place to spend your hard-earned. Extremely well-priced, but don't even think of finding a free parking space nearby. Instead, take the trolley straight there and get off at the 5th Avenue stop.

Opening hours: Mon-Fri, 11:30am-1:30am; Sat, 3pm-1.30am; Sun, opens when American football is on

McDini's (39)

105 East 8th Street, National City, CA 91950
T 619 474 6771

If you like corned beef then we suggest you go and snaffle-down some of the many hearty corned beef dishes and sandwiches served at this self-proclaimed 'corned beef capital of the world'. If you don't like corned beef then you should still swing by. It's a quirky, bustling and downright crazy place where the service is frantic yet friendly and the beer selection plentiful, with more than 80 beers available on tap and in bottle.

Opening hours: Mon-Fri, 11am-2am; Sat, noon-2am

Moondoggies (40)

832 Garnet Avenue, CA 92109
T 858 483 6550
www.moondoggies.com

Lively, open-air Pacific Beach bar where being blonde, beautiful and barely clothed is presumably a condition for entry. Sierra Nevada, Widmer and New Belgium's Fat Tire represent the 'craft beer' community, but most of the clientele are swigging Budweiser, Coors and some pretty loopy concoctions that they'll surely regret in the morning. Tsk-tsk.

Opening hours: daily, 11am-2am

O'Brien's (41)

4646 Convoy St., CA 92111
T 858 715 1745
www.obrienspub.net
Highly recommended

O'Brien's is to great beer what Evil Kneivel was to the needless breaking of bones. It professes to be the 'Hoppiest Place On Earth', and it's difficult to argue otherwise. Never mind its unremarkable strip-mall setting, this lively neighbourhood bar is a fine fusion of American and English and is an absolute must for even the most fair-weather beer drinker. The passionate, hugely knowledge-able and titanic owner Tom Nickel is chair-man of the San Diego Brewer's Guild and was a brewer at Oggi's for eight years. Tom knows the San Diegan beer scene like the back of his rather big hand. He has compiled a stunning beer selection. Hop-heavy West Coast and local beers dominate the two dozen tap hand-les, while the bottled range incorporates various European imports, including some rare Belgian beauties and numerous American micros. If you're eating, and it might not be a bad idea after all the big beers, then there's plenty of hearty and typically Californian chow to soak up the suds. Make sure you go.

Opening hours: Mon-Wed, 11am-10:30pm; Thu-Fri, 11am-11pm; Sat, noon-11pm; Sun, noon-6pm

Moondoggies open-air beach bar is a cool place to hang out.

The PB Tap Room (42)
1269 Garnet Ave., Pacific Beach, CA 92109
www.pbataproom.com

Surrounded by the thumping bass and hedonism of nightclubs and student bars, the Pacific Beach Tap Room is an oasis of lovely beer in a desert of madness and mayhem. This shrine to televised sports should be a haven for micros but is anything but. It showcases beer from nearly every local brewery (35 taps) and soaks it up with belt-expanding sandwiches, salads and pizza. Hordes of 20-something guys and girls seemed to get more attractive as we sipped the vast array of microbrews.

Opening hours: daily, 11am-late

Penny Lane Pub & Grill (43)
1001 W. San Marcos Blvd., San Marcos, CA 92069
T 760 744 8782
www.pennylanepub.biz

Cor Blimey guvnor. San Marcos has two Brit pubs. Loaded with Irish pub signs and Beatles paraphernalia (hence Penny Lane),

the draw at this warm and welcoming (if a little plain) pub is the fish and chips, a decent European and American beer selection and a nice enough outside area. Not an essential destination on San Diego's beer map – especially with Churchill's up the street. WiFi available.

Opening hours: daily, 11am-2am

Princess Pub and Grille (44)
1665 India St., CA 92101
T 619 702 3021
www.princesspub.com

A slice of Britain in the Little Italy area of downtown San Diego. Owned by a British couple, the Princess shows English footy and stocks a slightly lackluster selection of brews from Blighty with Fuller's ESB on keg arguably the highlight. No surprises here but a good place to catch a game.

Opening hours: Mon-Wed, 11am-midnight; Thu & Fri, 11am-1am; Sat 9am-1am; Sun 9am-midnight

Wit's End (45)
420 Robinson Ave., CA 92103
T 619 294 4848

Unassuming and affordable restaurant buried in an uninspiring Hillcrest strip mall. The wide range of simple food is complemented by a huge and carefully curated array of bottled beers and 22 taps.

Opening hours: Mon-Wed, noon-10pm; Thu, noon-11pm; Fri, noon-late; Sat, 2pm-late

The Yard House (46)
1023 4th Ave., CA 92101
T 619 233 9273
www.yardhouse.com

As Shakespeare never wrote: 'Alas, riches of ale alone doth not maketh a fine taverne'. The cavernous, sports-heavy Yard House has the biggest selection of taps in the city, yet somehow fails to muster much excitement. The concept, clearly dreamt up by a boardroom suit and not a brewer, is one that should work but, somehow, doesn't. The vast majority of the mainstream downtown crowd tends to ignore the eclectic selection in favour of Coors, Bud and Miller. It's a free country and they can bloody well do what they like. But

The Yard House likes to do things big but lacks a little atmosphere.

if our visit is anything to go by, such ale apathy renders the quality unpredictable and means the more adventurous beer drinker is left playing Russian roulette.

Opening hours: Sun-Wed, 11.30am-11pm; Thu, 11.30am-midnight; Fri & Sat, 11.30am-1.15am

BEER AND FOOD

Kaiserhof (47)
2253 Sunset Cliffs Blvd., CA 92107
T 619 224 0606
www.kaiserhofrestaurant.com

A family-owned Germanic restaurant with a bier garden and a dozen-strong selection of genuine imported German beers, including Spaten Optimator, the Bavarian Paulaner Hefeweizen and the crisp, clean Warsteiner. Perfect for washing down some unfeasibly large sausages and the odd schnitzel or two.

Opening hours: Tue-Thu, 4pm-midnight; Fri-Sun, 11.30am-midnight

Recommended beer & food match:
The sausage platter and Warsteiner will have you slapping your lederhosen with delight.

The Linkery (48)
3382 30th St., CA 92104
T 619 255 8778
www.thelinkery.com
Highly recommended

You'll find excellent made-from-scratch artisan food at this charming North Park restaurant, which is famed for making its own sausages, curing its own meat and cultivating its own sublime cheese selection. A melting pot of influences shapes the imaginative and ever-changing menu – from Mexico to the Pacific Rim – but every effort is made to ensure that the ingredients are sourced locally from independent, ethically aware suppliers. And that includes the beer. Owner Jay Porter champions the San Diego beer scene in the shape of a rotating draught beer menu, frequent beer and food matching dinners hosted by head brewers and, most admirable of all, a rare devotion to the joy of cask ale. Casks of local beers are tapped regularly and lovingly looked after with a strong focus on darker interpretations such as porters, stouts, Scottish ales and the occasional barley wine to accompany the meat-heavy menu. The sausage selection is incredible, ranging from basic bangers to Polish, Sicilian and super

The Linkery: great beer + sausages = very nice time.

spicy varietals. You'd be a fool not to eat at The Linkery, but you can just pop in for a quick drink and kickback in the cosy, candle-lit surroundings. Definitely worth a visit.

Opening hours: Mon–Fri, 11am-midnight; Sat & Sun, 9am-midnight

Recommended beer & food match
The rotating menus make a precise pairing difficult. However, the beer is unlikely to disappoint and neither is the scrumptious artisan cheese selection. Put the two together and you'll have a lovely time. We promise.

The Ritual Tavern (49)

4095 30th St., CA 92104
T 619 283 1618
www.ritualtavern.com
Recommended

Sadly, The Ritual Tavern opened in the blossoming North Park district long after we'd departed San Diego. However, our reliable agents in the field have returned with reports as glowing as ET's index finger. Owners Michael and Stacy Flores are revered local restaurateurs and serve superior scrumptious food (gumbo, Colorado lamb and sublime cheesecake) at this richly decorated, gothic gastronomic haunt. The food is accompanied by a carefully considered beer and wine selection. Port Brewing, AleSmith, Green Flash and Stone feature on draught,

while the great bottled beer menu showcases a number of beauties from Belgium (Foret Organic Saison), Canada (Trois Piostoles), Germany (Ayinger 'Celebrator') and America (Lost Abbey's Judgement Day, Avery's Salvation). We missed out on The Ritual but, if rumours are to be believed, it's probably best if you don't.

Opening hours: Tue-Sun, 5.30pm-11:30pm
Recommended beer & food match
Strawberry Shortcake with peaches and drizzled cream accompanied by **Ballast Point's Black Marlin Porter** *(6%). A thinking man's Black Forest Gateau.*

The Vine (50)

1851 Bacon St., CA 92107
T 619 222 8463
www.theobvine.com

With its white tablecloths, fancy wine list and even fancier food, you'd be forgiven for thinking this small, upscale eaterie is a beer-free zone. Forgiven yet also ridiculed and ordered to say sorry for being such a fool. After all, both hops and grapes grow on vine so it's only right that, as it is here, the former is championed with as much passion and knowledge as the latter. A grandiose bottled beer list sees Californian craft classics such as AleSmith's Horny Devil and Stone Ruination rub shoulders with a handful of out-of-state domestic delights, including Avery's Hog Heaven Barley Wine, Ommegang Witte from New York and Doggie Style from the Flying Dog pound in Denver, Colorado. And that's not all folks. The Vine also offers an impressive selection of European imports, including Gouden Caralus and Chimay Grand Reserve from Belgium, Young's Double Chocolate Stout from England, a couple of Canada's Unibroue beers and a trio of German stalwarts. Served predominantly in large, 750ml bottles, the beers are designed to enhance the equally ambitious Californian cuisine. It's a little on the dear side but worth every cent. During Happy Hour, the beers are half price. Worth the trip to Ocean Beach alone.

Opening hours: Sun-Thu, 4pm-10pm; Fri & Sat, 4pm-11pm
Recommended beer & food match
Crème Brulee served over chocolate covered bananas with **Bier de Miel** *(8%) – a honey-tinged ale from Belgium.*

Orange County & Beaches

Nestled between San Diego and Los Angeles, Orange County is named after the hue of its conservative, well-heeled citizens... probably. A playground for spoiled rich kids (and adults, too), the OC could do with a sobering and brutal boot camp but has Disneyland instead. Heading into LA, Highway 1 takes in the beach and commuter communities of Hermosa, Redondo, Long Beach and the harbourside San Pedro.

A trio of beaches – Huntingdon, Newport and Laguna – are dotted along the coastline and pretty much do what you'd expect: sun, sand, sea and shopping. South of Laguna, the principal points of interests are San Juan Capistrano, the big daddy of Spanish missions, and San Clemente – a cool and quaint surfing town with slightly more character than its northern buddies.

BREWERIES

Angel City (1)
833 W. Torrance Blvd., Suite #105, Torrance, CA 90502
T 310 329 8881
www.angelcitybrewing.com

Two-time 'California Homebrewer of the Year', former scriptwriter and jazz saxophonist Michael Bowe began brewing beer commercially in 1997 after striking a contract deal with Southern California Brewing (SCB) in Torrance. When SCB fell on hard times, Bowe rescued the brewery by buying the 8,000-barrel brew house on eBay for a six-figure sum and updating it with the introduction of an ex-Rogue Brewing bottling line. Tucked away in the unfancied Torrance district, Angel City has no taproom or pub attached, but its range of nine bottled beers has slowly gained a foothold in LA drinking destinations.

In the neighbouring Alpine Village, faux-German delicatessen and restaurant, diners wash down pork knuckle with the 'Alpine Village Oktoberfest'. German influences are called upon elsewhere in the shape of the Angel City Pilz, Angel City Dunkel and the Angel City Vitzen wheat beer brewed with Angel City own proprietary yeast. Bowe salutes Belgian and British brewing with an Abbey Ale and a forceful, floral IPA. There's a couple of LA friendly lagers too – one dedicated to the to the Bolivian beret-wearing troublemaker Che Guevara.

Recommendation
Angel City Abbey (8%)
A wacky interpretation of a Belgian Dubbel with a kinetic coming together of fruit, spice and honey flavours.

Ocean Avenue Brewery (2)
237 Ocean Ave., Laguna Beach, CA 92651
T 949 497 3381
www.oceanbrewing.com

Lively little brewpub just a couple of blocks from the shore with an outdoor patio and a chef and brewer that certainly know their onions from their IBUs. The consistent house beers tend to refresh rather than raise eyebrows, but the Amber and the Ludicrous Stout stand out. There are half a dozen European and American micro choices in the chiller, too.

Opening hours: Mon-Thu, 11am-10pm; Fri & Sat, 11:30am-2am

Recommendation
Red Sunshine (5.3%)
Appetising amber ale, twinges of blood orange and a refreshing tart finish.

BREWPUBS

Alcatraz Brewing Company (3)
The Block at Orange, 20 City Blvd. West Suite R-1, Orange, CA 92868
T 714 939 8686
www.alcatrazbrewing.com

As well as the Alcatraz watchtower at the entrance, jail-related memorabilia is smeared all over the walls between numerous blaring plasmas. The quartet of house beers were gaunt and predictable, the vibe a little sterile and the food fine if not fantastic. Positive points? The staff were helpful, and it's a decent enough place for a pint if you don't want to be dragged around the shops.

Opening hours: Mon-Thu, 11am-11pm; Fri & Sat, 11am-1am; Sun, 11am-10pm

Recommendation
Pelican Pale Ale (5%)
Authentic and golden West Coast pale ale full of resinous spice and a clipped floral finish.

Bayhawk Ales @ McCormick & Schmick's Pilsner Room (4)
2000 Main St, Irvine, CA 92614
T (Bayhawk) 949 442 7565
T (McCormick & Schmick) 949 756 0505
www.bayhawkales.com

Reeling in a well-groomed business clientele amid rather soulless surroundings, this seafood restaurant and bar doubles up as an upmarket taproom for the oft-overlooked Bayhawk Brewery. Bayhawk's bread and butter is contract brewing for bespoke restaurants and bars, but it also brews a range of its own ales – all of which are available in the adjacent Pilsner Room alongside a surprisingly decent yet pricey microbrew menu.

Through a curved glass screen, the brewmaster rustles up an unchallenging amber, Hefeweizen, pale ale, sprightly honey blonde lager and an IPA – all clearly tailored for widespread appeal. It's not the most inspiring of venues but worth a visit if you're passing.

Brewery tours: call ahead

Opening hours: daily, 11.30am-11pm

Recommendation

Chocolate Porter (5.4%)

The most adventurous Bayhawk beer doesn't overplay the chocolate. Try pairing it with the M&S oysters.

Huntington Beach Brewery (5)

201 Main St., Huntington Beach, CA 92648

T 714 960 5343

www.hbbrewco.com

This place is a pretty standard beach bar with lots of plasma screens, typical brewpub food and five uninspiring draught beers. The roof gardens are blessed with a great vista of the Pacific Ocean and palm trees, and the bar staff was equally pleasing on the eye. Pop in if you're passing but do so more for the sights than the suds. Free WiFi, regular beer appreciation nights and more adventurous guest beers on tap.

Opening hours: daily, 11.30am-11.30pm

Recommendation

Pier Pale Ale (5%)

Hearty, hop-driven personality with pinewood on the nose and a brusque, bitter finish.

Main St. Brewing/Lamppost Pizza (6)

300 N. Main St., Corona, California 92880

T 951 371 1471

www.lamppostpizzacorona.com

The less than uplifting location and drab frontage hide a tidy little set-up, one that's been peddling pizzas and pints for more than ten years. Annexed to the main pizza parlour, the ten-barrel brewery and oval-shaped bar keeps a friendly Corona crowd content with nine fresh beers on tap, bartender banter and TVs showing balls of various guises being thrown around. Brewer Bob Culver's delicate Hefeweizen is the local favourite followed by the pale ale, but it's the Black Pearl Stout and Hop Daddy IPA that recently bestrode the podium at the Great American Beer Festival.

Opening hours: daily, 11am-close

Recommendation

Katarina Wit (5%)

Balanced Belgian-style wheat beer spiced with coriander, orange peel and an ingredient that Bob refused to divulge.

Manhattan Beach Brewing Company (7)

124 Manhattan Beach Blvd., Manhattan Beach, CA 90266   **T** 310 798 2744

www.manhattanbeachbrewingcompany.com

This palm-tree flanked spot reworks the classic brewpub recipe with a touch more cool than most. The service is cheery, the brews are approachable and the food eschews grease for taste. The beers change regularly but there are four core ales all year round: a Blonde, a Pale Ale, a Hefeweizen and a Red.

Recommendation

Manhattan Beach Blonde (5%)

Straddling a blonde ale and lager in style, it's crisp, clean and an ideal post-beach thirst-slaker.

Newport Beach Brewing Company (8)

2920 Newport Blvd., CA 92663

T 949 675 8449

www.nbbrewco.com

Myriad food choices, friendly staff and a couple of standout beers make this a justified Newport Beach hotspot. Grab yourself a seat on the patio, where you can watch sports in the sun and enjoy a range of refreshing beers. Head brewer Kirk Roberts also offers some seasonals worthy of further inspection.

Opening hours: Sun-Thu, 11:30am-11.30pm; Fri & Sat, 11.30am-12.30am

Recommendation

Bisbees ESB (5%)

Fronted by toffee-sweetness, it doesn't overdo the astringent hops and leads with a nutty aroma.

Pizza Port San Clemente (9)

301 N. El Camino Real, San Clemente, CA 92672
T 949 0005

In the Hispanic seaside village of San Clemente, acclaimed by many as the birthplace of surfing (and also home to some mean looking Marines), you'll find a Pizza Port sprawled across three levels. Sticking close to the tried and tested formula employed by its San Diegan counterparts, this one knocks out terrific pizza and more than two-dozen ales from a glistening bar and rather battered brewery. Gnarly and a little gruff, it lures in a young surf crowd with plenty of piercings, body art and tall tales of wave-catching. The best place in town.

Opening Hours: Sun-Thu, 11am-10pm; Fri & Sat, 11am-midnight

Recommendation

Trestles Special Golden (4%)
Liberty hops leap from this lip-smacking lager, bringing you up as the sun goes down.

Red Car Brewing (10)

1266 Sartori Ave., Torrance, CA 90501
T 310 782 0222
www.redcarbrewery.com

This is a cracking little brewpub tucked away in Old Town Torrance. The Thirties building, an old tram depot that used to house the Red Car trolley, has retained its character. The industrial décor (exposed brick, wooden rafters and flourishes of steel) is toned down with Sepia-photographs from yesteryear, great music and a friendly welcome. The huge brew kettles, which loom behind an L-shaped bar partitioned from the restaurant, produce half-a-dozen forward-thinking ales. The English-style beer choice incorporates all the usual suspects with a wheat, porter, a light golden ale, an impressive Motorman Reserve ale dedicated to the Red Car drivers and the popular Big Red Ale.

Opening hours: Mon-Thu, 11.30am-9.30pm; Fri, 11.30am-11pm; Sat, noon-11pm; Sun, noon-8.30pm

Recommendation

South Bay IPA (6.5%)
This may just be the best IPA you'll encounter on your travels between San Diego and San Francisco. A big, dark orange ale with plenty of orange and lemon – aimed squarely at hop heads.

Redondo Beach Brewing Company (11)

1814 Catalina Ave. Redondo Beach, CA 90277
T 310 316 8477
www.redondobrewery.com

This better-than-average two-floored brewpub set two blocks back from Redondo Beach is the sister brewery to Manhattan Beach. The bespoke beers aimed predominantly at the mainstream palette have been crafted on the gleaming brewery since 1990 and served alongside a menu that exceeds the standard brewpub grub. Bright and sea-breezy, it attracts surfers, families and the odd sports enthusiast. The outdoor space, which is blooming in flowers, is great for al-fresco ale enjoyment.

Opening hours: Sun-Thu, 10.30am-11.30pm; Fri & Sat, 10.30am-1am

Recommendation

Blueberry Wheat (4.5%)
Refreshing Blueberry beer, sweet but not overly cloying. Tight, tart finish.

San Pedro Brewing Company (12)

331 W. 6th St., San Pedro, CA 90731
T 310 831 5663
www.sanpedrobrewingy.com

This bright and breezy, family-friendly red-brick brewpub can be found in the pleasant seaport suburb of San Pedro. The venue attracts a largely local crowd with live music, friendly staff, unobtrusive sports screens, a comprehensive food menu and, lest we forget, some tasty if unspectacular beers brewed on site. As well as a rotating guest beer, the core selection includes Longshoreman Lager, a light lawnmower thirst-slaker; a floral 'Point Fermin Ale'; and the decent Cascade-hopped 'Shanghai Red Ale'. From the food menu, the 'Classic Shrimp Cocktail' features prawns simmered in the Longshoreman lager and served in a martini glass. Delicious.

Opening hours: Sun-Thu, 10.30am-midnight; Fri & Sat, 10.30am-2am

Recommendation

Harbor Hefeweizen (5.2%)
This unfiltered wheat beer exudes cloves and bananas. The best example of a beer style on the list.

BEER BARS

Café Boogaloo (13)
1238 Hermosa Ave., Hermosa Beach, CA 90254
T 310 318 2324

Hermosa Beach hangout specialising in live music, fresh food sourced from the Santa Monica Farmers Market, Cajun cuisine and more than two dozen microbrews and pilsners on tap. Bartenders chalk up what's on special.
Opening hours: Mon-Fri, 5pm-1.30am; Sat, 1pm-1.30am; Sun, 10am-midnight

Goat Hill Tavern (14)
1830 Newport Blvd., Costa Mesa, CA, 92627
T 949 548 8428

Bring a date here and you'll be going home alone... but happy. Goat Hill calls itself 'Beer Heaven', and the cluttered bank of 141 taps, running from the obvious to the obscure, is a bleary-eyed utopian vision for beer lovers. Despite the expansive variety, however, Coors Light and its kind are the biggest sellers and, consequently, the consistency of more complex brews has been known to suffer. But with bargain-basement prices, table football and pool, the Goat Hill is a must-visit if you want to experience a rare slice of Californian counter-culture. No food but you can bring in bites from outside.
Opening hours: Mon-Fri, noon-2am; Sat & Sun, 11am-2am

Hollingshead Delicatessen (15)
368 S. Main St., Orange, CA 92868
T 714 928 9467
www.hollingshead4beer.com

Nestled deep in a strip mall far off the well-trodden tourist path, the Hollingshead Delicatessen belies its inauspicious appearance by serving up sublime suds and scrumptious sandwiches with a sardonic smile. Chicago-born owner Ken Hollingshead is an affable and entertaining host whose depth and breadth of beer knowledge is as vast as the tasty torpedoes he serves.

Half a dozen rudimentary tables are wedged between chillers and shelves bursting with more than 450 bottled beers from all four corners of the globe. On draught, a rare and eclectic selection of micros is poured, with no small amount of passionate patter at $4.50. Ken is only too happy to suggest a brew to complement your sandwich and, every quarter, invites West Coast brewers to come and host dinners and beer tastings.
Opening hours: Mon-Thu, 10am-8pm; Fri, 10am-9pm; Sat & Sun, closed

Naja's Place (16)
154 International Boardwalk, Redondo Beach, CA 902777
T 310 376 9951
www.najasplace.com

This waterside watering hole claims to have the biggest selection of beers in LA. With 77 taps and more than 250 bottled beers, many of them Belgian, they're up there with the best-stocked. Located at the end of a marina jetty, it's a little difficult to find and attracts a fairly rough and ready crowd but worth the effort for the impressive brews and views. Regular live entertainment, decent food menu (Hebrew Polish Sausage went down like the Titanic) and friendly staff.
Opening hours: Mon-Thu, 2pm-midnight; Fri & Sat, noon-2am; Sun, noon-10pm. Call ahead to check for winter opening hours.

The line of taps at the Goat Hill Tavern offers a fantastic range of great beer.

Oggi's Pizza & Brewing Company (17)

19461 Main St., Huntington Beach, CA 92648
T 714 969 8000
www.oggis.com

You know the score.
Beer, enormous pizza
and a unwavering
dedication to American
sport. An improvement
on other Huntingdon
Beach beer joints and
the patio is a decent
addition. The house
beers come from San
Clemente and are
served alongside a few
interesting guest beers.

Opening hours:
daily, 11am-10pm

Yard House (18)

1875 Newport Blvd., Costa Mesa, CA 92627
T 949 642 0090
www.yardhouse.com

It's difficult to pick faults with Yard House.
The food is ample and very tasty, there's a
100-strong beer selection (with a lot of
macros) poured from a wall of shiny kegs,
the staff are courteous, professional and
knowledgeable and there's a nice raised
balcony to eat and drink outdoors. But,
somehow, there's something missing.
Perhaps it's just a bit too polished? Eat here
but go to the Goat (see previous page) for a
more down-to-earth drinking experience.

Opening hours: Sun-Wed, 11.30am-11pm; Thu,
11.30am-11.30am; Fri & Sat, 11.30am-1.15am

Yard House (19)

160 South Brea Blvd., CA 92821
T 714 529 9273
www.yardhouse.com

This Orange County link in the bar chain
has a vast selection of beers but not the most
exciting environment in which to drink
them. Happy hour (weekdays, 3–6pm) is a
great opportunity to pick-off some pints you
may not have sampled yet but, otherwise, it
doesn't hold much surprise.

Opening hours: Sun-Thu, 11.30-midnight; Fri & Sat,
11.30am-1.30am

BEER AND FOOD

Brea Tap Fish House (20)

101 E. Imperial Hwy., Brea, CA 92821
T 714 257 0101
www.tapsbrea.com
Highly recommended

With its high ceilings, premium surf 'n'
turf menu, upscale New Orleans–style
décor and cosy fireplaces, this popular
fine-dining brewpub and restaurant is a
smart place to impress a romantic fella or
filly, tuck into terrific food with a buddy
or even just to watch the game on the
giant plasma screen. Towering behind
screens in the main lounge is a state-of-
the-art brewery overseen by the talented
and award-winning brewmaster Victor
Novak. Inspired by the European brewers
of yesteryear, Victor calls upon German
and British malt to craft an array of old
world beer styles, including Biere de Garde,
Helles, Imperial Russian Stout (2007 GABF
Silver Medal winner), Schwarzbier, Vienna
Lager, and Oscura – a beer traditionally
brewed in Mexico by Austrian immigrants.

There are always seven beers on tap,
one on genuine cask handpull, and the beer
sampler tray comes with all you need to
know about what you're drinking. What's
more, there are quarterly beer dinners, and
the courteous staff comes armed with beer
and food recommendations. The prices are
a bit higher than most but, all in all, Brea Tap
Fish House is a real gem. November 2007
saw the opening of a second Taps house in
the Promenade Shops at Dos Lagos, Corona.

Opening hours: Mon-Thu, 11am-10pm; Fri & Sat,
11am-11pm; Sun, 10am-9pm
Recommendation
Jefferson Ale (9.5%)
*Only using ingredients that Jefferson would have
had at his disposal, Victor has breathed life back
into a 200-year-old recipe. Rum and raisin on the
nose, a taste of mellow toffee and a rich, lingering
and vinous port-like finish.*

Los Angeles

The rather soulless yet spellbinding, smog-laden sprawl of Los Angeles is a quite absurd and unique metropolis if ever there was one.

The history of LA and the Central Coast

Once upon a time the Chumash and Tongva people hunted and gathered in Southern California. That all changed in 1781 when the Spanish arrived. They built Franciscan missions up and down the coast, and their legacy remains in the shape of the principal coastal towns: Santa Barbara, San Luis Obispo, Monterey and Santa Cruz. The biggest settlement was 'El Pueblo de la Reina de Los Angeles' which, thankfully, has been abbreviated into Los Angeles.

Initially a series of multicultural farming settlements, LA and its coastal satellite siblings only began to develop in the late nineteenth century with the completion of the railroad in the 1870s and the discovery of oil in 1892. Lured by promises of a paradisiacal lifestyle based upon a flourishing petroleum industry, hordes of new arrivals flocked to Southern California. By the turn of the century, the population in LA alone had soared to six figures. By this point, Santa Barbara was a flourishing port and fertile agricultural outlet, Monterey was a teeming fishing port while limes and logging kept Santa Cruz busy.

A second wave of expansion followed with the advent of the movie and aviation industries in the early 1900s. By 1932, there were more than one million people dwelling in LA and its increasingly fragmented environs. Commerce and population was boosted with the construction of Highway 1, a scenic coastal highway that joined the dots from Santa Barbara to Half Moon Bay.

At the end of the Second World War, LA sucked in even more new arrivals. Military types, who'd passed through on their way to fight in the Pacific, returned to settle in the sun. Spreading farther into the San Fernando Valley, LA was now home to a buoyant real-estate market and the glamorous allure of the silver screen.

Strangely, the boom years of the Sixties and Seventies coincided with some of the city's worst racial conflicts –the 1965 Watts Riots being the most notorious. Post Cold-War cutbacks in the military and aeronautical industries precipitated an economic dive, and this further stoked the flames of racial strife.

LA in the Nineties was like a bad film. There were floods, earthquakes and fires, unemployment was at an all-time high and there was a crack cocaine epidemic. Racial tension exploded in 1992 with full-scale rioting following the notorious beating of Rodney King by LAPD officers. While there remains a gaping chasm between the haves and the have-nots, generally drawn across racial lines, the political, financial and social climate of LA in the new millennium is more stable than it's been for quite some time.

LA today

LA is a city of contrasts and confusion. It's unrivalled in its affluence but also harbours shamefully poverty-stricken neighbourhoods. Look beyond the smog and inflated egos of those in the movie business and you'll find an enthralling mix of different cultures, characters and quirky nooks and crannies.

The nearest you get to the heart of LA is the mish-mash of impressive architecture and urban chic that is Downtown. It's infringed upon by a variety of neighbourhoods – the notorious South Central, soaring Angelino Heights and the Latino-stronghold that is Macarthur Park.

Save the pretty town of Pasadena and the San Gabriel Mountains beyond it, North LA is a nebulous network of strip malls, low-rise neighbourhoods and drive-thrus cloaked in a blanket of nothingness. To the east lie

Compton, East LA and Watts – districts notorious for gang violence, drugs and general debauchery.

From Downtown, a better bet is to head for the ocean. At first, you'll hit Hollywood. Few famous folk reside in Hollywood itself, preferring to peer down on the masses from their mansions in the hills above. Wealth abounds in West LA, home to a huge pink dollar, and the spotless, poodle-clad boulevards of Beverly Hills. Meanwhile, Sunset Strip remains an unashamed display of decadent ostentation.

Beyond this are the beach towns. Santa Monica has cutesy shops, funky bars and manicured boardwalks, while Venice scores high on the fun and freak factor. And it's easy to see why the serene Malibu has lured so many millionaires to its shores.

Orientation

American writer Dorothy Parker wrote 'Los Angeles is 72 suburbs in search of a city' and she wasn't wrong. There's no rhyme or reason to its layout, there are no clear boundaries nor is there a city centre to speak of – merely an urban jumble of neighbourhoods that seem to have been arranged by a blindfolded, two year-old monkey on acid.

The automobile is king in LA. Almost a quarter of the city's land is dedicated to the motor car and its planet-destroying requirements – highways, freeways, flyovers, garages, gas stations and drive-thru burger-joints, banks, coffee-shops and pharmacies.

Yet, incongruous to its driving fixation, LA is inexplicably difficult to get around. Not only is it a navigator's nightmare, with freeways and highways changing names every few miles, but it also grinds to a gridlocked halt between 6–10am and 3–8pm. Driving on the freeway can be a fairly daunting affair, too. It's dog-eat-dog driving, folks, where everyone adopts a 'my way on the highway' mantra and where things can get pretty scary. We left skid-marks all over LA, in both senses, so be safe, assertive and don't be scared to flip the bird once in a while.

Public transportation requires patience and time should you decide to park the car. The LA Metrorail has four colour-coded lines that spray in different directions, and the Metrolink links Downtown LA with the suburbs – both are frequent and reliable.

The bus system, meanwhile, has wide coverage yet stutters from one stop to another. It's a good way to see the 'real' LA but keep your wits about you late at night.

Taxi drivers in Los Angeles seem to confuse 'the knowledge' with knowledge. If they knew as much about the streets of Los Angeles as they do about world peace, politics and the secret to life, perhaps fewer people would drive themselves.

Accommodation

LUXURY

Mondrian Hotel 8440 Sunset Blvd., West Hollywood, CA 90069; T 323 650 8999; www.mondrianhotel.com
Things don't get much more LA than this über-fashionable Ian Schrager hotel. Not content with some super-swish rooms, the poolside views across the LA skyline are spectacular. Though not a great beer bar, The Sky Bar is a magnet for your stereotype cocktail-sipping LA glitterati.

MID-RANGE

Farmer's Daughter Hotel 115 S. Fairfax Ave., CA 90036; T 800 334 1658; www.farmersdaughterhotel.com
Trendy boutique hotel opposite CBS Studios, which is decorated with retro-imagination. Colourful rustic rooms, a pool, patio and lounge with free WiFi rooms.

BUDGET

USA Hostels (Hollywood) 1624 Schrader Blvd. Hollywood, CA 90028; T 323 462 3777; www.usahostels.com
Hooray for Hollywood's dirt-cheap digs slap bang in amongst all the glitz. Clean and expertly run, it throws in lots of nice little extras such as free WiFi, free storage after you check out, free shuttle bus from the airport if you're staying more than one night and, best of all, free pancakes in the morning. And it's got a nice patio, too.

The LA beer scene

For all the adulation received elsewhere, boutique beer has never met with a particularly warm Angelino welcome, and the beer scene is rather Mickey Mouse. No one really knows why. Some blame the climate: LA's hot and sweaty weather stifles pub culture and big beers wilt whenever the mercury rises.

But if this were really the case, neighbouring San Diego wouldn't be such a scorching hotbed of craft-brewing creativity.

What's more, craft beer plays to a tough crowd in LA. The hop simply isn't hip in Hollywood, while the city's huge Latino and African-American communities are, for whatever reason, not the most dedicated followers of craft beer. Many date this ale apathy back to the early days of the craft-brewing revolution. Goodwill created by a number of start-ups in the Eighties was wiped out when Eureka, a sizeable and well-supported brewery owned by celebrity chef Wolfgang Puck, over-stretched itself and hit the wall in quite spectacular fashion saddled with more than $1 million debt. Eureka's failure alienated bars and drinkers and, almost overnight, blacklisted LA as a craft-beer market.

Having somehow remained oblivious to the West Coast's love affair with craft beer for quite some time, Angelinos are finally getting the right idea. A handful of pioneering bars, such as Father's Office and Lucky Baldwin's, are no longer fighting a lonely beer battle. High-end restaurants, swanky bars and working men's watering holes are all waking up to the benefits of fine beer drinking. Doors that were previously closed to out-of-town craft brewers, such as New Belgium and Stone, are now edging open, while Craftsman, the finest brewery in LA, finally seems to be getting the credit it so richly deserves. Angel City and Skyscraper, the two other stand-alone breweries, are also gaining a loyal following.

"Things are definitely improving and there's a lot of great beer and great places to drink it in," said Craftsman's Mark Jilg, "but you just have to look a little harder in LA than you do in other cities."

BREWERIES

Craftsman Brewing Company (21)
See feature on page 82.

Skyscraper Brewing Company (22)
3229 Durfee Ave., El Monte, CA 91732
T 626 575 0770
www.skyscraperbrewing.com

Disillusioned with the LA craft-beer scene and inspired by his homebrewing days in Utah and the suds available while working in San Francisco, Phillip Sutton constructed Skyscraper Brewing in 2006. Currently, Phillip brews and bottles two beers at a modest El Monte brew house in an industrial unit in East LA. Inspired by the legendary Anchor Steam, Lug Nut Lager (5.2%) is teamed with a wheat beer fortified with wildflower honey. More beers are planned. Call ahead if you want to visit the brewery.

Recommendation
Bulldog Honeyweizen (5%)
Sweet honey helps rather than hinders this quirky take on a Bavarian wheat beer. Spicy hop aroma.

The beer inspector at Craftsman Brewing Company.

Craftsman Brewing Company [21]

1270 Lincoln Ave. #800, Pasadena, CA 91105
T 818 298 2437
www.craftsmanbrewing.com

It's been a lonely job brewing beautiful beer in LA, but someone's got to do it. And that someone is Mark Jilg – owner and head brewer at Craftsman. Mark has been working from his hand-built brewery in a labyrinth of Pasadena industrial units since 1995. There's no pub, no taproom and no bottling line (there will be soon), just three hard-working chaps making super beer. If Mark had been working his mashfork magic all these years in San Francisco, he would have long been riding a microbrewing wave. But in LA, he's been swimming against the tide of ale apathy and ploughing the lonely furrow.

"Historically, LA is a brewing wasteland and trying to make a beer work here is frankly a crazy idea," said Mark. *"LA is a difficult place to make a brewery work. It's not a get-rich-quick scheme, it's a lot of hard work and it requires a lot of commitment and money."*

It's taken more than a decade for Craftsman to seep into the LA consciousness. Mark and his two assistants have braved the quite insane LA freeways in a retro Forties Studebaker truck, delivering beer to a growing number of switched-on bars and restaurants. Slowly but surely the word is finally spreading into all the right places. If you walk into an LA bar and see Craftsman's wooden tap handles, chances are it knows what it's doing when it comes to beer.

Craftsman beers are subtle, delicately hoppy and brewed with integrity and all the balance of a level-headed ballerina. Mark brews a quartet of year-round beers all brewed with a twist. '1903', the biggest seller, is a strapping pre-Prohibition lager brewed with a dose of corn and a complexity that belies its pale appearance. Brewed with rye, Craftsman's Pale Ale is a peppery, oaky drop. The IPA pricks the tongue with pine needles and then soothes it with a mellow sweetness. The Heavenly Hefeweizen, bursting with all the clichéd yet requisite banana, bubble gum and clove, is arguably the best wheat beer we tasted on our travels. For two-thirds of the year, don't miss a strong Belgian-ale brewed using sage, Triple White Sage; Orange Grove Ale, a unique fruit beer that attains its bitterness from the pith of carefully selected Californian oranges; and a deliciously dry and peaty Smoked Black Lager that proves dark can be very drinkable.

But that's not all folks. Craftsman really picks up the pace with its two dozen or so seasonal and specialty beers, released on a monthly basis. Mark experiments with oak-ageing and blending, lavender, spruce, cherries and other fruits, spices and botanicals – they're one-off ales that challenge and charm in equal measure. The most impressive effort is, in our opinion, the Burgundy-coloured Cabernale. Huge quantities of Californian Cabernet Sauvignon grapes, de-stemmed and crushed, are added to the mash and fermented for a week to ten days.

Tours of the brewery are not available but Craftsman's quaff is available at the following locations (amongst others): Lucky Baldwins, Father's Office, The Other Room, Barney's Beanery, The Village Idiot, The 3rd Stop, Martel and the Delirium Café.

THE BEERS

Poppyfields Pale Ale (4.8%)
With Eucalyptus at one end, caramel at the other, it stretches the boundaries beyond your usual pale ale.

1903 (5.6%)
Imagine the middle ground in a Venn diagram of a Vienna lager and a Czech pilsner. Pale but potent.

IPA (6.25%)
Hazy, orange-amber beer promoting pine, grapefruit, pear drops and a delicate hop finish.

Cabernale (7.5%)
A flavoursome fender-bender between grain and grape with summer berries, spice and a lovely tannin-coated finish.

Orange Grove (8%)
A light, bitter amber beer with zesty citrus aroma and swathed in flavours that can, quite frankly, only be described as... orange.

Triple White Sage (9%)
If you like sage, you'll absolutely love this beer. But if you don't, you probably won't.

Aurora Borealis (11%)
Bombastic strong Belgian ale that tingles your mouth with mint, pine and fierce freshness.

BREWPUBS

Belmont Brewing Company (23)

25 39th Place, Long Beach, CA 90803
T 562 433 3891
www.belmontbrewing.com

The BBC's doing the world a service with one of the most serene and affordable ocean views in all of LA – and the beer isn't bad either. While the Pale Ale lacked piquancy, the lightly hopped Long Beach Crude (6.5%) impressed. Drink in the stunning sunsets and handcrafted ales on the picturesque, wind-sheltered patio or shoot the breeze with Long Beachers at the busy bar. A sister venue to the Bonaventure Brewing Company, BBC does all the things a brewpub should and does them rather well. Keep your eye out for the well-attended Beer and Food Dinners.

Opening hours: Mon-Fri, 11pm-1am; Sat & Sun, 5.30pm-1am

Recommendation
Strawberry Blonde (4.5%)
Nicely balanced fruit beer presumably aimed at the ladies. But even hetero-masculine tigers such as us will like it. Especially when it's hot.

Crown City (24)

300 S. Raymond, Pasadena, CA 91105
T 626 577 5548
www.crowncitybrew.com

The predominantly dark house beers play second fiddle to a bountiful selection of recognizable microbrews both in bottle and on tap at this two-tier Pasadena pub. It's pretty standard brewpub business with lots of TVs, generously proportioned pub food, beer stuff on the walls and attentive staff. Just two blocks down from Lucky Baldwins, it makes for a pleasant Pasadena pit stop. Crown City's beers are brewed by craftsmen.

Opening hours: Mon-Thu, 11.30am-11.30pm; Fri & Sat, 11am-1am; Sun, 11am-10pm

Wolf Creek Brewing (25)

27746 McBean Pkwy., CA 91354
T 661 263 9653
Recommended
www.wolfcreekbrewco.weekly.com

This neighbourhood brewpub out in the 'burbs has a bit more going for it than most. A clean and uncluttered venue off the beaten track, Wolf Creek lures in locals with very good pizzas, an outdoor patio and a batch of beers brewed with invention. It also offers some top-notch guest beers.

Opening hours: Mon-Thu, 11am-10pm; Fri & Sat, 11am-11pm; Sun, 10.30am-9.30pm

Recommendation
Yellowstone Wolf Pale Ale (6.2%)
Crammed with copious amounts of Cascade, it's bitter yet balanced with plenty of grapefruit on the nose

BEER BARS

Barney's Beanery (26)

8447 Santa Monica Blvd., West Hollywood, CA 90069
T 323 654 2287
www.barneysbeanery.com

A Hollywood institution, Barney's Beanery was founded by John 'Barney' Anthony in 1920 on what was then Route 66 (now the Santa Monica Boulevard). Once a pit stop for parched pioneers who'd refuel on its famous chilli, Barneys Beanery went on to lubricate Hollywood's freewheeling hedonism during the Sixties and Seventies.

Janis Joplin had her last drink here (booth number 34), the staff kicked Jim Morrison out the Doors after he urinated on the bar, Hendrix drank himself into a purple haze, Quentin Tarantino scribbled *Pulp Fiction* while sunk in the technicolor booths and the Red Hot Chili Peppers have propped up the bar, too. Amid the hipster grunge and dive-bar décor, there's little room for pretension or poseur posturing – a rare thing in these parts. The long, dark bar takes centre stage among threadbare booths, video games, a kick-ass jukebox and pool tables.

Famed for its onion soup, 45 different kinds of chilli and a million interpretations on the fried potato concept, Barney's menu is an unfeasibly big 'un. And so, too, is the beer list. There are nearly 140 ales and lagers hailing from America and elsewhere and incorporating mainstream and micros, but nothing overly obscure for the adventurous beer buff. Since being taken over by more corporate-minded patrons, two new versions have opened in Santa Monica and Pasadena. Sadly, you can't reproduce a classic and neither rivals the original. Free WiFi.

Opening hours: daily, 11am-2am

Barney's Pasadena (27)

99 E. Colorado, Pasadena CA 91105

T 626 405 9777

Sports-friendly Pasadena outpost with a mainstream draft selection supported by an eclectic bottled list that'll satisfy, but maybe not surprise, a beer geek.

Barney's Santa Monica (28)

1351 3rd St. Prom., Santa Monica, CA 90401

T 310 656 5777

Touristy take on the original, drawing a younger, baseball-capped crowd with a lengthy list of beers and karaoke on Wednesdays from 10pm. The patio is a prime location for people-and-performer watching.

Daily Pint (29)

2310 Pico Blvd., Santa Monica, CA, 90405

T 310 450 7631

A touch of welcome grit amid the Santa Monica glamour, the Daily Pint is a drinking den with darts, shuffleboard, table football and a jolly fine beer selection. All that's good about Belgian, Czech and Californian brewing is here, and there's whisky a go-go too.

Opening hours: daily, 2pm-2am

Good Microbrew & Grill (30)

3725 Sunset Blvd., CA 90026

T 323 660 3645

www.goodmicrobrew.com

The Good's list of boutique bottled beers is so MASSIVE it'll make your eyes water. Lost Abbey, Meantime, Thomas Hardy, Schneider Aventinus, Ommegang from New York, Polygamy Porter from Utah and even Old Engine Oil from Scotland are just a drop in the bar's barrel of bottled delights. And there

are some alluring taps, too (Angel, Lagunitas, Firestone). Unfortunately, it's all let down by the atmosphere, or rather the lack of it. It's like going for a drink inside a ping-pong ball.

Opening hours: Mon-Thu, 11am-10pm; Fri, 11am-11pm; Sat, 9am-11pm; Sun, 9am-10pm

Library Alehouse (31)

2911 Main St., Santa Monica, CA 90405

T 310 314 4855

www.libraryalehouse.com

Highly recommended

A stylish yet cosy L-shaped boutique beer bar and bistro clad in wood with a spacious sun-kissed patio out back. Owner Leo Stanton has focused on quality not quantity with approximately 50 beers (29 crafts on tap and many hard-to-find bottled beers), mostly American microbrews, on offer. Short tap-lines are used to ensure a greater level of freshness and samplers are available for the undecided. The food menu is quintessentially Californian with a Latin twist. Beer is used in the jambalaya and the battered fish and chips.

One of the few bars in California that's free of blaring TVs, and there's an impressive wine selection, too. Very popular, among both surfers and suits, so you might like to think about booking ahead.

Opening hours: daily, 11.30am-midnight

Library Bar (32)

630 W. 6th St., CA 90017

T 213 614 0053

www.librarybarla.com

Highly recommended

This place gives beer the discerning drinking credit it deserves. Devised by a switched-on female beer sommelier, the beer list is cleverly divided into bibliographical sections; Belgian Trappist beers such as Chimay and Rochefort come under 'Religion'. 'American Authors' is home to Craftsman, Rogue and AleSmith. You can study Samuel Smith under 'English Authors' and flick through seasonal beers in the 'Periodicals' section. Meanwhile, you'll find some decent lagers and the mainstream lite beers in 'Light Reads' and the amusing 'Kid's Corner'.

For the well-read beer buff, 'Epic Novels' offer big beers. All zinc and well-groomed upholstery and swarming with people who

The beer list in the Library Bar will get you thinking before you start drinking.

look great and smell nice, the Library Bar puts the 'shhhh' into chic. With shelves holding several hundred books, it's just like a proper library... just much better and less boring.

Opening hours: Mon-Fri, 3pm-2am; Sat & Sun, 7pm-2am

Little Bar (33)
757 S. La Brea Ave., CA 90036
T 323 937 9210
www.littlebarlounge.com

Funky, dimly lit neighbourhood bar with an East Coast feel, plenty of well-known micros and a range of sake, which (and you may not know this) is actually beer. Good place for a game of 'arrers' (darts), too.

Opening hours: daily, 5.30pm-2am

Lucky Baldwins (34)
17 South Raymond Ave., Pasadena, CA 91105
T 626 795 0652
www.luckybaldwins.com
Highly recommended

The path that leads to Lucky Baldwins is a well-trodden one among the beer-drinking cognoscenti. English owner David Farnsworth, who swapped the Lake District for LA in 1996, has grown Lucky Baldwins into more than just a jingoistic British pub to watch the football or wolf down fish and chips. The decoration (patriotic paraphernalia, British football memorabilia and enough breweriana to make a beer geek implode) may not be particularly special for visiting Brits, but David's almost evangelical

dedication to educated and enlightened beer drinking is certainly unique.

When David started, Lucky Baldwins had ten taps. Today it has 63, of which a dozen or more are American microbrews (including several Craftsman), even more are Belgian and British, and one, on handpump, is always Fuller's ESB. The hundred bottled beers include a smattering of classic British ales (Thomas Hardy, Bluebird, Old Engine Oil) and a wealth of sumptuous Belgian classics. In fact, such is David's unswerving dedication to Flemish and Walloon beer-making, he was recently inducted into the Belgian Brewers Guild in Brussels – no mean feat, folks.

Sierra Nevada's Big Foot Barley Wine is a favourite here (several vintages are available), drinkers flock to the regular beer festivals (Belgian – 51 beers on tap, IPA, barley wine, Oktoberfest and Christmas) and local breweries are often championed on cask.

Opening hours: Mon-Fri, 8am-1.30am; Sat, 7am-1.30am

Lucky Baldwins' Delirium Café (35)
21 Kersting Court, Sierra Madre, CA 91204
T 626 355 1140

Lucky Baldwins's Delirium Café, named after the legendary Brussels bar, opened in 2005 in Sierra Madre. A little smaller and with a Belgian rather than British vibe, it still has 45 different beers on tap and hosts several small beer festivals.

My Father's Office (36)

1018 Montana, Santa Monica, CA 90401
T 310 393 2337
www.fathersoffice.com
Highly recommended

If every office was like this, getting up in the morning wouldn't be such a chore. A small, buzzy and bustling neighbourhood bar set back from the seafront whose reputation has been built on fine food and a seductive draught beer selection. The burgers are said to be the finest in all of LA, and the mainly West Coast craft beers are served by knowledgeable staff. A little hectic and service can be a bit brusque but worth a visit – your dad would be proud.

Opening hours: Mon-Thu, 5pm-1am; Fri, 4pm-2am; Sat, noon-2am; Sun, noon-midnight

Recommendation
'**Office Burger**': *Dry-aged beef with caramelized onion, applewood bacon compote, Gruyere, Maytag blue cheese and aragula. Eat with* **Bear Republic Racer 5 IPA** (7%).

The Otheroom (37)

1201 Abbot Kinney Blvd., Venice, CA 90291
T 310 396 6230
www.theotheroom.com

A wealth of well-respected, West Coast craft names (Craftsman, Bear Republic) adorn the bar at a young, trendy hangout where, under atmospheric candlelight, the fine-looking denizens of Venice look even finer. It's incredibly swish, incredibly busy and, after 11pm, incredibly difficult to get into. No food though.

Opening hours: daily, 5pm-2am

The Redwood Bar & Grill (38)

316 W. 2nd St., CA 90012
T 213 680 2600
www.theredwoodbar.com

Swashbuckling downtown nautical-themed bar where fishing nets, planks of driftwood and pirate paraphernalia deck the walls. A bank of beers includes a good spread of Craftsman and other West Coast suds. Craftsman is also used to make the fish batter.

Opening hours: Fri, 11am-2am

Snake Pit (39)

7529 Melrose Ave., CA 90046
T 323 852 9390

It may only hail the ale in moderate fashion, with a modest selection of conventional and slightly alternative taps such as Firestone and Anchor, but the Snake Pit is one of the better bars on this trendy thoroughfare. In truth, it's a dive bar. Check out the rather attractive eye-candy slinging the beers.

Opening hours: daily, 11.30am-2am

Stuffed Sandwich (40)

1145 E. Las Tunas Drive, CA 91776
T 626 285 9161
www.stuffedsandwich.com

Ronald Reagan–worshipping, moustache-sporting and highly opinionated owner Sam Samaniego has collated an extraordinary selection of more than 800 bottled beers from all around the world (many highly sought after) and some first rate crafts on draught.

If you don't know what to drink, Sam will give his upper-lip fluff a contemplative twiddle and tell you what he thinks. In fact, there's nothing Sam likes more than telling people what he thinks. Famed as much for his sarcastic and brusque customer service (done with tongue firmly wedged in cheek) as his peerless beer knowledge, unfeasibly large sandwiches and bowls of spaghetti, Sam and his wife Marlena have turned this basic beer bar and sandwich shop into an elbow-bending institution since they began in 1976. Beer only served with food. Uninspiring outdoor area.

Opening hours: Tue-Sat, 11am-8pm

Recommendation
Ask Sam, he knows best.

T. H. Brewster's Bar (41)

The Sheraton 4 Points, 9750 Airport Blvd., CA 90045
T 310 649 7024
www.fourpointslax.com

There are lots of corporate hotels near the airport, but this is the only one with its own beer sommelier and a remarkable two-dozen strong beer range. The transient atmosphere is shrink-wrapped and the music cheesy, but there's a fine flow of draught and bottled artisan ales, barley wines and Lambics sourced from Belgium, Britain, Germany and closer-to-home. The small plate food is cleverly matched with the likes of Chimay, Spaten and Duvel, and a beer tasting is held every third Wednesday of the month. TVs showing sport, a jukebox and a plastic darts board fight a losing battle against the sterile surroundings, so take your beer to the pool.

Opening hours: noon-1am

BEER AND FOOD

Beechwood Restaurant (42)
822 W. Washington Blvd., Venice, CA 90292
T 310 448 8884
www.beechwoodrestaurant.com

Oozing chic, this restaurant is technicolor stools, polished beech wood, clean-lines, subtle lighting and no small amount of minimalist showmanship. It's not a place where you'd expect beer to feature highly, but the list of ales is thoughtfully compiled. The complete absence of mainstream micros leaves room for two taps (Stone was on when we visited) and a chiller packed with a handful of discriminating European lagers and ales (Pilsner Urquell, Ayinger Weiss), some British standards (Newcastle Brown) and big Belgian and American beers. Budgets didn't stretch to the food but it looked as good as the Venetian babes on the swish patio.

Opening hours: Sun & Mon, 6pm-midnight; Tue-Sat, 6pm-2am

Boneyard Bistro (43)
13539 Ventura Blvd., Sherman Oaks, CA 91423
T 818 906 7427
www.boneyardbistro.com

Aficionados will be in hop-heaven with an overwhelming choice divided neatly into style sections. Bourbon barrel-aged Allagash Curieux from Maine and Shiner Bock from Texas complement a whole host of American counterparts from the West Coast, there's a full selection of Belgian Trappist Ales, a pan-Atlantic choice of Lambics, stouts, porters and an 'Oddballs' section featuring Crafts-man's Cabernale and Rogue's Crustacean Barley Wine – both delicious with the bistro's

mouth-watering cheese board. Gleefully, the food here is just as creative.

Opening hours: Mon-Thu, 6-10pm; Fri & Sat, 6-11pm Sun, 5-9pm

Hungry Cat (44)
1535 N. Vine, CA 90028
T 323 462 2155
www.thehungrycat.com

This swish seafood restaurant casts its beer net further than most and hauls in a modest catch of American microbrews beers seldom seen in Californian waters. Tecate from Mexico, Abita Springs from New Orleans, Pennsylvania's Victory Brewing and the big beers of Boulder's Avery Brewery feature alongside the likes of Stone, Firestone Walker and Green Flash. All of which is entirely irrelevant information as by the time

you befriend this ravenous moggy, the sommelier will have freshened things up with more downright attractive ales.

Opening hours: Mon-Sat, 5:30pm-midnight; Tue-Fri, 11:30am-2.30am; Sun, 11am-3pm & 5pm-11pm

Lucky Devils (45)
6613 Hollywood Blvd, CA 90028
T 323 465 8259
Highly recommended
www.luckydevils-la.com

Notorious for its awe-inspiring burgers, this modern Californian diner is the brainchild of former Diet Coke model Lucky Vanous – and, by both name and nature, he certainly is. The bar-cum-open-plan kitchen is festooned with a standout selection of taps (Victory, Stone, Northcoast and Bear Republic), pulled by attentive, knowledgeable staff as well as a flurry of Californian and Belgian classics.

If your belt and bank balance can take the strain, order the legendary $14 Kobe Hamburger and the indulgent Belgian Beer Buttermilk Pancakes. Good brunch menu and homemade sodas are nice extra touches.

Opening hours: Sun-Wed, 11am-midnight; Thu-Sat, 11am-3am

Osteria Mozza (46)
6602 Melrose Ave., CA 90036
T 323 297 0100
www.mozza-la.com

This incredibly fashionable Italian gastro-nome-magnet successfully pairs beer with fancy-pants food. Cherry-picked efforts from an array of European and American artisan brewers are served with the same fanfare as the wine. If you haven't booked ahead (and you should if you want a table), chance your arm at nabbing one of the sought-after stools at the bar. Careful though, the stools have no backs, which could prove dangerous when the bill arrives.

Opening hours: Mon-Sat, 5.30-11pm

Spring Street Smoke House (47)
640 N. Spring St., CA 90012
T 213 626 0535
www.sssmokehouse.com

Grill skills pay the bills at this basic but popular, ramshackle downtown restaurant and bar. In-the-know, beer-loving carnivores flock here for a feast of flesh and fluids that include the entire range of Angel City brews on draught, a handful of Californians, four Belgians and a few less challenging choices.

Opening hours: Mon-Fri, 10:30am-9pm; Sat, noon-9pm

The 3rd Stop (48)
8636 W. 3rd St., CA 90048 3323
T 310 273 3605
Recommended

This beer-revering bar and restaurant is a slick operation populated by a hotchpotch clientele. Furnished with a mish-mash of influences – a chandelier dangles from the roof and a portrait of William Burroughs looms large – the room flickers with candlelight. More smoking jacket than beer anorak, it may be a bit forced for some but you certainly don't need a monocle to see that the beer selection is really rather wonderful.

Upon the bar stand 36 taps showcasing a wealth of Euro and American talent, including AleSmith, Craftsman, Delirium, Duvel, Shiner, Stone and lots more too numerous to mention. At $6 a pint, it's a bit expensive. But when big, well-crafted beers are served with knowledge and a bit of banter, it softens the blow. The tapas-style finger food and dainty dishes were a refreshing departure from brewpub food that can bloat and bore.

Opening hours: Mon-Fri, noon-2am; Sat & Sun, 4pm-2am

Village Idiot (49)
7383 Melrose Ave., CA 90046
T 323 655 3331
www.villageidiot.com

Part French bistro, part restaurant and (a small) part beer joint, the Village Idiot is certainly no fool when it comes to quality quaff. There are eight taps sat on the bar, four of which pour ubiquitous lagers and four which know better and shower Californian suds (mostly Craftsman) from their steel spouts. Flipping font-tastic.

Opening hours: Sun-Thu, 11:30am-midnight; Fri & Sat, 11:30am-1am

The York (50)
5018 York Blvd., Highland Park, CA 90042
T 323 255 9675
www.theyorkonyork.com

The York is what we Brits would describe as a gastropub, but not in a poncey, pejorative way. Huge windows lighten the dark brick walls, the service is spick and span and the choice of food and drink, chalked up on a blackboard, is small, yet perfectly formulated. Craftsman, Firestone and Stone pour alongside some trendy European lagers on the bar while thrillers from the chiller include Chimay, Fullers, Hobgoblin, Rogue and Unibroue.

Opening hours: daily, 5pm-2am

The Yard House (51)
401 Shoreline Village Dr., Long Beach, CA 90802
T 562 628 0455
www.yardhouse.com

Eleven years ago, this is where the Yard House began and now there are seven LA venues each with more than a hundred taps and the same reliable recipe of slick service, consistent cuisine and slightly manicured ambiance.

Opening hours: Sun-Thu, 11am-midnight; Fri & Sat, 11am-2am

Central Coast

THE SPECTACULARLY rugged Pacific coast – one of the most famous and scenic seaside stretches in the world – is what Californian dreaming is made of. While LA tends to delight and disgust in equal measure, chilled-out solace can be sought in the slower-paced towns of Santa Barbara, 'socialist' Santa Cruz, Monterrey and, our favourite, San Luis Obispo – not to mention the bucolic bosom of Big Sur where the waves are big, the trees are tall and the locals are a little bit leftfield. The coastal highway provides a ready-made ale adventure and effortlessly drinks in some superb suds and stunning scenery.

Today

From the white-washed, red-roofed splendor of Santa Barbara to the muted uprisings of Santa Cruz, the Central Coast makes for an enjoyable acclimatisation chamber whether you're heading north or south. Santa Barbara, the first port of call north of LA, is a soothing, rather splendid antidote to the insanity and smog below. Felled by an earthquake in the Twenties, Santa Barbara was rebuilt with a Mediterranean theme, like a posh Spanish fishing village, and is home to a curious chic mix of blue-rinse conservatism and youthful student exuberance. Santa Barbara is the Patron Saint of Firefighters, and the city's accommodation and boutique stores will burn a hole in your pocket, but it's well-equipped to extinguish one's thirst for impressive beer.

Beyond the one-horse agricultural town of Guadalupe lies the brilliant town of San Luis Obispo. This classic mid-way stop-off buzzes with students and punches well above its weight in the partying stakes. Thursday nights are especially fun with a fabulous farmer's market and, if it's the first Thursday of the month, a big biking ballyhoo when locals pedal around town in fancy dress, making whooping noises and annoying us grown-ups by being young and carefree.

Don't be surprised if you can't find Big Sur as, well, it's not really there. Less a town and more an area of awesome natural beauty, Big Sur is all jagged rocks, towering redwood forests and mazy two-lane roads. Its relative isolation has inspired many a hippy scribe and artist to pick up a pen and paintbrush and it's still swathed in left-leaning liberalism.

By contrast, Carmel takes itself rather too seriously. Thanks to a law passed by former Mayor Clint Eastwood, it's illegal to eat ice cream on the boardwalk, but you can browse the prim town's galleries and art shops.

Beyond the affable Monterey, home to an awesome aquarium, is Santa Cruz, a radical surf-town that likes to think of itself as San Francisco's naughty little sister. With rowdiness, a touch of attitude, great bars and restaurants and a legendary beach, Santa Cruz is an anarchic aperitif to the main course that awaits 90 minutes up the coast.

At the Central Coast's northern tip, tucked under the belt of San Francisco, is Half Moon Bay, home to the world pumpkin championships, some of the world's best surfing and a terrific little brewpub.

Orientation

With its feet in the smog of LA and head in the free-thinking mist of San Francisco, the Central Coast is a sea breeze to get around in comparison with the cities that top and tail it. Along with Amtrak's celebrated, and notoriously tardy, Coast Starlight (humorously nicknamed the Starlate), the finest way to see central California is undoubtedly by a leisurely cruise on the legendary Highway 1.

The tarmac path between LA and San Francisco may be a well-trodden one, but popularity hasn't tarnished its dashing, natural good looks nor detracted from its meandering magic. Flanked by an ocean filled with frolicking sea lions and wallowing whales on one side and magnificent mountain ranges on the other, Highway 1 weaves around hair-pin bends and swoops and undulates from shoreline to dramatic giddy cliff highs. It blusters sea breeze through your hair, sun-blushes your cheeks and uplifts your mood with incredible ocean vistas – especially when drenched in that distinctive, dusky Californian glow.

The beer scene

The film *Sideways* may have thrust Californian wine into the limelight, but what that pair of foolish goons failed to mention, during their shamelessly indulgent and thinly disguised binge-drinking jaunt, is that the beers are equally qualified to whet your whistle in style. Half-a-dozen micro-breweries can be had in Santa Barbara alone. Firestone-Walker is brewing up an Anglicised storm amidst the vineyards, and the bars and brewpubs of Santa Cruz and San Luis Obispo certainly know a brew or two. Good beer spots are dotted all along the Pacific Coast Highway and also rather helpfully, if we say so ourselves, detailed below.

BREWERIES

Central Coast Brewing (52)

1422 Monterey St., San Luis Obispo, CA 93401
T 805 783 BREW
www.centralcoastbrewing.com

This multi-tasking venture brews its own beer, brews ales under contract for Californian bars and restaurants and even offers individuals the opportunity to craft their own suds using its array of mini copper brew systems. A good place to discover the latest local beer news or knock back a few pints while your own beer languidly matures.

Opening hours: Tue-Thu, 2pm-9pm; Sat & Sun, noon-6pm

Recommendation
Topless Blonde (5%)
Beer and babes in a bottle. Genius.

Firestone Walker (53)

See feature on pages 92–93.

Island Brewing Company (54)

4187 Carpinteria Ave. Carpinteria, CA 93013
T 805 745 8272
www.islandbrewingcompany.com

Incredibly friendly owner and brewer Paul Wright, a former naval submarine veteran and business insurer from the Bay Area, became smitten with Santa Barbara when visiting his three daughters at university and decided to set-up his own family-run brewery. A former home brewer who cut his teeth at Marin Brewery for more than two years, Paul crafts West Coast interpretations of European beer styles, including a caramel-coated winter warming Jubilee Ale, a strong Starry Night stout, a Bavarian-style Weissbier and a top-selling, Kolsch-style Blonde. Paul also plays to the surfer crowd with a Tropical Lager.

Island's kegs and bottles are confined to the Santa Barbara coast but if it's the cask you're after (the Jubilee Ale is especially good), you need to pop by the brewery and sample it fresh. Yards from the coastal railway track and overlooking the kind of classic ocean view that California does so well, the brewery is home to a 15-barrel Hungarian brew house (steam fired boiler, five fermenters and a trio of finishing tanks) and a bright and airy taproom, bedecked in art and merchandise, with a few stools and a great outdoor drinking area. If you're not driving, the brewery is minutes from Carpinteria train station on a line that links Santa Barbara with San Luis Obispo. Brewery tours available.

Opening hours: 11am–close

Recommendation

Avocado Honey Ale (5%)

Seasonal ale brewed to coincide with the local avocado festival. A delicious sweet honey aroma, medium bodied like a Kolsch, with molasses and more honey on the palate but, interestingly, no real avocado flavour.

Santa Cruz Mountain Brewing Company (55)

402 Ingalls St., Swift St. Courtyard, Santa Cruz, CA 95060

T 831 425 4900

www.santacruzmountainbrewing.com

The beers of Santa Cruz Mountain Brewing Company are dotted about the town's bars, but we recommend swinging by the brewery at the Westside Swift St. Courtyard to sample them at source. Chad and Emily Brill, along with the latter's brother Nick, brew entirely organic ales on a rudimentary brewing system within a small business unit. On bruised and battered grundies, Chad and Nick brew, and then hand-bottle, an assortment of food-friendly, accessible ales including a deep, dark stout, a pale ale, the well-liked Amber, an even-handed IPA (7.5%), a wheat beer and a ballsy barley wine.

Tasting room hours: daily, noon–10pm

Recommendation

Dread Brown Ale (5.4%)

Dark, stout-like colour with caramel and coffee up front, plenty of roasted malt warmth throughout and a finish resembling oat biscuits.

Brian Thompson and assistant brewer Patrick Slain of Telegraph Brewing Co.

Telegraph Brewing Company (56)

416 N. Salsipuedes St., Santa Barbara, CA 93103

T 805 963 5018

www.telegraphbrewing.com

Tired of chasing the white-collar dollar on Wall Street, Brian Thompson created Telegraph Brewing in January 2006. The former homebrewer, backed financially by some banking buddies, has embarked on a mission to brew some uniquely Santa Barbara /Californian beers that, in his words, "are a bit different". And we think these beers are indeed handsome little rogues.

Using Santa Barbara water, hard with a good balanced mineral profile, and ingredients sourced as locally as possible, Brian's beers are inventive, session-friendly and – easy on the hops – won't strip the enamel from your teeth. Telegraph brews a quartet of year-round ales, packaged in stylish 750ml cork and wire bottles,. The pleasantly hoppy California Ale (6.2%) is an unfiltered, medium-to-full bodied amber ale brewed with orange peel and Cascade and Centennial hops. Imagine the well-mannered lovechild of a Bavarian Weissbier and a Belgian Wit and you're close to the Golden Wheat Ale (brewed to 5% using 30% wheat) while the Oatmeal Stout has a rich, enveloping mouth-feel. From a tidy industrial unit on the outskirts of town, the Telegraph brewery dispatches its beers to around 60 bars and restaurants from Santa Barbara to San Luis Obispo.

Brewery tours: call ahead

Recommendation

Stock Porter (5.7%)

Unlike most American porters, just stouts in disguise, Stock uses a 80/20 blend of fresh porter and wood-aged porter taken from American oak barrels previously used for Californian Zinfandel.

Firestone Walker (53)

Brewery & Taproom
1400 Ramada Drive, Pasa Robles, CA 93446
T 805 238 2556
www.firestonewalker.com

They say you should never mix the grain and the grape, but try telling that to the folks at Firestone Walker – a brewery ploughing a lonesome and flavoursome furrow amongst the vineyards deep in the heart of Californian wine country. Founder Adam Firestone – son of the plonk pioneer Brooks Firestone and great grandson of tire titan Harvey Firestone – had witnessed the Californian wine boom of the Eighties and the harmonious marriage of Old World wine-making traditions and New World techniques. Always more happy with a tankard than a tulip glass in his hand, Adam embarked on a similar game plan in the realm of beer-making with his English brother-in-law, David Walker.

Initially, things didn't go to plan. It was 1996, with many small breweries hitting the wall, and there was no call for dodgy-tasting beer. Sadly, Adam and David's first attempt was just that.

"They wanted to do oak-fermented ales. So the original concept was to take chardonnay barrels and use beer in them," recalls head-brewer Matt Brynildson. *"But the beer oxidised and it was basically all malt vinegar."*

Following the chardonnay shambles, the duo hired brewmaster Jeffers Richardson who rejected wine barrels in favour of a unique adaptation of the famous Burton Union system. Invented in the 1830s and based upon a medieval technique established by monks, the Burton Union system separates beer from unwanted frothy yeast using a row of linked casks and troughs. Technical stuff aside, Firestone Walker tweaked the Burton Union system and patented a similar oak barrel brewing system called 'Firestone Union' on which its flagship Double Barrel Ale is crafted.

"Double Barrel Ale represents 50% of our production. It's a very English beer in its origins – in fact, it's about as English as American beer gets," said Matt. *"We're closer to Burton than California and we're the only brewery in America to use the Union system. The biggest difference between Firestone and Burton is that we're using new oak and different types of barrels."*

On the back of the runaway success of Double Barrel Ale within the Central Coast area, Adam and David unleashed Firestone Pale Ale, Firestone Lager and, more recently, Walker's Reserve. Incorporating 40 60-gallon, medium-toast American oak barrels, the Firestone Union also ferments a selected section of other Firestone beer batches.

"The Union system," says Matt, *"amplifies the hop character and makes the beer more bracing while the oak imparts delicate notes of vanilla, chocolate and wood. There are a lot of brewers who are working with wood but we're different because we use oak for the primary fermentation."*

In 2002, Firestone Walker moved from a humble brew house on a wine estate to a comparatively enormous brewery in Pasa Robles, formerly home to the recently deceased and aptly named Slow Brewing Company. Although it inherited a state-of-the-art brewery with seven 200-barrel fermentation tanks, Adam and David introduced smaller fermenters and bright tanks in order to maintain its small-batch brewing methods. The gravity-driven brewery system was modelled on the Deschutes Brewery in Bend and produced more than 55,000 barrels in 2007. At the 2007 GABF, when Firestone Walker was named mid-sized brewery of the year, few will have been surprised as its beers have been bubbling under the big time for quite a while.

"We really focus on drinkability and balance and that can be a little pedestrian for the beer geeks, but we're a traditional regional brewer," added Matt. *"We tend to stick with cleaner hop flavours and not the earthy, grassy and vegetal aromas that you can find in other Californian beers."*

The Brewers Association honoured Matt with the 2007 innovation award for being a leader in barrel-aging experimentation. A year earlier, Matt had masterminded the crafting of the Firestone Walker Fine Ales' commemorative 10th anniversary ale, which consisted of ten separate batches brewed over 10 months and aged in oak barrels, then blended like a fine wine with input from local winemakers. Released in limited batches, the beer has been fetching sums of $100 among bartering beer boffins.

"We've learned a lot (from winemakers) about toast levels, oak and we're moving beer in and out of barrels," said Matt. "We're not trying to make Belgian beers, but I'm interested to see what oak ageing does to the ales. So we're taking very clean beers and ageing them in all kinds of whisky and wine barrels, blending them like wine and experimenting with racking and different toast intensity. The consumer is pushing breweries to go outside of the lines," he added. "But we don't intend to lose sight of drinkability."

Firestone's English-style beers, untarnished by success, medalled five times at the 2007 GABF and are now widely available up and down the Californian coast. To catch them at their most sprightly, however, there's both a taproom at the brewery and also in nearby Buellton.

Tours: Available every Saturday at 3pm in Paso Robles. Contact the brewery at least a week in advance for large groups or to enquire about tours on another day or time.

THE BEERS

Lager (4.2%)
A golden lager with toffee and spice in the aroma, delicate and bittersweet on the palate with a brusque hop conclusion.

Pale Ale (4.6%)
All hail to this phenomenal pale ale! It takes all the good bits of American and British brewing and deftly fuses them together with balance and style. Sprightly floral American hop notes tip-toe all over a delicious malt base reminiscent of light caramel and a touch of vanilla. Gorgeous.

Double Barrel Pale Ale (5%)
Rich, fragrant, bracing and brisk, this classic English-style pale ale is piqued with hop-spice and underscored with soft, warm malt flavours. Familiarity may have bred a smidgeon of contempt among beer snobs but it's an extremely well-made beer. The unfiltered version, often available at the Firestone taprooms, is even better.

Walker's Reserve (5.9%)
Bridging the gap between a porter and a stout, it's opaque and overloaded with espresso and chocolate aromas. The taste is a touch of roasted nuts, licorice and a sweetish tinge of raisin and caramel. Brewed with five different malts and Cascade and Golding hops, it's one for the aficionado.

IPA (6.5%)
Dry-hopped with a blend of Amarillo, Cascade and Centennial, it's a classic Californian interpretation that swaps bitterness bravado for balance and drinkability. Golden-hued, it ushers in pine, honey and grapefruit flavours.

Bravo (11%)
A limited-edition, bourbon-barrel aged porter that shouts about oak, coconut, oak, chocolate, more oak and vanilla before being muffled with a velvet glove.

Firestone Walker 'Ten'
Is it a barley wine? Is it a port? Who knows, but this highly complex, rich and sought-after concoction teems with potent flavours of port, molasses, roasted chestnuts, winey fruit and a dry, roasty bitter finish.

Nectar Ales

Firestone's Nectar Ales previously belonged to Humboldt Brewing – a set-up that once out-brewed Sierra Nevada in the mid-Eighties but running before it could walk hit hard times. The Nectar Ales, more hop-driven West Coast beers than Firestone's, are brewed nearby and available at the Firestone Walker Taproom.

Pale Nectar (4.9%)
Modestly hopped with Cascade, Centennial and Mt. Hood, it's a golden gulp that slips down nice and easy.

Red Nectar (5.2%)
An excellent amber ale that flirts with a more reddish and ruby hue. Sweet, fruity notes on the nose, plenty of spice and fruit poke through on the palate followed by a slight cherry finish.

IPA Nectar (5.3%)
Floral, fruity and hoppy, it's a golden example of a West Coast IPA in both colour and character. Buttery malt sweetness brings balance and sticks around for a flourishing finish.

Nectar Hemp Ale (5.7%)
An American Brown Ale brewed with hemp seeds toasted in Canada and mashed in the beer. Two pounds of seeds, packed with loads of anti-oxidants, give the beer a nutty flavour and stabilise the beer – so it's not just a gimmick.

BREWPUBS

Anacapa Brewing Company (57)
472 E. Main St., Ventura , CA 93001
T 805 643 2337
www.anacapabrewing.com

Manufactured brewpubs can often be soulless places, but this red-brick beer hall buzzes more than most. Behind the long curved bar stand the row of tanks and switched on staff that kept the craic flowing like drug-peddling junkies. For good, middle-range, sensibly priced beer and food you can't go wrong.

Recommendation
Pierpoint Pale Ale (4.8%)
Slightly grassy, golden ale that swerves into the IPA lane on the finish. Succinct and dry.

The Brewhouse (58)
229 W. Montecito St., Santa Barbara, CA 93101
T 805 884 4664
www.brewhousesb.com

Geared towards locals, Brew house has been brewing beers in the Santa Barbara back streets since 1998. The beers shine under the knowledgeable touch of accomplished brewer Pete Johnson, who keeps things exciting and experimental on a seven-barrel brew-system behind the bar.

Johnson complements a core trio of year-round ales (a Pilsner, IPA and Pale Ale) with one-off editions (he brewed a James Brown Ale the day after he died and a beer brewed with Habanero peppers), specials and a number of strong monastic Belgian beers under the 'Saint Barb' banner: a Dubbel, Trippel and an Abbey Ale. Check out the eye-watering Habanero Chilli Pilsner, too. It's sold for $1 a shot or drunk in pints by what we can only presume are local lunatics.

The vibe is unpretentious, the décor basic and the gastropub food a marked improvement on the textbook belly-bloating burgers and Buffalo wings – there's also blues, rock and reggae on Wednesday to Saturday nights.

Opening hours: Sun-Thu, 11am-10pm, Fri & Sat, 11am-10.30pm

Recommendation
Condor Pilsner (5.2%)
Superb piny and resinous aroma with juicy, tangy malt.

Cameron's English Pub (59)
1410 S. Cabrillo Hwy., Half Moon Bay, CA 94019
T 650 726 9613
www.cameronsinn.com

We didn't quite know what to make of this British enclave owned by Cameron and Lisa Palmer. But we do know that you should check it out. With a rusty old London taxi and a genuine Sixties double-decker bus in the car park, an original telephone box outside the door and a Union Jack and St. George's flag fluttering in the Californian breeze, it's as if a bomb has gone off in a factory of British clichés.

Inside, things remain similarly bizarre and ramshackle. More than 3,000 beer cans deck the walls (Cameron started collecting them when he was just 10 years old), there's a little shop selling Coleman's Mustard, Marmite and other iconic English food stuffs, there are British beer mats everywhere and a full-scale attack of random bric-a-brac.

Cameron, the shrewd son of a Geordie, has circumnavigated the Californian smoking laws by creating a puffing area on the double-decker bus. Every other seat has been taken out, carpets laid and TV and music installed. On our visit there were 20 beers on draught and 65 bottles, including Cameron's very own 'Double Decker Pale Ale' and 'Mavericks Amber Ale'.

Opening hours: Sun & Mon, 11am-11pm; Fri & Sat, 11am-midnight

Coastline Brewery (60)

120 Union St., Santa Cruz, CA 95060
T 831 459 9876
www.coastlinebrewery.com

Youthful downtown beer-led pub, restaurant and music venue serving Germanic-style brews produced in nearby San Carlos. The relaxed surfer-dude vibe infiltrates the rather tardy, albeit friendly, service while the beers play to the crowd and are mainstream in character with a Blonde, an Amber and a Lager. The food is a tad elementary, but the ramshackle patio makes a nice sun spot, and the folk are friendly.

Opening hours: Sun-Wed, 4-10pm; Thu-Sat, 4pm-midnight

Recommendation
Half Pipe Lager (5%)
Lawnmower lager with touch of butterscotch.

Downtown Brewing Company (61)

1119 Garden St., San Luis Obispo, CA 93401
T 805 543 1843
www.downtownbrew.com

Look up brewpub in the dictionary and you should find a picture of Downtown – a big old two-floored red-brick building that does everything a brewpub should do... and with gusto. Set down a street off the main drag, Downtown's ground floor drinks bar is a shade groovier than upstairs where food, pool and sports draw in a student following. Creating accessible ales with modest ABVs, the brewery plays to a college crowd – a drinkable Honey Blonde (4.4%) and Wheat Beer (3.5%). A good drinking circuit stop features regular live music.

Opening hours: Sun-Thu, 11am-11pm; Fri & Sat, 11am-midnight

Recommendation
Blueberry Ale (3.3%)
A little thin but packing a pungent fruit punch.

Half Moon Bay Brewing Company (62)

390 Capistrano Rd., Half Moon Bay, CA 94019
T 650 728 2739
www.hmbbrewingco.com

Like star-spotters heading for the Hollywood Hills, Big Wave riders from around the globe breathlessly converge on Half Moon Bay in search of a spiritual surfing high.

Mavericks Point, visible from the brewpub on a clear day, is arguably the most notorious surfing location in the world, with waves that routinely crest at more than 25 feet and top out at over 50 feet. Created by a cluster of bizarrely shaped rocks, the surf here make the scenes from 'Point Break' look like a dip in a children's paddling pool. It is the exclusive domain of the world's premier, and frankly insane, big wave surfers. While locals have known about Mavericks since the Sixties, it didn't rise to prominence until the Nineties, when filmmaker Gary Mederios released a movie about Mavericks called *Waves of Adventure in the Red Triangle*. Every few winters or so, Mavericks holds an invitation-only contest when lunatics do battle amid the breaks and try not to drown.

A far safer way to pay tribute to Mother Nature's undulating bathtub is to raise one of a number of surf-themed suds at the superb Half Moon Bay Brewpub. Paddle Out Stout, Sandy Beach Blonde and the flagship Mavericks Amber Ale are just three great beers crafted by the Virginia-born brewer Alec Moss.

You may recognise Alec from *Celebrator* magazine – the monthly American beer bible. Every year, for the tongue-in-cheek 'Swimwear Issue', Alec is pictured surrounded by gorgeous bikini-clad girls draped seductively over the brewing equipment – he's the one with a smile on his face.

Much to our disappointment, the ladies were absent on our visit, but the 15-barrel brew house remained, steadfastly supplying locals, tourists and shell-shocked surfers with a batch of malt-driven session beers whose roots lie mainly in English brewing traditions. The seven core beers, which spectrum from pale ale to extra stout, tend to play it solid and safe and leave the showboating to the esoteric seasonals such as Half Moon Bay Bourbon Solstice – a Bourbon-barrel aged barley wine.

If you're eating, veer towards the seafood and fish. Not only are you by the sea, it's also ethically sourced as part of a 'Seafood WATCH Program' to ensure no endangered ocean-dwellers are scoffed. The slight nautical theme of the restaurant is a little cheesy, but the ocean views are stunning and the patio, also blessed with an incredible vista, is well worth a short haul off Highway 1. Live music from Wednesday to Sunday and a great selection of tequilas.

Opening hours: daily, 11.30am-10pm

Recommendation

Mavericks Amber Ale (4.8%)

More influenced by malt than hops, it's no surprise that Moss does a rather lovely Amber. With hints of apricot, digestive biscuits, tangerine and a touch of caramel, it's quenching when it's hot yet comforting when it's not.

Hollister Brewing (63)

6980 Marketplace Drive, Santa Barbara, CA 93117

T 805 968 2810

www.hollisterbrewco.com

Former brewer at the Santa Barbara Brewing Company, Eric Rose has gone it alone in Goleta. Our men on the ground report good things from this bright, modern gently sports-leaning brewpub, with special mention of the delicious fries cooked in duck fat and a regularly rotating range of entirely organic ales.

Opening hours: daily, 11am-close

Recommendation

Hip Hop (8.6%)

Good name, big and brawny and lots of hops.

Santa Barbara Brewing Company (64)

501 State St., Santa Barbara, CA 93101

T 805 730 1040

www.sbbrewco.com

SBBC takes the basic brewpub concept and buffs it up a little. The red brick, the tiled floor, the TV screens, the mainstream menu and the service are all professional, polished and perfectly acceptable if a little predictable. Things get a bit more charismatic in the annexed pool hall, accessed through an alley out the back, with plenty of decent beer to go with the billiards. The spectrum of different-coloured house ales warrant praise for consistency, loads of lapulin action and no small amount of showboating, especially with the seasonals.

Recommendation

Anti-Freeze (7.2%)

Sweet and stocky Scotch ale with butterscotch, biscuity-malt and a layer of toffee. A seasonal winter warmer.

Seabright Brewery (65)

519 Seabright Ave., Santa Cruz, CA 95062

T 831 426 BREW

www.seabrightbrewery.com

Celebrating its twentieth year in 2008, this slick, whitewashed brewpub was created by a duo of New Yorkers and is still regarded by many as the best brewery in Santa Cruz. The award-winning venue, a few blocks from the beach, has stepped onto the GABF podium on several occasions, and its core selection is regularly enlivened by a handful of home-brewed one-offs. Seabright's upper-end ales and eats (the Spinach and Blackened Salmon salad was a scrumptious spouse to the snappy Sandpoint IPA) draws a substantial local following especially, we're told, on a Tuesday night when live bands crank things up. The sun-drenched patio is an especially attractive crowd-puller.

Opening hours: 11.30am-11.30pm

Recommendation

Oatmeal Stout (5%)

Mocha and milky hot chocolate front this sweet, creamy and roasty stout that doesn't cower in the sun.

The Taproom at Firestone Walker Brewing Company (66)

620 McMurray Rd., Buellton, CA

T 805 686 1557

www.firestonewalker.com

There's a taproom at the brewery in Paso Robles but to really satiate your Firestone thirst, this British saloon bar, decked out in oak tables and an antique bar from London's

Liverpool St. Station, is worth a trip. In addition to the regular Firestone lineup and four guest beers, it serves taproom-only brews such as the terrific Unfiltered Double Barrel Ale and India Pale Ale on a rotating basis. Food made with locally sourced ingredients also available.

Opening hours: Mon-Thu, 5-9pm; Fri-Sun, 11am-9pm

BEER BARS

Brittania Arms (67)
444 Alvarado St., Monterey, CA 93940
T 831 656 9543
www.britanniaarms.com

Note to American bar-owners. If you're going to replicate a British boozer, for goodness sake pick a decent one. Cutty Sark curried chicken is one of a number of faux English dishes. Reasonable beer selection but nothing beyond the usual suspects. Fine for a pub crawl pit-stop or early morning English football matches, but walk the plank after one pint.

Opening hours: daily, 11am-2am

The Maiden Publick House (68)
Highway 1, Village Center Shops, Big Sur, CA 93920
T 831 667 2355
www.themaidenpub.com

This cosy, understated former Laundromat deep in California's 'squeal like a pig' country was bought on eBay by owners who'd tired of their East Coast hamster-wheel existence. Bereft of any airs and graces, the gruff locals in this British-themed drinking den fell silent when we walked in but soon warmed up with talk of soccer, beer and our quite hilarious accents. Despite its relatively remote Big Sur location in a forest clearing, the Maiden's beer list spans the entire spectrum of European beer styles and top-notch American craft twists thereof. The bottled selection nearly reaches one hundred, and there's four ever-changing taps. With pub snacks on the go, it's an ideal place to refuel on Highway 1 (don't drink and drive though).

Opening hours: Mon-Thu, 3-10pm; Fri & Sat, noon-midnight; Sun, noon-10pm

The rural retreat that is the Maiden Publick House.

97

The Mucky Duck (69)

479 Alvarado St., Old Monterey, CA 93940
T 831 655 3031
www.muckyduckmonterey.com

Single and ready to mingle? Then head down to the Mucky Duck where, we were told, there's plenty of potential for dancin' and romancin'. Our visit witnessed lots of lively young whippersnappers larking about to the eardrum-bursting tunes of a passable AC/DC covers band yet very little chin-stroking beer connoisseurship – kids these days eh? The pub food, though hardly haute cuisine, soaks up a beer range totalling more than 60 and featuring mostly mainstream lagers and well-established craft names.

Opening hours: daily, 11.30am-2am

The Original Spike's (70)

570 Higuera St., San Luis Obispo, CA 93401
T 805 544 7157
www.originalspikes.com

A bonafide beer bar where the good drinking gospel has been preached for more than 25 years. The intimate, laid-back coffee-shop demeanour –cosy booths occupied by student types sporting trendy hats – gets livelier by the hour thanks to a shrewd array of ales selected by owner Mark Prichett. He'll be only too pleased to lead you on a whirlwind, whistle-stop tour of more than 80 West Coast and European delicacies. But not in a geeky way, he's a splendid fellow and this, folks, is a splendid place that warrants your undivided attention.

Opening hours: daily, 11am-late

BEER AND FOOD

Bouchon (71)

9 W. Victoria St., Santa Barbara, CA 93101
T 805 730 1160
www.bouchonsantabarbara.com

Bouchon is a properly posh, starch white table-clothed kind of place where the phenomenal food is presented high rather than horizontal. Renowned primarily for its first-class wine offering, the sommelier is thankfully as skilled in the art of the grain as that of the grape, and the beer list makes for an enthralling read. Belgian-style beers dominate with Duvel, Chimay, Orval, Karmeleit Tripel and Lindemans Lambics sharing the billing with Ommegang Rare VOS and Abbey Ale. Others include Sierra Nevada, Anchor, Firestone and local hero Telegraph. Pick your poison, attack the heavenly cheese board and then brace yourself for the bill.

Opening hours: daily, 5.30pm-close

99 Bottles Of Beer On the Wall (72)

110 Walnut Ave., Santa Cruz, CA 95060
T 831 459 9999
www.99bottles.com

Town centre pub and restaurant that stocks (yes you've guessed it) 99 beers (and more). Not all of them, however, are bottled with 40 dispensed on draught. Mickey's Big Mouth and MGD rub shoulders with Gonzo Imperial Porter, Orval, Ayinger Celebrator, Westmalle Dubbel ($8) and Mendocino's Eye of the Hawk amongst many others.

Take your choice at The Original Spike's

There's also a Mystery Beer option whereby staff will pick out a suitable bottle, just for you. The standard pub food plays second fiddle to the beer selection, and the vibe is affable and friendly. Tuesdays is 'Pint Night'.

Opening hours: Mon-Sat, 11am-2am; Sun, 11am-midnight

Novo (73)

726 Higuera St., San Luis Obispo, CA 93401
T 805 543 3986
www.novorestaurant.com
Highly recommended

This tremendous little tapas restaurant serves a tempting array of superior international dishes, local and European wines and an excellent assortment of boutique beers. A dreamy, romantic creek-side setting and friendly, switched-on staff make the Novo a really must-go.

Opening hours: Sun-Wed, 11am-9pm; Thu-Sat, 5pm-midnight; Sun, 10.30am-5pm

---

Red Bar & Restaurant (74)

200 Locust St., Santa Cruz, CA 95060
T 831 425 1913
www.redsantacruz.com
Highly recommended

The Red Bar & Restaurant is certainly not your usual Californian beer joint. Part Moulin Rouge, part Berlin bordello, it's a sexy and sultry late-night dining venue above the historic Santa Cruz Hotel. Velvet drapes, plush purple sofas and dark wooden partitions blush under flickered candlelight. Beautiful folk buzz at the bar, and the untroubled staff smoothly swishes from intimate table to intimate table, furnishing diners with fine wines, perfected patter and Mediterranean and Californian cuisine – Rib-eye steak rubbed with espresso and chilli, hazelnut-encrusted Portobello mushroom and a deliciously delicate seafood risotto. The phenomenal beer menu is similarly inviting, showcasing a mouth-watering roster of brewing excellence. A magnum of Chimay Grand Reserve ($49), Port Brewing's Devotion and the rare yet revered Moonlight's 'Bombay By Boat' all feature alongside some brilliant craft drafts from Belgium and California, small bottled classics and bigger 75cl beers designed to share. The stupor-shifting Bloody Mary, made with organic garlic vodka, hits the spot the morning after. An almost faultless drinking and dining experience that we can't recommend highly enough.

Opening hours: daily, 5pm-1am

Recommended beer & food match:
The full-bodied, malt-driven **Craftsman Oktoberfest** *dovetails effortlessly with the sweet marmalade in the gourmet Bluto Burger, neatly wrapping up the indulgent textures.*

SOUTHERN CALIFORNIA

NEVADA

CALIFORNIA

PACIFIC OCEAN

Brewery
Brewpub
Beer bar
Beer and food

LOS ANGELES, ORANGE COUNTY & BEACHES

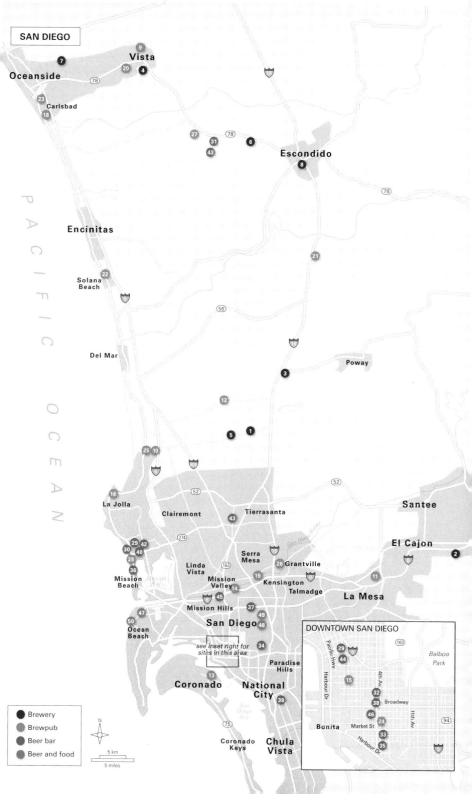

SAN DIEGO

PACIFIC OCEAN

Oceanside

Vista

Carlsbad

Escondido

Encinitas

Solana
Beach

Del Mar

Poway

La Jolla

Clairemont

Tierrasanta

Santee

El Cajon

Serra
Mesa

Grantville

Linda
Vista

Mission
Valley

Kensington

Talmadge

La Mesa

Mission
Beach

Ocean
Beach

Mission Hills

San Diego

see inset right for
sites in this area

Paradise
Hills

DOWNTOWN SAN DIEGO

Balboa
Park

Pacific Hwy

Harbour Dr

4th Av

Broadway

11th Av

Market St

Harbour Dr

Bonita

Coronado

National
City

Coronado
Keys

Chula
Vista

Coronado

- ● Brewery
- ● Brewpub
- ● Beer bar
- ● Beer and food

N

5 km

5 miles

Northern California

NORTHERN CALIFORNIA is a truly mesmerising part of the world. From San Francisco, the home of Californian brewing, to the Napa vineyards, and from the Sierra Nevada mountains to the stunning coastal runs, deep pine forests and glorious countryside views, Northern California, or NorCal for short, bestows upon you a spectacular experience of rugged America.

If you're coming for the beer, NorCal's main attraction has got to be San Francisco. However, we would recommend taking some more time to explore farther afield. You won't be disappointed.

Defining the land

But what exactly is Northern California? Well, there's no right or wrong answer. To some people, NorCal refers to the area north of San Luis Obispo County or the Tehachapi Mountains. Other people talk of the Central Coast area, which covers the land from San Luis Obispo County to Santa Cruz County. Still others, usually residents of the northern reaches of NorCal, define their homeland as those areas north of the San Francisco Bay Area and Sacramento metropolitan areas. But there's a problem combining the coastal and inland areas, since the Central Valley is considered to be a distinct region in itself, set apart both culturally and geographically from the coast. Division of the Sierra Nevada and Eastern California throws up even more problems.

But we're not going to get caught up in all this geographical pedantry. In our version of events, NorCal starts with San Francisco, draws a rough line going east to the Nevada border at White Mountain (14,246 feet), and then encompasses everything north up to the state of Oregon.

Cross cultures

Will Rogers, the legendary Cherokee-American cowboy and all-round entertainer, once said:

"Children in San Francisco are taught two things: love the Lord and hate Los Angeles."

Spend a bit of time here and you'll soon notice the cultural divide between the citizens of North and South. Whether they admit it or not, this division pretty much exists in the heads of the NorCal bunch, some of whom scorn their SoCal counterparts. You might be forgiven for accepting their argument when you balance it with the *Baywatch*-style beaches of LA and the image-obsessed models and musclemen who frequent them. And then there's the porn industry that's spilling out of 'Silicone Valley', where the preponderance of breast implants props up a multi-billion dollar industry.

Natural beauty

SoCal's apparent infatuation with celebrity culture and the plastic surgeon is a world away from the natural beauty that characterises the northern half of the Golden State. There's a wealth of stunning natural beauty in the north, from the rugged sandstone cliffs and golden beaches that stand between Highway 1 and the Pacific Ocean between Jenner and Mendocino, to 'Redwood Country' at the extreme northern tip of NorCal – home of the world's tallest trees. Not only that, but NorCal boasts a city that's so cosmopolitan it positively drips a cultural mix of people who know they're living in the right place. That would be San Francisco – with the world-famous Golden Gate Bridge and the infamous prison island of Alcatraz, the colourful streets of Chinatown and the vibrant gay community at Castro. Oh, and NorCal boasts some pretty tasty beer, too.

Left: At 853 feet, Transamerica Pyramid is the tallest building in San Francisco.

San Francisco

JUST AS LA is home to vacuous movie stars, San Diego to Ron Burgundy and Corcoran (the California State prison), so too is San Francisco the home of Californian brewing. In fact, beer is such an integral part of the city that you can't fail to find a decent drink there. Nor will you struggle to find something to do in between since this is the gem of the West Coast. Full of culture, history, stunning architecture and sunshine – miss it at your peril.

The history of San Francisco

True to form the Spanish were the first outsiders to arrive here way back in 1769, but they typically struggled to hold on to the land, elbowed out by the Mexicans 50 years later. Possibly a bit upset by a chilly sea breeze, the Mexicans, too, were swept aside in 1846, when the Americans arrived and succeeded in a bout of fisticuffs.

The population quickly expanded – the Gold Rush inspiring thousands to leg it from the East. Railroad development facilitated the influx, but the spurt hit a wall when the gold ran dry. To make matters worse a 1906 earthquake left San Francisco rather shaken. Somehow these two negatives combined to keep locals positive, and as savvy folk like Levis Strauss discovered straight cuts and chocolateer Domingo Ghirardelli attracted sweet-tooths, the city became a major international player.

While the Twenties was a decade of prosperity, the Wall Street Crash in 1929 again left San Francisco feeling the pinch. Along with Prohibition, crime started to pay, and so Alcatraz Island found its calling as a prison resort, hosting bad asses like Al Capone. The Great Depression piled on the pressure, but ambition overcame poverty as the Golden Gate Bridge and Oakland Bay Bridge stretched out across the bays. By the end of the Second World War, the city was enjoying its ship-building role – an industry that would again swell the population.

Good news, except the industrialisation and urban Fifties development gave rise to a green backlash and the first rumblings of left-wing politics. The world watched as the Sixties saw this explode into a counter-culture revolution – middle class students from Berkeley 'dropping out' to become hippies and congregate at Haight-Ashbury.

The city calmed and danced the California hustle into Seventies, witnessing the proud erection of the Transamerica building and momentum gathered around the Gay Rights movement. The Eighties were less care-free though, as AIDS cast its shadow and protests against ugly urban regeneration. A big earthquake minutes before game three of the 1989 World Series certainly dampened spirits. The Nineties didn't fare much better and while a nerd-fest in the nearby Silicon Valley saw the rise of the Internet, the dot.com crash signalled economic disaster as significant as the gold bust had done some 150 years prior.

A roller coaster ride then, and in just over 150 years, but the downs in the city have always been followed by ups, and as the city's residents hit the Millennium, they were nothing if not positive.

San Francisco today

With its strong blend of culture and European outlook, San Francisco is one of the most exciting and liberal cities in the world. At every turn there's a museum or gallery. The Museum of Modern Art is particularly rewarding, as is a trip to Alcatraz – now a museum. Experiences as diverse as this help make it a city as moving and grooving as an episode of *Fame*.

At the last census there were just over 700,000 people living in San Francisco, and one quarter of them were aged between 25 and 34, which explains the vibrant scene on the streets of this amazing city. There is live music in a venue every night, with everything from rock and jazz to blue grass and gypsy brass. There are clubs for dancing, film festivals and a theatre, bars and bike rides, ferry rides and even an 'Escape from Alcatraz' triathlon. Eating out is a joy, with more variety and quality in the cuisine than in most American cities, and its devotion to grub can be experienced at numerous wonderful restaurants as well as places like the Ferry Plaza Farmers' Market.

The climate is also lively, famous for its fog and weather that proves consistently inconsistent, with cold spells in the summer and warm spells in winter. Whatever the temperature, the sun often shines long enough to enjoy the 1017 acres of its famous Golden Gate Park or a football game with the 49ers at Candlestick Park. And cautious low-rise development up to the Seventies means you can also use those sunny days to find a high vantage spot and enjoy the stunning views from a number of vistas.

Whatever the colour of Congress, San Francisco remains a politically liberal place. The rise of the hippy movement and gay rights are testament to the tolerant nature of the city's inhabitants, where the homeless seamlessly rub shoulders with the suits. This 'anything goes' approach to life makes San Francisco the perfect place to sit back and enjoy a pint as the world buzzes by.

Orientation

Unlike many West Coast hotspots, San Francisco boasts the Bay Area Rapid Transit (BART) – a subway system to whizz you around with much more efficiency than London's ageing Tube. If you'd rather take in the sights as you travel from A to B, try the quaint and historic tram system. San Francisco is relatively small, but it expands through its various neighbourhoods, so you might want a hire car to explore. Parking on anything other than a meter is pricey, however, so you might prefer to take your chances with a cab.

Locals are proud of the neighbourhoods. Each offers something different, with a specific identity shaping the atmosphere. For example, Union Square is very swanky and a central shopping area – shop till you drop stuff. Meanwhile, North Beach is a Boho show complete with the best view of the city at Telegraph Hill. Elsewhere there's the Embarcadero and financial area with the old waterfront and Ferry Building Marketplace, where suits and sailors dodge foreigners on their way to Fisherman's Wharf. Chinatown does exactly what it says on the tin, and spectacularly so. South of Market/Yerba Buena has gardens and views with the Museum of Modern Art; the Mission is trendy; and Haight Ashbury/Golden Gate Park – home of the 'Summer of Love' – still clings to its left-wing roots. Nob Hill is more than just a funny name, where you can take a cable car for more spectacular views. You can see the stunning architecture and museums of the Civic Center from the top, and the Castro District/Upper Market, famous for its gay community.

All this is simply an appetizer. It doesn't even take in Oakland or Berkeley, both of which are across the water and boast not only unique histories, but also some fantastic bars to boot. And beyond that is the greater Bay Area with places like Fairfax and San Leandro, again offering great beer drinking opportunities. In short, San Francisco is a very busy place. If you're only here for a couple of days, go and think about what to do in a bar – that's our advice – but here are some of our highlights.

Alcatraz: Everyone who's been to San Francisco ends up at Alcatraz. Go and you'll see why. It's a thoroughly interesting location and involves a ferry ride out into the bay (see www.nps.gov). An afternoon tour costs around $20.

Cable cars: The city's most famous form of transport scales the San Francisco Hills and offers a great way to see the sites. The cars can be picked up from stops along Powell and Mason and Powell and Hyde streets as well as along California. A day pass costs $9.

Chinatown: A must see. This neighbourhood boasts the biggest Chinese community outside of China. Packed with everything you'd expect, it's an incredible assault on the senses. For more information visit www.sanfranciscochinatown.com.

Sausalito: This small community on the other side of the Golden Gate Bridge has great architecture, great restaurants and perfect views of the city. It's worth hiring a bike and cycling over to it for the afternoon (around $30 a day – see www.blazingsaddles.com) or stop off when you check out the bars in Marin County.

Telegraph Hill: One of the most impressive vistas to take in the city. Drive up or take a walk through the Telegraph Hill neighbourhood – once the home of artists and poets.

Accommodation

LUXURY

Kensington Park Hotel 440 Geary St., San Francisco, CA; **T** 415 292 6473; www.personalityhotels.com
Set in the heart of the Union Square shopping district, this is a bit like staying in London's West End. Rooms from $149.

Marriott San Francisco 55 4th St., San Francisco, CA 94103; **T** 415 896 1600; www.marriotthotels.com
Another upmarket option in Union Square with good access to local sites and a sports bar next door offering reasonable beers and food. Rooms from $185.

MID-RANGE

Hotel Aida 1087 Market St., San Francisco, CA;
T 415 863 4141

For the price you won't get a better place to stay near the Civic Centre and all its cultural offerings. The reviews aren't up to much, but we say stop moaning. Rooms from $50.

BUDGET

Elements 2524 Mission St., San Francisco, CA 94110; **T** 866 327 8407; www.elementshotel.com
If you're young you might chance your arm at this hostel. If you take advantage of all the bars on the doorstep you won't even notice how budget it is. Rooms (dorms) from $25.

The beer scene

San Francisco is the spiritual home of American beer, and many attribute this to a beer revolution started by one Fritz Maytag, owner of Anchor Steam. Fritz bought the brewery when the beer was bad and he subsequently made it, and craft brewing as a whole, good. Suffice it to say, where Fritz stepped others followed, and the scene is now as vibrant as a herd of pink elephants on LSD.

One of the keys to this success has to be the unity of the San Francisco Brewers Guild. There are many proactive guilds all along the West Coast, but this outfit warrants a special mention. Their passion is unrivalled, and there is a genuine support for each other. While the vast array of brewpubs and beer bars makes San Francisco an incredibly competitive beer city, the Guild is delighted to show off each and every one.

"The San Francisco beer culture has so much going for it..." says Guild member and owner of Magnolia, Dave McLean. "... the history as the West Coast's brewing center, the city's early role in the birth of the American craft beer movement, and the fact that it's the epicenter of today's larger artisan food and beverage renaissance.

"So the members of the Guild work together to share the collective story with the public and do our best to uphold the great beer traditions we've inherited. In a city with so much going on, so much vying for the public's attention, the Guild's all about strengthening the role good beer plays in our community."

Check out the Guild's website before you go (www.sfbrewersguild.org), and it'll show some of our highly recommended spots and a flavour of what this great beer city has to offer.

BREWERIES

Anchor Brewing Co. (1)
See feature on pages 108–109.

Speakeasy (2)
1195 Evans Ave., Suite A, San Francisco, CA 94124
T 415 642 3371
www.goodbeer.com

Those bums down at City Hall couldn't stop this speakeasy from getting popular, and the brewery's clever painted labels with their gangster themes and shifty eyes have raised a few eyebrows. Fortunately they back the marketing up with the quality of the beers. The Double Daddy Imperial IPA (9.5%) peppers the taste buds like a shower from a Tommy gun, while in the Untouchable (5.4%) they have a pale ale that Eliot Ness himself would've broken ranks to drink.

This is a big regional brewery that's growing at a rate of knots. Having shifted more than 7,000 barrels in 2006, Speakeasy is expecting to expand capacity. The reputation lies in the Prohibition Ale (6.1%) – a firm favourite. Having established a name on this beer, they are proving they have depth in the likes of Bootlegger Black Lager and Old Godfather Barleywine-Style Ale. Well worth checking out either at the brewery or in many of the beer bars in the city.

Opening hours: call ahead
Recommendation
Prohibition Ale (6.1%)
An amber that offers more malt than most - a nice hop hit and a dry finish.

Anchor Brewing Co. ⁽¹⁾

1705 Mariposa St., San Francisco, CA 94107
T 415 863 8350
www.anchorbrewing.com

If the city is like a spiritual home to beer, then this place is its church, so go prepared to offer the respect it deserves. They make Anchor beer here.

Anchor's inauspicious surroundings can be misleading. The brewery is set in urban surroundings outside the city, and a rainy day can cast an industrial cloud upon the brewery. Step inside, however, and it disrobes as effortlessly as Clark Kent to prove appearances can be deceptive.

Fritz Maytag bought a majority share in the Steam Brewery in 1965. While brewing had been taking place here since 1896, when Fritz picked it up it was a shambles, the machinery archaic, beer rank, sour and so bad locals thought the place had closed – even Fritz wouldn't touch it.

"I was never into beer really," admits Fritz. "I drank light US beers such as Lucky Lager, Olympia and Dos Equis and didn't think much about what I was drinking until looking at The Steam Brewery.

"When we first stepped in the brewery had no refrigeration at all; everything was pumped and gravity-pulled. It was dusty, rundown, ramshackle, very primitive."

As heir to the famous Maytag washing-machine empire, Fritz at least had a bit of spare change. By the time he took full ownership three years later, Fritz had already taken it from washed up to gleaming.

By then he had started to use traditional brewing methods, sugar was taken out of the brew kettle, whole hops were introduced alongside two-row imported barley and additives were impolitely asked to leave. Fritz centrifuged, pasteurised and made cleanliness God's right-hand man. So, when he had his first batch of Anchor Steam ready in 1971, it was smashing. Well received, it was quickly followed by a Porter in 1972 (at a time when no one in the world was making one) and Liberty Ale in 1975 alongside Old Foghorn Barleywine and Christmas Ale.

By then Fritz was running a profit and had earned a reputation as the starting pistol for an entire re-think on beer in America. Modest about his impact, this success proved a storm lantern during dark drinking days. Anchor had become an inspiration for home brewers and, thanks to Fritz's efforts, the Eighties saw a craft beer boom.

"We've been doing it for years and we were saved by the competition," Fritz modestly reports. "Between us all, we've met the tremendous demand for small craft beer. Today, this is a great time for beer drinkers. There's integrity, passion, variety, it's a wonderful time."

Today Fritz runs a stunning brewhouse, perspiring authenticity, its beating chest a copper brewhouse handmade in Germany 50 years, all of it visible from the taproom and indeed Fritz's office.

The beer it produces remains a fine example of American craft, interpretations of other styles now including a big and nutty Anchor Bock Beer, Anchor Small from the mash of the Old Foghorn, and the all-malt Summer Beer. Still craft in attitude, Anchor has seen newcomers supersede it in terms of production. While Fritz expands his enterprise in other directions with spirits and cheese, the brewery deliberately maintains a small-scale feel.

"I don't want to lose control or sell out," admits Fritz. "I know what it feels like to risk a lot of money. I would rather be small and comfortable, keep our growth modest and keep doing what we're doing. I just have a wild enthusiasm for making stuff."

Small is beautiful though, right girls? Well it is here, and if you make it to town and miss this place then buy a screwdriver, put it to your head, and tighten that screw. It's loose. You have a screw loose. Get it?

Opening hours: by reservation (call 415 863 8350). Popular so book a month in advance.

THE BEERS

Anchor Small (3.3%)
Using the traditional small-beer techniques, this one is born from the sparging of the Old Foghorn mash. It's a light offering with some citrus notes.

Summer Beer (4.6%)
A newer addition to the Anchor stable, the Summer Beer uses a wheat malt to keep it light and dry. Not as much bite as the Steam or Liberty but still a bit of bitterness and a good quaff for the warmer months.

Anchor Steam (4.9%)
Held up as the forerunner for many of today's Anchor beers, Anchor Steam was first brewed in 1896. The version Americans know and love today was first bottled in 1971. The prominent 2-row barley malt is nicely balanced by a citrus hop. At 4.9% it's a great session beer.

Anchor Bock Beer (5.5%)
A seasonal to celebrate the spring, the Bock is a sweet and malty offering. Whole hops give it a punchy finish.

Anchor Porter (5.6%)
The Anchor Porter is another early Seventies creation, and a trendsetter in a style that was generally being ignored at the time. All the toffee and chocolate you'd hope for and, with whole fresh hops in the equation, all the coffee bitterness, too.

Liberty Ale (6%)
Using a special top-fermented yeast and dry hopped, this is a spicy and more bitter effort from Anchor. With the 2-row barley malt, it still retains a lot of the balance.

Old Foghorn (8-10%)
As you'd expect from a barley wine, this one is strong and sweet, but the heavy dose of Cascade hops means there's a nice bitter balance. The flavour is rich, as is the colour, and Old Foghorn stands up as one of the best examples of a barley wine.

Christmas Ale (ABV varies)
A seasonal offering that's different every year, this one defies explanation.

BREWPUBS

21st Amendment (3)
563 2nd St., San Francisco, CA 94107
T 415 369 0900
www.21st-amendment.com
Highly recommended

It's good to see Americans can hold a grudge like the best of us – in this case owners Shaun O'Sullivan and Nico Freccia seem to have used their bar to flip the bird at the ludicrous period of Prohibition in America. Actually, the pair are rather jolly fellows and the name of the bar, and the venue in general, celebrates the end of this unforgivable law and the resurgence of the local bar and brewpub. As a result, it's a splendid place, a vast loft-style interior offers a warm, inviting atmosphere, and the busy beer garden means there's plenty of cheer to accompany the beer. A stone's throw from the San Francisco Giants baseball ground, it's particularly lively on a game day and has a fantastic food menu that will satisfy the belly before you head over. More importantly, it has some very tasty brews on sale, all conceived on location. There are as many as 11 varieties here, with a useful ESB integrating a water profile that nods to Burton on Trent, and a well-attenuated pale (3.6%) that's a great session beer. There's even beer in cans here with the Watermelon Wheat proving exceptionally refreshing. As a brewer, Shaun would probably argue his way out of a 'beer geek' bag, but it's an inescapable label when you witness his devotion to quality here. All in all, this place is a must.

Opening hours: Sun-Thu, till midnight; Fri & Sat, till 1am

Recommendation
21A IPA (7.2%)
Four-hop hit – you'll think you've been slugged in the mouth by Barry Bonds.

Beach Chalet Brewery and Restaurant (4)
1000 Great Hwy., San Francisco, CA 94121
T 415 386 8439
www.beachchalet.com
Highly recommended

Not many visitors regard San Francisco a beach town, but they're dummies since it's clearly coastal. What is equally unsurprising is that, for a bit of California coast, this area is stunning. In the Beach Chalet Brewery and Restaurant you have the perfect place to suck it all in. The venue also sits above the Golden Gate Visitor's Center, so not only can you enjoy your dinner in the restaurant facing the ocean, you can also order drinks and food downstairs and bask in the sun on the edge of the Golden Gate Park. The food here is excellent, with a mouth-watering selection for breakfast, lunch and dinner. And in the beer they have a selection to match the views and cuisine. The ambitious brewing team produces a full compliment of styles and also tries their hand at an English bitter with the Zero Elevation ESB. This is a great accompaniment to any of the dark meats on the menu, and Fleishhacker Stout (5.5%) can be matched against the sweeter dishes.

Opening hours: check website

Recommendation
Playland Pale Ale (4.3%)
Great session beer with a fruity malt edge to compliment the bitterness of the hops.

Gordon Biersch (5)
2 Harrison St., San Francisco, CA 94105
T 415 243 8246
www.gordonbiersch.com

A great example of how a Gordon Biersch can be an independent operator despite the pretext of a franchise. This particular venue benefits from an ambitious brewer called John Tucci, who is such an advocate of the German styles we suspected he was wearing a dirndl under his uniform. Located on the Embarcadero along the waterfront, this venue has fantastic views of the Bay Bridge and is conveniently located near a metro rail stop and 21st Amendment. It's a Biersch so expect the same crowd, design and menu, but when the beer is this good that can hardly be a bad thing.

Opening hours: Sun-Thu, 11:30am-midnight; Fri & Sat, 11:30am-2am

Recommendation

The **Winter Bock** *(7.5%) on a brisk winter or indeed brisk San Francisco summer day is well worth a bash.*

Magnolia Pub & Brewery (6)

1398 Haight St., San Francisco, CA 94117
T 415 864 PINT
www.magnoliapub.com
Highly recommended

This one perfectly embodies the vibe on the city's famous Haight Street. A keen eye for craft, brewer Dave McLean has a love for beer and the Grateful Dead. McLean's interpretation of British beers means he wouldn't look out of place donning a bowler hat and stiff upper lip. He imports ingredients from the UK where possible, including Maris Otter from Yorkshire, London ale yeast and Golding from Kent. These British ingredients are marvelously showcased in the Blue Bell Bitter (4.9%), but there is still an American feel with ingredients like the Cascade hop-infused Spud Boy's IPA (6%). There's a fantastic array of styles in Magnolia, and with five British beer engines transporting the beer from a cellar that's home to 20 casks, it's a real homage to the styles across the water. But it really comes into its own during strong beer week when Dave, along with fellow brewer Shaun O'Sullivan at 21st Amendment, remind beer fans that the double IPA is still very much an American winner. Indeed the Magnolia is a mainstay of the brewing scene in San Francisco and an obligatory destination if you're in town. Well-mannered staff matches a genteel decor and decent grub, and the crowd is more middle-of-the-road than some of the surrounding dive bars.

Opening hours: Mon-Thu, noon-midnight; Fri, noon-1am; Sat, 10am-1am; Sun, 10am-midnight

Recommendation

Old Thunderpussy Barleywine (11.9%)
Incredible rich fruity quality and a lovely amber colour. Top-rate beer with a top-quality name.

San Francisco Brewing Co. (7)

155 Columbus Ave., San Francisco, CA 94133
T 415 434 3344
www.sfbrewing.com
Highly recommended

Situated in the heart of what used to be the Barbary Coast, the San Francisco Brewing Co. has surely seen some action. It retains all the charm and mystique from the days of yore, and while it has needed a few renovation jobs this hasn't masked the authenticity. You'll certainly feel you're in a real San Francisco bar here.

It helps that the beer is equally impressive. Current owner Allan Paul took on the bar in 1985. By setting up the brewpub, Paul instantly became a pioneer of the craft beer scene in San Francisco and indeed the entire country. Today he continues to fight the good fight with his magnificent beers and is a slave to the traditions of beer, with each creation faithful to the style by which it has been inspired. The emphasis here is on a fresh and tasty product, unpasteurised and unfiltered, none of it highly carbonated, served at cellar temperature. What you get is exactly that.

Opening hours: daily, noon-1am

Recommendation

Emperor Norton Lager
Malty and full-bodied, this is a great interpretation of a Munich-style amber lager.

Thirsty Bear (8)

661 Howard St., San Francisco, CA 94105
T 415 974 0905
www.thirstybear.com
Highly recommended

Ay Caramba, it's a tapas bar! Well, it's not *just* a tapas bar. It's a brewpub with a great selection of beers carefully matched with a fantastic Spanish menu. And it's called the Thirsty Bear, which refers to a circus bear in the Ukraine who, having escaped his trainers, rocked up to a man with a beer in his hand and stole it off him. Fortunately owner Ron Silberstein hasn't simply relied on a funny story – his beers are well worth a try.

We found nine hand-crafted beers on tap. Seasonals rotate around the standard American range with lager, brown ale, ESB,

IPA and Stout making the list. There's also the interesting Golden Vanilla infused with whole vanilla pods. More importantly, though, there's a cask-conditioned beer evening every Tuesday from 5.30pm. The beer is brewed on site and is limited to one keg, but it's the real deal and is easily polished off on the same night so arrive early if you fancy a try.

Thirsty Bear is half a block east of Moscone Convention Center, the San Francisco Museum of Modern Art and Yerba Buena Center for the Arts, so there's plenty around it to enjoy before, or after, you gleefully stuff your face.

Opening hours: Mon-Thu, 11:30am-10pm; Fri, 11:30am-midnight; Sat, noon-midnight; Sun, 5pm-10pm

Recommendation

A taste of Spain in the **Valencia Wheat** *beer provides a nice clean accompaniment to some of the smashing seafood here. Match it with Calamares Fritos – fried calamari with parsley, capers & lemon herb aioli. With a hint of coriander and Spanish orange peel it's a worthy representative of its Belgian Wit cousins.*

BEER BARS

Alembic (9)

1725 Haight St., San Francisco 94117 CA
T 415 666 0822
www.alembicbar.com
Highly recommended

Dave McLean is a determined chap when it comes to delivering choice. Not content with brewing fantastic beer at Magnolia, he's decided to take on the fancy-dan market with this stunning little venue down the road. As well as an informed back bar, including 28 tequilas, locally distilled spirits, an enormous array of bourbons, American whiskeys, rye and small-batch Bourbons, a well-versed bartender and an impressive cocktail list (gasp), the Alembic also has a first-rate range of beers matched with a thoughtful menu. The Magnolia beers are on here if you were a fan, and they are next to around 18 Belgians, a handful of Germans and a selection of the American competition. Artisan is the watchword in Dave's business, and this place does it justice. A younger cooler crowd than the Magnolia, tones of Milk & Honey and some industrial chic touches all make it a trendy

venue to be in. Being on Haight, it remains unpretentious with all comers very welcome.
Opening hours: Mon-Fri, 4pm-2am; Sat & Sun, noon-2am

Amnesia (10)

853 Valencia St., San Francisco, CA 94110
T 415 970 0012
www.amnesiathebar.com

This 'unforgettable' bar is a must and anything but a play on words. Live acts with styles that range from bluegrass to indie rock, Twenties and Thirties hot jazz to wild gypsy brass (whatever the hell fire that is), all help Amnesia earn a big 'thank you for the music' – although we heard no Abba. Amnesia is a bit of an enigma, having won best dive bar and best swanky bar in consecutive years. Either way you can ponder its identity over a range of 22 beers, which includes the highly regarded Racer 5 IPA, Moonlight's Death and Taxes and local favourite Speakeasy Prohibition Ale.
Opening hours: daily, 6pm-2am

The Argus (11)

3187 Mission St., San Francisco, CA 94110
T 415 824 1447

The chicks here are more stunning than Captain Kirk's phaser, and the dudes more chilled than an Arctic scientist's cool box. Pool out back, a fairly obscure contemporary soundtrack, and plenty of beer on as well with a dozen decent taps to try – the Trumer Pils is as fresh as it is in the Berkeley brewery.
Opening hours: Mon-Sat, 4pm-2am; Sun, 5pm-2am

Connecticut Yankee (12)

100 Connecticut St., San Francisco, CA 94107
T 415 552 4440
www.theyankee.com

There's a proud tradition of serving up beer in this bar. Even Prohibition officers struggled, although the bar's brief stint as a speakeasy in the Twenties was brought to an end when the pesky Feds killed the joy. These days it can operate in a more conducive beer-selling environment and does so excellently. Just around the corner from the Anchor Brewery, Connecticut Yankee makes a fine fist of serving up a range of beers on tap should you fancy something different. There's a strong sports scene here, and it's not simply a TV in the corner with historic images adorning the walls to provide some authenticity. There's good pub fodder on the menu with lunch, brunch and dinner. Before you leave, ask to see the table tennis DVDs. They're not from Thailand – the barman has a genuine passion for the sport, which actually is more like an obsession.

Opening hours: daily, 11am-2am

Doc's Clock (13)

2575 Mission St., San Francisco, CA 94110
T 415 824 3627
www.docsclock.com

The sign says 'beer, cocktails, happy hour, music, shuffleboard' and if that ain't good enough for you then God help you. It's good enough for us, particularly as the beers are good and the crowd included lots of lovely ladies – far too discerning for a couple of beer-writing reprobates, but very nice to look at all the same.

Opening hours: Mon-Sat, 6pm-2am; Sun, 8pm-midnight

Elixir (14)

3200 16th @ Guerrero, San Francisco, CA
T 415 420 3532
www.ElixirSF.com

A neighbourhood saloon bar that smacks of a post-modern Islington boozer during the day but by night has more allure than Sharon Stone's interview room (thanks to a firm shake of cocktails). Beer lives here, too, with 15 on tap and more in the fridge, all to be supped to the soundtrack of a jukebox. Established in 1858, this is one of the oldest venues in town. In the spirit of San Francisco, every second Thursday is 'Green Drinks' night, supporting sustainable businesses and organic products.

Opening hours: Mon-Fri, 3pm-2am; Sat, noon-2am; Sun, 11am-2am

Homestead (15)

2301 Folsom St., San Francisco, CA 94110
T 415 282 4663

A neighbourhood feel with a pleasant mix of locals and some local beer on offer. Probably best enjoyed during a quiet weeknight, since it brings in a more raucous crowd at weekends.

Jacks Cannery (16)

441 Jefferson St., San Francisco, CA 94133
T 415 931 6400

Down by Fisherman's Wharf, this bar has more than 80 beers on tap and provides a great stop if you fancy trying a few different tipples. Part of the bar has a wall made from 400-year-old oak panels. The subsequent austerity somehow manages to blend with a real dive bar feel, which also helps the place rise above the tourist hangout stereotype. In fact, it's a bit of an oasis from an otherwise tourist clichéd strip.

Opening hours: daily, 10am-2am

The Knockout (17)

3223 Mission St., San Francisco, CA 9411
T 415 550 6994
www.theknockoutsf.com

Retro, urban and chic, The Knockout is quite a blend, but it certainly seems to pull it off, with stunning and crazy art covering the walls. Throbbing most nights with a young, happy crowd, there are around 12 draft beers to complete a typically cool venue for the Mission.

Opening hours: Mon-Sat, 5pm-2am; Sun, 5pm-midnight

Latin American Club (18)

3286 22nd St., San Francisco, CA 94110
T 415 647 2732

There's a kitsch post-war feel to this place, which is a bar rather than a club as the name suggests. A few beers are possibly worth a peek if you're passing.

Opening hours: Sun-Thu, 6pm-2am; Fri & Sat, 5pm-2am

Lucky 13 (19)

2140 Market St., San Francisco, CA 94114
T 415 487 1313

This scruffy venue boasts fantastically nonchalant pierced and tattooed bar staff who are only moderately ruffled by the bang of punk tunes from the juke box. A former brothel and speakeasy, Lucky 13 has maintained some of its carefree past with a popular photo booth and with it some of the lurid traits to be enjoyed in a dodgy black book. You'll have to be well liked to see it though, and contrary to commonly held views we're not buff enough to get in it. Excellent bar skills on a variety of drinks and a strong selection of beers to marry with the experience, there's also a dog who orders at the bar, and that folks is about as good as it gets.

Opening hours: Mon-Thu, 4pm-2am; Fri-Sun, 2pm-2am

Mojo Bicycle Café (20)

639-A Divisadero St., San Francisco, CA 94117
T 415 440 2338
www.mojobicyclecafe.com

Beer and bikes for serious riders who like to chill with a coffee or beer while the bike gets checked out. Good grub and beer to go with it.

Pig and Whistle (21)

2801 Geary Blvd., San Francisco, CA 94118
T 415 885 4779
www.pig-and-whistle.com

This is a reasonably traditional English-style pub – there's even bangers and mash and curry on the food menu, not to mention Bass beer. There is a list of local microbrews on draft as well, including Anchor, Drakes and Speakeasy. From 4–6pm, the drinks are cheap thanks to the happy hour.

Opening hours: daily, 11.30am-2am

Rogue Ale House (22)

673 Union St., San Francisco, CA 94133
T 415 362 7880
www.rogue.com

This is as far south as Rogue heads with its beers. Nicely positioned near Chinatown, the traditional style American pub has more than 40 ales on tap. It also offers a classic Rogue pub menu, including salads, sandwiches, burgers (including Kobe Beef) and fish 'n' chips.

Opening hours: Mon-Fri, 11am-midnight
Recommendation
Rogue Imperial Stout (11%)
Plenty of depth, strong roasty chocolate and some dark fruit flavours.

Toronado (23)

547 Haight St., San Francisco, CA 94117
T 415 863 2276
www.toronado.com
Highly recommended

As one of the most highly regarded beer bars in the city, you're guaranteed to sample the best of West Coast. If you're after something decent, then they know how to keep it. The knowledge of the staff is unparalleled, and you'll do very well to find somewhere more authentically advocating the craft scene. Despite its historic reputation, Toronado is quite an unkempt establishment, often crowded and occasionally seedy, so don't go with romantic intentions. It's a bar with no designs on entertaining high society, and while everyone is welcome, you don't go here to marvel at interior design. Like it or lump it we say. You're allowed to bring in food from the nearby takeaways, and we'd recommend Rosamunde next door for some fantastic sausages. Turn up before 6pm and the beer is a dollar cheaper – every day.

Opening hours: daily, 11:30am-2am

Tunnel Top (24)

601 Bush St., San Francisco, CA 94108
T 415 986 8900
www.tunneltop.com

This is the sort of place where someone will be dancing by the end of the night, even though they really shouldn't be. A young hip crowd blends to make a mix of dive and lounge/club, so it's a reasonable stop for a beer, but particularly useful if you've got to wait for a table in the excellent Bar Crudo nearby (see right).

Opening hours: Mon-Sat, 5pm-2am

12 Galaxies (25)

2565, Mission St., San Francisco, CA 94110
T 415 970 9777
www.12galaxies.com

The first of many listings in the trendy Mission District where there are more bars than makes sense in this part of town. This one offers a young indie scene, with live music the focus and the local talent performing on a stage at the far end. A handy mezzanine offers fans a bird's-perch view of proceedings, and it's all served up with a few of the equally talented local brews.

Opening hours: Tue-Fri, 4pm-2am; Sat & Sun, 11am-2am

Zeitgeist (26)

199 Valencia St., San Francisco, CA 94103
T 415 255 7505

Zeitgeist has transformed from lesbian bar to gay biker bar and now all variations on a theme are welcome. There's a razor edge to it these days, but it's worth heading in to see a real bar at work. A German feel to the beer menu doesn't get in the way of local craft beers, and its general devotion to good beer makes it one of the most feted beer joints in the city, frequently packed until 2am. We were told no frat boys or hippies, and we were pretty sure we were neither, they might have subsequently said no devilishly handsome Englishmen, but perhaps not.

Opening hours: daily, 9am-2am

BEER AND FOOD

Bar Crudo (27)

603 Bush St., San Francisco, CA 94108
T 415 956 0396
www.barcrudo.com
Highly recommended

Get fresh at the weekend in a restaurant that offers a fantastic array of cooked, chilled or raw food with marvellous Belgian and local beers. The seafood is particularly notable, with a sexy crudo sampler giving you an excellent taste of what's on offer. By Union Square, it's a must after a draining day of shopping. The intimate venue is popular so book ahead.

Opening hours: Mon-Thu, 6-10:30pm; Fri & Sat, 6-11pm; closed Sun

Recommendation
Match the Japanese Kiuchi Brewery's **Hitachino Classic Ale** *with the steak crudo, complete with poached quail egg, Spanish anchovy, horseradish, cream, mustard oil and peppercress.*

Ferry Building Marketplace (28)

One Ferry Building, San Francisco, CA 94111
T 415 693 0996
www.ferrybuildingmarketplace.com

There's more taste and flavour than a tongue in this place, so expect your senses to get a smackdown hit when you walk in. Located at the foot of Market Street, the Ferry Building Marketplace was restored in 2004 and now offers the finest in fresh gourmet food, not to mention a few stands providing interesting beer lists with their exhibits. Among them is Farm Fresh to You (**www.farmfreshtoyou.com**) – where you can sample organic olives with some equally organic beers from the likes of Eel River – and the Hog Island Oyster Co. (**www.hogislandoysters.com**) – where you can match baked oysters with a beer from the North Coast Brewing Co. Elsewhere there's Taylors Automatic Refresher, with great burgers in a diner-style restaurant, and outside you'll find the Ferry Plaza Farmers Market on Tuesdays from 10am–2pm and Saturdays between 8am–2pm.

Opening hours: Mon-Fri, 10am-6pm; Sat, 9am-6pm; Sun, 11am-5pm

Front Porch (29)
65A 29th St., San Francisco, CA 94110
T 415 695 7800
www.thefrontporchsf.com

If you turn up when this place is busy you'll get to know the outside front porch very well, since this is where you'll be sat while waiting for a table. The wait should prove worth it, since the food is fashionable but good with a Caribbean feel to much of the menu. There's a modest beer list to match, including a couple of locals, Belgians and UK bottled beers.

Opening hours (kitchen): Mon-Sat, 5:30-10:30pm; Sun, noon-9pm
Opening hours (bar): Mon-Sat, 5pm-midnight; Sun, noon-9pm

Gestalt (30)
159 16th St, San Francisco, CA 94110
T 415 560 0137

Very basic but cool bar with an excellent sausage selection. 'Brats', as they are known here, come as pork, beef and lamb varieties, as well as organic hot links, Italian and

chicken jalapeno. There are also 20 taps and a good selection of German brews to go with the locals. No TV, this is all about the bikers, mainly push bikes, and there's a huge rack for them inside the venue.

Opening hours: Thu-Sat, 5pm-2am; Sun-Wed, 5pm-midnight

NoPa Restaurant (31)
560 Divisadero @ Hayes, San Francisco, CA 94117
T 415 864 8643
www.nopasf.com

A bright, breezy restaurant in one of San Francisco's up-and-coming neighbourhoods, NoPa has a modest beer offering to pair its Californian Mediterranean cuisine.

Opening hours (kitchen): daily, 6pm-1am
Opening hours (bar): from 5pm

Suppenkuche (32)
525 Laguna @ Hayes and Laguna, San Francisco, CA 94102
T 415 252 9289
www.suppenkuche.com

Trying to come up with lazy German stereotypes for every example of a German bar is likely to become boring for all concerned, so let's just say this is the *hunde's nusse* and you translate if you need to. Faithful to German ways, the menu here has a strong Bavarian feel with everything from *Kartoffelsuppe* to *Jägerschnitzel*, and a beer menu with appropriate matches in the shape of Paulaner and Franziskaner. Plenty of atmosphere to match the hearty cuisine means it comes recommended by beer and food enthusiasts alike.

Opening hours: dinner served daily, 5-10pm, brunch served Sun, 10am-2.30pm

Recommendation
Match the sautéed venison medallions in red wine plum sauce with red cabbage and Spätzle with a traditional Dunkel.

Berkeley, Oakland and Bay Area

IT TAKES about three or four days to get into the San Francisco groove. If you can spare a little more time, hop on the BART and head out into the wider Bay Area in Marin County and take in some of the delights this area has to offer. Then there's Oakland and Berkeley in the East Bay, with a host of great brewpubs, beer bars and celebrity restaurants.

BREWERIES

Drake's Brewing Co. (33)
1933 Davis St., Suite 177, San Leandro, CA 94577
T 510 562 0866
www.drinkdrakes.com
Highly recommended

San Francisco prides itself on being alternative, and at Drakes you get the full salute. Daily experimentation is encouraged in the quest to find that massive hop hit that so many Californians love. With their recognition growing, the able-bodied brewers are proving this can be achieved without damaging the flavour. With the IPA being the quintessential Californian quaff, it comes as no surprise that the Drake's interpretation is an award winner. For a real experience, get your hands on some of the barrel-aged stuff. Like their seafaring namesake, the team scours the globe for all things beer and, as it was founded in 1989, they've got their adept hands on plenty of kit with which to brew.

Opening hours: call ahead, beer tastings every Fri, 4–7pm

Recommendation
15th Anniversary Bourbon Lager (13.7%)
They've nailed this one to the mast.

Experience a barrel-aged IPA at Drake's Brewing Co.

Trumer Pils Brauerei (34)
1404 4th St., Berkeley, CA 94710
T 510 526 1160
www.trumerbrauerei.com

The Trumer has been helping West Coast drinkers fill their boots with an authentic European Pilsner for five years now. Deep in the heart of Berkeley, it's providing a slice of Salzburg on the West Coast, and the not-very-Austrian-sounding American Bart Malloy oversees brewing it to exacting tradition. It might seem an odd choice for the Austrians, except Berkeley has water that is nearly identical to that in Salzburg. As we all know how important water is to beer, this makes a bit more sense out of it all. True, it's still finding its feet and expanding, but there's plenty of investment behind it. It's so popular in San Francisco it should have a set of Roadrunner pins. It is what it is – a good clean Pils. And at 4.9%, you can expect some good clean fun.

Opening hours: call ahead

BREWPUBS

The Blue Frog and Grog (35)
1750 Travis Blvd., Fairfield, CA 94533
T 707 429 2337
www.bigbluefrog.com

The beer is brought to you courtesy of one of the few female brewers in the town, and she certainly knows her stuff. There's a full compliment of styles on the menu as well as a selection of seasonals to look out for, all brewed with plenty of care, affection and expertise. They can be enjoyed in the restaurant inside, which has an open kitchen to fill the place with plenty of cooking smells, as well as atmosphere, or on an outdoor patio (heated when necessary).

Opening hours: Mon-Thu, 11:30am-late

Recommendation
Hefeweizen (6.2%)
Nicely balanced and bursting with banana and clove.

Broken Drum Brewery (36)
& Wood Grill
1132 4th St., San Rafael, CA 94901
T 415 456 4677

A brewer who likes to have a bit of fun with the creations with a dark IPA, a Whamber dark wheat beer and a Hemp Porter – all worth a try. Bright and airy venue, well-behaved kids are welcome and there's a good brewpub food menu to enjoy inside or on the patio out front.

Opening hours: daily, 11am-1am

Recommendation
Holiday Nut Brown Ale (8.1%)
Plenty of toffee and nut to this one.

Buffalo Bills (37)
1082 B St., Hayward, CA 94541
T 510 886 9823
www.buffalobillsbrewery.com

One of California's first brewpubs, this 1983 creation is a stone's throw from the Bistro (see page 122) and a trip combining the two is well worth the 30 minute BART ride out of San Francisco. It's a typical example of its kind – red brick, polished wood, a standard brewpub food menu and a family feel. But with its heritage this is a trendsetter rather than follower. Among the tasty beer selection is the 20th century Ale, which the owners claim came from a Thirties brewing book, discovered during renovation.

Buffalo Bills, one of California's first brewpubs.

It's good stuff, as is the selection of mainstays and seasonal offerings, particularly the Pumpkin Ale and Orange Blossom.

Opening hours: Sun-Thu, 11am-10:45pm; Fri & Sat, 11am-11:45pm

Recommendation
Tasmanian Devil (6.8%)
Strong ale with a hit from Ringwood Tasmanian hops as well as Cascade.

Iron Springs (38)
765 Center Blvd., Fairfax, CA 94930
T 415 485 1005
www.ironspringspub.com
Highly recommended

A great stop on the way to the nearby beauty spot Point Reyes. The emphasis here is firmly on 'hand-crafted', with 12 beers and even four unique sodas on the taps. The pub is big and airy but also has a coffee-shop feel, certainly a nice retreat for a bit of a read with your drink.

All the beers are very tasty and lovingly created by brewer Mike Altman. In each there seems to be a classy touch, be it the lemongrass and chamomile in the White's Hill Wheat or the local honey in the Honey Bunny Blonde. The Flat Hat Dopplebock won three golds in a row at the GABF, and the Altman's Alt comes from a recipe handed down by Mike's great great uncle. Plenty of quirky character behind each and interesting flavours to back it up.

Opening hours: Mon-Thu, 4pm-close; Fri-Sun, noon-close

Recommendation
Barstow-Lundy Barleywine (8%)
Strength doesn't substitute flavour in this delicious and complex barley wine.

Jupiter (39)
2181 Shattuck Ave., Berkeley, CA 94704
T 510 THE TAPS
www.jupiterbeer.com

A stunning copper bar is the prominent feature of Jupiter, with the taps adding a Liberace-style sparkle. The beers are good as well, with an impressive 12 house offerings to cover the gamut you'd expect, all very quaffable and sat next to some of the familiar craft beers from other parts of the West Coast. The beer is brewed elsewhere, so don't expect

a glorious system to geek around, but it does mean there's space here. There's seating upstairs and in a garden patio, with heat lamps if it's brisk. Jazz hums most evenings in the summer to accompany a menu that includes some perfect wood-fired pizza. Nicely located opposite the Berkeley BART but tucked away down a side street. Keep your eyes open for it.

Opening hours: Mon-Thu, 11:30am-1am; Fri, 11:30am-1:30am; Sat, noon-1:30am; Sun, 1pm-midnight

Recommendation
Quasar Double IPA (8.2%)
A big hitter.

Marin Brewing Company (40)
1809 Larkspur Landing Circle, Larkspur, CA 94939
T 415 461 4677
www.marinbrewing.com

Another seasoned campaigner in California, this brewpub dates back to 1989, and the beers have been winning awards ever since. The IPA is a great American-style version, as is the Hefe Weiss, the 'Old Dipsea' Barleywine makes the perfect after-dinner quaff and the Point Reyes Porter carries Bobby Vinton velvet quality. The food isn't bad either – wood-fired pizza and all your standard brewpub fare such as burgers, fish and salad. The traditional pub décor makes it a relaxing environment in which to take it all in.

Opening hours: Sun-Thu, 11.30am-midnight; Fri & Sat, 11.30am-1am

Recommendation
Blueberry (5%)
Not too sweet - natural and even a bit earthy.

Moylan's Brewery & Restaurant (41)
15 Rowland Way, Novato, CA 94945
T 415 898 4677
www.moylans.com

Brendan Moylan's second creation maintains all the values of his first. The beer has obvious Celtic feel to flavours and labels, and the award-winning roots set by Marin Brewing Co. have been transferred.

Opening hours: Sat-Thu, 11.30am-midnight; Sat, 11.10am-1pm

Recommendation
Moylans IPA (6.5%)
Well worth a try.

Pacific Coast Brewing is the only brewpub in Oakland – a must-see if you're in the area.

Pacific Coast Brewing (42)

906 Washington St., Oakland, CA 94607

T 510 836 BREW

www.pacificcoastbrewing.com

Like a bad guy in a woeful prequel, the dark side prevails here. The mantra 'light is shite' might be applied, but only by us since the brewers are far from aggressive chaps. Still, they do like a dark beer and subscribe to an 'if in doubt make it stronger' policy with plenty of big beers on the menu – the Code Blue Barleywine (10%) standing out and matched by the Imperial Stout. Food, music and an outdoor area complete the package to make this, the only brewpub in Oakland, a must see if you're in the area.

Opening hours: Mon-Thu, 11am-noon; Fri & Sat 11am-1pm; Sun, 11am-11pm

Recommendation
Pacific Coast Killer Whale Stout (5.5%)
Killer coffee bitterness but just enough vanilla and chocolate to make it an interesting choice.

Pyramid Brewery and Restaurant (43)

901 Gilman St., Berkeley, CA 94710

T 510 528 9880

www.pyramidbrew.com

Pyramid has surged through the West Coast since its creation in 1984 and will be found on taps all over the place. This is one of five alehouses where you can sample the beer fresh on a brewing site and at the same time match it with a standard brewpub selection of grub. Pyramid offers quite a range from an Amber, Apricot and Hefe Weizen; an Imperial Hefeweizen; and an IPA, Pale and Porter. They even mix some of them to create 'Beertails' – not so sure if it was to our tastes but it adds something a bit different to the menu. The restaurant is grand with plenty of covers in the impressive shadow of the brewhouse.

Opening hours: Mon-Thu, 11.30am-10pm; Fri & Sat, 11.30am-11pm; Sun, 11.30am-10pm

Tours: Mon-Fri, 5.30pm; Sat & Sun, 2pm & 4pm

Recommendation
Apricot Weizen (5.1%)
Sweet but balanced.

Rafters Grille and Brewery (44)

812 4th St., San Rafael, CA 94901

T 415 453 4200

Light and airy with local art adorning the wall, Rafters also serves up a decent wood-fired pizza and has a friendly buzz to make it a worthwhile stop.

Opening hours: Mon-Fri, 11am-midnight; Sat & Sun, 11am-2am

Schooner's Grille & Brewery (45)

4250 Lone Tree Way, Antioch, CA 94531
T 925 776 1800
www.schoonersbrewery.com

Antioch is a 'bedroom' community, which doesn't mean the residents are lazy, much to our disappointment. It's east of Berkeley, and a bit of a drive, but if you do your home-work there are plenty of national parks to visit, particularly in nearby Mount Diablo. And if you get a thirst on it's worth popping in to Schooner's. A good brewpub with a big brunch, lunch and dinner list, all of which sits nicely next to a beer menu boasting the full compliment, including Red, Pale and IPA, and seasonal offerings, including a winter Scotch Ale and Summer Pils.

Opening hours: Mon-Thu, 11am-10pm; Fri & Sat, 11am-midnight; Sun, 10am-10pm

Recommendation
Irish Oatmeal Stout (5%)
Gold winner in the 2006 Great American Beer Festival.

Steelhead Brewing Company (46)

333 California Drive, Burlingame, CA 94010
T 650 344 6050
www.steelheadbrewery.com

A native of Oregon, Steelhead moved south in 1995, and this typical red-brick brewpub is credited with bringing new business to Burlingame. If not all agree, at least it brings plenty of life to one of the wealthier suburbs of San Francisco. Set on the coast it's a nice spot for a drink, and the large windows and granite bar make it an impressive venue, especially with its fine collection of brewed-on-site beers. The Hairy Weasel Hefeweizen, Barracuda Blonde, Raging Rhino Red and Bombay Bomber IPA are all mainstays, and if you get a chance try something off the seasonal menu, they have a good reputation and for good reason.

Opening hours: Sun & Mon, 11:30am-9pm; Tue-Thu, 11:30am-10pm; Fri & Sat, 11:30am-11pm

Recommendation
Half Moon Porter
Lovely colour, nut and coffee on the nose, plenty of chocolate up front with a pleasant bitter finish.

Triple Rock Brewery & Alehouse (47)

1920 Shattuck Ave., Berkeley, CA 94704
T 510 843 2739
www.triplerock.com
Highly recommended

There's something about Berkeley brewpubs that makes them stand out, and this one is no exception. Opened in 1986, Triple Rock goes head-to-head with the San Francisco Brew-ing Co. as the oldest brewpub in San Francisco, and consequently one of the oldest in the country. Inside, the antique-wood interior proves refreshing against the tide of red-brick brewpubs, conferring a sense of craft. The collection of 'breweriana' also tips a nostalgic nod to the past. It comes as no surprise that the owners' work was recognized with an 'Outstanding Restoration and Renovation' award from the Berkeley Architectural Heritage Association.

The classic beers compliment the sur-roundings. The Pinnacle Pale Ale weighs in at 3.8–4.4% and provides respite from the bigger beers in this part of the world. The Black Rock Porter (4.6%) is roastier than a

Great taps at Triple Rock Brewery & Alehouse.

leg of lamb. And the Red Rock (5.5%) is all nut and grass tones. Enjoy some lunch and choose from the brewpub cuisine you'd expect – burgers for the carnivores, salads for the veggies and plenty in between. Triple Rock is on the doorstep of the University of California at Berkeley, and there's an incredible buzz as a result. When the sun is shining on the marvelous roof terrace there are few places better in town.

Opening hours: Sun & Mon, 11:30am-close; Tue-Sat, 11am-2pm

Recommendation
Bug Juice (5.8%)
Balanced beer with an ESB yeast strain backs strong fruity floral aromas with malty caramel character and plenty of Cascade bitterness to linger.

Ben & Nicks, plenty of Oakland style.

BEER BARS

Albatross Pub (48)
1822 San Pablo Ave., Berkeley, CA 94702
T 510 8843 2473
www.albatrosspub.com
A proper pub complete with six dartboards and a cracking selection of beer – 50 in bottles and more than 10 on draft. There's a local neighbourhood vibe but not in a discordant sense. Jazz and blue grass get a run out on selected live music evenings, dogs welcome before 8pm and unlimited popcorn handed out from a phone booth in the pub, this is a quirky addition to the Berkeley scene.

Opening hours: Sun-Tue, 6pm-2am; Wed-Sat, 4.30pm-2am

Ben & Nick's (49)
5612 College Ave., Oakland, CA 94618
T 510 923 0327
Right by Rockridge BART station, this neighbourhood hangout catches the young commuters on the way home. Often quiet during the day, there's a buzz by night. The likes of Russian River and Drake's seem mainstays, but there is plenty of variety and chancing your arm with whatever is recommended is never a bad idea.

Opening hours: daily, 11:30am-2am

The Bistro (50)
1001 B St., Hayward, CA 94541
T 510 886 8525
www.the-bistro.com
The owners of The Bistro made their love of beer perfectly clear when they started organizing their legendary beer festivals. One of them is the double IPA festival, which occurs every February, and also the appropriately named 'Strong Beer Week', where they showcase and judge the brawny beers. Sampling the 200 offerings of mostly 10% ABV beer from 10am is punishing – trust us, we've done it – but it does wonders for the local beer scene and is the best way to enjoy this bar. If you can't make it along for this or any of the other festivals throughout the year (check on the website calendar), then it's still well worth a visit. With the offer of a fantastic range of the very best local beers, a Belgian Beer Café, reasonable grub and live music every night, you won't be disappointed.

Opening hours: Mon-Sat, 9am-midnight; Sun, 2-10pm

Cato's Ale House (51)
3891 Piedmont Ave., Oakland, CA 94611
T 510 655 3349
www.mrcato.com
Highly recommended
Designed by a man with a passion for the New York Speakeasy, this place is based on

Cato's Ale House... it's got beer and glasses and everything.

the no-nonsense McSorley's Old Ale House and has a cucumber cool house band and dark wood interior with various signs, boxing pics and glasses hanging from the ceiling to keep it scruffy. Devotion to craft is highlighted by a strong spirits back bar that includes Chipotle infused Soju from Korea and Los Cabos Agave wine from Mexico. But there are great beers on offer here, too, with a fantastic array of local offerings. The owner is a former brewer so his selections are wise. While the food seems standard bar fare, he's also a chef. He was making the sausages when we popped in so even the basics on the menu are done right.

Opening hours: Mon-Thu & Sat, 11.30am-midnight; Fri, 11.30am-1am; Sun, 11.30am-10pm

The Hopyard (52)

3015-H Hopyard Rd., Pleasanton, CA 94588
T 925 426 9600

At 25 miles east of Oakland, this is quite a distance from San Francisco, but if you're heading out this way then stop in at the Hopyard. This place is located near what was once the largest hop farm in the world, and consequently The Hopyard unsurprisingly shows a strong commitment to the local beer scene. As well as plenty to try from the taps, there's also a great food offering to enjoy with the drinks.

Opening hours: daily, from 11am

The Hopyard (53)

470 Market Place, San Ramon, CA 94588
T 925 277 9600

Same crowd as the previous listing and the same qualities apply – commitment to good beer and food and worth checking out if you're in the area.

Opening hours: daily, from 11am

Noonan's Bar & Grill (54)

2233 Larkspur Landing Circle, Larkspur, CA 94939
T 415 464 8711
www.noonansbarandgrill.com

A high-end offering from Brendan Moylan, with a formidable 85-foot bar and a spirits shelf boasting around 1,000 spirits. There's also a great selection of beer – American styles from the Moylan stable and Belgians in bottles – all of which can be matched with some excellent contemporary American cuisine.

Opening hours: Mon, 11.30am-11.30pm; Tue-Thu, 11.30am - midnight; Fri & Sat, 11.30am-1am; Sun, 10.30-11pm

Pete's Brass Rail (55)

201 Hartz Ave., Danville, San Ramon, CA
www.petesbrassrail.com

Set in one of California's most expensive neighbourhoods, this bar has a huge selection of artisan beers paying deference to the West Coast scene. A neighbourhood favourite, it should provide you with a lively night, and there's plenty of hearty pub grub on the menu with sports screens coming as standard.

Opening hours: daily, 11am-late

BEER AND FOOD

Barclays (56)

5940 College Ave., Oakland, CA 94618
T 510 654 1650

A great pub with hearty food to match a decent beer selection. Plenty on the menu that will be familiar, but it's all cooked with care, making it a great stop for lunch. There's a monthly firkin event here as well as regular beer dinners, and its neighbourhood feel and lack of frills make it a winner.

Opening hours: Mon-Fri, 11am-midnight; Sat & Sun, 10am-midnight, brunch served from 10am

Lanesplitter Pizza (57)

2033 San Pablo Ave., Berkeley, CA 94702
T 510 845 1652
www.lanesplitterpizza.com

New York–style pizza seems a trend in Berkeley, and while there are plenty of places to pick up a slice while on the run between beer joints, this one enables you to have a beer at the same time, which can't be bad.

Opening hours: Mon-Thu, 11am-1am; Fri & Sat, 11am-1:30am; Sun, 11am-1am

Looney's Smokehouse (58)

2190 Bancroft Way, Berkeley, CA 94704
T 510 649 0628

Big on sport and meat, this barbeque paradise also holds a useful beer list. The Looney's Girly Man Sauce that leaves out the kick made us laugh, but we're men so we recommend the full tilt Texas Barbeque Sauce, a real kick best served with a Firestone Pale Ale off the tap.

Opening hours: Sun-Thu, 11am-10pm; Fri & Sat, 11am-11pm

Luka's Taproom and Lounge (59)

2221 Broadway, Oakland, CA 94612
T 510 451 4677
www.lukasoakland.com

French/Belgian cuisine with a stunning array of mussels and oysters on the menu to match with draft Belgian and American beers and a healthy bottle list that also includes some English offerings. The beer and food matching experience is well worth the visit, but with pinball and pool in a separate room with a jukebox, some screens for the sport and a 1,200-foot dance floor serviced by DJs playing everything from funk to punk, this venue offers pretty much anything you need for a night out.

Opening hours: Mon & Tue, 11:30am-midnight; Wed-Fri, 11:30am-2am; Sat, 5:30pm-2am; Sun, 11am-midnight

Rest of NorCal

NORCAL remains a huge body of land. As a result, there's no rule to it in terms of climate and culture. San Francisco's liberal leanings seep out towards Concord, home town of Tom Hanks, and up into the lower vineyards around Sonoma. But the rise of the grape as you head north has made the wine regions more affluent and arguably more conservative. Meanwhile, the racial mix becomes less diverse and more white and European. All of which makes it as impossible to generalise about politics as it does about the weather.

Lower house prices have been a major contributor to growth in cities outside San Francisco – Sacramento in particular proving an attractive alternative. Driving north from Sacramento you'll find rows of orchards and flat farm land before you reach Chico – a town that's home to Sierra Nevada, the largest craft brewery in America and previously recognised in *Playboy* magazine's Top 10 college party communities. This was not why we visited – 'twas the beer you understand – and the beautiful blondes, but mainly the beer. Fun times in Chico either way, with hippie vibes and the historic landmark Bidwell Mansion to boot.

Things tend to get quite weird up by Anderson Valley, but not in an entirely *Deliverance* way. It's certainly deep country. And with the Boonville massive boasting their own language, it's safe to say things are a little different in this part of the world. Hiking and biking are great ways to take in the surroundings, and the apple orchards offer a stunning spring bloom.

Elsewhere are towns with small communities – some very local and most very welcoming. Eureka provides the American oddity of an entire town seemingly built along a dual carriageway, yet somehow retaining a bit of charm. The impact of these expanding towns can't dent the countryside – there's simply too much of it in NorCal. Spells of driving will leave you feeling very lonely on the roads. Unspoiled scenery, occasionally prehistoric in appearance, will keep the eyes amply occupied.

Down the middle of the country the mountainous Sierra Nevada is breathtaking. There's the occasional ski resort as you hit the likes of Mammoth Lakes or Lake Tahoe, which means you can work off some of that beer. Elsewhere, national parks have become tourist hotspots. Yosemite's camp-sites are a particular favourite, with the occasional grizzly bear a rather unnerving accompaniment to a night under the stars. Spooning a bear is no bad thing though. Trust us. Impossible to sum up, it's safe to say you won't be bored in NorCal, even if you haven't got a beer in your hand.

Orientation

Northern California is a vast swathe of land. If you plan to see every venue on the list, you'll need a serious amount of time. Expect a bit of driving to get around, and consequently a plan is wise. Rest assured, aimlessly driving around in search of a Best Western with vacancies at 10pm is not an efficient use of time. We can vouch for that.

Like all of California, speed limits will be enforced. Despite the distinct isolation with few cars, let alone pedestrians, on many of the extremely large roads, speed limits will rarely exceed 65 miles an hour. If you take your chances and get caught then you know the drill and good luck. There's nothing like a highway patrolman barking at you in the middle of nowhere with his twitching finger on the trigger. Just remember they'll be bored. Who knows what goes through their heads out there? So remember, be polite.

Finally, in what must be one of the most comprehensive orientation pieces in this book: buy a map. The direction you decide to follow is obviously down to your destination, our guide therefore zigzags northerly across east and western towns, almost as if it were written when drunk...

The beer scene

The passion for good beer is strong in this part of the world, and the beer is some of the best in the country. Many towns offer a brewpub, and while some are obviously better than others, you should be able to find a beer of reasonable quality during most stops. The region is represented by a guild with some crossover into San Francisco. However, the growing enthusiasm and reputation outside of the city means brewers are developing their own identity.

"There are so many great brewers in Northern California," says Glynn Phillips of the Rubicon Brewing Company in Sacramento. "We're in a city with a few of them, and the rest of the West Coast is starting to take more notice of us as we enter competitions and win awards. The guild is becoming a tighter operation, and we've held our own events. If people venture out of San Francisco they'll see evidence of that and definitely enjoy our beer."

There aren't so many dedicated beer bars, but with everything spread out over such a large area the best bet is to find a hotel near a brewpub and decamp there for the evening. A few of the gems you should hit are Sonoma with Russian River; Chico, which has lots of good, lively bars (too many to mention in fact); and Boonville – home to the Anderson Valley Brewing Co. – a West Coast favourite.

Anderson Valley Brewing Co. – don't touch it, it's important.

But we're pleased to report gloriously good manners and hospitality in this part of the world, as well as some Bahl Hornin' ('good drinking' before you jump to conclusions). Set in the heart of the region, in the beautiful Anderson Valley, this is one of the more stunning breweries you're likely to visit. Anderson Valley Brewing Co. is surrounded by breathtaking landscape. The site is set on a huge expanse of land complete with a zoo, golf course, shire horses and a fantastic tasting room and beer garden.

Owner Ken Allen was inspired to set the place up 20 years ago, having witnessed other success stories in America. Today his quality beer matched with good distribution means it is being enjoyed up and down the West Coast. If you get the chance to take a tour do so, the copper brew kettle is particularly impressive, as is the incredible solar power generator on the roof, making this an environmentally sound operation.

The now legendary Boonville Beer Festival is regarded as one of the best occasions on the beer calendar (check the website for dates). And if you're there and are asked for some 'burlap' with an attractive local, that's a good thing. We'll leave you to discover why.

Opening hours: Sat-Mon, 11am-6pm; Tue-Thu, 1pm-6pm; Fri, 11am-7pm
Recommendation
Anderson Valley Hop Ottin (7%)
Well balanced with a hoppy hit, fruity flavours and enough malt in there to cover it.

BREWERIES

Anderson Valley Brewing Co. (1)
PO Box 505, 17700 Hwy. 253, Boonville, CA 95415
T 707 895 BEER
www.avbc.com
Highly recommended

When we heard they speak their own language in Boonville, we had our concerns.

notice. The beers are distributed to 30 States and are also sold in Whole Foods, so there's plenty of opportunity to give them a pop. The offering here is very good – floral, hoppy but balanced. The IPA isn't necessarily a crowd pleaser but worth a sample.

We visited this brewery after a night in Chico, so apologies to the guys at the brewery for our green complexions!

Opening hours: call ahead

Recommendation

Organic Porter (5.5%)
Sweet, dark fruit in a sweet, dark beer.

Feather River Brewing Company (4)

PO Box 443, Magalia, CA 95954
T 530 873 0734
www.featherriverbrewing.com

This little set up is tucked away in the foothills of the Sierra Nevada and really is a one-man operation. Although brewer Roger Preecs gets help from neighbour, Paul Williams, the hand-built set up out of his house makes this almost homebrewing on scale. But size doesn't matter, right girls? Roger is fighting that corner by producing a few good beers from humble resources. Not yet making massive noises with the beer community, there are three core beers from this stable: a honey, ale and a dark. While they don't necessarily match up to the neighbouring brewers, they're being bottled and available in stores nearby, and in Chico.

Recommendation

Honey Ale
Quite heavy on the honey but hopefully more proof that size doesn't matter.

Black Diamond (2)

2470 Bates Ave., Suite C, Concord, CA 94520-1294
T 925 356 0120

Things had looked a bit bleak for this Walnut Creek–based brewery when the owners decided to move on a few years ago. But brewer Grant Johnston's decision to take it to Concord has been a good one, and the beers continue to flow. Johnston has brewed in Blackheath, London, among other places, so knows a thing or two about a cask, and while we didn't sample it, fans were quick to celebrate his English Pale Ale. Beers that are well worth trying if you're heading out of, or indeed are in, the Bay area.

Opening hours: Mon-Fri, 3-7pm

Recommendation

Blonde Ale (5.2%)
Belgian-style beer that is particularly good on the nose with a surprising dry finish.

Butte Creek Brewing (3)

945 W. 2nd St., Chico, CA 95928
T 530 894 7906
www.organical.com

When you're based in Chico it's fair to say the local market is dominated by Sierra Nevada Brewing Co., but Butte Creek's beers are lovely, so don't dismiss this fine establishment. The USP at Butte is organic, and the commitment to organic is unfaltering –even the inflated price for the ingredients doesn't put them off. The set up is quite basic, but tours and tastings are available with a bit of

Lagunitas Brewing (5)

1280 N. McDowell Blvd., Petaluma, CA 94954
T 707 769 4495
www.lagunitas.com
Highly recommended

These beers are nothing short of marvellous. A growing reputation for their fantastically original labels and the liquid inside, Lagunitas rightly strikes a chord right across America. Like all good beer dudes, the team hails from homebrewing roots and has applied some of the most basic and equally effective principles. The flagship is the now legendary IPA, the piney hit sparking off against a maple caramel, amber hue and floral nose making it a perfect example of its breed. But this is simply one of many. The Stout has a lovely grape quality blended with the cocoa bitterness, the Pils a malty sweetness and the Amber a fluffy head with some Rolling Stone brown sugar. That remark isn't an accident by the way (contrary to oft-held views of the writers of this book), these chaps also have a beer called Brown Shugga, which really does 'taste so good' thanks to the molasses sticky toffee quality. Each one is worth a sample, making this a must as you head north into wine country.

Opening times: call ahead
Recommendation
Lagunitas Gonzo (8.5%)
A tribute to one-time San Francisco resident and legendary journalist Hunter S. Thompson. Strong ale with all the golden brown malt and earth needed to take on the citrus bitterness of the hops.

Lockdown Brewing Co. (6)

317 Leidesdorf St., Folsom, CA 95630
T 916 608 9204
www.lockdownbrewingcompany.com

We found ourselves on a bus heading out this way and one of the passengers was chatting about how he'd killed his wife, which we found rather odd. Then we saw we'd been chained to the seats and remembered a police incident. Yes, we were going to Folsom, home to the notorious Folsom prison, 'popularised' by the song from Johnny Cash and more so his performance there. Also known for incarcerating Charles Manson. If you, like us, find yourself uncontrollably drawn to the place, or you're just passing through, you

can check out the Lockdown beers in a number of local restaurants and shops. Although difficult to vouch for from behind bars, we can say they're good and include the Folsom Breakout Stout – a fair representation with a useful name for the territory – as well as the Represa Red Ale – an American ESB not afraid to refer to itself as a 'bitter'.

Opening hours: call ahead
Recommendation
Stony Bar Scotch Ale (6.5%)
Sweet and fruity on the nose, with a decent tawny colour and a caramel palate.

Mad River Brewing Co. (7)

T 707 668 4151
www.madriverbrewing.com

Opened in 1989, this microbrewery has produced a number of award-winning beers over the years, helping it garner a decent West Coast reputation. The simple set up (brewery and tasting room but no shop) is based in the small town of Blue Lake. Tours are very welcome with a call in advance. And if you're looking for a reason to tie in the visit, then visit the nearby nature reserve at Mad River Slough and Dunes in Arcata.

Perhaps most interesting on the menu is the Jamaica Red (6.6%). Named in honour of the annual Reggae River Festival in Humboldt County, this amber has a sweet front but spicy bitter finish. At 9%, the Mad River John Barley Corn is definitely a barley wine, but the alcohol is covered with plenty of malty sweetness, making it another fine effort.

Opening hours: Tue-Fri, 10am-5pm; Sat, noon-4pm
Recommendation
Steelhead Extra Pale Ale (5.7%)
An award-winning beer with plenty of citrus hop and a sweet, malty precursor for the bitter aftertaste.

Mendocino Brewing Co. (8)

1601 Airport Rd., Ukiah, CA 95482
T 707 463 2087
www.mendobrew.com

In Don Barkley, the Mendocino Brewing Company has American brewing history personified. Don was one of the founders of the movement when he started working at the legendary New Albion – a pioneering craft brewery where he was paid with beer for his efforts. At Mendocino Brewing, Don is using his years of expertise to run a state-of-the-art facility built for the team when it moved from its Hopland homeland in 1983.

The new site houses a huge brewery that produces 50,000 barrels a year (with a theoretical capacity for as many as 200,000). Unlike the days of New Albion, computers run this brewery. Traditionalists might say they miss the romance of the early Hopland brews, but Don is quick to point out that the beer is equal in quality these days and more consistent.

The flagship Red Tail Ale (6.1%) is an amber beer that as early as 1988 was being distributed to more than 300 destinations, now popular in the six pack form it makes up 40% of the brewery's sales. It's a full bodied beer, in keeping with Don's inspiration from the British beers, but blending the American desire for hops. The Blue Heron (6.1%) has also attracted fans with its medium body and smooth finish. Meanwhile Red Tail's younger brother, Eye of the Hawk (8%), proves another balanced offering, with lots of fruit (even apple) and a malty counter.

Don certainly knows what he's doing. While his facility might not have the 'stickin' it to the man' air of the New Albion, it brews some lovely beers.

Opening hours: visit the nearby famous Hopland Ale House (see page 144) to sample the beers.

Recommendation
Black Hawk Stout (5.2%)
A fair representation of a European-style beer.

Moonlight Brewing Co. (9)

PO Box 316, Fulton, CA 95439
T 707 528 2537
www.moonlightbrewing.com

Moonlight Brewing isn't open to the public. If it was you'd be able to witness what the early days of the brewing revolution must have looked like. Set in a beautifully peaceful corner of the Sonoma Valley, the only sound encroachment at the brewery is the toads frequenting a nearby pond. Nestled between vineyards brewmaster Brian Hunt raises a middle finger to any wine snobs by growing hops on his land and has his say on beer by inviting guests to relive themselves on a Budweiser can hanging on string from a tree round the back.

This is a one-man operation that looks fairly disorganised at first glance. Equipment cobbled together, crammed into a rickety building, debris everywhere, it's hard to believe it's a brewery at first sight. However, Brian is using what is at his disposal to serve his public very well with some tasty stuff. The beers are distributed throughout the immediate area and will be found in cities like San Francisco, where you should easily chance upon the Death and Taxes – a 5% dark lager, light and full of roasted flavour. The better beer bars will also tap. The Double Vision IPA (8.6%) has a stunning aroma that reminds you why the plant has hemp for a cousin, the bitterness countered by plenty of sweet fruit. The Lunatic Lager is a lip-smacking fresh and crisp offering, reigned in at 5% to ensure you can enjoy a few.

Recommendation
Moonlight St. Humulus Pale Ale
Caramel mixes with citrus and roasted notes to resemble marmalade on toast – orange jelly for our American cousins.

Sierra Nevada Brewing Co. (10)

See feature on pages 130–131.

Sierra Nevada Brewing Co.

(10)

1075 E. 20th St., Chico, CA 95928
T 530 893 3520
www.sierranevada.com

Drive into this place one term-time evening and you'll witness a remarkable college party scene. Revellers spill out from frat houses, music blares and girls dance. The next day life saunters past at a beautifully relaxed rate, hippies float along the sidewalks, coffee shops buzz and terraces fizz. The sun shines and kisses your alcohol-tortured brow, helping you forget about the 'buck-a-beer' foolery of the night before. Welcome to Chico.

These are not guarantees you understand, just our experience and what others describe as the norm in a town that sits as an oasis in NorCal. Whatever you find during your trip, however, you're sure to see most people enjoying Sierra Nevada beer.

Sierra Nevada produces great beer. Most beer enthusiasts in America, and a growing number internationally, agree. So good is the flagship Sierra Nevada Pale Ale that it has become the frame of reference for the American style. As a result, brewer Ken Grossman is credited with pioneering status on craft brewing.

Ken is the young contender to the founding fathers of Anchor Steam and New Albion, and he is only too happy to pay tribute to them as his inspiration.

"Anchor and New Albion were starting to come into the market, and I was intrigued and excited by this," recalls Ken. *"I went and had a look at what they were doing and returned knowing I could do something similar here.*

"I'd been a homebrewer who made all sorts of beers, and the Pale Ale was a favourite. What we liked about it was that it was relatively reproducible and significantly different to what people were drinking at the time – so we ran with it."

A chemistry and physics graduate, Ken obviously knew a thing or two about making beer. The interest in his first batches encouraged him to move from homebrewing to invest in a brewery. Like most, the first set up was rudimentary; the brewery was rented and tools claimed from dairies. What has now become his flagship beer – this bottle-conditioned beer with such distinctive hop character and an IBU of 37 – seemed audacious for an aspirational brewer in 1980. Ken was on to something though and quickly moved up to an annual production of 14,000 barrels as word of mouth swept it along the West Coast.

In fact, such was the demand that he moved again nine years later, buying a second-hand 100 barrel copper Bavarian brewhouse to put on the current site. This move represented the start of the second coming – a foundation for the beer and the brand. Marketing and distribution picked up, production picked up, investment in equipment picked up and in less than 30 years this modest start has reached an annual production of almost 700,000 barrels. The brewery has become a behemoth. The bottling line alone is a gem – a massive, clinking monster of a system.

Today, Ken is a green brewer, using state-of-the-art 250KW fuel cells to generate electricity by combining fuel and air in a clean, efficient and combustion-free process. He recycles water at every opportunity – even the water used to wash the delivery trucks is recycled and purified. The installation of a carbon dioxide collector has reduced emission by 59 per cent with fermentation gases gathered, re-used or sold elsewhere. Ken even uses a bike to get to work!

Despite the investment though, Sierra Nevada still brews craft beer with integrity. The brewery is still the biggest consumer of whole hops in the whole of America, and their use is at the centre of Ken's unwavering brewing principles, as well as a steadfast commitment to bottle conditioning.

The flagship remains Sierra Nevada Pale Ale, endowed with copious Magnum and Perle hops and finished with bundles of premium Cascade. This is the beer that made hops hip again. Many other beers impress: the 2007 Celebration full of citrus and hop hit; the barley wine chewy, malty and hoppy; the Schwarzbier earthy and roasted. An impressive list goes way beyond the Pale and reminds beer fans why Ken has had enduring success. All of them can be enjoyed at source in a fantastic brewpub on site. This is one of the busiest restaurants in Chico, with a standard brewpub menu, with one off innovations on tap, and the food has been approached with the same care as the beer, making it the perfect place to enjoy a spot of lunch.

Opening hours (tap room and restaurant): Mon, closed; Tue-Thu, 11am-9pm; Fri & Sat, 11am-10pm; Sun, 11am-9pm
Opening hours (brewery): Mon-Fri, 2.30pm; Sat, noon-3pm; Sun, 2.30pm

THE BEERS

Pale Ale (5.6%)
The flagship beer and the quintessential American pale, with a fantastic expression of the Cascade hops that give it the spicy, fruity profile that beer fans have come to love.

Porter (5.6%)
Lovely smooth mouthfeel, a decent balance of caramel and burnt flavours, and finishing with dark fruits and bitterness from the Golding and Willamette hops. A great example of the style.

Stout (5.8%)
Another creamy full-bodied effort that tastes as good as it looks. The dry and bitter notes are not overpowering, and there's superb balance to cater for most tastes.

Anniversary Ale (5.9%)
The two-row Pale, Caramel & Munich dominate in this sweet, malty beer that hits shelves in the autumn and provides a warm IPA-style beer for the cooler northern California months.

Harvest Fresh Hop (6.7%)
It's essential to catch this seasonal offering. The fresh wet hops provide an overwhelming flavour profile that includes an almost oaky quality to go along with the citrus grapefruit. Beautifully balanced and one of our firm favourites.

Celebration (6.8%)
To hit the winter months, this hearty offering combines a malty warmth with a spicy, hoppy finish.

A shining tribute to top brewing at Sierra Nevada.

BREWPUBS

3rd Street Ale Works (11)

610 3rd St., Santa Rosa, CA 95404
T 707 523 3060
www.thirdstreetaleworks.com

This busy brewpub isn't far from the town's leading light – Russian River. There's a standard brewpub grill house feel to the menu, although the Taco selection stands out, and regular brewmaster dinners are a reminder that the staff take beer and food matching seriously. Plenty of beers on tap, as many as 13 when we visited, and most were good. For anyone missing home, the Annadel Pale Ale has English ingredients and at 5.2% makes a nice change from hop hitting. Meanwhile the One-Ton Blackberry (4.9%) is a great stab at a fruit beer, light with subtle blackberry on the nose and palate.

Opening hours: Sun-Thu, 11:30am-midnight; Fri & Sat 11:30am-1am

Recommendation

Blarney Sister's Dry Irish Stout (4.6%)
Dry and roasted, but this stout is very nicely balanced with the caramel.

Auburn Ale House (12)

289 Washington St., Old Town Auburn, CA
T 530 885 2537
www.auburnalehouse.com

This red-brick, loft-style venue is a pleasant place to enjoy a menu that goes a bit further than the standard, featuring the likes of grilled swordfish and pub pickle chips. The beers are good, too, with a list you will come to expect in a standard brewpub. The Pilsner wheat and IPA are all reasonable representations. They also had a 'hard cider', which made a nice change. This place won't blow minds but worth a stop if you're out this way.

Opening hours: Sun-Thu, 11am-10pm; Fri & Sat, 11am-midnight or later

Recommendation

Old Town Brown
Coffee and toffee notes, the blend of hops making an appearance as well.

Bear Republic (13)

345 Healdsburg Ave., Healdsburg, CA 95448
T 707 433 BEER
www.bearrepublic.com
Highly recommended

The beers from this lot are in high demand, particularly the Racer 5 IPA (7%), which has growled its way along the West Coast. As a result of its success, the team here will open a massive new brewing plant in nearby Cloverdale to compliment the Healdsburg site.

This brewpub is standard, the brewery is visible, there's a shaded outside area welcome in the summer months and stuffed bears everywhere give Bear Republic an eerie and unique edge over its rivals. The food menu is hearty, with chili specials and home-made bread to boot, but you're here for the beer and what you get is very good.

Known largely for the Racer 5 IPA, there are a number of worthy counterparts, not least the Red Rocket Ale (6.9%). A medal winner, Red Rocket Ale is a real mishmash of flavours, with five different grains alone, including the likes of Belgian Caravienne and Hugh Bairds Crystal malts. If you fancy something lighter then the Special XP Pale Ale weighs in with a lower 5.4% ABV, yet another medal winner, it

HEALDSBURG, CA

The guys at Bear Republic

Brew It Up! Personal Brewery & Grill: put your money where your mouth is and brew your own

delivers a balanced light bodied beer. Also on the menu among the specialty beers is an ESB (4.8%) based on Fullers and Bass, which has more of a hoppy kick than its predecessors, making a nice change from the big Americans on the menu. There's a hell of a lot to choose from here. If you plan to head this way, book into a nearby hotel to enjoy the full selection. Alternatively, the team at Bear Republic bottles and distributes up and down the West Coast.

Opening hours: Sun-Thu, 11am-9.30pm; Fri & Sat 11am-10pm

Recommendation
Racer 5 IPA (7%)
Multi-award winner, the hops are native Cascade and Columbus, married with American grains, to deliver a full-bodied, hop-head delight.

Beerman's Beerwerks (14)
8284 Industrial Ave., Roseville, CA 95678
T 916 781 2337
www.beermans.com
The address gives the game away: it's on another business park location. You should try the beer though (they bottle). The Rip Roaring Red (6.3%), has been recognized in local competitions. A mix of chocolate malts with Centennial and Northdown hops, making it sweet and refreshing at the same time; the Lincoln Lager a decent nod to the Helles style.

Opening hours: Thu-Fri, 3-8pm

Recommendation
Hefe Weizen (5.5%)
Clean, crisp and not too heavy on the yeasty fruit, this is a refreshing choice.

Brew It Up! (15)
Personal Brewery & Grill
801 14th St. @ 14th & H, Sacramento, CA 95814
T 916 441 3000
The David Bowie of brewpubs, this is a place so unabashed by experimentation they even let you have a go. A collection of 12 gallon kettles line one side of the building and with recipes, ingredients and staff assistance all provided for a fee, you get to put your money where your mouth and brew your own. You'll need a week to do it, and if you find your money tastes like a badger's arse, then the house has 22 of its own. There's a nice range of styles, particularly with the European lagers and an unusual Vanilla Cream Stout standing out. In the tradition of giving most things a go here, they also offer a series of beer cocktails – the Port in a Storm blending Sandeman's Port with their Oatmeal Stout to good effect.

Overall this place offers a novel touch in a brewpub market that can sometimes seem a bit one dimensional. It's a buzzy venue, if reasonably archetypal in design, and one that offers a conventional but substantial and well-prepared menu – the onion rings having won local recognition in the 'Best Onion Rings in Town' category.

Opening hours: Sun-Wed, 11am-10pm; Thu-Sat, 11am-midnight
Brewing hours: Mon & Wed 4-7pm; Tue & Thu (groups); Sat & Sun, 11am-1:30pm
Recommendation
Raspberry Trippel (9%)
Nice balance of tart and sweet.

Dempsey's Restaurant & Brewery (16)

50 E. Washington St., Petaluma, CA 94952
T 707 765 9694
www.dempseys.com

The emphasis seems to be more on food, with ingredients coming from the nearby Red Rooster Ranch – a small organic farm also run by the brewpub owners. The food menu included pork chop with garlic mash, which was far from a sad attempt at an English dish but rather delicious and indeed unique.

While the beer list modest, there is enough range here to keep things interesting. Brewmaster Peter Burrell knows his organic onions, having picked up GABF medals at his previous operation Sieben's River North Brewery in Chicago. The staff was also trained to discuss the beers and kindly suggested the Ugly Dog Stout with their chocolate dessert.

Downtown Joe's American Bar and Grill (17)

902 Main St., Napa, CA 94559
T 707 258 2337
www.downtownjoes.com

Polished for the affluent wine buffs, this is a smart venue with an upmarket food menu, American classics but with a touch of chic. Jazz was the almost clichéd music offering, but rock was on the calendar as well and sport on the screens keeps it rooted and local, in fact, it hummed with a mixed crowd, and even a dog on our visit at least. Beer is standard, perhaps not the key concern, but still worth a quaff. The ESB had more to it than expected, nice fruity flavours, and the Lazy Summer American Wheat proved refreshing on a hot evening.
Recommendation
Tantric IPA (6.8%)
Nicely named beer that tasted very nice too.

Eel River (18)

1777 Alamar Way, Fortuna, CA 95540
T 707 725 2739
www.eelriverbrewing.com

Another outfit very proud of its organic roots, the organic recognition came from the California Certified Organic Farmers in 1999. A beautiful 30-foot bar made from recovered Californian redwood is a prominent feature in the brewpub, which is set on the banks of Eel River. A huge beer garden for more than 100 customers makes it a pleasant summer setting for a quaff.

The food is great – it's a meat-eater's paradise with locally sourced beef next to plenty of veggie options. The beer isn't bad either – balanced offerings that won't blow your head off and styles that sit nicely next to the food. The Climax California Classic (5.6%), crisp and balanced, is a gentle introduction to American styles. It's a summer seasonal so if you're fortunate enough to find it then give it a go. The Organic IPA (7%) has been well-received by beer fans. Not overly bitter, it has the hops aroma you should be used to now and a hint of strawberry flavour courtesy of the house yeast. And the rather strong Ravens Eye Imperial Stout (9.5%), with its rich, dark espresso notes, is the perfect match to some of the meat on the menu and evidence that this is a brewing team well capable of mixing it up.
Opening hours: call ahead
Recommendation
Eel River Certified Organic Porter (5.5%)
Full and rich, beautiful dark copper colour, plenty of chocolate and coffee notes. A perfect match with some of the locally reared beef on the menu.

Elk Grove Brewing Co. (19)

9085 Elk Grove Blvd., Elk Grove, CA 95624
T 916 685 2537
www.elkgrovebrewery.com

Beautiful copper kettles dominate the interior of this venue. With weathered walls and wooden panels, this feels like something straight out of the Wild West. The beers are starting to grow in reputation thanks to a number of GABF awards picked up by brewer Bill Wood. The Otis Alt (5.3%) and Eagle Pride Pilsner indicate the Germans are where his strength lies, but the Sloughhouse

Pale (5.5%) and Diamondback Wheat (4.8%) display versatility.

Opening hours: Mon-Thu, 11.30am-10pm; Fri & Sat 11.30pm-midnight

Recommendation

Otis Alt (5.4%)

Plenty of fruit with plenty of malty balance.

Fifty Fifty Brewing Co. (20)

11197 Brockway Rd., Truckee, CA
T 530 587 BEER
www.fiftyfiftybrewing.com

A stone's throw from skiing resorts, Fifty Fifty is evidence the beer revolution is reaching into every crevice of California. Dedication to beer is the order of the day, with multi-GABF medal-winning brewer Todd Ashman drafted in from Green Bay. A keen experimenter with barrel aging, Todd plans to develop this side of the beers in Truckee but meantime offers a host of core beers all with a skiing theme.

The Base Camp Golden Ale is probably your best bet after a day sweating it out in the 'ski pants'. At 4.9%, it's a reasonable session beer, light on the bitter with a dry finish. The foggy goggle Belgian White is a bit stronger at 5.3%. With a Belgian yeast strain, it offers plenty of spice and fruit. For a bit of extra punch the Trifecta Belgian Style Trippel comes in at 8% and includes locally grown purple sage honey to add a bit of sweetness to the spice.

There's plenty of food on the menu, too, including some mussels to go with the Belgians. There's live music during the busy times so all-in-all it's a cracking little hang out.

Opening hours: daily, 11am-2am

Recommendation

Donner Party Porter (6.7%)

Plenty of alcohol warmth, and the roasty malts give a sweet toffee to counter a bitter coffee.

Hoppy Brewing Co (21)

6300 Folsom Blvd., Sacramento, CA 95819
T 916 451 4677

Opened in Sacramento back in 1993, Hoppy Brewing Co. is a firm fixture on the beer scene and draws a crowd from the university. Set on a lot, it's not exactly inspiring to look at, and the inside is quite pub basic. There's a big bar for the flies and more spacious tables for the families, with brewpub fare on the

menu. The beer is worth a chug or two. The Amber (6.1%) is piney and sweet in equal measure, but has something of an American IPA about it, and the Total Eclipse (5.6%) shows they can brew a stout here. Light and dry, it has plenty of nice bitter coffee notes to shout about.

Opening hours: Sun-Tue, 11am-11.30pm; Wed-Sat, 11am-midnight

Recommendation

Stony Face Red Ale (5.6%)

This one's got lovely malt characteristics with grapefruit and a bit of spicy hop to take the edge off the sweetness.

Lodi Beer Company (22)

105 S. School St., Lodi, CA 95240
T 209 368 9931
www.lodibeercompany.com

True to its wine environs, this is an upmarket gaff. Sat next to shops in the downtown area, there's a good vibe, and if you're in Lodi for lunch it offers a standard brewpub menu but delivered with panache. There's plenty of choice on tap, including a rather extensive range – a Southern English Brown Ale, deep brown malt with plenty of caramel finish, a Doppelbock and Eisbock, a Gilt Edge Marzen and an IPA so clear about its roots it's called a Western Pacific IPA.

Opening hours: Sun-Thu, 11am-10pm; Fri & Sat, 11am-midnight

Lodi Beer Company: a lovely lady carrying some lovely beer. Nice!

Lost Coast Brewing (23)

617 4th St., Eureka, CA 95501
T 707 445 4480
www.lostcoast.com

Inspired by visits to the UK, the owners decided heritage was crucial when they selected this 100-year-old building. What they have created is a lovely little site on the coast with a genuine local feel, a friendly one, too, with plenty of seafood on the menu.

The Lost Coast 8 Ball Stout (6.3%) has an incredible burst of nutty flavour with additional coffee, chocolate and smoky qualities you'd expect from the style. This is one of the stand out beers on the West Coast. And it's only one of many from this house of flavours. The Lost Coast Double Trouble IPA (8.5%) not only has citrus notes but a whole host of fruity layers, including grapefruit as well as a hearty alcohol glow. The barley wine has grape and berry qualities next to gorgeous ginger malts. The Chocolate Porter has an awesome creamy finish over the bitter cocoa. And the Great White is a Belgian that has spent plenty of time thrashing around West Coast bars.

Opening hours: daily, 11am-1am

Recommendation
8 Ball Stout (6.3%)
This is strong, but not so much that you can't go back for second. A creamy smooth surprise.

Mammoth Brewing Company (24)

Minaret Rd. & Main St., Upstairs,
Mammoth Lakes, CA
T 760 934 2337
www.mammothbrewingco.com

A small microbrewery in the popular ski resort, so unsurprisingly Mammoth Brewing Company has an alpine feel to it. The beers aren't bad, and if you're looking for an apres-ski vibe when you come off the slopes there's plenty to try, usually accompanied by live music.

Recommendation
Mammoth IPA (7.6%)
Plenty of aroma and citrus tang.

North Coast Brewing Co (25)

5 N. Main St., Fort Bragg CA 95437
T 707 964 2739
www.northcoastbrewing.com

The beers are strong here. Famous faces to watch out for include Old Rasputin on the Russian Imperial Stout, the label featuring the man himself giving a friendly wave, possibly during happier, less mad times. It's a firm favourite on the West Coast. It's strong (weighing in at 9%) and with 75 IBUs doesn't let you down on bitterness either. Elsewhere the Brother Thelonious is a Belgian dark paying tribute to the jazz legend. As smooth as the vibes off Monk, this one is strong and sweet with a blend of caramel but also a fresh finish. The Red Seal amber is a subtle offering in the face of these two beers, and at 5.5% more of a session, meanwhile the PranQster is a Belgian using a traditional yeast strain and offers fruit and floral in equal nature.

If you decide to eat, you'll be subjected to some serious beer and food matching advice in the restaurant. Among the stand-out matches is the Blue Star Wheat Beer with the lobster salad; the Belgian PranQster with Tenderloin of Beef with Marsala and Hot Pepper Sauce; and the Russian Imperial Old Rasputin with the Imperial Chocolate Cake.
Recommendation
Russian Imperial Stout (9%)
Asks a lot of questions with roasty coffee beautifully complimenting the rich fruit flavours.

Placerville Brewing Co. (26)
155 Placerville Dr., Placerville CA 95667
T 530 295 9166
www.placervillebrewing.com

You might hit Placerville running from the guards at Folsom. If you need a pit stop you can get craft beer here. It's not the most attractive spot and looks like a fast-food restaurant from the outside with pine canteen style décor on the inside, but the food menu presents the staple brewpub tucker. There are some interesting creations on the beer list, not least the Tangerine Ale and Vanilla Stout.
Opening hours (kitchen): Mon-Thu, 11am-9pm (kitchen closed Tue); Fri & Sat, 11am-9.30pm; Sun, 11am-9pm
Recommendation
Boysenberry Ale (6.4%)
Try it just for the boysenberries!

Pyramid Alehouse, Brewery & Restaurant (27)
1029 K St., Sacramento, CA 95814
T 916 498 9800
www.pyramidbrew.com

No real surprises here, a gleaming moneyed brewpub that offers the standard Pyramid fare. Plenty of beer on offer, good grub, live sports and all in an impressive building with that 'we're in an industrial setting except we paid a few quid to make it look like that' feel.

Opening hours: Mon-Thu, 11.30am-9.30pm; Fri, 11.30am-11.30pm; Sat, noon-midnight; Sun, 11.30am-5pm
Tours: Mon-Fri, 5.30pm; Sat & Sun, 2pm & 4pm
Recommendation
Snow Cap Ale (7%)
Strong English ale with a bit of toffee sweetness and spicy bitterness at the end.

Pyramid Alehouse, Brewery & Restaurant (28)
1410 Locust St., Walnut Creek, CA 94596
T 925 946 1520
www.pyramidbrew.com

Seen one seen them all? Maybe, although we feel this isn't as impressive as the others. The beer garden is nice enough, and it's bright and breezy, but there's a feel of office canteen and training room about it. The beer and food are as you'd expect from a Pyramid, if you've seen them elsewhere.
Opening hours: Sun-Tue, 11:30am-10pm; Wed & Thu 11:30am-10:30pm; Fri & Sat 11.30am-11pm
Tours: Mon-Fri, 5:30pm; Sat & Sun, 2pm & 4pm
Recommendation
Tilted Kilt (6.3%)
The hops are high but balanced with an oaky, smoky touch.

Rubicon Brewing Co. (29)

2004 Capitol Ave., Sacramento, CA 95814
T 916 448 7032
www.rubiconbrewing.com
Highly recommended

The team at this well-loved brewpub is a key exponent of the NorCal Brewers Guild and takes the beer scene very seriously. A compact brewpub, Rubicon is conveniently located in the centre of Sacramento. It doesn't shout anything unique at you in décor, and the food menu has the appearance of other brewpubs, but it's a 'fun joint' and the mange is very bon. The beer is where the strengths lie, and there's plenty of range. Larger-than-life owner Glynn Phillips is a genuine beer enthusiast and is comfortable enough to present guest beers next to his own. Meanwhile capable brewer Scott Cramlet has plenty of space to experiment, a Rauch beer next on his list of creations.

The Czech Pilsner (4.8%) is brewed with strict coherence to its history and is faithful to the style because of that, equally the ESB ('T.C.B. E.S.B. R.I.P. E.A.P. Have One For The King' to give it its full title), using ingredients from across the pond and meeting expectations. The IPA is also very drinkable, offering plenty of citrus fruit and pine and enough caramel malt to balance the bitterness. The seasonal Great Lakes Rubicon is a must if it's on, the amber Belgian-style beer pitching a hop flavour that has just the right level of earthiness.

Opening hours: Mon-Thu, 11am-11.30pm; Fri, 11am-12.30am; Sat, 8.30am-12.30pm; Sun 8.30am-10pm
Recommendation
Monkey Knife Fight Pale Ale (4.3%)
Plenty of Mount Hood hop hit, the almost IPA quality makes for a great session beer.

Russian River Brewing Co. (30)

See feature on pages 142–143.

Sacramento Brewing Company (31)

Town and Country Village, 2713 El Paseo Lane, Sacramento, CA 95821
T 916 485 4677
www.sacbrew.com

This local favourite has been in keeping customers well oiled since 1995 and has won a glut of medals for its beers. Strip-mall surroundings make the environment unimaginative, but they fade into obscurity in the shadow of an ornamental kettle strutting from the top of the brewpub.

The stronger beers make the biggest impression here. The barley wines are full and sweet, garnering a decent durable reputation over the years. The Sac-Squatch Scotch Ale and its smoked peat malt delivers a body as roasted as a moist brunette on Copacabana beach. With the occasional cask thrown in as well, there's plenty to get your tongue around. The beer can be enjoyed with standard brewpub grub that includes some standout ribs. The venue serves as a local bar and family restaurant simultaneously, with regular events for patrons.

Opening hours: Mon-Thu, 11.30am-10am; Fri & Sat, 11.30am-midnight; Sun, 10am-10pm
Recommendation
Russian Imperial Stout (8.1%)
Fantastic dark, chocolate, biscuity stout with a lovely bitterness and just the right amount of carbonation.

Rubicon Brewing Company: made up of brewers who like to brush their teeth.

Sacramento Brewing Company Oasis (32)

7811 Madison Ave., Citrus Heights, CA 95610
T 916 966 6274
www.sacbrew.com

Sister to the previous listing, this venue has more of an Egyptian feel to it, perhaps slightly unusual. But the Pharaohs have been credited with some of the earliest beer recipes in history, so perhaps appropriate. Similar beers on the list, but this place has its own identity and warrants a peep.

Opening hours: Mon-Thu, 11.30am -10am; Fri & Sat, 11.30am-Midnight; Sun 10am-10pm

Silverado Brewing Company (33)

3020 St. Helena Hwy., St. Helena, CA 94574
T 707 967 9876
www.silveradobrewingcompany.com

Another brewpub in the heart of wine country, literally surrounded by wineries in fact, although the brewers will only be thinking about grapes if the hemorrhoids are in town. The Silverado lies in the charming town of St. Helena and is set in a century-old stone building, making it one of the more rustic venues on the NorCal tour. There's standard grill house food, with an interesting selection of beers.

Recommendation
Amber (5.7%)
Core beer, sweet and roasted in equal measure.

Valley Brewing Company (34)

157 W. Adams St., Stockton, CA 95294
T 209 464 2739
www.valleybrew.com

Valley Brewing Company opened its doors in 1853, and so enjoys plenty of heritage here. The fact that it closed in 1955 shouldn't matter, it's still testament to a period of American brewing and well worth a trip. Dark wood interior, spliced with red brick, a sports bar feel, nice patio and decent tucker make it an otherwise standard offering, but the beers stand out. The Black Cat Stout (6.6%) is particularly chocolaty with a lovely bitter end to it. The London Tavern Ale has a hint of good Ol' England about it. At 4.1%, it's manageable and with the Kent Golding and Fuggles, boasts plenty of flavour, too.

Recommendation
Hitman Gold (5.5%)
Inspired by Bret 'The Hitman' Hart himself, this beer pays homage to wrestling with an equally airy lift up front before a smackdown hop hit.

Russian River Brewing Co. (30)

725 4th St., Santa Rosa, CA 95404
T 707 545 BEER
www.russianriverbrewing.com

Deep in the heart of California's wine-making region, Vinnie Cilurzo of Russian River Brewing is making a difference with beer. Russian River Brewing Co. was actually conceived by the Korbel Champagne Cellars in Guerneville, set by the Russian River. Korbel recruited Vinnie in 1997. Five years later, they decided to leave beer behind and also left the brewing equipment with Vinnie. He decided to take it on with his wife Natalie and move it to Santa Rosa. This wasn't exactly a risky punt. Only two years into the gig with Korbel, Vinnie had established Russian River as the Small Brewing Company of the Year at the GABF. But if you go back even further to 1994, the real birth of Vinnie's legend can be found at the Blind Pig Brewing Company in Temecula. It was here that the young brewer created the eponymous double IPA, believed to be the first of its kind in the style, and started a West Coast hop revolution. Fast forward to Russian River today, Vinnie's double IPA, Pliny the Elder, has been a multiple award winner. With his Lambic expressions, he's proving that beer is as complex as wine.

"As well as about 500 wineries in 50 miles, Sonoma Valley actually has a number of places selling great beer," says Vinnie. *"People here naturally have a good palate because of the wine traditions and we're converting a lot of them to the range and subtleties of beer."*

Modest but atmospheric, the brewpub itself offers food as well as entertainment. The main source of sustenance on the menu is pizza, and live music each week jumps from jazz to hard rock and reggae.

While it buzzes away, Vinnie is brewing his beer next door so it doesn't get any fresher. Despite the phenomenal success of his beer, the set up is surprisingly small, producing around 3,000 barrels a year (1,800 through the restaurant). Of the ales and lagers, the Aud Blonde Pils (4.5%) is nice and light but balanced; the Lap Dance Pale Ale (5.3%) is an amber with an orange, malty blend; and for those who can't take the hop hit of a double IPA, the Russian River IPA (6.7%) has plenty of piney nose and citrus on the taste buds.

Vinnie's flair for innovation and creativity has recently taken on a Belgian bent, and his knowledge is phenomenal.

"I'm always experimenting here and head over to Belgium once a year to learn more about how to get the best out of the beer."

The enthusiasm has paid off. His first barrel-aged release, Temptation (7.25%), has been a roaring success. The blonde ale is aged for twelve months in used chardonnay barrels with *Brettanomyces* and has wonderful sour notes over citrus. The Supplication (7%), second out of the barrel, has been aged for twelve months in used pinot noir with sour cherries, *Brettanomyces* and two strains of bacteria to naturally sour the beer – all offering a wonderfully sour and oaky beer.

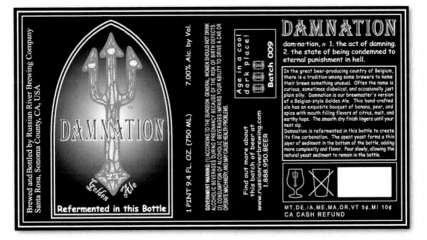

The beer community rightly regards Vinnie as one of the foremost creative forces in craft beer, and he has become a spokesperson for the movement as it slowly but surely eats into the profits of the big-boy brewers that dominate the market. Much of what is on offer is limited release. As a result, it's not only best enjoyed on site, it could prove the only place it's available – making a visit even more crucial.

Opening hours: Sun-Thu, 11am-midnight; Fri & Sat, 11am-1am

THE BEERS

Dr. Zues (5.9%)
Mixing it up with the hops, this seasonal is brewed with 100% Zues hops and is somewhere between a Pale Ale and an IPA – perhaps more approachable if you've been blown away by the double IPAs.

Russian River Blind Pig IPA (6%)
Another fantastic example of an American IPA, Blind Pig has a beautiful golden colour and all the bitter grape-fruit qualities you'll have become accustomed to.

Damnation (7%)
A big-hitting award-winning Belgian strong golden ale with all the banana flavours the hungriest monkey would demand – not to mention hearty hops for balance and generous carbonation for decent mouthfeel.

Suplication (7%)
Aged with sour cherries in French oak Pinot Noir barrels for one year, Suplication will screw most mouths up thanks to the three strains of Brettanomyces yeast and

Lactobacillus and Pediococcus bacteria in the mix. Great balance though.

Temptation (7.3%)
Aged in French oak for one year, this blonde ale has the oak characteristics you'd expect along with tart taste you want from the Bret style. It's an excellent addition to the beer list and unsurprisingly another multi-award winner.

Pliny the Elder (8%)
A firm favourite with American beer fans, this latest yardstick for a double IPA is brewed with 40% more malt and over twice the amount of hops in the standard IPA. Lip-smackingly good!

Pliny the Younger (11%)
A seasonal that's hopped three times more than the standard IPA and is dry hopped four different times to give some serious bitter hit. A fantastic flavour experience if you can hack the hops.

BEER BARS

Ausiello's 5th Street Grill (35)
609 5th St., Santa Rosa, CA 95404
T 707 579 9408

No mistaking what this place is about, with a plethora of TV screens committed to sport. The food is representative – burgers and sandwiches – but there is a good selection of beer, too. All in all, a good place to hit if there's a major sporting event on the box.

Opening hours: call in

Buck's Crazy Horse Saloon (36)
3rd & Main Chico, CA
T 530 342 7299
www.buckscrazyhorse.com

Good-looking barmaids, cowboy country singers and a mechanical bull... What else could you want? Decent beer? OK, it's a bit Bud Light, but you read mechanical bull, right? For a 'bucking good time'? Surely that's sufficient...

Opening hours: Tue-Sat, 8pm-2am

Clocktower Cellar (37)
6080 Minaret Rd., Mammoth Lakes, CA 93546
T 760 934 2725

There's a fantastic beer selection in this dive-style basement bar. There was a snowboarding crowd in when we visited, so perhaps a younger scene although all are undoubtedly welcome to enjoy a host of regional West Coast beers. There's pool and table football as well, and the place generally provides a lot more atmosphere than the nearby Mammoth Brewing Co.

Opening hours: daily, 11am-2am

Gallaghers Irish Pub (38)
1201 K St., Sacramento, CA 95814
T 916 444 3444
www.thebroilersteakhouse.com

Irish pub with Guinness, steak and oysters on the menu and a strong selection of whisky.

Opening hours: Mon-Sat, 11am-10pm; Sun, closed

The Graduate (39)
344 W. 8th St., Chico, CA 95928
T 530 343 2790

This bar is a good pool hangout with a good selection of American craft beers. If you catch it on a student night then you know what to expect. Get it when one of the many other Chico bars is rocking, though, and you'll find it as mellow as Simon & Garfunkel.

Opening hours: daily, 11am-late

Hopland Ale House (40)
13351 S. Hwy. 101, Hopland, CA 95449
T 707 744 1361
Highly recommended

This is one of the first establishments that started the brewpub revolution and craft beer scene. Hopland Ale House is affiliated with Don Barkley and the Mendocino Brewing Company and acts as a tasting room for his beers. You'll see a lot of red brick and dark wood in brewpubs across the West Coast but only a few that aren't overly polished. This is one of them.

Opening hours: Thu-Mon, noon-7pm; Tue & Wed, closed

Lakanuki (41)
6201 Minaret Rd., Suite 200, Mammoth Lakes, CA 93546
T 760 934 7447
www.lakanuki.com

This lively venue is a 'party hang-out' with a modest craft beer selection, and great for a nightcap if you find yourself skiing in Mammoth Lakes. The entertainment comes in the form of DJs, karaoke and live bands, and in December they have been known to host a Naughty Santa Lingerie party...

Opening hours: daily, 11am-2am

The Madison Bear Garden (42)
316 W. 2nd St. Chico, CA
T 530 899 1639

A college bar, good burgers, pseudo-psychedelic interior design and a great range of the Sierra Nevada beers. That's about all we remember, it was towards the end of a bar crawl in Chico, and they had cheap pitchers.

Piaci Pub and Pizza (43)

120 W. Redwood Ave., Fort Bragg, CA 95437
T 707 961 1133

They call it 'the home of adult pizza', and we weren't disappointed. The food is served up next to a very impressive list of American craft and European beers. In terms of size it's not a big place, but it packs a big punch and is very reasonably priced.

Opening hours: Mon-Fri, 11am-2pm; Fri & Sat, 4pm-10pm; food served Sun-Thu, 4pm-9pm

Riley's (44)

706 W. 5th St. Chico, CA
T 530 343 7459
www.rileysbar.com

Home to the original 'buck-night' apparently, which means a (one, single) dollar for a pint of Sierra Nevada. And tequilas are the same price if you're there on a Tuesday. It's crazy talk and as a consequence this place has made it into *Playboy* magazine's top 100 college bars on two occasions. If you sample the drinks on Tuesday, you'll be drowning in impossibly beautiful students, so drink responsibly.

Opening hours: daily, 11am-late

Sudwerks (45)

2001 2nd St., Davis, CA 95616
T 530 756 2739

Davis is a town made famous in beer circles for its university's brewing course. Indeed many of the significant brewing brains attended, and the future elite is being spewed from its yeasty pipes each year. So it's worth a pilgrimage. While you're there take in Sudwerks. The German themed local has a great selection of Germanic beers, a loyal following and fantastic cuisine.

Opening hours: daily, 11am-11pm

Sweet Spot Pub & Lounge (46)

619 4th St., Santa Rosa, CA
T 707 528 7566
www.sweetspotpub.com

Another Santa Rosa sports bar, where locals line the stools on a game day. There's a good selection of beers to accompany the action, including a devotion to the fine collection of Lagunitas. Enjoy them with a menu that includes a Belizean Beach Club. If you're here late, watch out for live music.

Opening hours: Mon-Sat, 4-10pm; Sun, 10am-10pm

The inviting shores of Lake Tahoe in north-eastern California

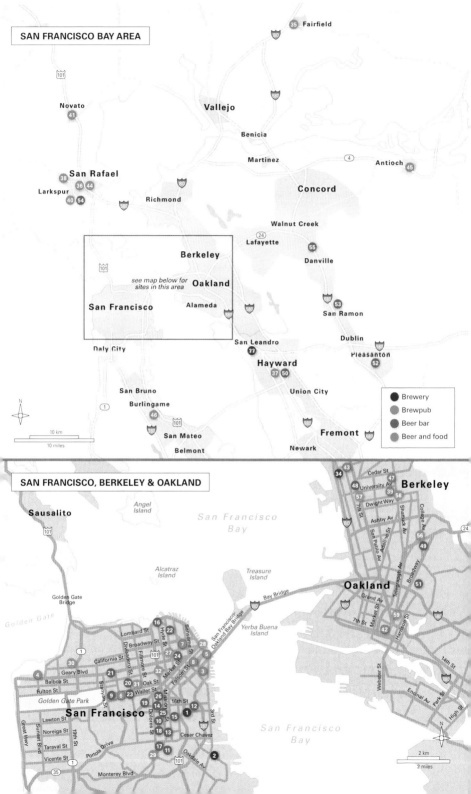

SAN FRANCISCO BAY AREA

Fairfield 35

Novato 41

Vallejo

Benicia

Martinez

Concord

Antioch 45

San Rafael
38 36 44
Larkspur
40 54

Richmond

Walnut Creek
Lafayette
Danville 55

Berkeley

see map below for
sites in this area

Oakland

San Francisco

Alameda

San Ramon 53

Daly City

San Leandro 77

Dublin

Pleasanton 52

Hayward
37 50

Union City

San Bruno
Burlingame 46
San Mateo
Belmont

Fremont

Newark

Brewery
Brewpub
Beer bar
Beer and food

10 km
10 miles

SAN FRANCISCO, BERKELEY & OAKLAND

Sausalito

Angel
Island

San Francisco
Bay

34 43 Cedar St
48 University Av Berkeley
57 39 58
Dwight Way
Ashby Av
College Av

Golden Gate
Bridge

Alcatraz
Island

Treasure
Island

Bay Bridge

Yerba Buena
Island

56
49

Oakland
51

Grand Av
59
42

Golden Gate

San Francisco-Oakland Bay Bridge

16 22
Lombard St
Broadway 7
California St 27 24
30 32
Geary Blvd
21
Balboa St
20 31
Fulton St
9 6 23
Golden Gate Park 14
San Francisco 19

28
5
8
3

Oak St
Waller St
26
25 15
10 18
13
17 11
29

16th St
1 12

Cesar Chavez

2

San Francisco
Bay

2 km
2 miles

NORTHERN CALIFORNIA

OREGON

- Brewery
- Brewpub
- Beer bar

Crescent City

Yreka

Goose Lake

Alturas

McKinleyville
Arcata

7

Eureka
23
Fortuna
18

Shasta Lake

Shasta Lake

Redding

Red Bluff

Susanville

Orlando

Chico

Paradise

3 10 36
39 42 44

Willows

Thermalito

Reno

Fort Bragg
25 43
Willits

CALIFORNIA

NEVADA

Ukiah
1 8

Clearlake

40

Cloverdale

13 9

Santa Rosa
11 30 35 46

St. Helena

33

5 16 Petaluma

Napa

17

Grass Valley

20

Lake Tahoe

Carson City

Yuba City

Auburn

26

Placerville

South Lake Tahoe

Woodland
Davis

Sacramento

14 32 12 6

15 21 27

19 29 31 38

Vacaville

(see p146 for San Francisco and Bay Area)

Novato

San Rafael

Berkeley

2

Concord

28

Oakland

San Francisco

Daly City

Redwood City

Sunnyvale

San Jose

Fairfield

Vallejo

Antioch

Lodi

22

Stockton

34

Manteca

Tracy

Turlock

Patterson

Los Banos

Merced

Sonora

Mammoth Lakes
24 37 41

PACIFIC OCEAN

Gilroy

Santa Cruz

Watsonville

Monterey Seaside

Salinas

Madera

Fresno

Visalia

Hanford

N

50 km

50 miles

Oregon

FOR GOODNESS SAKE, go to Oregon. Seriously. Go. Go for the ballistic beer; go for the breathtaking beauty; go for Portland – a fantastically funky, fiery whizzbang of a place. Just go.

A short history

The Pacific Northwest was one of the last places to be explored by Europeans. English explorers Francis Drake (1579) and James Cook (1778) had popped their heads around Oregon's door in the name of curiosity before Captain Robert Gray weaved his way up to the Columbia River in 1792 and whacked an American flag in Oregon soil – presumably to the chagrin of the indigenous Chinook, Klamath and Bannock native Americans.

The fur trade initially attracted settlers and the fur-trapping British Hudson's Bay Company was the region's dominant economic force, yet Oregon didn't really establish itself on the map until hordes arrived along the Oregon Trail. Two chaps called William Overton, a Tennessee wanderer, and Massachusetts lawyer Asa Lovejoy, are widely considered as the founding fathers of Portland. They arrived by canoe on the banks of the Willamette in 1843, and Overton was immediately struck by the timber-rich, mountainous landscape. While Overton had the vision, it was Lovejoy who had the money – it cost just 25 cents to lay claim to the undiscovered 640-acre site.

Before long, however, Overton got itchy feet and moved on. He sold his share to Francis W. Pettygrove and a new partnership was born – but one unable to agree on a name for the new land. Lovejoy was determined to name the site after his hometown of Boston, while Pettygrove was equally adamant about

his native Portland, Maine. They settled the argument with a flip of a coin, now known as the 'Portland Penny'. Pettygrove won two tosses out of three.

The 33rd state was admitted to the Union in 1859. Prior to that time, the Oregon Territory stretched from California to Canada along the Pacific Coast and east to the Rocky Mountains from the Pacific Ocean – an area that now encompasses the states of Washington, Idaho and Montana.

Lovejoy and Pettygrove's vision of Portland as a prosperous and pleasant port failed to materialise. In the late 1800s Portland was a dastardly place where skulduggery, mayhem and mischief reigned. Things improved by the turn of the nineteenth century. A large slice of the million visitors who came to Oregon's Lewis and Clark Exposition in 1905 ended up staying and over the next 50 years the advent of railroads and the automobile further expanded Oregon's population and commercial prowess – mainly in the lumber and wheat trade.

Economic buoyancy was deflated by the Depression of the Thirties, and there was no recovery until the Second World War, when war production revitalised the shipyards and Oregon became a major supplier to the American forces in the Pacific. Thousands of newcomers arrived to work in the factories, and then settled after the war.

During the Fifties, the wheels of Oregon's industrial growth were oiled by the completion of the McNary and Dalles dams and the introduction of natural gas to the state. Industrial growth, however, came at agricultural cost, and a green backlash ensued in the Sixties. Huge strides were taken, and laws passed, to preserve Oregon's natural resources. In the Eighties, Oregon was hit by further economic depression

Left: Vista House overlooking the Columbia River

and the logging industry bore the brunt. The farming focus switched to the fruit, nut and wine industries, and the agriculture of wider Oregon has continued to thrive.

Portland, meanwhile, enjoyed an influx of young, creative graduates as part of the dot-com boom in the Nineties. Although the bubble burst shortly after, the creative vibe remained and Portland became renowned for its artistic and creative communities. It also gained a reputation as a city whose political and social outlook often clashed sharply with the rest of Oregon.

Today

Oregon is stunningly beautiful, blessed with a hugely diverse array of natural delights. The 400-mile coastline is simply awesome. Raw, rugged and jutting, it cuts a snaking swathe through lush, evergreen forests, taking in a smorgasbord of sublime sights. With rolling sand dunes, craggy coves, wallowing whales, quirky fishing villages and boundless sandy beaches it is, we reckon, the most dramatic part of the Pacific Highway's coastal drive – eclipsing California's well-trodden thoroughfare. It really shouldn't be missed.

To the south lies the even more spectacular Crater Lake National Park. The eponymous lake, formed by a collapsed volcano, is the deepest in America and famed for its gleaming sapphire sheen and water purity. Mt. Hood, located 50 miles east of Portland, is another volcanic wonder and home to half a dozen gnarly ski areas and countless kick-ass climbing routes. The Hood River valley below, enriched by the run-off from Mt. Hood's volcanic slopes, is a plentiful source of fruit where apricots, apples, blueberries and wine grapes grow.

Hood River flows into the awe-inspiring Columbia River Gorge where funky riverfront towns, numerous waterfalls and some of the world's finest windsurfing waters can be found. The Willamette Valley, meanwhile, is the most densely populated area of Oregon. It's also wonderful wine country with more than two hundred wineries producing some of the world's finest Pinot Noir.

On the other side of the Cascade mountain range, things change again. The high desert country of central Oregon is drier than a sawdust Martini. Kissed with 300 days of sunshine a year, and swathed with virginal powder in the winter, it's a magnet for sporty types with Mt. Bachelor and Smith Rock especially popular with skiers and climbers respectively.

Awaiting one further east is uplifting isolation. Yet amid the bone-dry scrublands, parched prairies and arid desert plateaus lie the peculiar Painted Hills, the immense Steens Mountains (the biggest continental geological fault) and the plunging depths of Hells Canyon – North America's deepest river gorge.

Beer scene

Oregon is not called 'Beervana' for nothing. No other American state, or arguably European country, can lay claim to a richer, more diverse beer scene and wherever you find yourself, be it in central Portland or trundling about the Eastern wilderness, rest assured you're rarely far from a delectable drop. While it's arguable whether the state was present at the birth of the craft brewing revolution, it has certainly been an integral figure in its upbringing. Without Oregon, American craft beer certainly wouldn't be the upstanding paragon of diversity, taste and innovation that it is today.

Up until 1980, however, Oregon beer was hopelessly one-dimensional. Drinkers could drink any beer style they wanted as long as it was yellow, fizzy lager. Henry's, Olympia or Rainier were the only 'local' brews and pretty much identical in everything but name. (Henry's should however be applauded for opening people's eyes with its admirable Henry Weinhard Private Reserve). As for dark beer, it was available but about as popular as gout.

Yet Oregonians couldn't help noticing Washington and California's embryonic ale endeavours and, with the 1978 legalisation of homebrewing, Oregon quickly developed a thirst for more enlightened beers. Fred Eckhardt, Oregon's revered beer writer, was an influential figure throughout, and he stoked the fire of intrigue through his beer column in *The Oregonian* – the state's leading newspaper.

In 1981, winemaker Charlie Coury opened Cartwright's, Oregon's first commercial craft brewery. Yet, like so many pioneering pacemakers, Charlie was unable to go it entirely alone and conceded defeat on New Year's Day 1983.

Later that year, Oregon legalised brew-on-premise establishments which transformed brewing from a loss-making labour of love into a potentially feasible way of making a buck or two. With a key barrier to market removed, a number of entrepreneurs upgraded their interest in brewing from merely passionate to professional.

The debate rages as to Oregon's first brewery. Some claim that it was Rob and Kurt Widmer's concept in Portland in 1984, while others argue that Widmer's was preceded, by a matter of days, by the BridgePort Brewery – a neighbouring venture fronted by winemakers Nancy and Dick Ponzi. In 1985, Mike and Brian McMenamin opened their first brewpub in Hillsdale, Portland, and this was followed in 1986 by Portland Brewing on Northwest Flanders, owned by Fred Bowman and Art Larrance. Beyond Portland's perimeters, Hood River Brewing opened and the McMenamins began their empire building with two more venues in Lincoln City and Hillsboro. Over the next decade, numerous craft breweries opened.

Oregon's perpetual precipitation advanced the cause of craft beer. The mild, rainy and grey climate encouraged the burgeoning pub culture and endowed the state with some rather helpful natural beermaking resources: soft Bull Run water, locally grown barley and native Oregon hops are all the requisite ingredients brewers needed to craft pale ales, IPAs, velvety smooth Porters, silky Stouts and more.

In 1992, the Oregon Brewers Guild (OBG) was formed with the primary goal of promoting the brewing industry in Oregon. In 1996, it introduced the 'Quality & Integrity Mark', the nation's first craft beer quality-assurance program and, in 2001, it forwarded the cause of smaller players by freeing access to market through a collective distribution initiative.

Championed by the Oregon Brewers Guild and unencumbered by the state's hands-off brewing legislation, Oregon's craft beer scene flourished through the 1990s and after 30 years of expansion the number of breweries in Oregon now numbers more than 80.

Of the 50 largest breweries in the nation, five are craft breweries located in Oregon: Widmer Brothers Brewing Company, Deschutes Brewery, Full Sail Brewing Company, BridgePort Brewing Company and Rogue Ales.

Oregonian brewers are hardly resting on their laurels either. Between 2004 and 2007, more than a dozen breweries eagerly flung open their doors while the founding fathers of the scene – such as Widmer, BridgePort, Deschutes, Rogue and McMenamins – continue to grow from strength to strength.

When it comes to beer knowledge, Oregonians are an enlightened bunch. Sit at any bar in any town, from Astoria to Zena, and marvel at the sheer beer passion on both sides of the bar. Bartenders tend to be clued-up beer sommeliers capable of telling you everything about the beer from its strength and hop flavour to the inside leg measurement of the guy – or girl – who lovingly brewed it.

Portland, the jewel in Oregon's brewing crown, is home to more than 30 breweries alone. Michael Jackson (the legendary and late beer writer rather than the baby-dangling dude) once described it as "Munich on the Willamette", as Portland surpasses the German city in terms of the number of breweries.

While craft beer sales account for just below 4% of the entire beer market in America, in Portland they represent a staggering 45% of all beer drunk.

"If you like beer there's no better place in the world than Portland," says Rob Widmer of Widmer Brothers Brewing. "Within a mile of Downtown you can find the best examples of a beer style in the world whether that's a domestic brew or an import."

Such is the quality, sheer quantity and kaleidoscopic range of Portland's beer, even the most mainstream watering hole boasts the kind of beer selection to make a British beer buff weep into his pint glass.

This makes the task of identifying Portland's finest beer establishments an unfeasibly tricky one. We're nothing if not brave soldiers, dear readers, and so we've courageously –and some would say selflessly – done just that. All for you.

Portland

Nestled in the state's northwest corner at the confluence of the Willamette and Columbia rivers, Portland is an amiable, attractive and unashamedly alternative city. With a wonderfully quirky underbelly and infectious edge, it blends the maverick spirit of San Francisco with the bohemian, funky microbreweries, coffee shops and cutting-edge music scene of Seattle... and does so with a devious twinkle in its eye.

While big branded business has managed to wheedle its way into town (Nike and Intel are based here), Portland champions the little guy with no small amount of zeal. Small independent grocery shops, book stores (Powell's is legendary), bars, cafes and eateries are everywhere and enthusiastically frequented by locals. Compared to most American cities of its size, Portland's food is fantastic. Fresh, varied and usually locally sourced, gastronomes won't want for decent, affordable grub here. Nor will drinkers be disappointed. In addition to the brilliant beer (don't worry, there's plenty more of that later), Portland's wine scene is in fine fettle, albeit, by European standards, a little pricey.

What else? Oh yes, how could we forget? Thanks to the city's unique freedom of speech legislation, Portland also has more strip clubs per capita than Las Vegas, Reno and San Francisco. If the strip clubs turn you blind then use your ears and tune into Portland's music scene. Helped by low rents and copious rainfall (always a friend to artistic innovation), Portland has proudly usurped Seattle from the Indie throne and become a veritable hotbed of guitar-plucking talent. Not a night goes by without a gig so check out the listings in the various weeklies.

More refined culture vultures are in for a treat too. With its ever-expanding list of galleries, public artworks and venues, Portland's visual arts scene is undoubtedly a work in progress. Its continuous infusion of fresh talent, artistic style and creative energy has landed Portland on *AmericanStyle* magazine's list of the country's 'Top 25 Arts Destinations' for seven years running.

Once you've dawdled around the Portland Art Museum (fresh from a $125 million refurbishment) and the Portland Institute for Contemporary Art, the best time to explore Portland's other galleries is on the first Thursday of every month during the aptly, if a little unimaginatively, titled 'First Thursday Gallery Walk'. On these nights, galleries and shops in Portland's Old Town, Pearl District and Downtown neighbourhoods stay open late and invite the public to chat with the artists. Most art dealers use First Thursday to stage new exhibitions and artist receptions.

On the last Thursday, don't miss Northeast Alberta Street's 'Last Thursday' art walk where galleries showcase their wares amid a carnival atmosphere with bands, comedians, jugglers, food stalls and a small boy who tells jokes for 25 cents. It's pretty bonkers.

Portland also boasts arguably the strangest selection of museums in the world. Stark's Vacuum Cleaner Museum is exactly what you'd assume it to be – namely America's most extensive selection of vacuum cleaners. Then there's Kidd's Toy Museum for all you big (and little) children out there; the Rice Northwest Museum of Rocks and Minerals for all you geeks; and last (and very much) least, there's Velveteria, a bizarre collection of more than a thousand velvet paintings.

There are plenty of other cultural offerings in Portland including an established regional theatre (Portland Center Stage), a resident symphony (Oregon Symphony), an opera company (Portland Opera), touring Broadway shows (the Best of Broadway Series), and a vibrant collection of smaller organisations. For those willing to scratch below the surface, the city tenders an impressive range of progressive, smaller-scale programming.

Portland also plays host to myriad festivals throughout the year such as the Oregon Seafood & Wine Festival (January), Cinqo de Mayo Fiesta (May), the Portland Rose Festival (June), the Waterfront Blues Festival (July) and, best of all, the Oregon Brewers Festival (July).

Oregon Brewers Festival

The inaugural Oregon Brewers Festival took place in 1987, organised by a trio of local microbreweries – Portland Brewing Co, Widmer Brothers Brewing Company and Bridgeport brewing company.

The initial aim was to be a showcase for the embryonic nationwide microbrewing scene and introduce the adventurous drinkers of Portland to beers from outside the local market. With only 124 craft breweries in the entire nation, the first festival was a modest affair with 13 participating breweries and a total of 16 beers on tap – but it still attracted 15,000 visitors. Twenty years later and the Oregon Brewers Festival, a four-day event over the last weekend in July, has become one of the most popular beer festivals in America.

In 2007, the Oregon Brewers Festival served 73 different craft beers from 14 states and more than 60,000 poured through the gates. While the festival's focus is fresh craft beer, there's live music, an educational tent, lots of lovely food and all manner of alfresco entertainment by the river at Portland's Gov. Tom McCall Waterfront Park.

Getting around

Once you've got your bearings, Portland is an easy place to get around. It's home to a clean, cheap and efficient public transport system, it is compact in size and its streets are laid out alphabetically and numerically. So long as you've a basic grasp of counting and spelling, you should be OK.

Unlike other American cities, Portland doesn't peter out rather forlornly into an endless, bleak wasteland of car lots and identikit drive-thru fast-food joints. In 1979, the authorities prudently set up an urban growth boundary that made a stark distinction between urban areas and traditional farmland.

As well as curbing urban sprawl, strict planning has also heavily restricted the construction of ungainly skyscrapers. Instead, they seemed to have built bridges – and lots of them too.

The Willamette River, which slices through the middle of Portland, is traversed by the city's multitude of bridges including the world's only telescoping double-deck vertical lift bridge (Steel), the world's oldest lift bridge (Hawthorne) and America's longest tied-arch bridge (Fremont).

Plod Portland Ditch the car. All that's needed to get around Portland is legs. Downtown is lovely and condensed. Half-size city blocks (200-foot rather than the standard 400-foot behemoths) and a plethora of parks and public spaces make Portland an ideal city to explore on foot. While some might opt to venture where their feet happen to take them, Portland walking maps are available at Powell's Books and the visitor information centre at Pioneer Courthouse Square.

There are also walking tours that leave Pioneer Courthouse Square daily, guided by knowledgeable locals armed with all manner of fascinating facts and historic did you knows? Choose from 'Best of Portland' and 'Underground Portland' for two hour jaunts. On weekends, sample 30 items in three to five hours on the 'Epicurean Excursion'. Don't forget to keep your eyes open for Quimby and Flanders Street and Montgomery Park – Matt Groening, creator of The Simpsons – named several of his characters after Portland's avenues. www.portlandwalkingtours.com

Pedal Portland Named 'Best Cycling City in North America' by Bicycling magazine two years in a row, Portland is a breeze on two wheels. In addition to wide, clearly marked bike lanes on nearly every commuter and Downtown thoroughfare, there are municipal bike racks, easy access over the multitude of bridges and respect from both drivers and pedestrians.

Adding to the bike-friendly atmosphere, TriMet buses are equipped with bike racks, while bikes are also welcome aboard all MAX light rail trains. Bikes (including lock, helmet and maps) can be hired from Waterfront Bicycle Rentals (315 SW. Montgomery, **T** 503 227 1719) and Citybikes Workers Cooperative (734 SE. Ankeny, **T** 503 239 6951).

Cycling routes

Vera Katz Eastbank Esplanade
For a year-round bridge experience, cyclists (and pedestrians) can enjoy the Vera Katz Eastbank Esplanade, which opened in May 2001. This one and a half-mile pedestrian/cycling corridor extends along the east side of Downtown Portland's Willamette River, affording dramatic views of the city. The esplanade connects to the sea wall at Gov. Tom McCall Waterfront Park via the Steel Bridge (on its pedestrian/bicycle river crossing at riverbank level) and the Hawthorne Bridge. The resulting loop is just under three miles in length.

Springwater Corridor
Cyclists who opt to continue south on the Eastbank (rather than turning onto the Hawthorne Bridge) can follow a three-mile path between OMSI (Oregon Museum of Science and Industry) and the Sellwood Bridge opened for recreation. This is the westernmost leg of the Springwater Corridor. A testament to Oregonians' zest for recycling, the Springwater Corridor is one of Portland's most notable bike developments. This former rail corridor was reborn as an alternative transportation and recreational trail that winds for 17 miles from Portland to Boring (it's not though). The corridor is part of a 170-mile loop from the city centre to gorgeous wilderness (Mount Hood National Forest).

Forest Park
There are 30 miles of bikeable terrain in the 5,100 acres of Forest Park – the largest forested urban park in America. One of the most popular routes for bikers is the 11.2-mile Leif Erikson Drive, with views of the Columbia River, Mt. Hood and Mt. St. Helens.

MAX (Metropolitan Area Express) **Light Rail** The MAX is a clean, cheap and efficient light railway system with three lines (red, blue and yellow) and two more planned (green and orange). The MAX Yellow Line (opened in 2004 at a cost of $350 million) is a five mile track along Interstate Avenue, linking the Portland Metropolitan Exposition Center to the Oregon Convention Center/Rose Quarter area and the hotels of the city's Downtown. It will soon stretch as far south as Portland State University. The Blue Line connects Downtown to a number of Portland's principal tourist destinations while the Red Line links the city centre with Portland International Airport (PDX). MAX will expand its reach to even more residents and visitors to the Portland area with its new Green line, due to be finished in September 2009 at a cost of $557 million.

Portland Streetcar Project The rather fancy European-style Portland Streetcar orbits a five-mile loop that begins and ends at the Portland State University campus. It links up a number of Portland's neighbourhoods including Nob Hill, Pearl District, Downtown's cultural quarter and the city's busy River Place district.

'Fareless Square'

Fareless Square is a 330-block area in Downtown Portland where transportation on all MAX light rail trains, buses, trolleys and streetcars is free – all part of Portland's drive to reduce air pollution, parking problems and street congestion in the central city. 'Fareless Square' now stretches across the Willamette River to include stops at the Rose Garden arena (home to the NBAs Portland Trail Blazers), the Oregon Convention Center and Lloyd Center mall.

Portland Aerial Tram Opened in January 2007, the Portland Aerial Tram throws up some spectacular cityscape views. The two custom-designed Swiss-made cabins, which can accommodate up to 78 people, travel between the OHSU Center for Health & Healing and the university's main campus on Marquam Hill. It takes just three minutes to travel 3,300 linear feet and rise 500 feet in elevation. A round-trip ticket is $4 and

cyclists can board with their bikes. At the lower terminal, the Portland Streetcar station is just a few steps away.

Amtrak With buses and MAX making stops at Union Station, travelling by train to and from Portland makes sense. Amtrak's legendary Cascades Train departs Portland's historic train depot several times daily for points north, including Vancouver, Washington; Seattle and Vancouver, B.C., and for cities south of Portland, including Oregon City, Salem, Albany and Eugene. Passengers ride in comfort with movies, laptop power access and cold drinks. Throw in some staggeringly beautiful scenery and it's a wonder why people don't use it more often.

Orientation

Portland is an assortment of sharply defined districts, all with their own distinct personality and vibe. But, such is their proximity, you can also hop from one to another with relative ease. **Downtown** has been gently tapped with the wand of regeneration and transformed by the money of big retail brands, business and mainstream bars and restaurants. **Pearl District**, a former industrial section of northwest Portland, is now a gentrified, artsy and achingly cool quarter full with a knowingly stylish blend of art, business and warehouse residents. Exposed brickwork and girders, uber-fashionable restaurants, cutesy little boutiques, elaborate haircuts

and skin-tight trousers – they're all here. As well as the BridgePort BrewPub & Bakery, Oregon's oldest craft brewery, Pearl is home to Powell's City of Books, the largest independent bookstore in the world. It spans a full city block and houses more than a million used, new and rare books.

Nob Hill/Northwest offers turn of the century Victorian architecture, tree-lined streets, food markets and an impressive array of restaurants, pubs and cafes. Nestled into the base of Portland's west hills, it's also a shopping Mecca with Northwest 23rd ('Trendy-third') being a particularly fine avenue on which to flash your cash.

Separated from Downtown by the Willamette River, **Hawthorne** puts the hip into hippy. Live music, ethic eateries, retro clothing boutiques and brews (both caffeinated and alcoholic) line Hawthorne Boulevard – an ideal destination for after-hours antics. The **Cultural District**, meanwhile, is swathed in greenery and flanked by the city's major cultural institutions such as the Arlene Schnitzer Concert Hall, the Portland Center for the Performing Arts, the Portland Art Museum and the campus of Portland State University.

The **Old Town/Chinatown** area is a bustling arts and entertainment district and the site of some of Portland's best music spots and art galleries. Every weekend from March through December, Old Town hosts the well-known Portland Saturday Market – open on Sundays, too.

Perfect for a Sunday stroll or a romantic night out is **Sellwood** in southeast Portland – a lovely little neighbourhood awash with antique shops and a handful of bars and restaurants.

Northeast Alberta, meanwhile, is a culturally diverse and vibrant district that comes alive on the last Thursday of every month. On the second Thursday each month, the rejuvenated **North Mississippi** also cranks up the volume with 'Second Thursday Social' – a shindig made up of music, art, food, wine and beer.

Not content with boasting Oregon's smallest brewery (Clinton Street Brewery), **Division/Clinton** is now home to some pretty funky bars and eateries. For food, folk flock to 28th Avenue ('Restaurant Row'), where a gamut of international gourmet delights awaits. The Laurelhurst Theater, an art deco movie palace serving microbrews and pizza, is a local landmark.

Accommodation

EXPENSIVE

Ace Hotel 1022 SW. Stark St., Portland, OR 97205; **T** 503 228 2277; **E** reservations.pdx@acehotel.com www.acehotel.com
Ace Hotel is sleek but retains the character of the old building from which it emerged. The 79 rooms mix uncluttered comfort with a bohemian vibe using industrial salvage, a clear eye for contemporary design and a clever economy of style. Ace gives everything you need and nothing you don't so there's no pay-for-view TV or trouser press but there is free Wi-Fi and retro-bikes for guests to pedal about town. Prices range from $95–$250 for a very 'Portland' experience.

MID-RANGE

Jupiter Hotel 800 E Burnside St., Portland, OR 97214-1221; **T** 503 230 9200
Around $100 will reward you with a room in this cool, kitsch hotel that's been given a lick of retro verve. The 80 designer rooms have platform beds, fluffy pillows, free Wi-Fi and eyebrow-raising colour schemes. After a night's cavorting at the adjacent Doug Fir, one of Portland's leading music venues, you can detox and unwind with a spa style rubdown or a personal yoga mat. Shabby chic on a shoestring.

BASIC

White Eagle 836 N. Russell St., Portland, OR 97227; **T** 503 335 8900; www.mcmenamins.com
Book into one of the White Eagle's 11 basic rooms that brim with typical ye-olde McMenamin charm and go downstairs to the bar for a beer and a damn good boogie! More for low-budget living-it-up folk than light sleepers, the White Eagle offers bunk rooms with bunk beds ($40) or 'full rooms' from $45. Room rates are for single or double occupancy. Rock on. Free Wi-Fi Internet too.

BREWERIES

Hair of the Dog Brewing Company (1)
4509 SE. 23rd Ave., Portland, OR 97202
T 503 232 6585
www.hairofthedog.com

Hair of the Dog beers are really rather special. In 1993, home brewer Alan Sprints set out to brew strong, maverick bottle-conditioned beers that pay homage to long-forgotten beer styles. Adam, Hair of the Dog's first ever offering, is a rich and mellow top fermented take on the rarely brewed German Adambier style. Before a languid cold conditioning, whole hop flowers are introduced alongside intensely roasted barley. The result? A warm, fruity and complex ale that treads gently on the toes of harvest ales and barley wines. Drink from an after-dinner snifter and marvel as prunes, coffee, liquorice, raisins and caramel all come out to play.

Fred, meanwhile, is a golden-hued, malt-driven tribute to beer writer Fred Eckhardt, brewed with rye grain, ten different varieties of hop and no concern for Father Time. After a long maturation period, Fred gets better with age, its complexity increasing in the bottle.

Rose is Hair of the Dog's honey-tinged interpretation on a Belgian Tripel which, at 8%, drinks in a dangerously deceptive manner. Don't let Doggie Claws get stuck into you until it's been laid down for a while. This beast of a barley wine, like all Hair of the Dog's beers, gets better when left alone and then consumed in celebration of one's restraint.

Look out for Hair of The Dog's 'From the Wood' limited selection of beers aged in barrels that previously housed bourbon, brandy and other generous elixirs.

Sadly, there's no bar or restaurant at the brewery, but Hair of the Dog's bottle-conditioned beauties can be found all over Portland. Higgins Restaurant, Horse Brass and Belmont Station are a good bet. Beer boffins keen to see the brewery in all its glory should definitely call ahead.

Widmer Brothers Brewing Company (2)
929 N. Russell St., Portland, OR 97227
T (brewery) 503 281 2437
T (Gasthaus) 503 281 3333
www.widmer.com

The Widmer brothers, Kurt & Rob, were there at the start of all this lovely craft beer business.

Along with BridgePort, the Widmer Brothers Brewing Company spearheaded the tasteful revolution in 1984 and it's currently the eleventh biggest brewery in the entire nation. The driving force behind the brewery's success has undoubtedly been the award-winning Widmer Hefeweizen, Oregon's best-selling craft beer.

"Some people think that it should be more like the European style," says Rob Widmer. "But we intended to brew it as a northwest interpretation and we've done it in the way we believe it should be done."

Beers playing a supporting role include the velvet-textured Drop Top Amber Ale; an Oud Bruin ale aged in port barrels for six months and more; and the modestly hopped Broken Halo IPA with an IBU count of 45.

Also, every year, the Widmer brothers release a new boundary-pushing beer as part of the 'W' Brewmaster Series.

Brewery tours: Fri, 3pm; Sat, 11am and noon

BREWPUBS

Downtown/Pearl

BridgePort Brewpub & Bakery (3)
See feature on pages 160-161.

Full Sail Brewing Company at RiverPlace/McCormick & Schmick's Harbourside Pilsner Room (4)
RiverPlace Marina District, 0307
SW. Montgomery, Portland, OR 97201
T (brewery) 503 222 5343
T (Pilsner Room) 503 220 1865
www.fullsailbrewing.com

If time doesn't allow a sojourn to the delightful Hood River, this riverside outpost of the Full Sail Brewing Company is a picturesque alternative. Situated next door to McCormick & Schmick's Harborside Pilsner Room restaurant, this small brewery offers cityscape views across the Willamette River and RiverPlace Marina (pretend the rumbling bridge traffic isn't there). As well as all Full Sail's specialty and seasonal beers on draught in the adjoining Pilsner Room restaurant, it's here where Full Sail's brewing mastermind John Harris is given free rein to experiment to his heart's content. Cask beers are served next door too, alongside a rotating selection of Oregon beers.

Rock Bottom Restaurant & Brewery (5)
206 SW. Morrison St., Portland, OR 97204
T 503 796 2739
www.rockbottom.com

A huge, corner site in Downtown Portland is where you'll find the only Rock Bottom in Portland. This archetypal chain brewpub, with all the requisite copper and exposed brickwork, attracts suits and families with a bustling upbeat feel and impeccable service. There are five pool tables upstairs (free before 4pm), plentiful pub tucker and thankfully the kind of experimental brewing mantra one would expect from a smaller, independent brewery. Half a dozen core beers are offered alongside the occasional cask and speciality guest beer.

Opening hours: daily, 11am-2am
Recommendation
Velvet Pale Ale (5.9%)
While the house brews generally hit the spot, this citrus-scented seasonal – a hoppy pale ale brewed with flaked oats – really impressed at the nearby Oregon Brewers Festival. Lovely and creamy with a dainty Simcoe hop bitterness. Purists beware: it's a nitro. We know, it's awful isn't it?

Rogue Ales Distillery and Public House (6)
1339 NW. Flanders St., Portland, OR 97209
T 503 222.5910
www.rogue.com
Highly recommended

Superb pub perched at the peak of the Pearl District serving more than two dozen Rogue beers and home to Oregon's first and only rum distillery. Spread over two levels, the restaurant serves delicious Kobe beef burgers, halibut fish and chips and gator gumbo up top while, below, Rogue's irreverent ales and infused spirits stir things up at the bar. Outdoor seating, too.

Opening hours: Mon-Fri, 11am-midnight;
Sat, 11am-1am; Sun, 11am-11pm

Tugboat Brewing Company (7)
711 SW. Ankeny St., Portland, OR 97205
T 503 226 2508
www.d2m.com/Tugwebsite

This former art gallery and coffee shop was converted into a brewery by watchmaker turned brewmaster Terry Nelson in March 1993. On a four-barrel system, Nelson cultivates hearty northwest ales that are unapologetically big in every way. The largely Tex-Mex food menu hovers around the $6 mark and there's free Wi-Fi, nightly live jazz jams and a hotch-potch collection of comfy furniture. A cosy venue with a beatnik vibe.

Opening hours: Mon, 5-10pm; Tue-Thu, 4pm-midnight; Fri & Sat, 5pm-1pm; Sun, closed
Recommendation
Chernobyl Stout (14%)
Only served in half-pint measures, there's no rushing this opaque, immense Imperial stout. It's strong, sweet and full of molasses, raisin and chocolate flavours.

BridgePort Brewpub & Bakery

(3)

1313 NW. Marshall St., Portland, OR 97209
T 503 241 7179
www.bridgeportbrew.com
Opening hours: Mon-Thu, 11:30am-11pm;
Fri, 11:30am -midnight; Sat, 9am-midnight;
Sun, 9am-10pm

"The wonderful thing about Portland is that everyone's doing something different," says Karl Ockert, BridgePort's head brewer. *"Americans are doing mores styles than any other country in the world and Portland is the largest craft beer maker in the US."*

It wasn't always that way. In 1984, Portland was a brewing wilderness. Superior beers were, like a supermodel that's toppled off her high heels, rather thin on the ground. Ockert, a former wildlife manager, had just graduated from UC Davis with a brewing degree when he and the winemaking Ponzi family set up a brewery in a nineteenth century old rope factory. Having started out as the 'Columbia River Brewing Company', the name was changed in 1986 following the success of Portland's first microbrew – a Scotch Ale called Bridgeporter. Over the next few years, BridgePort became renowned for what were, back then, pretty way out and wacky ales. Following the 1988 bottled release of Blue Heron Bitter, a sublime citrus sip, Ockert then raised the bar even further with his high-octane Old Knucklehead Barley Wine.

Yet it is the India Pale Ale for which BridgePort is rightly and nationally renown. First brewed in 1996, a year after the brewery had been bought by Carlos Alvarez of the Texan Gambrinus Company, Bridgeport IPA now accounts for 75% of the brewery's production.

"When we made IPA in 1996 with 50 IBUs, people thought we were out of our minds," recalls Karl. *"But now it's pretty pedestrian and I think it offers good balance compared with other IPAs. We were one of the first who pushed the IPA style and we thought that it was nothing but a fringe style. But we live in the biggest hop-growing area in the world and so it's no surprise that it's taken off."*

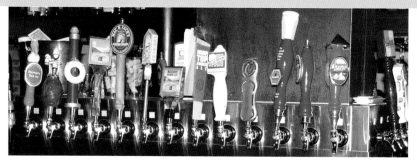

Bridgeport IPA is a classic IPA and one of the West Coast's finest beers. It's been placed on the podium at numerous brewing competitions, scooping two golds and one silver in the Brewing International Awards since 2000. It's also the inspiration for St. Austell's Proper Job, a lovely ale from Cornwall.

While its Northwest neighbours have stretched the boundaries of bitterness and brawn, BridgePort has continued to brew single-infusion beers that wouldn't look out of place in a British brewery – simple yet elegant.

"We cover the spectrum but balance is our key word," adds Karl. "We don't want to be cloyingly sweet or so hoppy that it takes the hairs off your tongue."

The brewery capacity was expanded to 100,000 barrels in 2001 and BridgePort's beers are now available in 18 states. In Portland, meanwhile, the brewpub has been renovated from a rundown pizza shack into a rather funky fusion of iron, red brick, timber and shafts of natural light.

While locals talk fondly of its former guise, the new BridgePort headquarters is a striking, sleek 12,000 square foot minimalist venue softened by candlelight, shafts of natural sunshine and the delicious aromas emitted from the bakery (a slice of marketing genius if ever there was one). In addition to three separate bars, there's an outside area perfect for Pearl people watching, a conference room and a vibe altogether different from your usual brewpub.

BridgePort IPA and others are drawn straight from the finishing tanks while cask versions of the Bridgeport beers are available here (every Tuesday is cask night) and in the smaller, rather cosier BridgePort Ale House in Portland's Hawthorne district.

THE BEERS

Blue Heron (4.9%)
Soft and rounded pale ale with a lip-smacking finish.

Beertown Brown (5.2%)
A moreish brown ale with a spicy undercurrent and a sweet, malty mouthfeel. Hints of chocolate and toffee too. Rich and robust.

Haymaker (5.3%)
An extra pale ale that comes out with the sun in the summer. Drinks like a smooth Kolsch but with a crisper finish. BridgePort's latest addition.

BridgePort IPA (5.5%)
A delectable, double-fermented drop brewed with a quintet of hops that adorns it with a delightful floral hop bitterness yet doesn't pucker the mouth with intense astringency. For many, the Northwest's finest IPA.

Ropewalk (5.6%)
Amber ale brewed in awe of the BridgePort HQ, a former rope factory. Laced with Crystal malt, it's lightly hopped and a reliable all-rounder when it comes to accompanying BridgePort's food menu.

Black Strap Stout (6%)
Smoother than a cashmere codpiece, it overflows with rich dark molasses, cocoa and an acerbic Northwest hop finish. Capped off with a thick, moustache-bothering creamy white head.

ESB (6.1%)
An English-style dry-hopped extra special bitter with an underplayed hop-driven Northwest twist.

Ebenezer (6.4%)
Four types of malt take centre stage in this rich, bronze-coloured Christmas ale. Goes down like a slim Santa in a chimney.

Old Knucklehead (9.1%)
BridgePort's underbelly gets scratched here in the shape of a stonking great barley wine. Old Knucklehead, labelled with a picture of Oregon beer writer Fred Eckhardt, takes all the normal ingredients needed for a beer and doubles the amount. Ideal as an after-dinner tipple.

Northeast Portland

Alameda Brewing Company (8)

4765 NE. Fremont St., Portland, OR 97213
T 503 460 9025
www.alamedabrewhouse.com

Sage, juniper and Willamette Valley fruit – all ingredients used by Alameda's head brewer John Eaton to create some rather impressive ales. A trio of stainless steel tanks takes centre stage at this high-ceilinged warehouse-style brewpub, located in the trendy Beaumont-Wiltshire district. Swift and smiley service and marvellous munch (don't miss the terrific Brewhouse Reuben) complement Eaton's array of adventurous yet approachable ales.

Special mention must be made of the food-matching recommendations on the beer list. The best-selling Klickitat Pale Ale, for example, is paired with salmon gyros, while the multi-award winning Black Bear XX Stout finds a foodie friend in the colossal shape of the Seven-Barrel Burger. More brewpubs should follow this gastronomic lead.

Opening hours: Sun-Thu, 11am-11pm; Fri & Sat, 11am-midnight

Recommendation
Irvington Juniper Porter (5.1%)
Smooth and full-bodied. Complex cocoa and coffee flavours finished with a fleck of floral juniper spice.

BJ's Pizza, Grill & Brewery (9)

Lloyd Center District, 825 NE. Weidler St., Portland, OR 97232
T 503 288 0111

Beer and decent pizza in comfortable, commercial and cookie-cutter surroundings. Straightforward yet consistent house ales complemented by a handful of guest beers. Rather impersonal, however, with an atmosphere to embarrass the moon.

Opening hours: Fri & Sat 11am-11pm; Sun-Thu 11am-10pm

Alameda Brewing Company: *(top)* interior; *(above)* outside

Broadway Grill & Brewery (10)
1700 NE. Broadway, Portland, OR 97232
T 503 284 4460

A sister venue to the Old Market on a corner site on the bustling NE Broadway. Trying to write something complimentary about the food here is like trying to describe the taste of cinnamon through the medium of dance. It was pretty awful and the beer wasn't much better.

Opening hours: daily, 11am-close

Edgefield (11)
2126 SW. Halsey St., Troutdale OR 97060
www.mcmenamins.com
T 503 669 8610/800 669 8610
Highly recommended

Edgefield is quite possibly the most unique drinking destination in the whole of the Pacific Northwest.

The extraordinarily grand main building, housing a hundred charming, comfy TV and telephone-free guest rooms, is a national landmark whose 38 acres of sweeping grounds have been renovated into a relaxed, rural wonderland. In addition to the peaceful ponds and gorgeous gardens, there's a fine-dining restaurant, the terrific Power Station Pub and summertime grill, a winery, movie theatre, lots of tiny boutique bars and snugs holed up in dens and sheds, and a terrific basement bar with immaculate pool tables – all decked out with McMenamins' signature whimsy.

McMenamins' largest brewery and principal distillery can also be discovered here along with regular live music, a luxurious spa and outdoor pool, an on-site glass blower and pottery maker and a par-three golf course. All in all, it's a veritable kingdom of fun just a 15-minute drive out of Portland that should, under no circumstances, be missed.

Opening hours: daily, see website

Laurelwood Brewing Company
E info@laurelwoodbrewpub.com
www.laurelwoodbrewpub.com

Not one, not two, but three Laurelwood brewpubs can be found in Portland serving up organic beers alongside conscientious cuisine.

In 2004, Laurelwood hit the big beer time when it scooped the Champion Brewery award at the prestigious World Beer Cup. The grain used in several of the house brews is cultivated without the pesky interference of artificial fertilisers, pesticides and such-like. Ditto for the food. Oregon country beef, Draper valley chicken and Carlton Farm pork are just some of the locally sourced and ethically aware farmyard features on the menu. A starter is more than enough for the modest European belly. But don't worry, if you can't finish your food then it's composted and so won't damage the planet.

In addition to the core selection of beers, Laurelwood's team of brewers are constantly conjuring up seasonal delights.

Recommendation
Free Range Red (5.9%)
Brewed with 100% organically-grown malts, this rich copper-coloured ale has loads of fresh hop flavour. A balanced, super drinkable beer.

Laurelwood Pizza Company (12)
1728 NE. 40th Ave., Portland, OR 97212
T 503 282 0622

The latest addition to the Laurelwood empire rolls a modern diner, sports bar and pizza parlour neatly into one sizeable venue. When we visited, it was very new and could have done with a bit of scuffing-up. But the food and beer were great. Free Wi-Fi.

Opening hours: Mon-Fri, 11am-midnight; Sat & Sun, 10am - midnight

Laurelwood Public House & Brewery (13)
5115 NE Sandy Blvd., Portland, OR 97213
T 503 282 0622

From here's where Laurelwood's ales hail. Peer down at the gleaming brewhouse as you munch on breakfast or belt-loosening burgers and marvel at the stained-glass window or chuckle at children making noise and utter fools of themselves in the kids' play area.

Opening hours: daily, 11am-11pm

Mashtun Brewpub (14)
Junction of 22nd & Alberta St., Portland, OR 97211
T 503 548 4491

A newcomer to the city's brewing ranks (opened in 2005), this big, bright and breezy brewpub is a modest looking place with concrete floors and wooden tables. Yet livened-up by a shiny brew-system and quirky and colourful murals, it lures in locals with its terrific, locally sourced food, free Wi-Fi and funky jukebox, a sizeable patio and unaffected atmosphere. While the decent, often daring, beers don't quite compete with Portland's best, the Bohemian Pilsner and Razorback Red stand out.

Recommendation
Mash Tun Alberta Pale Ale (5%)
A juicy jumble of flavours here with pear drops, blood orange and apple skins undercut by a shy hop bitterness and crystal malt sweetness.

McMenamins Kennedy School (15)
5736 NE. 33rd Ave., Portland, OR 97211
T 503 249 3983/888 249 3983

A nostalgic smell remains in this former grade school dating from 1915 where you can sleep in converted classrooms and drink in detention (a former janitor's closet is now a hole-in-the-wall bar). As well as 35 rooms and a school dining room, there are several dinky drinking spots, a movie theatre, a soaking pool and, best of all, a working brewery. Ideal for a last night stay should you be heading for the nearby airport.

Opening hours: daily, until late

McMenamins on Broadway (16)
1504 NE. Broadway, Portland, OR 97232
T 503 288 9498

Corner pub and restaurant with elevated views of Broadway's hustle, bustle and babes. Swing through the stained glass doors into a welcoming pool hall.

Opening hours: Mon-Sat, 11am-1am; Sun, noon-midnight

Northwest & North Portland/Nob Hill

Amnesia Brewing Company (17)
832 N. Beech, OR 97217
T 503 281 7708

Amnesia is a welcome and marked departure from your average brewpub. Since its opening in 2004, it has grown in parallel with a hip and regenerated northern Mississippi Avenue neighbourhood and gained a cult following. It's like a mini-Oktoberfest here but without all those pesky Germans being sick on their lederhosen. The only food is juicy, locally sourced saucrkraut, sausages and burgers sizzled on a BBQ. Locals hang-out under the outdoor marquee; inside, there's a small bar and a seven-barrel brewsystem. The full-bodied beers, underpinned by a Marris Otter base grain, are unfiltered and include two dry-hopped IPAs, an ESB, a Pilsner and a Porter.

Opening hours: Mon-Thu, 4pm-midnight; Fri & Sat, 2pm-2am; Sun, 4pm-midnight

Recommendation
Copacetic IPA (5.8%)
Floral Amarillo-hopped IPA with a bountiful nose and juicy, citrus-fruit flavour. Don't worry about the hazy amber hue, that makes it taste even better. Only available at the brewery.

BJ's Pizza, Grill & Brewery (18)

Jantzen Beach, 12105 N. Center Ave., Portland, OR 97217
T 503 289 5566
www.bjsbrewhouse.com

Opening hours: Sun-Thu, 11am-11pm; Fri & Sat, 11am-midnight

Below: the unforgettable Amnesia Brewing Company

Crystal Ballroom (19)

1332 W. Burnside, Portland, OR 97209
T 503 225 0047
www.mcmenamins.com

Elegant and hip, the 90-year-old Crystal Ballroom is a unique Portland live music venue with a 'floating' dancefloor, terrific sound and a strong Indie following. Underneath in a former mechanics' garage is the Ringlers Pub, a spacious pool hall with regular DJs and a glowing chandelier.

Opening hours: daily, 11.30am-2am

McMenamins

430 N. Killingsworth, Portland, OR. 97217
T (503) 223 0109
www.mcmenamins.com

The McMenamins pub empire or, as they call it, 'Kingdom of Fun', consists of more than 50 venues. The only thing that unites them is that each is diverse, distinctive and – more often than not – restored to its former glory. Schools, prisons, theatres, cinemas, country piles, residential houses and tattered old taverns, dotted all over the Pacific Northwest, have all been given a trademark fun, funky makeover by Brian and Mike McMenamin, two Portland-born and bred brothers who have bumbled their way to success. They direct multi-million dollar operations, rather fittingly, from a former mortuary in the north of the city. Their first pub, The Barley Mill, was bought in 1983 after dabbling in various ventures including a wine business and café.

"Back then, bars were pretty daunting places," recalls Brian. *"Windows were boarded over; they were smoke-filled rooms with men hunched over the bar holding a beer. We wanted to open them up, make them more family-friendly and make them a more important part of the community."*

Keen home-brewers, with plenty of European tours of beer-drinking duty under their belts, Mike and Brian were instrumental in cultivating Oregon's celebrated beer culture. In 1984, along with the Bridgeport Brewing Company and Widmer Bros Brewing Company, Brian and Mike successfully lobbied Oregon legislature to relax its ban on brewing and selling beer on the same premises.

Having kickstarted the brewpub revolution, McMenamins brewed their first beer in 1984 at the Hillsdale Brewery and Pub. *"When we started, it was illegal to have a brewpub, but we got behind Portland micro-brewers as we wanted food and drink that was fresh and local,"* says Brian. *"In 1985, we had 30 taps and then we began brewing McMenamins beer – as it couldn't get more fresh and local than that!"*

With money tight, the brothers scoured their home city for new venues to revamp.

"In the olden days we knew Portland and places would just crop up," added Brian. *"You couldn't really plan anything and we just had to work with what was in front of us. Some of them were plain dumb ideas from a business sense but we're stubborn Irish types and when they don't work we just work at them until they do. We experiment and we get there eventually."*

On buying a new site, McMenamins arms its very own team of five artists and two historians with the task of dressing the pub and brewery in a way that befits its past and roots the pub back into its surroundings. Known for their psychedelic murals on the walls, exotic sculptures, esoteric ironmongery and all-round quirkiness, McMenamins pubs epitomise the amiable peculiarity of the Pacific Northwest.

They're all heavily family-friendly places that play down TVs, sports and loud music in favour of having a decent drink, a bite to eat and a chat with buddies in unique surroundings. While anecdote suggests that the food and drink can fluctuate, the prices at McMenamins are extremely reasonable and the staff were, without exception, on fantastic form.

With more than 20 different breweries, the selection of house beers differs from venue to venue yet each brewer is given the freedom to develop his or her own unique style.

Having kicked off with a green energy program in September 2005 for just the seasonal ales, the McMenamins breweries are now using 100%, eco-friendly wind power to brew their ales and committed to using entirely green energy all year round.

McMenamins' brewers are trained in house and tend not to be recruited from brewing school. *"We like to get in homebrewers who know what it's like to brew at grass roots,"* adds Brian. *"Most of our brewpubs have pretty rudimentary six barrel systems but there's plenty of creativity going on.*

"Our beer and food are sold at working men's prices. We're sensitive. We don't want to be the cheapest nor the most expensive in town – but stick to the middle ground."

As well as the brewing operations, McMenamins also owns a winery and a distillery (whisky, brandy and gin) at its magnificent Edgefield venue and even roasts 40,000lbs of its own coffee beans.

THE BEERS

Ruby (4.4%)
Using more than 50lbs of hand-macerated fruits, this er... ruby coloured beer blows raspberries all over your palate and then leaves with a crisp, tart farewell.

Cascade Head (4.5%)
Don't be hoodwinked folks, Cascade is not made with Hallertau hops and not Cascade. Named after the National Wildlife Preserve in Lincoln City, Oregon, it's a refreshing stepping stone to more robust hop-heavy ales.

Nebraska Bitter (4.6%)
A better-behaved younger sister to Hammerhead with a more subdued Cascade influence.

Edgefield Wheat (4.7%)
Clear and crisp hefeweizen that gives the glad-eye to those with a taste for a less fruity drop.

Bagdad Ale (5%)
An ale masquerading as a lawnmower lager, Bagdad is a solar-powered Sterling-hopped seller that slips down easy in the summer.

Crystal Ale (5.1%)
The malt triumvirate (Pale, Munich and Crystal) give a rich enough backdrop for the sprightly Hallertauer hops to do its spicy stuff.

Black Rabbit Porter (5.5%)
Smoother and sweeter than Hammerhead, this approachable porter flies out the tap at Edgefield where an elusive black rabbit once roamed.

Hammerhead (5.9%)
Cascade-heavy classic Northwest pale ale and McMenamins signature best-seller. Check out the lovely creme caramel malt base, or is that just us?

Terminator Stout (6.5%)
A firm favourite with coffee, nuts and lots of toasty roasty-ness softened by bitter Cascade. To paraphrase Arnie: "I'll Be Black".

Sunflower IPA (6.7%)
A citrus scent introduces a palate of lime jelly, marmalade and grapefruit in a pale ale that won't intimidate the average Joe but should make the radar of hopheads.

Laurelwood NW Public House (20)

2327 NW. Kearney St., Portland, OR 97210
T 503 228 5553

Nestled in the debonair neighbourhood of
Nob Hill, Laurelwood's other home is a
relaxing Victorian venue with extensive
outdoor seating, seven Laurelwood beers
(and one seasonal) on tap and the same chow
as its parent brewpub. Good after a hard
day's flashing the cash in the nearby shops.

Opening hours: daily, 11am-11pm

Lompoc 5th Quadrant (21)

3901-B N. Williams Ave., Portland, OR 97277
T 503 288 3996
www.newoldlompoc.com

A more family friendly, upscale northern
outpost of the Lompoc empire. Opened in
January 2006 in the up-and-coming 'Nickel'
part of Portland, the beers are brewed on-site
and matched to an inspiring array of dishes.
Lompoc Strong Draft (LSD), a smoky American strong ale, does a merry gastronomic jig
with the Chorizo penne pasta. They do a mean
Bloody Mary too (just $2 on the weekend).

Opening hours: Sun-Thu, 11am-11pm; Fri & Sat,
11am-midnight

The Lucky Labrador Beer Hall (22)

1945 NW. Quimby St., Portland, OR 97209
T 503 517 4352
www.luckylab.com

A vast former trucking warehouse (on the
street that gave the Simpsons' mayor his
name) is what the latest Lucky Lab calls
home. A huge industrial crane hovers over
the tables, pictures of dogs deck the walls
and the simple pub food ranges from bento
and sandwiches to salads.

Opening hours: Mon, 11am-10pm; Tue-Sat, 11am-
midnight; Sun, noon-10pm

MacTarnahan's Taproom (23)
(formerly Portland Brewing Company)

Northwest Industrial District, 2730 NW. 31st Ave.,
Portland, OR 97210
T 503 228 5269
www.macsbeer.com

Founded by more than 5,000 shareholders
in 1986, the Portland Brewing Company was

purchased in 2004 by Pyramid Breweries
and renamed MacTarnahan's Taproom
after the founder Robert Malcolm 'Mac'
MacTarnahan – the grand old man of
Oregon craft brewing who sadly passed
away in his sleep in October 2004 just
hours after celebrating the official opening
of the newly named brewpub. At this
well-established stalwart of the Portland
brewing scene a huge gas-fired Bavarian
brewhouse takes centre stage, including
two 40-barrel copper brewing kettles.
While the décor and food lean towards
Germany, the beers are underpinned by
British and American influences. Mac's
Amber Ale boasts a substantial following
while other popular brews include the
devilishly smooth Black Watch Cream
Porter and rasping Highland Pale Ale.

Opening hours: Mon, 11am-9pm; Tue-Thu,
11am-10pm; Fri, 11am-11pm; Sat, noon-11pm;
Sun, noon-9pm

Recommendation
MacTarnahan's Amber Ale (5.3%)
*The smooth malty tones of Portland's original amber
ale sharpened by the presence of dry-hopped Cascade.
Simple but very drinkable.*

Widmer Gasthaus (25)

955 N. Russell St., Portland, OR 97227
T (Gasthaus) 503 281 3333
www.widmer.com

The affable Widmer Gasthaus, situated opposite the brewery in a historically protected building, is a big old European place that serves up Germanic cuisine such as schnitzel, fondue, beer sausages and the rather scrumptious Bourbon Bock Cheese Burger. All the Widmer beers, fresh and in great nick, are available here.

Opening hours: Sun-Thu, 11am-11pm; Fri & Sat, 11am-1am

Recommendation
Widmer Hefeweizen (4.8%)
A very approachable American take on a Hefeweizen with less of the expected clove and banana fruitiness. Claiming to be neither Bavarian or Belgian in style, it is unfiltered and very refreshing yet may baffle Weizen-loving purists.

Left: The Lucky Labrador Beer Hall

The New Old Lompoc (24)

1616 NW. 23rd Ave., Portland, OR 97210
T 503 225 1855
www.newoldlompoc.com

Formerly a legendary tavern dating back to the Forties, and the 'Old Lompoc' brewery since 1996, the 'New Old Lompoc' gained its oxymoronic moniker in 2000 when new owners took it over, re-jigged the beer, added a kitchen and threw liquor behind the bar. There's a smashing suntrap of a garden out-back but if it's raining, and it will be, stick to the compact and cosy locals' bar where Lompoc's beers, and a quartet of guest ales, are slung by friendly staff. Mention must be made of the delicious Portobello Mushroom Sandwich – tasty enough to turn the head of even the most salivating, red-blooded carnivore.

Opening hours: Sun-Thu, 11am-1am; Fri & Sat, 11am-2.30am

Recommendation
C-Note Imperial Pale (6.9%)
Brought to you by the letter 'C'. Crystal, Cluster, Cascade, Chinook, Centennial, Columbus and Challenger – they're all Northwest hops and they're all in here. At 100 IBUs, it itches your brain and makes it wobble.

Southeast Portland/Hawthorne

Clinton Street Brewing (26)

2520 SE. Clinton St., Portland, OR 97202

T 503 238 5588

www.rubbergashproductions.com

Before setting up Oregon's smallest commercial brewery in 2005, brewer Michael Atkins was a legend among Portland students for supplying his beer to university house parties... allegedly. Now he's gone legit, conjuring up some fairly remarkable ales. The 'brewery' is no bigger than a home brewing set-up, and its modest size means the beer choice is forever changing. Whatever's on tap, however, can be taken to the Clinton Street Theater next door and savoured in front of a movie with a slice of pizza. Distinctive and balanced, the beers were in fine fettle on our visit and locals were waxing lyrical about Mike's efforts. The décor is staggeringly simple with a scattering of tables, a small four-stool bar area and a few pieces of funky art. A lively little place with great beer.

Opening hours: vary

Recommendation

Clinton Street Dunkelweizen (6%)

Dark, fruity and full-bodied with a touch of banoffee pie.

Highland Pub (27)

4225 SE. 182nd, Gresham, OR 97030

T 503 665 3015

www.mcmenamins.com

The stainless steel fermenting tanks you see in this Gaelic-leaning Gresham brewpub were once part of England's renowned Whitbread Brewery. One marked departure from most British boozers is the intricate psychedelic-Italianate chandelier dangling above the main bar.

Opening hours: Mon, 11am-10pm; Tue-Thu, 11am-11pm; Fri, 11am-1am; Sat, 11am-midnight; Sun, noon-10pm

Hopworks Urban Brewery (28)

2944 SE. Powell Blvd., Portland OR 97202

T 503 201 8957

www.hopworksbeer.com

One of Portland's newest craft breweries, Hopworks Urban is the brainchild of the award-winning brewer Christian Ettinger, formerly of Laurelwood Brewing. Although the eco-friendly brewpub was yet to open on our visit, locals at the Oregon Brewers Festival were getting really rather enthusiastic about the prospect of drinking the organic handcrafted brews. And if Christian's prototype IPA at the OBF was anything to go by, this eager expectation is by no means misplaced. A full line of fine beers including adventurous seasonals will be available and some inventive food dishes too. A beer garden and decking have also been built.

Opening hours: Sun-Thu, 11am-11pm; Fri & Sat, 11am-midnight

Recommendation

Hopworks Organic IPA (6.5%)

An exceptionally hoppy IPA (IBU 71) in the West Coast tradition using Amarillo, Centennial, Ahtanum but not Cascade hops. The malt spring board is all-organic.

Lompoc Hedge House (29)

3412 SE. Division St., Portland, OR 97202

T 503 235 2215

www.newoldlompoc.com

They say it's a pub but we reckon it's actually someone's house. As this is a great spot for a pint or three, let's hope the owners don't come back and tell everyone to clear off. There's a tiny bar serving Lompoc beers, a handful of simple booths and an impressive porch where you can watch the world drift by. It may feel like suburbia but it's easily incorporated into a pub crawl along with the nearby Clinton Street bars.

Opening hours: Mon-Fri, 11.30am-midnight; Sat & Sun, 11.30am-11pm

The Lucky Labrador Brewing Company & Brew Pub (30)

915 SE. Hawthorne Blvd., Portland, OR 97214

T 503 236 3555

www.luckylab.com

The Lucky Labrador Brewing Company started brewing at this old roofing warehouse in 1994, where dog art adorns the walls – portraits of Labradors at every turn – serving homebrewed hooch. There's a dog-friendly outdoor patio, the beers tend to have dog-themed names and, in October,

Roots Brewing Company – dedicated to organic beer

'Dogtoberfest' attracts both the two and four-legged to a charity dog wash and beer – man's second best friend. Full of flavour yet modest in strength and IBU, the core range of seven ales boasts a bark bigger than its bite. As well as several seasonals, there's a regular cask option, guest ale and (CAMRA members, look away now) rotating nitro tap.

Opening hours: Mon, 11am-10pm; Tue-Sat, 11am-midnight; Sun, noon-10pm
Recommendation
Hawthorne Best Bitter (4.5%)
Ahhh, a taste of home. A quintessentially English pint that's dry hopped, refreshingly drinkable and with a nose more delicate and aromatic than a potpourri-sniffing puppy.

Philadelphia's Steaks & Hoagies   (31)
6410 SE. Milwaukie Ave., Portland, OR 97202
T 503 239 8544

A tiny little Westmoreland café-cum-brewpub where the small three-barrel brewery plays second fiddle to the unabashed celebration of Philly Cheese Steak – an artery-clogging feast of grilled steak, onions and hoagies.

Opening hours: Mon-Thu, 9am-10pm; Fri & Sat, 9am-11pm; Sun, 10am-8pm
Recommendation
Ginger Hefeweizen (4.5%)
Cloudy gold ginger beer that's spicy and sweet and

made with wheat. Dare we say it, but this would be gorgeous poured over ice and sipped on the outdoor patio. (Beer snobs: please don't issue death threats, it's just a suggestion.)

Roots Brewing Company   (32)
1520 SE. Seventh Ave., Portland, OR 97214
T 503 235 7668
www.rootsorganicbrewing.com

A friendly and inviting Tiki-style Hawaiian bar and the only brewery in Portland dedicated entirely to organic beer. Craig Nicholls and Jason McAdam, formerly of Alameda and McMenamins breweries respectively, began the business in March 2005, brewing an enchanting hop-free Burghead Heather Ale and the bountiful black-cherry flavoured eXXXcalibur Imperial Stout which, weighing in at a hefty 8.6%, is only served in 10oz glasses. An impressive range of organic wines and food is available too – the jerk-rubbed smoked pork wrap flick works wonders with the beer below. Guest taps are rotated while kids are welcome till 8pm during the week and an extra hour on the weekends.

Recommendation
Woody IPA (6%)
Dry-hopped tree-hugging ale with shed-loads of Magnum hops and more than 70 IBUs. The 'Let Us Give You A Woody' T-shirt is worth a mention too.

Southwest Portland

The Fulton Pub (33)
0618 SW. Nebraska St., Portland, OR 97239
T 503 246 9530
www.mcmenamins.com

Cool and cosy Macadam neighbourhood hangout signed up to the McMenamins vision in 1988. Great garden and a refreshingly unpretentious crowd.
Opening hours: Mon-Thu, 11am-midnight; Fri, 11am-1am; Sat, 1am-midnight; Sun, noon-11pm

Hillsdale Brewery & Public House (34)
1505 SW. Sunset Blvd., Portland, OR 97201
T 503 246 3938
www.mcmenamins.com

A low-rise pub and McMenamins museum that holds the bowl-shaped planter that originally held the mash for the company's very first onsite brew (October 1985) and a framed scribbled note depicting the first brewing recipe. A legend in its own lunchtime, the Hillsdale also sports some funky neon on the ceiling.
Opening hours: Mon-Thu, 11am-midnight; Fri & Sat, 11am-1am; Sun, noon-11pm

John Barleycorns (35)
14610 SW. Sequoia Pkwy., Tigard, OR 97223
T 503 684 2688
www.mcmenamins.com

A cathedralesque and cosy cavern named after the 1960s Traffic album *John Barleycorn Must Die* and a ballad by 18th-century Scottish poet Robert Burns. You may have to step out into the serene garden after a glass of JCB Strong, the pub's velvet-gloved heavyweight ale with a strength of 8%.
Opening hours: Mon, 11am-midnight; Tue-Thu, 11am-1am; Sat, 11am-1am; Sun, noon-midnight

Lucky Labrador Public House (36)
7675 SW Capitol Hwy., Portland, OR 97219
T 503 244-2537
www.luckylab.com

A cosy 1920s kennel where we wanted to stay longer but, like the Littlest Hobo, we just kept moving on. Maybe tomorrow...
Opening hours: Mon-Sat, 11am-midnight; Sun, noon-10pm

Max's Fanno Creek (37)
12562 SW. Main St., Tigard, OR 97222
T 877 629 7273

Brewer Max Tieger opened his bouncing brewpub on the banks of Fanno Creek in 2007. The ten-barrel brewery, displayed behind two big windows, furnishes punters with more than 20 bold and adventurous standard and seasonal beers – mostly of a Belgian bent.

The Strawberry Blonde Farmer's Daughter stops short of sickly sweet, there were plenty of local plaudits for the viscous Vanilla Porter. Max's Nit Wit was one of the few Belgian wheat beers we encountered boasting both body and citrus bite.
Opening hours: Sun-Thu, 11am-9pm; Fri & Sat, 11am-11pm
Recommendation
Max's Fanno Kriek (7%)
Not just a clever jeux-de-mot, this cherry beer aged in French Oak is tart and sweet in all the right places.

The Old Market Pub & Brewery (38)
6959 SW. Multnomah Blvd., Portland, OR 97223
T 503 244 2337
www.drinkbeerhere.com

A 15-barrel brewhouse knocks out some solid if unspectacular suds at this brewpub in the Burbs. A former greengrocer, located in the leafy neighbourhood of southwest Portland, this standard beer-making bar and restaurant is best known for its first ever creation – Mr Toad's Wild Red Ale – and the appropriately titled HOP ON! There are more than 20 taps, ample pub grub, pool tables and shuffleboard too.
Opening hours: Mon-Thu, 11am-midnight; Fri & Sat, 11am-1am; Sun, 11am-11pm

Raccoon Lodge & Brew Pub (39)

7424 SW. Beaverton-Hillsdale Hwy., Portland,
OR 97225
T 503 296 0110
www.raclodge.com

Reminiscent of a hunting lodge, the Raccoon was created in 1998 by Portland Brewing pioneer Art Larrance and holds a ten-barrel brewery in which a selection of approachable ales are brewed. As well as the expected brewpub fayre, Raccoon offers five varieties of fries (sweet potato, shoestring, ale-battered steak fries, Yukon Gold and tater tots) accompanied by eight dipping sauces – delicious with the sweet and sturdy Blonde Bock. Pool tables are in the basement.

Opening hours: Mon-Sat, 11.30am-10pm; Sun, 11.30am-9pm
Recommendation
Ring Tail Pale (4.1%)
A quaffable golden stepping stone for any mainstream lager-swilling naysayers.

West Portland

Cornelius Pass Roadhouse & Imbrie Hall (40)

4045 NW. Cornelius Pass Rd., Hillsboro, OR 97124
T 503 640 6174

Former farmstead converted into a colourful brewery, big ol' pub, renovated 19th-century barns and a bar set in what can only be described as a shed. Drink beneath high wooden beams and rafters and next to wood stoves in the pub or betwixt the tall trees outside in the summer.

Opening hours: Mon, 11am-10pm; Tue-Thu, 11am-11pm; Fri-Sun, 11am-late

Oak Hills Brewpub (41)

14740 NW. Cornell Rd., Portland, OR 97229
T 503 645 0286
www.mcmenamins.com

Beer boffins will be bowled over by the multi-coloured brewery, complete with painted fermentation tanks, in this cosy L-shaped pub lined with booths and a bar and open kitchen.

Opening hours: Mon-Thu, 11am-midnight; Fri & Sat, 11am-1am; Sun, noon-midnight

BEER BARS

Downtown/Pearl

Apotheke (42)

1314 NW. Glisan St., Portland, OR 97209
T 503 241 7866

Austere, sparse, stark, whitewashed décor warmed by kaleidoscopic lighting, bass lines and beats and dangling works of minimalist art: it's a drinking scene like no other in Portland. The Apotheke is unique and bound to polarise opinion.

Predominantly a spirits bar with the feel of a modern art gallery, it refuses to serve cocktails or mixers. Instead, drinkers are encouraged to sample spirits in unadulterated form – either neat or on the rocks – or cherry pick from an astonishingly broad list of European elixirs, herbal liqueurs and lesser-known libations. Beware, they're sure to put hairs on your chest and daft thoughts in your head.

The beer menu, meanwhile, is a thoughtfully compiled showcase for European craft brewing with a fantastic selection of bottles from, for the most part, Belgium, Germany and Scandinavia. With all this alcohol sloshing around, you should also graze on a selection of European dishes.

Opening hours: Tue-Thu, 5pm-midnight; Fri & Sat, 5pm-2am

Bailey's Taproom (43)

213 SW. Broadway, Portland, OR 97205
www.baileystaproom.com

Bailey's is a Downtown bar serving artisan beer, wine, chocolate and cheese. Owner Geoffrey Phillips has cold-shouldered the mainstream in favour of a carefully compiled collection of American micros hailing predominantly from Oregon and the Pacific Northwest on 20 rotating taps and in bottle – Hair of the Dog Adam, Stone Vertical Epics and Dick's Imperial Stout to name but a few. The cheese is sourced from the West Coast (including the Rogue creamery), there are chocolate cookies and truffles from Eugene, Oregonian pinots and dessert wines and free Wi-Fi so you can email your friends and make them jealous. A true gastronome's delight.

Opening hours: Mon-Sat, 4pm-midnight

BridgePort Ale House (44)

3632 SE Hawthorne Blvd., Portland, OR 97214

T 503 233 6540

See BridgePort feature on pages 160-161.

Opening hours: Sun-Mon, 11.30am-10pm; Fri, 11.30-11pm; Sat, 11am-11pm

Henry's 12th Street Tavern (45)

10 NW. 12th Ave., Portland, OR 97209

T 503 227 5320

www.henrystavern.com

A vast Pearl District bar that brings micros to the baseball-capped masses. Encased in a portion of the historic Blitz-Weinhard Brewery, Henry's is home to more than 100 draft beers including 60 craft brews from across the States. The kegs chill in a glass cooler above the bar and there's even a chilled strip running the length of the bar to keep the pints cool. At 18,000 square feet, it exudes a rather impersonal corporate feel while the high-heeled crowd seems more interested in shots and mainstream fizz than the micros. Billiards upstairs and the outside courtyard is nice and lively in the summer.

Opening hours: Sun-Thu, 11am-11pm; Fri & Sat, 11am-midnight

Higgins (46)

1239 SW. Broadway, Portland, OR 97205

T 503 222 9070

Higgins advocates artisan beer in a manner that befits its true gastronomic status, and the beer menu makes for a drooling read. Bottled highlights include Poperings Hommel Ale and St. Bernadus Abt 12 (60th anniversary special edition) from Belgium; England's Samuel Smith's Imperial Stout; Aventinus Weizen Eisbok from Germany, Trois Pistoles from Canada and a champagne-style Brazilian brew called Eisenbahn Lust ($45). As well as 11 draft beers (including Hair of the Dog and Lindemans Framboise), Higgins boasts its very own knowledgeable beer sommelier among its friendly and immaculately turned out staff.

Artisan beer at Higgins

Diners and drinkers can eat in the genteel restaurant, take it a little more relaxed in the fine-dining bistro or simply grab a stool at the bar for a beer and one of its sublime sandwiches. Whether with a mate or a date, don't leave Portland without hitting Higgins.

Opening hours: Mon-Fri, 11.30am-12am; Sat, 4pm-2.30am; Sun, 4pm-midnight

Market Street Pub (47)

1526 SW. 10th, Portland, OR 97201

T 503 497 0160

Long and lively L-shaped urban bar in Downtown Portland attracting Portland State University students and nearby theatre-goers with the vibe of a no-nonsense British boozer.

Opening hours: Mon-Sat, 11am-1am; Sun, noon-midnight

Mary's Club (48)

129 SW. Broadway, Portland, OR 97205

T 503 227 3023

Portland's oldest strip club. This legendary nightspot, here since 1954, has its very own 'Mary's' microbrew along with a whole host of American ales. Adults only.

Opening hours: 365 days a year, 11am-2.30am

Strumptown: uber-trendy coffee shop in Downtown

McMenamins Mission Theater (49)
1624 NW. Glisan, Portland, OR 97209
T 503 223 4527
www.mcmenamins.com
This former Swedish evangelical Mission is
now a characterful movie theatre and live
music venue with a horseshoe-shaped mezzanine and huge light-streaming windows.

The Ram's Head (50)
2282 NW. Hoyt, Portland, OR 97210
T 503 221 0098
Red-bricked pub, bang-in-the-middle of the
trendy,urban 23rd shopping district, which
attracts hip locals with its wacky wall
doodlings, curvy booths and laid-back air.
Opening hours: Mon-Thu, 11am-midnight; Fri & Sat,
11am-1am; Sun, noon-11pm

Ringlers Annex (51)
1223 SW. Stark, Portland, OR 97205
T 503 525 0520
www.mcmenamins.com
This espresso bar, diminutive drinking hole
and bistro is ideal for people watching. For
those who don't want to see or be seen, head
downstairs to the underground cellar bar.
Opening hours: Sun-Wed, 4pm-midnight; Thu-Sat,
4pm-2.30am

Stumptown (52)
128 SW 3rd, Portland, OR 97204-2705
T 503 255 6194
Recommended
Bike messengers, hipsters and some seriously
silly haircuts tap away on laptops beneath
exposed brickwork, local artwork and dangling orbs of light at this long, airy and uber-
trendy coffee shop in Downtown. Together
with cakes, pastries and a baffling selection of
ornately named coffees, the long wooden bar
is home to an exceptional selection of bottled
beers including Aventinus, Orval, Young's
Old Nick Barley Wine and Westmalle Tripel.
The draught range leans towards
Belgium too with Chimay White, La Chouffe
and Rodenbach on the pour. Music comes
courtesy of twin turntables at the end of the
bar and there's a library of baffling cult
magazines to flick through.
Opening hours: Mon-Sat, 7am-9pm; Sun, 7am-8pm

Northeast Portland

Beulahland (53)
118 NE. 28th Ave., Portland, OR 97232
T 503 235 2794
www.beulahlandpdx.com
Beulahland is a glorious slice of Portland underbelly. This grimy, grungy coffee-and-ale house pours sessions, imports and local hop heroes to an, ahem, artistic crowd. Tap handles dangle from the ceiling and funky local art hangs on the wall; it's kitsch, achingly cool and, some would say, a little bit edgy at night. With good value food, live music acts, DJs and a pool table, it's an ideal stop prior to, or after, visiting the nearby Laurelhurst Theatre.
Opening hours: Mon-Fri, 8.30am-2.30am; Sat & Sun, 9am-2.30am

Bink's (Tavern/Pizza Joint) (54)
2715 NE. Alberta St,., Portland, OR 97211
T 503 493 4430
Comfy neighbourhood tavern that draws an upbeat Alberta crowd. The solid beer choice and cocktails slightly overshadow the simple pizza-led pub food but it's nevertheless a lively locals hang-out.
Opening hours: daily, noon-2am

Concordia Ale House (55)
3276 NE. Killingsworth St., Portland, OR 97211
T 503 287 3929
Highly recommended
Brilliant beer bar in the Alberta district with 22 constantly rotating taps and an unswerving dedication to the lesser-spotted delights of Belgium, the Pacific North-West and beyond. Extraordinarily vast range (featuring beers we'd never heard of nor sampled), overseen by educated and enthusiastic bartenders while the food ticks both the quantity and quality boxes.
Opening hours: Mon-Fri, 11am-2.30am; Sat & Sun, 9am-2.30am

Gustav's (56)
5035 NE. Sandy Blvd., Portland, OR 97123
T 503 288 5503
www.gustavs.net
If there's one thing the Germans do better than efficiency, automobiles and reliable trains, and attracting lazy national stereotypes, it's beer. And, nestled between the two Laurelwood bars on Sandy Boulevard, there's plenty of it here. Spaten beers, Franziskaner and Paulaner can all be found within the ornate walls of this German restaurant and beer house along with a meat-laden German menu, musicians and singing staff.
Opening hours: Mon-Fri, 11am-11pm; Sat & Sun, 11am-midnight

Moon & Sixpence (57)
2014 NE. 42nd Ave., Portland, OR 97213
T 503 288 7802
Another English-theme pub. There's nonsensical memorabilia on the walls, European footy on the telly and a couple of hand-pulled casks on the bar. The ubiquitous 'British' range (Stella, Boddingtons and Newcastle Brown Ale) is improved by two Belgians on tap, a host of hop-heavy micros and a bottled list comprising Trappists and farmhouse ales from Belgium.
Opening hours: Tue-Thu, 3pm-midnight; Fri & Sat, 3pm-1am; Sun, 4pm-midnight

Northwest & North Portland/Nob Hill

The Blue Moon Tavern & Grill (58)
432 NW. 21st, Portland, OR 97209
T 503 223 3184
www.mcmenamins.com
Pagoda-style roof caps a snug, arty and friendly pub on 'Trendyfirst' 21st Avenue.
Opening hours: Mon-Sat, 11am-1am; Sun, noon-midnight

Chapel Pub (59)
430 N. Killingsworth St., Portland, OR 97217
T 503 286 0372
www.mcmenamins.com
Welcome to McMenamins HQ! The stunning Little Chapel of the Chimes, created in 1932, now houses a family-friendly neighborhood pub with a picturesque outdoor patio.
Opening hours: Mon-Wed, 11am-11pm; Thu, 11am-midnight; Fri & Sat, 11am-1am; Sun, noon-11pm

La Bodega (60)

1325 NE. Fremont St., Portland, OR 97212
T 503 943 6099
www.labodegapdx.com

Spanish tapas bar and bottle store where both the grain and the grape are celebrated in style.

A dizzying array of imported beers from Belgium, Britain and Germany rubs shoulders with an equally eclectic range of micros and big beers of America. Once you've cherry-picked from the 100-strong selection, you can either sip them at the bar, on the patio or, for a 25% discount, take them away with you. You can bring in your own food but why would you when there's mouth-watering small tapas plates of delicious meats, artisan cheeses and sandwiches. The food is thoughtfully paired with the beer and wine while, on Sundays between 3-6pm, bespoke beer and wine tastings are hosted.

Opening hours: Tue-Sun, 11am-10pm

McMenamins Tavern & Pool (61)

1716 NW. 23rd, Portland, OR 97210
T 503 227 0929
www.mcmenamins.com

Plenty of elbow-bending and elbow room to be had at this arty, eight-ball eaterie just down the road from the New Old Lompoc.

Opening hours: Mon, 11am-midnight; Tue-Sat, 11am-1am; Sun, noon-11pm

Pix Patisserie

www.pixpatisserie.com

Extravagant epicurean enlightenment awaits at this trio of Portland patisseries. Specialising in elegant pastries, idyllic ice creams, mouth-watering chocolates and handsome, hand-crafted cakes, Pix's unshakable allegiance to the art of indulgent consumption also incorporates quality coffees, wines, spirits and, lest we forget, beautiful beer. To accompany the edible masterworks, Pix (aka pastry chef Cheryl Wakerhauser) carefully plundered the craft beers of Belgium and America and has come away with everything from US Pilsners to lesser-spotted Lambics.

Pix Patisserie (62)

3901 N. Williams Ave., Portland, OR 97227
T 503 282 6539

This northern outpost of the Pix Empire is a kitsch celebration of cakes, Stumptown coffee and a cornucopia of bizarre booze. Names on the outstanding bottled brew list include Chimay, Deus Brut des Flandres ($35), Goliath Tripel, a pair of Lindeman Lambics, Hair of the Dog Adam, Rochefort 10 and, if you're after something a little less 'big', Victory Pilsner. As well as pairing the beers with chocolates, this red-wallpapered lounge also serves up the much-neglected gastronomic triumph that is the beer float. Pix vanilla ice cream + Raspberry Lambic Beer = jolly good idea. Thursday is flight night during which various libations are poured with a little bit of education and knowledge thrown in for free. As if that's not enough, there are free movies on a Monday. Marvellous.

Opening hours: Mon-Thu, 7am-midnight; Fri, 7am-2am; Sat, 8am-2am; Sun, 9pm-midnight

St Johns Theater & Pub (63)

8203 N. Ivanhoe, Portland, OR 97203
T 503 283 8520
www.mcmenamins.com
Highly recommended

This impressive domed stronghold has been a Lutheran Church, American Legion Post, bingo parlour and home for Gypsy wakes before, finally, conversion into a hugely impressive bar and cinema showing art films, silver screen and cult classics for just $3 a throw.

Opening hours: Mon-Thu, 11am-11pm; Fri & Sat, 11am-1am; Sun, noon-11pm

White Eagle Saloon (64)

836 N. Russell St., Portland, OR 97227
T 503 282 6810
www.mcmenamins.com

Tequilla-slamming, serious-boogying and downright hedonistic hotel and live music venue that's one of the oldest in town. Outdoor deck and beer garden as well.

Opening hours: Mon-Thu, 11am-1am; Fri & Sat, 11am-2.30am; Sun, 4pm-11pm

Southeast Portland/Hawthorne

Acropolis (65)
8325 SE. McLoughlin, Portland, OR 97202
T 503 231 9611

Juicy five-dollar steaks, glamorous dancing ladies decanting themselves from their clothes on stage and, lest we forget, more than 50 microbrews on tap. Not for the faint-hearted and, needless to say, adults only.
Opening hours: daily, until 2.30am

Back Stage Bar (66)
3702 SE. Hawthorne, Portland, OR 97214
T 503 236 9234
www.mcmenamins.com
Highly recommended

This unfeasibly high Hawthorne hangout stretches eight storeys from floor to ceiling. A quite phenomenal pool joint and pub behind the Bagdad Theater & Pub, it is decorated with a giant mural telling tales of the building's previous guises.
Opening hours: Mon-Fri, 4pm-1am; Sat, 2pm-1am; Sun, 2pm-midnight

The Bagdad Theater & Pub (67)
3702 SE. Hawthorne Blvd., Portland OR 97214
T 503 236 9234
www.mcmenamins.com

This magical Mediterranean movie hall has been a shrine to celluloid adventure for four generations now. It's a fine-looking cinema where pizza and pints can be consumed amid barrelled arches, ornate wrought iron, colourful mosaic work and fairytale murals.
Opening hours: Mon-Sat, 11am-1am; Sun, noon-midnight

The Barley Mill Pub (68)
1629 SE. Hawthorne, Portland, OR 97214
T 503 231 1492
www.mcmenamins.com

No-fuss establishment with all the artefacts, eccentric neon and artwork you'd expect from McMenamins' oldest pub. Outdoor tables and a conservatory are good spots when the sun shines.
Opening hours: Mon-Thu, 11am-midnight; Fri & Sat, 11am-1am; Sun, noon-midnight

Basement Pub (69)
1028 SE. 12th Ave., Portland OR 97214
T 503 231 6068
www.basementpub.com

A straightforward yet friendly neighbourhood dive bar that attracts a mixture of locals and hipsters. It lacks airs and graces but with cheap and cheerful food, a handful of local craft beers, nostalgic video games and a rocking jukebox, it's a splendid setting for a serious session (drink responsibly though).
Opening hours: daily, 3pm-2am

Belmont Station Biercafe (70)
4500 SE. Stark, Portland, OR 97215
T 503 232 8538
www.belmont-station.com

Located just down the road from the legendary Horse Brass pub, the Belmont Bier Café is a chameleon venue that fuses a café, deli, corner store and bottled beer emporium neatly into one. There are nearly a thousand bottled beers (all stored lovingly under UV-filtered light) to take away or drink next door in the deli area where four draught beers, no-nonsense sandwiches, salads and soups with beer chips and chutney are served. A neat little place for lunch and a shrewd stop before a road trip out of town.
Opening hours: Mon-Sat, 11.30am-10pm; Sun, noon-9pm

The Blue Monk (71)
3341 SE. Belmont St., Portland, OR 97214
T 503 595 0575
www.thebluemonk.com

Italian restaurant and shadowy jazz basement bar on Belmont where drinkers can embark on a foot-tapping, goatee-stroking, globe-trotting tour of world brewing. Lesser-spotted American microbrews line up on tap while the vast bottled selection, numbering more than three dozen, throws up some seriously big beers (Stone, AleSmith and Deus from Belgium) alongside European and out-of-state imports (Chimay, Dogfish, Cooper's and Schneider).

Opening hours: Sun-Thu, 5pm-1am; Fri & Sat, 5pm-2am

Clinton Street Pub (72)

2516 SE. Clinton St., Portland, OR 97202
T 503 236 7137

This cracking old neighbourhood bar next to the Clinton Street Theater has been oiling the wheels of locals and movie buffs for more than 50 years. Two years ago, new owners spruced things up a little without wiping away the enduringly dingy, dive bar vibe. A dozen microbrews are on offer to wash down the greasy corndogs, plus a pool table, wall of pinball, good music and and fires. Friendly staff, quirky regulars and a lot of fun.

Opening hours: daily, 7.30pm-2am

The GoodFoot Pub and Lounge (73)

2845 SE. Stark St., Portland, OR 97214
T 503 239 9292
www.thegoodfoot.com

Jumping joint spread over two floors with a pub upstairs and a rug-cutting lounge and dancefloor below. As well as ten beers on tap (some organic and home-brewed), there's a substantial array of bottled beers. The waist-worrying food from the kitchen soaks up the suds while regular music and art shows draw in a lively mix of hipsters and locals.

Opening hours: daily, 5pm-2.30am

Greater Trumps (74)

1520 SE. 37th Ave., Portland, OR 97214
T 503 235 4530
www.mcmenamins.com

A cultured cigar and port bar with the look and feel of a war-time Parisian bistro. Wines, spirits and South American smokes take precedence over beers.

Opening hours: Mon-Sat, 4pm-1am; Sun, 4pm-midnight

Horse Brass Pub (75)

4534 SE. Belmont St., Portland, OR 97215
T 503 232 2202
www.horsebrass.com
Highly recommended

The Horse Brass Pub is a Portland drinking institution. Owner and publican Don Younger has been here for more than 30 years. He's credited with enlightening Portlanders during the dark drinking days of the late Seventies and early Eighties and the pub's dedication to British and German beers served as an inspiration for those who have gone on to further cultivate Portland beer culture. The Horse Brass is an authentic replica of an English boozer in everything from the mountains of memorabilia and English soccer to the basic yet beer-friendly food (greasy fry-up anyone?). The beer choice, however, is far more exciting than anything you'd find back in the UK with a mesmerising myriad of craft beers on offer. Arguably the most influential pub in Oregon.

Opening hours: Mon-Fri, 11am-close; Sat & Sun, 9am-close

Laurelhurst Theater (76)

2735 E. Burnside St., Portland, OR 97214-1757
T 503 232 5511
www.laurelhursttheater.com

Wonderful art-deco art-house cinema restored to its former Twenties glory, where local microbrews and pizza can be taken into the theatre. From the kitsch retro décor to the classic, independent screenings, it's a unique movie-going experience and, at $3 a flick, the best bucks you're likely to spend.

McMenamins Mall 205 (77)

9710 SE. Washington St., Portland, OR 97216
T 503 254 5411
www.mcmenamins.com

Inviting little place in a mall that's ideal for kicking back after a long day flashing the cash. Outdoor seating, too.

Opening hours: Mon-Sat, 11am-1am; Sun, noon-midnight

McMenamins Oregon City (78)

102 Ninth St., Oregon City, OR 97045
T 503 655 8032
www.mcmenamins.com

Come find epicurean enlightenment at this former turn-of-the-century church and sit alongside judges from the neighbouring courthouse on the outdoor patio.

Opening hours: Mon-Thu, 11am-midnight; Fri & Sat, 11am-1am; Sun, noon-11pm

McMenamins Sunnyside (79)

9757 SE. Sunnyside Rd., Clackamas, OR 97015
T 503 653 8011
www.mcmenamins.com

Archetypal McMenamins local on the fringes of the town centre.

Opening hours: Mon-Wed, 11am-midnight; Thu-Sat, 11am-1am; Sun, noon-11pm

Oaks Bottom Pub (80)

1621 SE. Bybee Blvd., Portland. OR 97202
T 503 232 1728

What this brightly-coloured bar lacks in size it makes up for in its top-notch burgers, beer and those wonderful gastronomic delights known as tater tots. Overseen by former Oregon Brewers Guild director Jim Parker and Jerry Fechter, one of the guys behind the Lompoc empire, the dozen-strong tap list is divided between Lompoc brews and local guest beers. The food is freshly prepared and locally sourced, they do a killer Bloody Mary and a few wines, too. Nice outdoor back patio. Kid and dog friendly.

Opening hours: daily, 11.30am-midnight

Pix Patisserie (81)

3402 SE Division St., Portland, OR 97202
T 503 232 4407

Vibrant café with gaudy yellow walls and comfy seats. The first Pix in Portland also boasts a 30-strong beer menu featuring big bottles of Belgian Lambics and Trappists, as well as delicious dessert wines. If you've got a sweet tooth, we suggest you bring it here.

Opening hours: Sun-Thu, 10am-midnight; Fri & Sat, 10am-2am

Pix Patisserie (82)
3731 SE. Hawthorne Blvd., Portland, OR 97214
T 503 236 4760

Petite pastry shop and cultured candy store in Hawthorne where you can grab yourself an absurdly complicated coffee, Spanish and French wines and a bottle or two of Belgian beer. Keep your eye out for the bingo nights where the numbers are called in French and chocolates are used as chips.

Opening hours: Sun-Thu, 10am-midnight; Fri & Sat, 10am-2am

Pub at the End of the Universe (83)
4107 SE. 28th Ave., Portland, OR 97202
T 503 238 9355

So laid-back you may have to check if it's breathing. Drawing in locals and students, the bar regularly revolves two dozen taps and brings in some rarely spotted ales from Oregon and beyond. Food is of the hearty, home-made variety with plenty of soups and meat-free dishes.

Opening hours: daily, 12.30pm-2am

Roadside Attraction (84)
1000 12th Av., Portland OR 97214
T 503 233 0743

It may only have four microbrews on tap and no great beer bottles to speak of, but this utterly funky, hidden gem located a few hundred yards from the Basement Pub must be paid a visit. The crimson brothel-like interior is bedecked with erotic art, a knackered old piano, pristine pool table, all manner of outlandish furniture and a Tiki-style bar serving a strong array of spirits. Outside, meanwhile, is a quirky cross between a Hawaiian shack, a florists and a surrealist Dali-esque scrap yard. Mental but marvellous.

Opening hours: daily, 3pm-1am

Skybox Pub & Grill (85)
7995 SE. Milwaukie Ave., Portland, OR 97202
T 503 731 6399
www.skyboxpub.com

The Skybox in Sellwood looks beyond the brands that lend their mainstream names to the game on TV. Around a dozen accessible microbrews (Widmer, BridgePort and

The crimson interior of the Roadside Attraction

Rogue) are joined by a number of imports and the odd cask-conditioned quaff. Eighteen screens and a gargantuan 55-inch plasma poke through mountains of sporting memorabilia meaning only those with their heads encased in concrete will miss the ball action or, indeed, the cheery pub food: the beer-battered mozzarella sticks are good.

Opening hours: Mon-Wed, 11am-10pm; Thu, 11am-11pm; Fri, 11am-midnight; Sat, 9am-midnight; Sun, 9am-9pm

Southwest Portland

McMenamins Cedar Hills (86)
2927 SW. Cedar Hills Blvd., Beaverton, OR 97005
T 503 641 0151
www.mcmenamins.com

Plenty of character and buzz at this Beaverton bar and restaurant situated just down the street from the world headquarters of Nike. As well as the usual hand-crafted ales, spirits and home-made food, features include a sporting shrine, with historic pool tables and pin ball under the flickering glare of televised sports, and a lovely, shaded outdoor seating area.

Opening hours: Sun, 12-11pm; Mon-Thu, 11am-midnight; Fri & Sat, 11am-1am

McMenamins Greenway Pub (87)

12272 SW. Scholls Ferry Rd., Tigard, OR 97223
T 503 590 1865
www.mcmenamins.com

Betty, a porcupine puffer fish, is just one of the highlights at this Tigard tavern – the second oldest McMenamins venue. It has recently been refurbished with the addition of a jumpin' jukebox, outdoor eating area, spanking new pool tables and, of course, an impressive aquarium in which Betty resides alongside Alfred III, a tang lionfish.

Opening hours: Mon, 11am-11pm; Tue-Thu, 11am-midnight; Fri & Sat, 11am-1am; Sun, noon-11pm

McMenamins Murray & Allen (88)

6179 SW. Murray Blvd., Beaverton, OR 97005
T 503 644 4562
www.mcmenamins.com

Beaverton brew gurus. A striking stained-glass windowed sun on the ceiling takes centre stage here.

Opening hours: Mon-Sat, 11am-midnight; Sun, noon-11pm

West Portland

The Grand Lodge (89)

3505 Pacific Ave., Forest Grove, OR 97116
T 503 992 9533/877 992 9533
www.mcmenamins.com

Built in 1922 and renovated in 2000, this impressive country pile wears its grand moniker with grandiose style. McMenamins has created an enormous house of fun where guests can wind down amid ostentatious surroundings of manicured lawns, ornate architecture and elaborate artwork. As well as 77 tasteful European-style rooms, there's a handful of restaurants and bars, a garden pool and the Compass Room movie theatre.

The Ironwork Grill @ The Grand Lodge

3505 Pacific Ave., Forest Grove, OR 97116
T 503 992-9533/877 992 9533

Spacious first-floor restaurant with stained glass windows, wrought ironmongery and elaborate artwork.

Opening hours: Mon-Fri, 11am-late; Sat & Sun, 7am-late

The Yardhouse Pub @ Grand Lodge

3505 Pacific Ave., Forest Grove, OR 97116
T 503 992 3442

Informal drinking den on the fringes of the Grand Lodge's immaculate front lawn, the Yardhouse hosts regular live music, outdoor seating and a 10-hole disc golf course as well as a cigar-smoking section.

Opening hours: daily, 11am-close

Raleigh Hills Pub (90)

4495 S.W. Scholls Ferry Rd. Portland, OR 97225
T 503 292-1723
www.mcmenamins.com

Comfy ski-lodge feel with high vaulted ceilings and warm wood beams and booths throughout and an eye-catching mural adorning one entire wall. The beer garden beckons thirsty punters in summertime.

Opening hours: Mon, 11am-11pm; Tue-Thu, 11am-midnight; Fri & Sat, 11am-1am; Sun, noon-11pm

Riverwood Pub (91)

8136 SW. Hall Blvd., Beaverton, OR 97008
T 503 643 7189
www.mcmenamins.com

The mixture of traditional wood booths, hanging plants, colourful murals and neon-lit ceiling shouldn't really work but, somehow, it does. The restaurant and deck affords water and woodland views from the banks of Fanno Creek.

Opening hours: Mon & Tue, 11am-10pm; Wed & Thu, 11am-11pm; Fri, 11am-midnight; Sat, 11am-11pm

Rock Creek Tavern (92)

10000 NW. Old Cornelius Pass Rd., Hillsboro, OR 97124
T 503 645 3822
www.mcmenamins.com

A Phoenix-like pub that has risen from the ashes of a fire in 2002. A rustic and rural retreat, this Hillsboro hangout lures in visitors with live music, a floating dance floor, pool tables and, of course, great food and ales.

Opening hours: Sun-Tue, 11am-10pm; Wed & Thu, 11am-11pm; Fri & Sat, 11am-1am

Columbia River and Northern Oregon

THE COLUMBIA GORGE region, to the east of Portland, makes for spectacular scenery and a beautiful, bucolic breather from the pleasures of Portland. The winding drive east on the I-84 hugs the picturesque Columbia River, a windswept natural watershed that separates Oregon State from Washington. Affording stunning vistas of the Cascade mountains, it passes the Multnomah Water Falls, the Bonneville Dam, the impressive Bridge of the Gods and a handful of picturesque picnic spots and hiking trails.

The 50-mile mark brings you into Hood River – the windsurfing capital of the world that doubles up as a small outward-bounding hillside town with plenty of get-up-and-go and a trio of breweries – not too shabby for a population of around 5,000.

Once fed, watered and windsurfed, there are two options. Either head south along the 'Mt. Hood Loop' on I-35 to Mt. Hood, the new Mt. Hood Scenic Byway, and back to Portland on the I-26. Or cross the river north into Washington and meander along the shore back to Portland via Stevenson and the Walking Man Brewpub. The latter is the shorter trip but both are dramatic days out.

On the west coast, Astoria is a scenic and historic town where the Columbia River flows into the Pacific Ocean. Founded in 1811 by Hudson's Bay Company fur trapper John Jacob Astor, it is the oldest American settlement west of the Rockies. It's also a great place to start exploring the rugged Oregon Coast, working your way southwards to Newport, home of Rogue Brewery.

Midway between the coast and Portland is McMinnville, a picturesque little tourist town full of antique shops, historic homes and art galleries. It is perched on the edge of the Yamhill Valley – home to one third of Oregon's vineyards and wineries and a rich source of fresh fruit.

BREWERY

Full Sail Brewing Company (1)
506 Columbia St., Hood River, OR 97031
T (brewery) 541 386 2281/1 888 244 BEER

Full Sail Tasting Room & Pub
506 Columbia St., Hood River, OR
T 541 386 2247
www.fullsailbrewing.com

Full Sail's story dates back to 1987 as the northwest microbrewery scene was just kicking off, dovetailing with the transformation of Hood River from a cute little town selling fruit into a windsurfing Mecca. The first year was mostly spent converting a derelict fruit cannery full of pigeons into a bona fide brewhouse with a brand new state-of-the-art brewery, but Full Sail still managed to fuel a burgeoning Hood River with almost 300 barrels of beer.

The following year they began bottling the beer by hand. For such a ripe business, it was an incredibly ambitious move but it enabled the brewery to navigate the industry's choppy seas during the mid 1990s.

Today, Full Sail is the tenth biggest craft brewer in the whole of America and its beers can be found throughout the Pacific Northwest and beyond. Despite its substantial size, Full Sail became a 47-strong employee co-operative in 1999. While the engine room of Full Sail's success has been its Amber Ale, an eight times gold medal winner at the World Beer Championships, it has branched out into more esoteric ales and lagers with Session, a retro pre-Prohibition lager, boasting a dedicated following among both beer geeks and board-heads.

In 2000, Full Sail headhunted maverick brewer John Harris and, every two months or so, he unleashes remarkable seasonal beers as part of The Brewmaster's Reserve series. These have included Bocks, bombastically hopped bitters, barley wines, imperial Porters and hedonistic holiday ales. Most of the beers are available in the taproom above the brewery. The food menu is simple and straightforward but the views from the balcony restaurant and sundeck are anything but. Bottles are available to go while a taster tray costs $5.

Brewery tours: daily, 1pm, 2pm, 3pm & 4pm; cost, free; duration, 20 minutes
Opening hours: 11.30am–close
Recommendation
Session Lager (5.1%)
A beer that certainly lives up to its name. Such an easy-drinking, well-constructed lager is manna from heaven in this heartland of heavily hopped ales. Ideal for sipping on the sundeck after a long day pretending you can windsurf.
Pale Ale (5.4%)
Floral ale made with two (secret) Northwest hops.
Amber Ale (5.5%)
A microbrew classic. One of the first to show that there's more to beer than Light or Regular. It may seem unadventurous now but it was once groundbreaking.
IPA (6%)
Citrus, summer sip with 60 IBUs.
Wassail (6.5%)
Mahogany-coloured, malt-driven winter warmer.
FS Ltd
Ever-changing range of small-batch beers named after Full Sail's motto. Living the Dream.

BREWPUBS

Big Horn Brewing/ (2)
Ram Restaurant & Brewery
515 12th St. SE., Salem, OR 97301-4034
T 503 363 1904
www.theram.com

This enormous venue, winner of 'Best large Brewpub of the Year' at the GABF in 2001, is one of the better bars that make up the 15-strong Ram restaurant empire. A local beer buff labelled Ram restaurants the 'Burger Kings of the brewpub world' but the staff are too friendly, food too decent and interiors too slick for that unfair comparison. All-in-all, the Rams are a little bland but are resolutely reliable. If you don't like surprises, they're perfect.
Recommendation
Total Disorder Porter
A thin initial mouthfeel contradicts the molasses, chocolate and warm coffee that follow. By far Ram's most accomplished beer - well, that's what we think anyway.

Big Horn Brewing/ Ram Restaurant & Brewery (3)

320 Oswego Pointe Dr., Lake Oswego,
OR 97034-3227
T 503 697 8818
www.theram.com

Imagine a picturesque, lakeside version of above.

Big Horse Brewing Company (4)

115 State St., Hood River, OR 97031
T 541 386 4411

Big Horse has been wedged into the foothills of Mt. Hood since 1987, first as the Horse Feathers Pasta House and then, from 1995, as Big Horse Brewing. Above the street-level brewhouse, the two-storey restaurant and bar has a ski-chalet feel complete with outdoor decking ideal for alfresco drinking and with some of the best vistas in town. The beers, while not quite as impressive, span a number of styles from seasonal Belgians to an ESB, while the food selection is vast – almost too vast in fact. Two big pool tables, chess and Jenga provide added entertainment but, in our opinion, it lacks the beers of Full Sail and the buzz of Double Mountain.

Opening hours: Mon-Thu, 11.30am-10pm; Fri & Sat, 11.30am-10.30pm; Sun, 11.30am-9.30pm

Recommendation
Nightmare Oatmeal Stout (6.5%)
Smooth and creamy and stacked with roast caramel, chocolate and a touch of sweet coffee. Try it with the Snickers Bar Pie – a criminally indulgent combination of fudge brownie, caramel, peanuts and a cream cheese filling.

Bill's Tavern & Brewhouse (5)

188 N. Hemlock, Cannon Beach, OR 97110
T 503 436 2202

Mosey on down I-101 and you'll arrive at Cannon Beach, a few miles south of the charming Ecola State Park. Famous for the Haystack Rock, Cannon Beach is a lovely little artistic hamlet renowned for its annual Sandcastle Contest held every June. After a hard day's sculpting with bucket and spade, Bill's Tavern & Brewhouse makes for a fine retreat. This cosy brewpub, set back a few blocks from the ocean, is decked in warm

wood with a separate bar and a restaurant. The upstairs brewery, visible from the bar, furnishes drinkers with eight house beers alongside local guest ales and interesting imports. A number of the beers are adorned with herbs and spices, and the brewery is renowned for using esoteric ingredients to nudge the boundaries of innovation.

Opening hours: Mon-Fri, 11am-11pm; Fri & Sat, 11am-2am

Recommendation
Duckdive Pale Ale (5.5%)
Golden in hue with an aroma of grapefruit, this archetypal Northwest pale ale sneaks into IPA territory. Spruce and pine with a floral finish.

Double Mountain Brewery & Taproom (6)

84th St., Hood River, OR 97031
T 541 387 0042
www.doublemountainbrewery.com

Neat and lively taproom pouring decent beers to a less touristy crowd than its Full Sail neighbour. Soups, salads, pizzas and sandwiches play second fiddle to a range of small batch beers brewed by former Full Sail head brewer Matt Swihart. It might not have the views of Matt's former employer but his beers and food certainly give it a run for its money. Definitely swing by if you're in town.

Opening hours: Mon-Thu, 4-10pm; Fri, 4-11pm; Sat, noon-11pm; Sun, noon-9pm

Recommendation
Double Mountain Altbier (5.6%)
Creamy caramel sweetness balanced out by back of the throat bitterness. Copper-coloured brew with Gambrinus organic Pilsner, chocolate, wheat and Munich malt. Robust Germanic ale.

Elliot Glacier Public House (7)

4945 Baseline Dr., Parkdale, OR 97041-8703
T 541 352 1022
Highly recommended

After Hood River, the next beer stop on the 'Mt. Hood Loop' is the Elliot Glacier Pub, a splendid brewpub housed in the charming Valley Theatre. The scenery on show through the back window, or from the terrific terrace if the weather allows, is quite possibly the finest of any pub on the West Coast. Sit back and enjoy with one of Elliot Glacier's beers or pick a dish from the inventive menu – compiled with more thought and creativity than most – specialising in fondue.

The seven-barrel brewery produces half a dozen core beers and a handful of seasonal ales, all with a slightly sweet signature. One suspects the spectacular views improve the beers with the drinking but the Porter, Scottish ale and pale ale were all entirely satisfactory.

Parkdale is linked to Hood River by the Mt. Hood Railroad, on which old-fashioned Pullman trains trundle, and the schedule leaves you just enough time to grab a couple of beers and a bite to eat. The stop is less than a block away from the brewpub.

Recommendation
Baseline Porter (5.8%)
This no-nonsense porter, darker than a coal miner's nightmares, will refresh or warm in equal measure.

Fearless Brewing (8)
326 South Broadway St., Estacada, OR 97023
T 503 260 2337
www.fearless1.com

Big home-brewing author and guru Ken Johnson turned his back on Portland in favour of the picturesque environs of Estacada in June 2003. On the scenic upper reaches of the Kayak-friendly Clackamas River, he serves up a perfectly drinkable selection of brewpub ales and a couple of brave rotating seasonals to parched pub-goers and paddlers.

Recommendation
Fearless Scottish Ale (5%)
The oh-so-sweet malt-inspired aroma jumps out of the glass to reveal toffee flavours on the tongue. Slightly fruity but, unlike a Scottish soccer fan, not bitter at all.

Fort George Brewery and Public House (9)
1483 Duane St., Astoria, OR 97103
T 503-325-PINT
www.fortgeorgebrewery.com

Opened in March 2007, Fort George Brewery is built on the site of the original 1811 Fort Astoria car dealership (renamed during the War of 1812 when the British seemed to be winning) and honours its origins with a washroom mural. Art-deco industrial lines are softened by a reclaimed wooden bar and

window frames made from an old boat while a glass garage door divides the restaurant from the bar.

Veteran brewer Jack Harris (a McMenamins' alumnus) and local lad Chris Newlowill bought a brewhouse in Virginia Beach and lugged it cross-country on a flatbed truck (not without incident – a tornado in Nebraska almost carried it away).

Jack and Chris make eight styles including Quick Wit, a white Belgian with lemongrass, elderberry and coriander; Vortex IPA and XVIth Chapel – both with IBUs over 100; Pi (3.1416) Beer, with strawberry and rhubarb; and a ginger ale with wasabi. They have also experimented with a Finnish-style Sauti, using juniper twigs. Never clarified, fined or filtered, all the beers are available in Mason jars.

Opening hours: Mon-Thu, 11am-11pm; Fri & Sat, 11am-midnight; Sun, noon-midnight

Recommendation
Vortex IPA (7.5%)
Dry-hopped and resinous with soft, woody undertones, Cascade and Simcoe hops, used in the kettle, are joined by Palisades for the hopping.

Golden Valley Brewery & Pub (10)
980 East 4th, McMinnville, OR 97128
T 503 472 BREW
www.goldenvalleybrewery.com

Golden Valley is a big old place with high wooden-beamed ceilings, a striking brewhouse and an antique 1920s bar that was previously installed in Portland's Grand Old Hoyt Hotel. Befitting its location within the heart of wine country, brewmaster Mark Vickery has borrowed techniques from the grape trade to brew 'IPA VS Brut' (9%/IBU 50), a champagne-style beer aged in local Argyle Chardonnay barrels for two months, racked and matured using 'Methode Champenoise'. He throws a couple of Argyle wines into the

Beer samples at Golden Valley

brew, too, and ages his seasonal Imperial Stout in wine barrels for two months. Beer samples (around ten ales tend to be on tap), are served perched on a hand-crafted stave previously used by Oregon's wineries.

The seven all-year-round ales, ranging from a robust porter to a brassy Irish red, don't overdo the IBU or ABV and make for solid session beers. The highlight of the food menu is Golden Valley beef and home-grown seasonal vegetables raised and grown on a local ranch belonging to the owners. There's a banquet room and a beer garden too.

Opening hours: Mon-Thu, 11am-10pm; Fri & Sat, 11am-midnight; Sun 11am-9pm

Recommendation

Red Thistle Ale (5.4%)

Brassy Irish-style red brewed with a quartet of rich malts backed up by a tidy bitter finish – courtesy of five different hops. Complex and balanced with enough power to rein in Golden Valley's prime beef.

Karlsson Brewing Company (11)

35900 Industrial Way, Suite 102, Sandy, OR 97055

T 503 826 8770

www.karlssonbrewing.com

Fun little brewery and taproom on the outskirts of Sandy. The place buzzes with locals playing shuffleboard, music, a couple of plasmas and banter from bartenders. Food consists of popcorn, peanuts, Scotch eggs and other simple beer-friendly tucker. Pop in if you're passing through and pick up a growler ($15 for 64oz).

Opening hours: Mon-Thu, 2pm-close; Fri & Sat, 10am-close

Recommendation

Pioneer Pilsner (5.8%)

Sometimes, a crisp, lip-smacking and full-bodied European-style lager and a handful of peanuts can make one very happy indeed.

The Lighthouse Brewpub (12)

4157 N. Highway 101, Lincoln City, OR 97367

T 541 994 7238

www.mcmenamins.com

Coastal brewpub with open fermenters and a superb seaside setting.

Opening hours: Sun-Thu, 11am-11pm; Fri & Sat, 11am-midnight

Main Street Ale House (13)

333 N. Main Ave., Gresham, OR 97030

T 503 669 0569

www.mainstreetale.com

The Main Street Ale House is the beer drinker's best bet in the suburban town of Gresham. The chefs conjure up the standard stuff such as pizza, burgers, seafood and salads. The beers are decent but not worth a detour alone – a dozen house ales cover the usual brewpub bases. Free pool from 6-9pm.

Recommendation

Eager Beaver IPA (5.5%)

Spick and span IPA with enough sweetness to take itself beyond the usual one-pint limit.

McMenamins West Linn (14)

2090 SW. 8th Ave., West Linn, OR 97068

T 503 656 2970

www.mcmenamins.com

Don't be hoodwinked by the drive-thru burger bar exterior for inside this family-friendly restaurant there's a marine-cum-golf mural on the walls and ceiling, a Hawaiian style shack bar and plenty of pastoral plants.

Opening hours: Mon-Thu, 11am-midnight; Fri & Sat, 11am-1am; Sun, noon-midnight

Mt. Hood Brewing Company/ Ice Axe Grill (15)

87304 E. Government Camp, Government Camp, OR 97208

T 503 622 0768/503 622 0724

www.mthoodbrewing.com

Befitting its location at the base of Mt. Hood, there's an outward bound vibe going on at this friendly brewpub. The company, named after a Portland brewery from 1905, opened in 1992 within the stone clad walls of a former ski rental shop and has been quenching the thirst of skiers, fisherman, hikers, tourists and locals ever since.

The ten-barrel brewhouse, located on the first floor, conjures up eight core draught beers, fusing local Northwest hops and malt with Mt. Hood's glacial water. The selection flicks between light and dark, with the emphasis on resinous hops, and there's a cask conditioned beer and a nitro too. The Ice Axe IPA is mighty popular and the Cascadian dry-hopped pale ale will also appeal to Lupulin lovers. You'll also find some of Mt. Hood's beers elsewhere in the state. The food? Plate-cracking portions that don't veer too far off-piste from brewpub cuisine. Brewery tours are available but call ahead.

Opening hours: Sun-Thu, 11.30am-9pm; Fri & Sat, 11.30am-10pm

Recommendation
Pinnacle ESB (5%)
Cask-conditioned amber ale. Mellow malt-driven ale with a rich mouthfeel.

Pelican Pub & Brewery   (16)
33180 Cape Kiwanda Dr., Pacific City, OR 97135
T 503 965 7007
www.pelicanbrewing.com
Highly recommended

At the Great American Beer Festival, American beer's version of the Oscars, Pelican was named 'Small brewpub of the Year' in 2005 and, following expansion, 'Large Brewpub of the Year' in 2006. In the same year, head brewer Darron Welch scooped gold in the 'Large Brewpub Brewer' category while his beers won five medals (three golds and two silvers). A dizzying selection of seasonal brews rotates around five flagship ales and tends to eschew the usual Northwest hop signature in favour of a sweeter, rounder and altogether more Flemish character.

Limited edition ales include a spicy Saison, a floral and fruity French farmhouse ale and a whole host of Imperial interpretations of European styles. The core range, meanwhile, includes an awesome American-style India Pale Ale (IBU 85); the quaffable Kiwanda Cream Ale; the dark and dangerously drinkable Tsunami Stout (7%); and MacPelican's Scottish Ale, given a Yankee slant with the use of Willamette hops.

While it's by no means cheap, the food is fresh and wonderfully varied with everything from pizzas and salads to fish and chips, shark tacos and crab-crusted Mahi-mahi.

Recommendation
Doryman's Dark Ale (5.8%)
Mahogany colour, sweet caramel-biscuit aroma with fruit cake, a touch of toffee and toasty on the palate. Mt. Hood and Cascade hops clip the sweetness nicely.

Rogue Ales Public House at Pier 39 (17)
100 39th St., Astoria, OR 97103
T 503 325 5964
www.rogue.com

The location is unique – perched at the end of a pier in a 19th-century fish cannery with views across the Columbia River. Opened in 2006, the pub sticks loyally to the brewer's radical recipe of irreverent ales, enthusiastic service and big, bold pub food including the renowned Kobe beefburger. Three dozen taps offer Rogue's range, a number of efforts from the brewer's Northwest neighbours and the mass-market lagers.

Opening hours: 11am-midnight

Thompson Brewery & Public House (18)
3575 Liberty Rd., Salem, OR 97302
T 503 363 7286
www.mcmenamins.com

This charming 1905 home of former Civil War soldier Franklin Thompson is now home to the first brewery in Salem since Prohibition. If it wasn't for the cute corner bar, you'd be mistaken for thinking you'd stumbled into someone's front room.

Opening hours: Mon, 11am-11pm; Tue & Wed, 11am-midnight: Thu-Sat, 11am-1am; Sun, noon-midnight

Wet Dog Café and Astoria Brewery Company   (19)
144 11th St., Astoria, OR 97103
T 503 325 6975

The Wet Dog Café, operated by Astoria Brewing Co. since 1995, is situated on the riverfront tram line. It's a cavernous warehouse of a place with uplifting views over the water. Brewer John Dahlgren and Manager Steve Allen are currently doubling its capacity but already produce an impressive line of nine ales (with ten guest taps and a selection of bottled beers), ranging from Volksweissen and Poop Deck Porter through Kick Ass Imperial Oatmeal Stout. Reflecting the Northwest's infatuation with hops are Shark Spit IPA (IBU 69) and Bitter Bitch Imperial IPA with a whopping IBU of 118!

Opening hours: Mon-Fri, 11am-11pm; Fri & Sat, 11am-2am

Recommendation

Bitter Bitch Imperial IPA (8.5%)
This quite crazy beer won the IPA category and People's Choice at the 2007 Portland Beer & Wine Fest. For the true hop freak only.

BEER BARS

Boon's Treasury (20)
888 Liberty St. NE., Salem, OR 97301
T 503 399 9062

Beer garden, a brick and wood interior, the full gamut of McMenamins booze and everything from live blues to funk at this boudoir of laid-back leisure sat on the northern periphery of central Salem. Once the official home of the Oregon treasury. Free Wi-Fi.

Opening hours: Mon-Thu, 11am-midnight; Fri & Sat, 11am-1am; Sun, noon-11pm

Hotel Oregon (21)
310 NE. Evans St., McMinnville, OR 97128
T 503 472 8427/888 472 8427
www.mcmenamins.com

Rather splendid hotel in the heart of wine country with 42 well-appointed guest rooms, a rooftop terrace and bar, a subterranean wine bar and a bustling ground floor pub as well as a pool and billiard room.

Rooftop bar: Sun-Thu, 11.30am-11pm; Fri & Sat, 11.30am-midnight
Pub: Sun-Thu, 7am-11pm; Fri & Sat, 7am-1am
Cellar bar: Fri & Sat, 5pm-close

McMenamins Sherwood Pub (22)
15976 SW. Tualatin-Sherwood Rd., Sherwood, OR 97140
T 503 625 3547
www.mcmenamins.com

Sherwood neighbourhood pub that puts the 'Mc' into McMenamins with its Scottish vibe: dark wood, salvaged memorabilia and dangling orbs of cosy light.

Opening hours: Mon, 11am-10pm; Tue-Thu, 11am-midnight; Fri & Sat, 11am-1am; Sun, noon-10pm

Old Chicago Pizza & Pasta (23)
850 NW. Eastern Parkway, Gresham, OR 97030
T 503 667 5101
www.rockbottomrestaurantsinc.com

This off-shoot of the Rock Bottom empire lures in beer drinkers with more than 100 different brews from all four corners of the world. Classics, the obscure, the mainstream and the local all feature: the choice is staggering. Sadly, the beer range doesn't compensate for the fact that this place is unadulterated, uncut 'Now You Have Yourself A Nice Day, D'ya Hear?' commercial cheese.

Opening hours: daily, 11.30am-2am

Wanker's Corner Saloon & Café (24)
8499 Main St., Wilsonville, OR 97070
T 503 682 9674
www.wankerscorner.com

Despite its absence from the American vernacular, the meaning of the word Wanker is not lost on the owners of the bar who have milked their moniker (oh behave) to the max. Wanker's has a wide selection of bottled beers (mostly domestic and imported lagers), half a dozen micros on draught and in bottle and even its own microbrew – Outback Ale, a toasty, tawny-coloured brown ale that drinks well enough and fuels the chuckles while reading a food menu that includes Wanker Special made with certified Wanker beef and Wanker Wraps.

Opening hours: Mon-Wed, 11am-midnight; Thu-Sat, 11am-1.30am; Sun, 11am-11pm

Western Oregon

FOR A MORE laid-back drinking experience, Western Oregon offers the coastal retreat of Newport and the liberal, alternative university-town vibe of Eugene.

Newport is a buzzy blend of tourist town and working-class fishing village. Nestled between the Coast range and the Pacific Ocean, it's been a holiday haven since 1856 and is home to a number of tourist attractions: the Oregon Coast Aquarium, the Hatfield Marine Science Centre, two historic light-houses, a bustling Bayfront and the sandy swathes and broadwalks of Nye Beach.

Situated at the confluence of the Willamette and McKenzie rivers, Eugene is renowned for athletics, academia and all things alternative. It was here that Matt Groening, founder of the Simpsons, was born, where the cult comedy *Animal House* was filmed and where the spaced-out strummers Grateful Dead are still widely worshipped. Home to the University of Oregon – a centre of liberal learning with quite a legacy – the University's legendary track and field coach Bill Bowerman oversaw a golden era for athletics in the Fifties, which earned Eugene the pseudonym of 'Track Town'.

In the Seventies, Eugene led the way in community and co-operative programmes and, even today, there's a heightened presence of hedonistic hippydom with mature Acid casualties living happily alongside bolshy, bushy-tailed students. The laid-back vibe is enhanced by the presence of some great brewpubs and breweries as well as lively pubs and bars. In 2007, Eugene was hailed by a leading American beer magazine as one of ten great beer towns that you wouldn't expect to be great beer towns.

BREWERIES

Ninkasi Brewing Company (25)

272 Van Buren St., Eugene, OR
T 541 543 1941
www.ninkasibrewing.com

Named after the ancient Sumerian Goddess of Fermentation, Ninkasi is fronted by Jamie Floyd – a professional brewer since 1990 and former president of the Oregon Brewers Guild. After 11 years at the Steelhead Brewery in Eugene, Jamie started Ninkasi using a leased brewery in nearby Springfield. In the summer of 2007, the equipment was shifted into a converted plumbing warehouse in the centre of Eugene. With a 7,000 barrel capacity and plans to double that output on its current site, Ninkasi is on a joint mission, with neighbouring brewpubs, to put Eugene firmly on the brewing map.

Its beers are well equipped to do just that. Unashamedly big in hops, they've flavour and complexity. The ales take the Pacific Northwest character and gleefully run with it and the seasonal lagers (a creamy Helles and a nutty Muncher Dunkel Lager) venture where most microbrewers daren't tread. The Tricerahops Double IPA is a mammoth and mean mouthful with an ABV of 9.7% while Total Domination IPA, weighing in at a mere 6.9%, is slightly mellower with a drop of caramel sweetness and a marvellous melee of pine, citrus and grapefruit. Ninkasi's beers also include a dry Irish stout, a pale ale and a light lager.

Brewery tours: call ahead
Recommendation
Believer (7%)
Complex caramel forms the foundation for this roasty Double Red Ale that's balanced out by a rich hop presence. Winter ale that, like Santa's elves, doesn't just work during Christmas.

Rogue (26)

See feature on pages 192–195

Siletz Brewery & Roadhouse (27)

243 North Gaither St., Siletz, OR 97380
T 541 444 2335
www.siletzbrewing.com

Siletz is a small one-horse town, 10 miles from Newport, surrounded by pine forests and rolling mountain rivers. It's a beautifully bucolic base for a brewery, and it's easy to see why, in 1995, Randy Kenyon and Mike French chose to swap the rat race for life in a beat-up brewery shoehorned into an old barn. Having cut their mash forks as members of the local 'Good Heathens' homebrewing club, Randy and Mike now pull all the strings at a 16-barrel brewhouse, crafting 800 barrels of awesome artisan and unfiltered ales and lagers a year.

The Siletz stable, made up of ten core beers and a number of seasonals, enjoys a strong state following, a small market in Ohio and, until recently, Japan. The battle for biggest sales is waged between the renowned Spruce Ale and elaborately hopped Paddle Me IPA. These two are shortly followed by the soft and silky, espresso-tinged Oatmeal Cream Stout.

The adjacent brewpub is a great little hangout for the locals. All the Siletz beers are served here and it does a roaring trade in gargantuan pizzas.

Brewery tours: Saturdays are best but visitors are always welcome if you call ahead
Brewpub: Fri & Sat, 11am-midnight; Sun-Thu, 11am-10pm
Recommendations
Lovin Lager (5%)
A prince among Pilsners, this crisp Czech lager is darker than most with a sweet malt base upon which a sharp and tongue-slapping hop bitterness is layered.
Spruce Ale (6.5%)
Light copper-coloured ale with an alluring haze, a delicate, fruity and flowery bouquet and woody, gingerbread and spice on the palate. The finish is dry, pine-like and quenching. Lovely.

Rogue (26)

2320 OSU Drive, Newport, OR 97365
T 541 867 3660
www.rogue.com

Opening hours: brewery tours daily 3pm; distillery
tours 4pm. Call ahead if you have a large group

Rogue celebrates its twentieth birthday
in 2008. In American craft brewing years,
that's pretty old. While countless others
have come and gone, Rogue has prospered
through the shrewd and mischievous
marketing of its kaleidoscope range of
experimental beers.

The brewery is fronted and co-owned
by Jack Joyce, a straight-talking qualified
lawyer and former director of the Nike
clothing empire. Tired of mounting
paperwork and pestering bosses, Joyce
became restless and left to start up his
own business. He teamed up with partners
Rob Strasser and Bob Woodell with the
intention of championing local Oregonian
produce across America.

"*It could have been cranberries or
hazelnuts but it was beer,*" added Joyce.
"*Two brewer guys came to us with the
idea, and we put the money forward.
We struck a deal whereby every year
they made a penny, they'd get 10%.
If they lost a penny, they'd get fired.*"

A Budweiser drinker with no
knowledge of homebrewing, Joyce
had never run a small business before.
"*If you look at the beer market from a
small guy's point of view, you're looking
at an industry dominated by three main
players and restrictive distribution.
You have to do something different.*"

And, my, Rogue was different.
Unpasteurised, hand-crafted, heavily
hopped and highly irreverent ales
packaged in tall, screen-printed 650ml
bottles adorned with a 'rogue' character
on the front. At the heart of Rogue
is a beer manifesto that sticks up for
the artesian principles and unrivaled
ingredients of craft brewing.

There are 26 edicts that make up the
beer manifesto ranging from the abstract:
"*We hold that beer is not an abstraction
but a concrete reality which occurred in
the past, occurs in this living present and
will occur in the future*"; the virtuous:
"*Small scale brewing means the salvation
of beer*" to the fervently straightforward:
"*We hold that beer is worthy of passion.*"

The manifesto also rattles the cage
of any micro or craft brewers who have
'sold out' to the behemoth brewing
companies. Such a subversive and image-
led modus operandi must, however,
be buttressed by first-rate beer.

"If you're going to be irreverent and do some crazy stuff then you better make damned sure that you're making great beer," said Jack. *"We're not in the beer business because that's a very staid, traditional, high bound business – we're in the entertainment business."*

Since the first brewpub was opened in Ashland in 1989, Rogue has expanded its community alehouse empire to ten. It tends to pick working class towns with a tight community and an established beer-drinking culture.

Rogue's beer roster, meanwhile, is staggering, with more than 60 different beers. These include the flagship Dead Guy Ale, a Mocha Porter, barley wine, an imperial Pilsner, a cream ale, a Belgian saison and chipotle ale. There's also a hazelnut brown ale served with a complimentary Oregonian hazelnut – crack open the shell to reveal a 'Rogue' condom. Head brewer John Meier also brews using buckwheat – a member of the rhubarb family – for Rogue's Signature Series, launched in association with acclaimed Japanese chef Masaharu Morimoto.

John, a softly spoken former system control analyst and homebrewer, came in from the cold of Alaskan brewing in the late 1980s after meeting Jack on a business trip. The opportunity to return to his native Oregon was too good to turn down and he now oversees Rogue's beer-making from the headquarters in the seaside town of Newport.

For such a small brewery, Rogue's reach is incredibly wide. It sent its beer east in 1992, it's available in 42 states and now ships beer to Japan, Scandinavia and the UK. With ready-made distribution, Rogue is one of several craft breweries currently getting spiritual. Employing the same maverick marketing, it has unleashed a gin made with spruce, a rum made from hazelnuts and an award-winning white rum and dark rum. With Pacific Northwest's vineyards on Rogue's doorstep, are plans afoot for a wine?

"Yes, we've just trying to figure what our take on it would be," said Jack. *"But I can't be doing with all that Terroir. What a load of bull. While brewers work their butts off, winemakers have time to make nonsense like that up."*

THE BEERS

Bullfrog Ale (4.8%)
An American style wheat beer and an Issaquah Brewhouse original. Light in both colour and body, it's a crisp, refreshing ale served with a wedge of lemon.

Honey Orange Wheat (4.8%)
Unfiltered wheat beer, brewed with Oregon wildflower honey and orange juice, balanced with a nice medium-sweet malt character. Medium bodied, mellow and a nice honey-orange finish.

Younger's Special Bitter (YSB) (4.8%)
A classic English-style special bitter boasting a triumvirate of caramel maltiness, full-on fruit flavours, and hop bitterness, with a dry, hoppy finish. Named after Don Younger of Portland's infamous Horse Brass Pub, commemorating its 30 year anniversary.

Half-e-Weizen (5%)
An unfiltered Belgian-style fusion of wheat and barley malts, spiced with coriander and ginger.

Kells Irish Lager (5%)
Irish-style lager with a smooth mellow flavour and an apple crisp finish. Perfect for floating Guinness.

American Amber Ale (5.3%)
John hasn't held back with the hops in this tawny-coloured amber beer that comes complete with a coffee aroma, a tight head and a delicate roasted malt accent. Pause after the first sip for a delayed hop hit.

Chipotle Ale (5.3%)
Roasted chipotle peppers afford this deep golden ale with an eye opening chilli flavour, a malty, smoky aroma and a tightly kept crispness. A spicy and rather hoppy interpretation of Rogue's American Amber Ale which blends amazingly well with Rogue Chocolate Stout.

Juniper Pale Ale (5.3%)
Floral hops on the nose and a spicy finish hewn from whole juniper berries. Dedicated to 'the turkey in each of us'.

Mocha Porter (5.3%)
One for the chocolate lovers out there. Hopped with Centennial and Perle, it treads the line between dark chocolate bitterness and smooth Mocha sweetness.

Morimoto Black Obi Soba (5.3%)
A richer version Soba Ale enhanced by the addition of specialty malts and a special blend of hops. A fuller, nutty flavour that retains a clean, crisp finish.

Morimoto Soba Ale (5.3%)
Delicately roasted Soba (buckwheat) bestows this light, refreshing ale with a nutty finish and a compatibility with refined cuisine.

Oregon Golden Ale (5.3%)
Deep gold in colour, a resonant malty aroma, silky smooth and crisp with a herbal hop finish. Oregon Golden Ale is the original Rogue brew dating back to 1988.

St Rogue Red (5.3%)
Reddish copper in colour, a roasty malty flavour with a hoppy-spruce finish.

Santa's Private Reserve (5.3%)
A double-hopped version of St Rogue Red. Roastier, toastier and with a fuller presence of Chinook, Centennial and a mystery hop called Rudolph.

Chocolate Stout (6%)
Mellow flavour of oats, chocolate malts and real dark chocolate balanced deftly with enough hops for a bitter-sweet finish.

Hazelnut Brown Nectar Ale (6%)
A traditional European Brown Ale gone properly nutty! Dark brown in colour with a hazelnut aroma, a mellow malty aftertaste and a flavour that can only be described as nuts. A 2007 World Beer Championship Winner.

Monk Madness (6%)
Belgian ale deftly constructed using a quintet of malts and five different hop varieties. Beautifully balanced.

Shakespeare Stout (6%)
Ebony in colour, fluffy creamy head, ballsy flavour and a melodious, chocolate finish.

Brutal Bitter (6.2%)
An Imperial bitter with exotic traditional floor malts, citrusy, hoppy flavour and a stupendous hop aroma. The official beer of the Rogue Nation combines the Oregon Crystal hop with English malts.

Dead Guy Ale (6.2%)
Brewed in the style of a German Maibock, using Rogue's proprietary Pacman ale yeast. Deep honey in colour with a malty aroma and

a rich, robust flavour. Especially popular with Grateful Dead fans, so we made it the label for our Maierbock ale. Great with pork and hot and spicy food.

Smoke Ale (7%)
Inspired by the fall of the Berlin Wall, this German style Rauchbier has an orange-amber hue, a delicate smoke aroma and flavour, with a concentrated hop finish.

Dad's Little Helper (8%)
A thinking man's malt liquor. Using Midwest corn and Oregon Crystal Hops, it's lagered long and hot to coax out the sweet and crisp corn flavours.

Morimoto Imperial Pilsner (8.8%)
Built around the strong, malty backbone of this golden-coloured lager is a dry hop floral aroma and a deep hop bitterness.

Imperial India Pale Ale (9.5%)
No-nonsense Imperial IPA that, with its eye-wateringly intense aroma and hop bitterness, will meet even the most hardy hop-head expectations.

Imperial Stout (11%)
The Emperor of Stouts. Rich in texture, broad, soft and dry with a dark fruit finish. The strongest and fullest of all stouts.

Old Crustacean Barleywine (11.4%)
A beast of a Barleywine. Unfiltered and unfined, it's intense, robust, malty and dark.

The Bier Stein stocks over nine hundred different beers

Willamette Brewery (28)

1574 Coburg Rd., Box 226, Eugene, OR 97401
T 541 688 4555
www.willamettebrewery.com

Under construction at the time of writing, Head brewer Todd Friedman, formerly of the Beer Stein, plans to initially brew a Northwest IPA and a Hefeweizen.

BREWPUBS

The Bier Stein (29)

345 E. 11th Ave., Eugene, OR 97401
T 541 485 BIER
www.myspace.com/thebierstein

With more than nine hundred different beers, the Bier Stein claims to offer the greatest selection in the whole of Oregon. Belgian classics, hard-to-get-hold-of Americans like Dogfish and Jolly Pumpkin, lesser-spotted Germanic lagers, Canadian craft ales, Stone's Vertical Epics, Thomas Hardy Ale and other bottle-conditioned Brits... the list goes on and on. There's a sensible and rotating selection of ten microbrews on tap, while the open-plan kitchen knocks out top-notch sandwiches, artisan meats and cheeses. It's not the cosiest place in town, but the owners Chip and Kristina are knowledgeable and friendly and it makes an ideal spot for an informal bite and an enlightening beer.

Opening hours: Mon-Sat, 11am-11pm; Sun, 4-11pm

BJ's Pizza, Grill & Brewery (30)

1600 Coburg Road #4, Eugene
T 541 342 6114

Standard BJ's with Chicago-style pizza and a decent selection of beers served in comfy, albeit, corporate surroundings. Lacks the character of other Eugene beer joints.

Opening hours: Sun-Thu, 11am-11pm; Fri & Sat, 11am-midnight

Calapooia Brewing Company (31)

140 Hill St. NE., Albany, OR 97321
T 541 928 1931

Anyone hunting for an informal, relaxed beer in the timber town of Albany could not fare better than here. The décor is staggeringly simple, the locals friendly, the food is standard pub stuff, there's regular music jams and the beers belie their straightforward surroundings. Check out the Calapooia Green Chili Lager, an exceedingly spicy sip made with Serrano, Anaheim and jalapeno peppers that will put hairs on your body where there really shouldn't be any.

Opening hours: Tue & Wed, 3-10pm; Thu & Fri, 3-11pm; Sat, 3pm-midnight; Sun, 3-8pm

Recommendation
Yankee Clipper IPA (6.5%)
Bold, crisp IPA that gets its huge hop nose from the use of a 'hop-back', which filters unfermented beer through a bed of Cascade and Centennial hops. Calapooia's biggest seller.

Eugene City Brewing (32)

844 Olive St., Eugene OR 97401
T 541 345 4155
www.rogue.com

At this Rogue outpost, opened in 2004, brewmaster Trevor Howard sets the pace with a bespoke selection of beers unavailable elsewhere in the Rogue empire. With around 30 taps showcasing both Rogue and other micros, it can stretch the stamina of any marathon beer drinker. Highlights include Track Town Common, a smooth and crisp Pre-Prohibition lager, and Track Town IPA, brewed with 100% Northwest hops, ABV 7% and IBU 85. The lively bar is cell-phone free and cooks up Rogue specials such as Kobe Burgers, Halibut Fish and Chips and Gator Gumbo. Outdoor seating, too.

Opening hours: Mon-Thu, 11am-11pm; Fri & Sat, 11am-midnight; Sun, 11am-10pm

Recommendation
100 Meter Ale (6.25%)
IPA that flies off the blocks with a heavy hop aroma that keeps on going until it reaches the back of the throat. Kettle-brewed with Chinook, Simcoe, Centennial, Palisade and Cascade with a dry hopping of Amarillo.

High Street Brewery & Café (33)

1243 High St., Eugene, OR 97401
T 541 345 4905

Housed in a renovated residential house on the fringes of the city's centre, this is Eugene's first post-Prohibition microbrewery. Beers taste best in the backyard beer garden under the shade of fir, ash, hawthorn and tulip trees in the summer.

Opening hours: Mon-Sat, 11am-1am; Sun, noon-midnight

McMenamins On Monroe (34)

2001 NW. Monroe Ave., Corvallis, Oregon 97330
T 541 758 0080
www.mcmenamins.com

Student hangout on the edge of Oregon State University campus that goes crazy with Beaver fans on big match days. Features a pool, colourful on-site brewery and sun-trap beer garden.

Opening hours: Mon & Tue, 11am-midnight; Wed, 11am-1am; Thu-Sat, 11am-2am; Sun, noon-midnight

Oregon Trail Brewery (35)

341 SW. 2nd St., Corvallis, OR 97333
T 541 758 3527
www.oregontrailbrewery.com

Oregon Trail has been brewing in the student town of Corvallis since 1987 but didn't really get into its award-wining stride until 1993 under the stewardship of new owners Dave Willis and Jerry Bockmore, a pair of movers and shakers from the early Northwest brewing crowd.

The seven-barrel brewery shares a spot with the European-style 'Old World Deli', a quirky and kooky Corvallis institution that does a roaring trade in delicious sandwiches and a leftfield line in live entertainment from belly dances to foot-tapping music acts. All the beers are available in the deli with the vanilla-esque, whisky-kissed Bourbon Barrel Porter a must-sip.

Opening hours: Mon-Sat, 8am-10pm; Sun, 11am-5pm

Recommendation
Oregon Trail Wit (4.2%)
Crisp and tangy Belgian-style wheat beer tinged with coriander and apricot hop flavours. Hazy, unfiltered and very refreshing.

Rogue Brewer's on the Bay (36)

2320 OSU Dr., Newport, OR 97365
T 541 867 3660
www.rogue.com

Drink and dine in the engine room of the rascal-like Rogue Nation. Blessed with grand views across the Yaquina Bay Marina, and marked with a towering red silo, visitors sidestep their way through the brewery, past flying fork-lifts, towering tanks and a shop selling all manner of Rogue beers and bumpf.

The upstairs bar and restaurant, moderately nautical in theme, has views of the harbour and the working brewery and offers more than 20 Rogue beers on tap including exclusive, limited-edition ales unavailable elsewhere. Local fresh seafood stands out on the food menu while there are daily tours of the neighbouring distillery at 4pm.

Brewery tours: daily, 3pm (call ahead if you're part of a large group)

Opening hours: Sun-Thu, 11am-9pm; Fri & Sat, 11am-10pm

Rogue Brewers on the Bay

Roseburg Station Pub & Brewery (37)

700 SE. Sheridan St., Roseburg, OR 97470

T 541 672 1934

A trainspotter's tavern drenched in railroad history, the Roseburg pub and brewery has set up home in what was once the city's bustling Southern Pacific train depot.

Opening hours: Mon-Thu, 11am-11pm; Fri-Sat, 11am-midnight; Sun, 11am-10pm

Steelhead Brewing Company (38)

199 E. 5th Ave., Eugene, OR 97401

T 541 686 2739

www.steelheadbrewery.com

Established in 1991, the original Steelhead is the second oldest brewery in Eugene and over the years has scooped nearly two dozen medals at the Great American Beer Festival. Steelhead brews a quartet of standard ales: a banana-like Hairy Weasel Hefeweizen; the approachable Barracuda Blonde cream ale; the intensely fruity Bombay Bomber Ale; and the award-winning Raging Rhino Red. As well as a flurry of seasonals and its own root beer, the brewer also fuses beers together to produce six 'Beer Blends' such as A-Bomb (Rhino Red and Bombay Bomber) and Bread Basket Ale – a corn and wheat concoction consisting of Hairy Weasel and Barracuda Blonde.

Opening hours: Sun-Thu, 11.30am-11.30pm; Fri & Sat, 11.30am-12.30pm

Recommendation

Raging Rhino Red (5.4%)

Deep red colour, plenty of hops up front with a cultured caramel base. Sweet aroma, a warm mouth feel and a super dry finish.

Enjoy award-winning beers at Steelhead Brewing

BEER BARS

Opening hours: Mon-Fri, 11am-midnight; Sat, 4pm-midnight; Sun, 4-9pm

Bay Haven Inn (39)
608 SW. Bay Blvd., Newport, OR
T 541 265 7271

There's all kind of nautical nonsense on the walls, live music, a pool table and plenty of grog does flow. But being lily-livered Limey land-lubbers, we only stayed for one pint before drinking up, me hearties, and walking the plank out of there. Smartly!

Opening hours: Sun-Thu, 8am-11pm; Fri & Sat, 9am-2am

Bombs Away Café (40)
2527 NW. Monroe, Corvallis, OR 97330
T 541 757 7221
www.bombsawaycafe.com

This café-cum-Mexican eatery is a lively Corvallis treasure, serving terrific burritos, tacos, chimichangas and other tasty home-made dishes, not to mention baked breads and guilt-inducing desserts. The bar stocks more than 20 types of tequila (whatever you do, don't chuck the good stuff down your neck – sip it) and around two-dozen well-chosen Western microbrews on the bar and a few gems in the chiller. Simple ideas, well-executed... it's easy to see why Bombs Away is so popular.

Cornucopia Bottle Market & Deli (41)
295 W. 17th Ave., Eugene, OR 97401
T 541 485 2300

Charming little neighbourhood deli and beer 'n' burger bar with a jaw-dropping selection of bottles sourced predominantly from the US microbrew scene. It's good value with reportedly the best burgers in town, a strong vegetarian slant, helpful staff and a cute patio garden out back.

Opening hours: daily, 8am-10pm

East 19th Street Café (42)
1485 E. 19th Ave., Eugene, OR 97403
T 541 342 4025

Hippy café frequented by tax-dodging, shower-shirking University of Oregon students and located on the edge of the campus. Expanded in 2007, it now offers pool tables, pinball, darts, a woodstove, new mahogany deck, an expanded kitchen and an updated menu. Free Wi-Fi.

Opening hours: Mon-Sat, 11am-1am; Sun, noon-midnight

McMenamins Corvallis (43)

420 NW. Third St., Corvallis, OR 97330
T 541 758 6044
www.mcmenamins.com

Boutique British boozer in a mock-Tudor building formerly occupied by a fish and chip shop. The batter and mushy peas have been replaced by a warm pub with open fires, a cosy vibe and outdoor seating when the sun comes out in Corvallis.

Opening hours: Mon, 11am-midnight; Tue-Sat, 11am-1am; Sun, noon-midnight

North Bank (44)

22 Club Rd., Eugene, OR 97401
T 541 343 5622

Restful wooded watering hole on the banks of the Willamette, with a gorgeous beer garden and superb views of the river. Splendid.

Opening hours: Mon-Thu, 11am-11pm; Fri & Sat, 11am-midnight; Sun, noon-11pm

Rogue Ales Public House/ House of Rogue Bed & Beer (45)

748 SW. Bay Blvd., Newport, OR 97365
T 541 265 3188

This bar, restaurant and hotel was where all the Rogue beers were brewed originally and is now the oldest of the Rogue pubs, dating back to 1989. In 1991 the brewhouse shifted across the bay. Over the following years, the brewpub expanded to include a big pool room, a casino and a 'Bed & Beer' – Rogue's unique interpretation of a Bed & Breakfast ($90–$130).

The one or two bedroom apartments are fully furnished with cable TV, microwave, dishwasher, coffeemaker, telephone, washer and dryer and queen size beds with private bath, a spacious kitchen and a comfortable living and dining area. You also receive two 22-ounce bottles of cold 'Rogue Ale' and two complimentary 'Rogue' pint glasses.

A wealth of Rogue beers are available to drink in or take away, and also feature heavily in the food menu: hazelnut ale bread; chicken marinated in lager; chocolate Stout beer floats; chipotle ale BBQ sauce; Shakespeare Stout Sauerkraut and a number of Rogue ale cheeses.

Opening hours: Sun-Thu, 11am-1am; Fri & Sat, 11am-2am

Sam Bond's Garage (46)

407 Blair Bvld., Eugene, OR 97402
T 541 431 6603
www.sambonds.com
Highly recommended

Sam Bond's is a brilliant bar, voted by *Esquire* magazine as one of America's best, with disco balls dangling from the rafters, a cool, kooky, mostly college clientele and a flurry of craft beers on tap, served in jam jars. There are regular live music acts, a delicious home-cooked organic menu, cocktails and a terrific beer garden out the back. Very popular and justly so. A bonkers, rather amusing and totally free bingo night takes place on a Monday.

Opening hours: 4pm-close

Southern Oregon

CLUSTERED ROUND the base of Southern Oregon's main artery, the I-5, you'll pass a handful of small towns worth taking your foot off the pedal for. Grant's Pass is a classic river town, home of the legendary Rogue River and a base for numerous boating excursions, rafting trips and all manner of aquatic explorations and forested forays.

The 'Fair City' of Central Point is not just home to the Walkabout brewing facility but also the Carter Park museum, Rogue Creamery and the Rogue Valley Family Fun Center. Medford, meanwhile, is Southern Oregon's largest city; a gourmet's delight with orchards, wineries and a wealth of speciality foods.

Famous for its Shakespeare Festival, Ashland is full of wide boulevards, rolling streams, lush gardens and parks flanked by high-brow book stores, chin-scratching coffee shops and plenty of antique boutiques and art galleries. And finally Klamath Falls, to the east, sits on natural geothermal springs within the Klamath Basin and at the gateway to the Cascades and incredible Crater Lake.

BREWERIES

Caldera Brewing Company (47)
540 Clover Lane, Ashland, OR 97520
T 541 482 HOPS
www.calderabrewing.com

With no taproom, no restaurant and no pub to rely on, the distribution-only, three-man Caldera Brewery has flourished since 1997 on the revered reputation of its ales and lagers alone. Head brewer Jim Mills, who trained with John Maier at Rogue and worked at Rogue's now-defunct Siskiyou Brewery,

inherited the 10-barrel brewhouse following the big Ashland flood of 1997.

Set up on the fringes of Ashland, Jim established Caldera as a key draught player before, in 2005, becoming the first brewery in Oregon to brew and can its own beer in 2005. Pale Ale and IPA, the two brews encased in aluminium, blow unflattering perceptions of canned beers clear out of the water.

While the cans are available in Oregon, Washington and California, a whole host of local watering holes host Caldera's beers on tap. Keep your tastebuds peeled for Dry Hop Orange, bursting with citrus hops; an authentic Pilsner lagered for eight weeks; and the best-seller, Ashland Amber, a thinking, drinking man's Fat Tire. Tours are not available but beer sales, from the dock, are.

Recommendation
Caldera IPA (6.5%)
Full-bodied, fruity and furnished with a forceful hop character (Crystal, Galena and Centennial). Archetypal Northwest IPA.

Walkabout Brewing (48)
5204 Dobrot Way, Central Point, OR 97502
T 541 664 7763

A modest seven-barrel garage brewery set up by Australian Ross Litton, a former Rogue brewer in Ashland. Producing nine ales, Walkabout supplies around a dozen Southern Oregon beer bars with a total of more than two hundred barrels a year, including the Siskiyou Micropub in Ashland. No tours are available.

Recommendation
Jabberwocky (6.5%)
Rip-roaring red English-style ale brewed with Northwest Willamette, Perle and Cascade hops. Nutmeg, spice and chewy mouthfeel laid over a sweet malt base.

BREWPUBS

Klamath Basin Brewing Company/ Creamery Brewpub & Grill (49)

1320 Main St., Klamath Falls, OR 97601
T 541 273 5222
www.kbbrewing.com

Located in the historic 1930s Crater Lake Creamery building, the brewery calls upon geothermal-heated water, Klamath Basin barley and Northwest hops to craft its beers. Owner Lonnie Clement has gently converted Coors Light-swigging locals with accessible, balanced ale, modest in strength and lacking the bitterness of rip-snorting hop monsters. More than 650 barrels were brewed in 2006 and, with distribution stretching north, there are expectations to double that. Butt Crack Brown, 5%, is more than just a funny name while the Cabin Fever Stout, 7.6%, made for a refreshing summer sip. Good food comes in gargantuan portions and the service is swift and smiley.

Opening hours: 11am-close

Recommendation
Crater Lake Golden Ale (6.2%)
Golden, medium-bodied ales fusing Cascade and Fuggles hops with Crystal and Munich malt.

Mia & Pia's Pizzeria & Brewhouse (50)

3545 Summers Lane, Klamath Falls, OR 97601
T 541 884 4880/541 884 0949
www.miapia.com

Former dairy farmer and rodeo king, Rod Kucera converted milk-making equipment into a brewhouse in 1996 and became a self-taught master of the mashfork. The brewery has since moved off site, but Rod's esoteric and oddly named libations remain – check out Country Bumpkin Pumpkin Ale, Watchamacallit Wheat and Old Goat Maibock. Popular with locals, there's an old-Western style charm, a long list of pizzas and more than a dozen beers, ranging from drinkable to the really rather decent. The limited edition Whisky Barrel Barley Wine kicked ass and, in a marked departure from most brewpubs, most of the beers don't exceed the 5% mark.

Opening hours: Mon-Thu, 11am-11pm; Fri & Sat, 11am-midnight

Recommendation
Linkville Lager (3.8%)
A refreshing change from bitterly-hopped bruisers. Punches above its modest weight.

Standing Stone Brewing Company (51)

101 Oak St., Ashland, OR 97520
T 541 482 2448
www.standingstonebrewing.com

Upmarket bar and brew-restaurant in a National Historic Registered building with a mezzanine ten-barrel brewery and a lovely outdoor area – great for alfresco ales and eating. Of the seven easy-drinking, small-batch ales, Honey Cream Ale makes for a mellow after-dinner tipple while the Hefeweizen impressed.

Standing Stone has not stood still when it comes to the environment. On average, 85% of the brewing grains used are organic and the first-rate food menu (wood-fired pizzas, soups, salads and sandwiches) includes local and organic greens, cheese and meat

Mia & Pia's – popular with locals

(including bison beef).It also passes on its used cooking oil to a local bio-diesel company, uses 100% recycled office paper and offsets its energy use with wind power and solar panels on the roof.

Recommendation

Double India Pale Ale

Unfiltered amber pale ale with intense hop bitterness and 100% organic malt that gives the five hop additions (Nugget, Crystal, Centennial, Cascade and Amarillo – IBU 95) something to hang on to.

Wild River Brewing & Pizza (52)

595 NE. E. St., Grants Pass, OR
T 541 471 7487
www.wildriverbrewing.com

Owner Jerry Miller floated Wild River back in 1994 with a CAMRA card-carrying brewer from England. Initially English in style, Wild River's beers now also embrace the German brewing tradition. Bock, Kölsch and Weizens rub shoulders with ales, Porters and bitters inspired by Blighty.

Wild River's flagship brewery, in the middle of Grant's Pass, serves wood-fired, hand-chucked pizzas with dough made with the spent grain from the 15-barrel brewery and beer features heavily in the food menu.

Many of the beers are based on recipes in old European brewing journals and executed using Northwest ingredients. Cask versions are occasionally available.

Opening hours: Sun-Thu, 10.30am-10.30pm; Fri & Sat, 10.30am-11pm

Recommendation

Blackberry Porter (5.7%)

Based on Whitbread's 1750 London Porter recipe, 16lbs of Oregon wild blackberries are thrown in the brew to create a deep oak-coloured, richly roasted and resinous drop.

Wild River Brewing & Pizza Company (53)

2684 N. Pacific Hwy., Medford, OR 97501
T 541 773 7487

Opened in November 2006, the latest addition to the Wild River portfolio serves wood-fired pizzas.

Opening hours: daily, 10:30am-11:00pm

Wild River Pizza & Brewery (54)

249 North Redwood Hwy., Cave Junction, OR 97523
T 541 592 3556

The original Wild River restaurant, here since 1975, added a 7.5 barrel brewery in 1990 and has a great outdoor deck.

Opening hours: Sun-Thu, 10.30am-10.30pm; Fri & Sat, 10.30am-11pm

BEER BARS

The Beau Club (55)

347 E. Main St., Ashland, OR 97520
T 541 482 4185

Smoky and just a little seedy, the Beau's long bar is home to a strong selection of spirits and a batch of Northwest brews on keg to the tunes of a rocking juke box. For late-night libations, locals say there's nowhere better.

Opening hours: daily, 11am-close

Black Sheep (56)

51 North Main St., Ashland, OR
T 541 482 6414
www.theblacksheep.com

A big, brash British pub above the plaza with views of the mountains, crammed to the gills

Alfresco dining at Wild River Brewing & Pizza

with Blighty-related bumpf. There's more excitement in the chiller than on the bar top, where a few standard 'macro-micros' reside (don't be fooled by the Fuller's hand-pull as it's keg not cask). Bottles include Melbourn Brothers, Lindemans, Lambics and Young's Double Chocolate Stout. Free Wi-Fi, English football on widescreen HDTV, darts, backgammon and a roaring wood fire are also thrown in.

Opening hours: daily, 11.30am-1am

Creekside Pizza Bistro (57)

92 N. Main St., Ashland, OR 97520
T 541 482 4131
www.myspace.com/creeksidepizzabistro

A pizza pie and a pint on the neat outdoor veranda, above a babbling brook decked in fairy lights, was really rather pleasant if truth be told. Bingo night on Monday and a quiz on Thursday.

Opening hours: daily, 11am-close

Jefferson State Pub (58)

31 Water St., Ashland OR
T 541 482 7718
www.thejeffersonstatepub.com

Lively music pub by the river with Caldera, Walkabout, Rogue and Deschutes on its

tap handles. As well as the live music and comedy nights, many come for its dedication to all things spiritual (try the local Cascade Vodka and Rogue rums) while others flock for the chef's speciality – fish and chips. With four types of chips, ten finger-licking dipping sauces, beer, tempura or chilli lime batter, and half a dozen fish and seafood choices, including Alaskan Halibut and Baby Scallops, the Piscean permutations are endless. Lovely.

Opening hours: daily, 3pm-1am

Wild River Pub (59)

533 NE. "F" St., Grants Pass, OR 9752
T 541 474 4456

Basic bar just round the corner from the brewery (see page 203).

Opening hours: Sun-Thu, 10.30am-10.30pm;
Fri & Sat, 10.30am-11pm

Wild River Pizza (60)

16279 Hwy., 101 S., Brookings Harbor,
OR 97415-9485
T 541 469 7454

Cosy, wood-clad restaurant with pizzas, pool and packaged Wild River ales to take away.

Opening hours: daily, 10:30am-11:00pm

Bend and Central Oregon

BEND is central Oregon's economic engine-room and, with a population of around 80,000, by far the largest city in the region. It is currently one of the top-ten fastest growing metropolitan areas in all of America and, in recent years, has boomed as the recreational capital of the Northwest.

Blessed with a high-desert climate (sunny days, crisp nights and low humidity), Bend's bucolic blue-sky backyard offers 1.5 million acres of National Forest, 500 miles of rivers and 150 lakes, including the famous Cascade Lakes. There are 25 terrific golf courses, mountain biking, fishing, hiking, camping, rock climbing at Smith Rock, white-water rafting on the daredevil Deschutes River and phenomenal powder skiing at Mt. Batchelor, an Olympic-calibre 9,065 foot ski mountain that averages more than 370 inches of the fluffy stuff every year, has 71 runs and 3,683 acres of gnarly vertical drop.

There's shopper's heaven in the form of Downtown Bend – home to brand-name retailers and bespoke boutiques, art galleries, outdoor outfitters and antique shops. Intense retail therapy can be further sought at the triple smoke-stacked Old Mill District – a funky, old-fashioned shrine to the leisure dollar.

Bend's nightlife is surprisingly buzzy, with a flourishing bar scene, several brew-pubs and beer friendly restaurants, a couple of cruising clubs and one of the finest McMenamins pubs in the whole of the Northwest. Bend is also the hometown of the legendary Deschutes Brewery.

Bend is smack bang in the middle of lots of fun and, being a bonza beer town, it's little wonder so many people are moving here in such large numbers.

BREWERY

Deschutes Brewery (61)
See feature on pages 206–207.

Deschutes Brewery ⁽⁶¹⁾

901 SW. Simpson Ave., Bend, OR 97702
T 541 385 8606
www.deschutesbrewery.com

Deschutes Brewpub (65)
1044 NW. Bond St., Bend, OR 97701
T 541 382 9242

Deschutes is the sixth biggest craft brewery in America, the second biggest in Oregon (two places behind Widmer) and unique in that its success has been founded on the popularity of a dark beer.

"A lot of industry pundits found it very hard to believe that a dark beer could sell so well and be the focus," says Deschutes' founder, Gary Fish. *"Our main flagship beer is Black Butte Porter – America's leading porter. We worked very hard for nearly two decades to make people realise that you shouldn't judge a beer by its colour."*

What also distinguishes Deschutes from other microbrewers is its exclusive use of whole, fresh hops. Mirror Pond Ale, first brewed in 1997 and a local favourite, is the only Oregon craft beer made exclusively with locally grown, whole flower Cascade hops. Named one of America's ten best beers by *Playboy* magazine, Mirror Pond Pale Ale also won a gold medal at the Brewing Industry International Awards in 2002.

"Mirror Pond Pale Ale is a strong, hoppy beer but nowhere near as aggressive as some of the Northwest beers which I find can be a bit off-putting," says Gary. *"We're not looking to make a lot of these wacky beers. We're trying to make traditional styles with a north-west influence and do them a little bit better than everyone else. We like to use hops but the more we taste these beers with heavy hop character the less we find balance and it's interesting to see whether that will last. We keep one eye on the history and tradition of brewing but the other on progress and we are always embracing new methods,"* he adds. *"We've grown but kept the micro personality. We still brew beer in very small batches at the brewpub."*

The vast majority of the 150,000-plus barrels brewed every year come from the Deschutes principal brewing facility, opened in 1993 with a 50-barrel traditional gravity brewhouse and a new one-of-a-kind 131-barrel Huppmann brew system from Germany.

On its 12.5 barrel system, the Deschutes Public House and Brewery in Bend is responsible for the 'Bond Street Series', a collection of limited edition, idiosyncratic ales released in small batches. These have included Hop Ale, made with wet hop flowers; Hop Henge Imperial IPA; a Huppmann-inspired German Pilsner called 18th Anniversary Pilsner; and the big bottom-fermented beauty Broken Top Bock.

As well as the Deschutes standards and a couple of cask conditioned versions, the brewpub continues to brew its own bespoke ales and rotates brewers every 12 weeks with each one armed with the task of creating 'something unique'. On our visit, for example, we sampled 4k Pils, brewed to celebrate the 4000th beer brewed at the pub; a Pilsner fermented with champagne yeast called Champizzle; an organic amber ale; an excellent abbey ale and a Coffee Double Bock (10.5%) brewed using a blend of Ethiopian and Sumatran coffee beans. It was great fun.

Such is the seductive selection of ales, there's no real need to mention the pub's buzzy vibe, marvellous food menu and amusing bartender banter but we thought you'd like to know anyway. Another Deschutes brewpub is due to open in Portland – check out the website for details.

Brewery tours: Tue-Fri, 1pm, 2.30pm, 4pm; Sat noon-4pm

Brewpub hours: Mon-Thu, 11am-11pm; Fri & Sat, 11am-midnight; Sun, 11am-10pm

THE BEERS

Cascade Ale (4.6%)
Herbal hop nose gives way to a medium-bodied malt smoothness and a clean, pear-drop finish.

Buzzsaw Brown (4.8%)
Oak-coloured ale underpinned with shortbread sweetness and a very delicate lingering bitterness.

Twilight Ale (5%)
Frisky and vigorous hop-thrusted ale that finishes sweetly.

Bachelor ESB (5.2%)
Big maltiness balanced by robust bitterness and a crisp, warm finish.

Cinder Code Red (5.4%)
Treacle-tasting tipple brewed with caramel malt, roasted barley and hops of the Amarillo and Tettnang variety.

Black Butte Porter (5.5%)
Beautifully balanced bitterness and chocolate-tinged sweetness. A slightly smoky finish like coffee brewed on a bonfire.

Mirror Pond Pale Ale (5.5%)
Archetypal American pale ale with pronounced caramel malt yet leaving plenty of room for a flurry of floral Cascade hops. Fantastic.

Obsidian Stout (6.4%)
Mocha and dark chocolate take centre stage in this chewy challenger to Deschutes dark beer throne.

Jubelale (6.7%)
Marvellously malty Christmas ale sharpened by hop bitterness derived from all manner of American & European hops.

Inversion IPA (6.8%)
Zesty grapefruit, bold citrus and pine flavours. Balanced out by soft and sweet malt. Very refreshing.

Reserve Series
In 2005, Deschutes officially launched its Reserve Series with Mirror Mirror, a formidable oak-aged barley wine inspired by a double batch of Mirror Pond Pale Ale. The following year, it launched an Imperial Stout, appropriately named The Abyss after its dark, deep and liver-destroying charm.

BREWPUBS

Bend Brewing Company (62)

1019 NW. Brooks St., Bend, OR 97701
T 541 383 1599
www.bendbrewingco.com

The BBC has been brewing in central Bend since 1995 and is slightly posher than other brewpubs in town. The ales of female brewmaster Tonya Cornett, a gradate of the World Brewing Academy, impress across the board and are certainly capable of standing toe-to-toe with those coming out of the Deschutes brewpub down the road. Tonya creates five signature beers and an array of seasonals, including the HopHead Imperial IPA, a GABF gold medal winner in 2005. In the summer months, take a sup on the surprisingly dry and refreshing Apricot Ale on the outdoor patio overlooking the Deschutes River.

Opening hours: daily, 11.30am–close

Recommendation

Outback Old Ale (c. 6%)
Wrap your gums around the plums and prunes of this dark copper coloured, malt-driven winter warmer with a fruity finish. Perfect after a day of powder carving.

Cascade Lakes Brewing (63)

2141 SW. 1st St., Redmond, OR 97756
T 541 923 3110
www.cascadelakes.com

Since 1994, Cascade Lakes Brewery has made its name with dependable beers and six unpretentious bars, restaurants and brewpubs in both Bend and nearby Redmond. What the core selection of beers lack in adventure, they make up for in across-the-board consistency and play to their core mainstream following. Monkey Face Porter, named after a famous Smith Rock ascent, improved as it warmed up, while the Pine Marten Pale Ale sported an uplifting floral aroma that also delivered on the palate. Tours of the 20-barrel brewhouse are by appointment only.

Recommendation

Rooster Tail Ale (5.2%)
Light bodied, golden style ale brewed with Cascade hops and two-row Vienna and Crystal malt. At just 30 IBU it's quenching and crisp in finish.

Cascade Lodge (64)

1441 SW. Chandler Ave. Suite 100, Bend, OR 97702
T 541 388 4998

Huge alpine-style brewpub that lures in locals, families and tourists with good value lunch and dinner specials, pool tables, darts, an outdoor heated patio in the summer and log fires in the winter months. A much better bet than Cascade West.

Opening hours: Sun-Thu, 11am-12pm; Fri & Sat, 11am-1am

Deschutes Brewpub (65)

See feature on pages 206–207.

Old St. Francis School (66)

700 NW. Bond St., Bend, OR 97701
T 541 382 5174/877 661 4228
Movie line 541 330 8562
www.mcmenamins.com

Highly recommended

Once a 1930s stoic Catholic schoolhouse, St. Francis has been transformed into one of the most remarkable beer destinations in all of Oregon. Acquired in 2004 by the McMenamin brothers, much of the original schoolhouse has been retained to house a bustling pub,

The alpine-style Cascade Lodge

brewery and bakery, a movie theater, a truly fantastic Turkish-style soaking pool and a handful of dainty drinking holes. Beers are brewed in an old kindergarten classroom where artwork from students still hangs from the walls. The main schoolhouse hosts the bar and the classrooms have been turned into lodging rooms. The gymnasium is an enormous movie theatre where you can drink, dine and drift off on comfy sofas.

Fireside Bar @ St.Francis
Cosy, late-night drinking snug with a duo of pool tables, a hearty food menu and a roaring fire.
Opening hours: Mon-Thu, 4pm-1.30am; Fri, 3pm-1.30am; Sat & Sun, noon-1.30am

O'Kanes @ St Francis
Located behind the main building, O'Kanes is a groovy little garage bar with a few tables and outdoor seating.
Opening hours: Mon-Thu, 4-11pm; Fri, 4pm-midnight; Sat, 1pm-midnight; Sun, 1pm-11pm

The Old St. Francis Pub
Roomy pub occupying the school's main building with a friendly, square bar and alfresco dining and drinking on the patio.
Opening hours: daily, 7am-1am

Seventh Street Brewhouse (67)
855 SW 7th St., Redmond, OR 97756
T 541 923 1795
Long, well-established restaurant, bar and

brewery that's a big favourite among Redmond residents. A garage door opens out onto a horseshoe pit and heated outdoor deck while inside, nestled next to a compact brewhouse viewed beyond a glass partition, the bar serves spirits, all the Cascade Lakes beers and a terrific line in comforting, indulgent pub cuisine and take-away pizzas.
Opening hours: Mon-Thu, 11.30am-11pm; Fri & Sat, 11.30am-12am; Sun, noon-9pm

Silver Moon Brewing (68)
24 NW. Greenwood Ave., Bend, OR 97701
T 541 388 8331
www.silvermoonbrewing.com
Silver Moon Brewing has been crafting beers in Downtown Bend since 2005 on the same site as a homebrew supply store. Five core ales are made at the 15-barrel brewhouse and poured at the sparsely furnished yet comfortable taproom, which hosts regular live music on Wednesday and Saturday nights and serves simple but perfectly decent pub food. The beers varied in quality with Bridge Creek Pilsner, Snake Bite Porter and the Hounds Tooth Amber the most impressive.
Opening hours: Mon-Sat, 2pm-11pm
Recommendation
Hounds Tooth Amber (4.4%)
Tangy, amber ale with a delicious creme caramel flavour. A delicate hop presence avoids any cloying cling to the mouth.

DownTowners coffee shop and deli

BEER BARS

Cascade West Grub & Ale House   (69)
64 SW. 14th St., Bend, Oregon 97701
T 541 389 1853
Scruffy sports bar and shrine to the Blue Collar dollar on a main drag. The focus is on at-the-bar drinking, TV screens, pool tables and gambling machines. A good place to watch sports with a decent beer but other than that...
Opening hours: daily, 10.30am-1am

DownTowners   (70)
852 Brooks St., Bend, OR 97701
T 541 388 2467
Small sandwich bar, coffee shop and deli down by the river where New Jersey-style subs, salads and soups can be chased down by a terrific selection of bottled and draught microbrews with great views of the park.
Opening hours: Mon, 11am-3pm; Tue-Sat: 11am-8pm

JC's Bar & Grill   (71)
642 NW. Franklin, Bend, OR 97702
T 541 383 3000
www.myspace.com/jcsbend
Customary sports bar and grill, opened in 2003 by twin brothers and Oregon State alumni Jeremy and Chris Cox. The bar was expanded in January 2007, and the Cox brothers started the Wildfire Brewing Company with ex-Deschutes brewer Paul Cook. The brewhouse, located out of town, proffers a trio of lager-friendly, rather

lightweight libations including Summer Seasonal, all citrus with a banana aftertaste, and Wildfire Logger, a malty Munich-style lager. The two-room bar, where students come to par-tay, has shuffleboard, pool, plenty of neon, well spoken-of burgers and more televised sports than you can shake a remote control at.
Opening hours: daily, 11am-2.30am
Recommendation
Code 24
Pale Ale with a resinous bite to it. By far Wildfire's finest beer.

Red Dog Depot   (72)
3716 SW. 21st Place, Redmond, OR 97756
T 541 923 6440
www.reddogdepot.com
The Red Dog opened in late 2007 as the latest drinking and dining missionary spreading the gospel according to Cascade Lakes. There's a strong canine theme with doggie décor throughout and even on the menu – try the Canine Cobb or drop in on 'Dawg Day' when Chicago-style hot dogs are on special. Outdoor seating, board games and free Wi-Fi make it a fine addition to Redmond's embryonic beer scene.
Opening hours: daily, 11am-11pm

Tumalo Tavern   (73)
64670 Stricker #103, Bend, OR 97701
T 541 330 2323
As well as the Cascade Lakes portfolio, there's a strong wine selection and an impressive back bar of spirits. Pool tables, too. No surprises but okay for a cheeky pint or two.
Opening hours: daily, 11am-midnight

Eastern Oregon

EASTERN OREGON is split into three distinct regions – the Northeast, the Southeast and the Columbia River Plateau – and they're all jolly beautiful places where stunning vistas surpass people in quite some number. In comparison with Western Oregon, the beer scene in the East is as barren as the wilds that make up the region.

One of the best ways to drink in brews and views is to embark on the dazzling Hells Canyon Scenic Byway, a 208-mile, 7–8 hour loop encircling the Wallowa Mountains; Hell's Canyon – north America's deepest gorge; hair-rising rapids; and some of the best rock formations since Led Zeppelin in their heyday. But best of all, at Baker City and then Enterprise, it incorporates Eastern Oregon's leading breweries.

BREWPUBS

Barley Brown's Brewpub (74)
2190 Main St., Baker City, OR 97814
T 541 523 4266

Baker is a quaint, old-fashioned town with museums, shops and a heightened awareness of its Wild West origins. It's also home to a bloody good brewpub, too. You'd be forgiven for assuming that the lack of nearby competition would lull Barley Brown's into complacency, but owner Tyler Brown and head brewer Shawn Kelso brew some appealing beers amid well-dressed décor.

Produced on a four-barrel brewhouse visible behind glass, just about every beer impresses, and there's a commendable commitment to daredevil drinking. Clam linguini, spinach frisee and mad pasta are just some of the tasty morsels to stand out on the meat-heavy food menu.

Opening hours: daily, 4pm-10pm
Recommendation
Turmoil Ale (7.6%)
A dark destroyer dripping in hop flavour and a touch of dry roasted peanuts. Fluffy head with impressive and ominously alcoholic lacing down the glass.

Terminal Gravity Brewing (75)
803 SE. School St., Enterprise, OR 97828-1674
T 541 426 0158
www.terminalgravitybrewing.com

Of all the brewpubs in all eastern Oregon, this one is by far the best. Terminal Gravity is essentially a suburban house and garage where people are welcome to pop by and chill out with a notably strong selection of superbly-crafted ales. The bar is very small, with just a couple of tables and stools. Upstairs things get a little roomier with sofas, darts and space to kick-back and relax. The best place to drink the beer is outside on the porch or in the gorgeous garden.

The most popular ale to come out of the adjacent brewery, plonked in a small garage, is Terminal Gravity IPA, but take the opportunity to sample TG's other fine ales – most of which have been zapped with heavy hop character. A beast of a barley wine called Bucolic Plague gets better with age, while the TG Triple is a strong Abbey ale indoctrinated with orange, coriander and a fabulously floral hop aroma. The staff are laid-back and incredibly friendly, there's simple pub food if you want it and make sure you check out the superb, bespoke hand-blown glasses.

Opening hours: Wed-Sat, 3-10pm
Recommendation
Terminal Gravity IPA (6.7%)
A brawny bottle-conditioned beer with a weighty mouthfeel and a deep shade of orange, conjuring up tastes of citrus, ginger, pine and fruity hoppiness. The finish is head-tiltingly bitter yet lovely and smooth.

GREATER PORTLAND

Vancouver
WASHINGTON

Columbia River

Portland
see map below for
sites in this area

Forest
Grove

Hillsboro

Gresham

OREGON

Beaverton

Happy
Valley

Tigard

Lake Oswego

Gladstone

5 km
5 miles

PORTLAND

Ainsworth St
Fernhill
Park

Killingsworth St

Alberta St

Freemont St

Willamette River

Nicolai St

Broadway

Pittock
Acres
Park

Lovejoy St

Glisan St

Glisan St

Everett St

Burnside St

Burnside St
Laurelhurst
Park

Washington
Park

Taylor St

Stark St

Belmont St

Hawthorne St

Marquam
Nature
Park

Duniway
Park

Division St

Powell Blvd

Holgate Blvd

Brewery
Brewpub
Beer bar

Willamette River

OREGON

WASHINGTON

OREGON

CALIFORNIA

IDAHO

PACIFIC OCEAN

Astoria
Kelso
Grandview   Richland   Pasco
Kennewick
Seaside
Columbia
Hermiston   Milton-Freewater
Portland
(see p212 for Portland)
Beaverton   Hood River   Pendleton
Gresham   The Dalles
La Grande   Enterprise
McMinnville
Lincoln City
Salem
Madras   Baker City
Newport
Albany
Corvallis
Canyon City   Ontario
Sweet Home
Santa Clara   Springfield   Prineville
Florence   Eugene   Bend   Caldwell
Redmond
North Bend   Burns
Malheur Lake
Roseburg
Green
Upper Klamath Lake
Grants Pass   White City
Brookings   Medford
Ashland   Klamath Falls   Lake View
Crescent City   Goose Lake

50 km
50 miles

● Brewery
● Brewpub
● Beer bar

Washington

KNOWN AS the Evergreen State, Washington is a beautiful and lush part of America, reaching from its pine-lined coast, across the mystical Puget Sound, up to the northern tip of America, across to the Cascade mountains and through eastern flatlands. With a more temperate climate than its southern West Coast cousins, there's a bit of rain knocking around, but that simply enhances the atmosphere and beauty. Besides, a rainy day is a great excuse to sit in a bar and enjoy a pint.

State history

When it comes to the northern reaches of the West Coast, the Spaniards started the standard 'Europeans beating up Native Americans' charge back in the eighteenth century, situating themselves on ports all the way up the seaboard. By 1790 the Brits had waded in so, in a bid to avert a European war over the land, the bigwigs from each nation got together at the Nootka Convention and amicably agreed on territory divisions.

When legendary explorers Meriwether Lewis and William Clark started sniffing around in 1805 it was clear the Americans wanted a piece of the action, but it took until the mid-1800s for the Spaniards and British to give up the land completely.

By 1889 the area previously regarded 'Oregon Territory' became Washington State, and it was then that the various towns and cities really began to develop, centring around the Puget Sound, a body of water that serves a number of towns with ports and thus access to the Pacific. Among them was obviously Seattle, but elsewhere southern towns like Olympia would become the state capital and Tacoma boomed as an industrial centre with its smelting of metals. In the north, the likes of Bellingham benefited

from gold rushes and Port Townsend become a centre for boat-building; while in the east Walla Walla (say it quickly and repeatedly) and Spokane continued to shelter travellers from the east and generate additional income from agriculture.

The industrial revolution provided the main source of income into the twentieth century and Washington really came into its own during the World Wars. Steady urban growth up to this point aroused itself to a sudden spurt and it was industrial giant Boeing that proved the lubricant. As well as planes the need for ships kept employment levels afloat and helped many towns around the Puget Sound recover from the Great Depression. This period also saw the building of the Grand Coulee Dam in 1941, the largest concrete structure in the country, and in 1954 the state saw the flight path turn commercial with the first Boeing 707 take off.

This commitment to technological advance continued well into the next few decades, particularly in the Seventies, when IT behemoth Microsoft moved its head office to Bellevue. It was a trend of techiness that continues to the present day, only once rudely interrupted in 1980 when the eruption of Mount St. Helens reminded all that computers aren't a patch on mother nature.

Today

Many of the towns that emerged from the twentieth century continue to prosper today but the emphasis of industry has obviously shifted, with most now benefiting from the fruits of tourism. The northern areas of the state enjoy a rich vein of interest from visitors both international and domestic, and the busy ferry services around the Puget Sound provide the opportunity to take in the spectacular surroundings.

Left: Snoqualmie Falls, one of a host of beauty spots in Washington State.

The beautiful northern climbs of Washington include the quaint conservative towns of Port Townsend and Bellingham showcasing some interesting Victorian architecture, all a must see.

Out east, the farming trade continues to flourish. Of the gems out here Walla Walla is possibly the best, although this is now an up-and-coming wine region, so not entirely devoted to beer.

Heading south to the Oregon border you'll hit the state capital Olympia, with a number of good beer bars and some fantastic architecture peppered around it. It's also a centre for fine arts and holds a film festival each year. Tacoma, the second largest city on the Puget, proves more blue collar, and its port remains a key economic driver. There's culture here, too, with the Washington State History Museum and America's Car Museum among places of interest.

If you make it to the border, the beautiful lakes and countryside around Vancouver and Stevenson prove the perfect setting for hiking, camping and, down on the Columbia, even a bit of kiteboarding.

Orientation

It's another 'get a map' job folks – we're talking about a massive state, and driving around it is akin to driving around the entire UK. If you're pushed for time we recommend you stay west around the coastal regions where you'll find the best beer. Most of the more significant tourist towns have motels on the outskirts, but if you want something more boutique book well in advance and expect to pay through the nose.

The beer scene

The Pacific Northwest is rightly proud of its brewing traditions, and as a result some of the standout names in the wider reaches of Washington state will be recognisable to those drinking in major towns such as Portland or Seattle.

Among the very best, not just in Washington but in the whole country, are Dick's and Boundary Bay, which should not be missed.

Beer history dates back to the 1850s in Washington, coinciding with much of the population growth and urban development of the state (building, and indeed reproducing, proving thirsty work). While prohibition rudely interrupted and ruined many of the businesses, the brewers remain proud of the heritage, so don't be surprised if you hear the likes of the Delin Brewery in Steilacoom (1854) and Leopold Schmidt and his Olympia Brewing Company (1896) mentioned.

The Nineties marked the most significant period of new growth, with the likes of Boundary Bay, Dick's and Port Townsend opening their doors and the movement as it is today really kicking in during this time. Although that makes things sound relatively young, brewers here have had more than ten years to perfect things, and as a result are producing some fantastic beers. They have the benefit of very fresh hops as well, with the Yakima Valley providing around 90% of the US supply. Washington's Hopunion looks after the farming of the crops and is one of the most important beer-related organisations in the country.

Most of the drinking holes you'll find in the state are brewpubs – selling beer on site is economically sound and enables increased revenue from food and entertainment. There are plenty of decent beer bars, but for the most unique beer experiences in this state you should try as many brewpubs as you can fit into your schedule.

While we're talking up Washington beer, we owe a debt of thanks to the Guild and the Brew-Ha map people. You can pick up a Guild list from www.washingtonbeer.com or a map from most of the brewpubs listed in the following pages. Read on...

Seattle

SEATTLE is a very cool American city. Regularly rocking out on its fine music scene, and bordered by a beautiful mountain range, this place is touristy, arty, fresh cuisine-y and liberally minded, there is plenty here for the holidaymaker and beer traveller alike. And while the weather has its critics, a bit of rain will not spoil the experience.

History

As we'll find later during this epic historical deliverance, Seattle is all about neighbourhoods, and interestingly the idea of small communities around a hub was something the first tribal explorers adopted thousands of years ago.

Back in the days of yore, there were villages on the foundations of Seattle, and they existed there for centuries, right up until the northern States started to lure Americans in the 1850s.

A movement to Washington state came shortly after California became passé, and migration up the coast became fashionable. The outcome proved the same as anywhere else: skirmishes with the locals leading to native displacement and American rule.

Logging enticed most people to the area with the convenience of a port proving the perfect outlet for shifting the abundance of wood south from the early 1850s. It was an industry that worked as a catalyst for development in the area and by 1860 there was a road and university, a newspaper by 1863 and a red-brick building (see most brewpubs) by 1872.

Fascination in precious metal encouraged more migration as the century drew to a close; the Klondike Gold Rush increasing economical and population growth in equal measure. A bust quickly followed, as was the trend, but by this point the city was on its way and the first ten years of the twentieth century saw more rapid urban growth.

In 1917, the aviation industry landed in Seattle with the establishment of Boeing. While it, too, would bust in the Seventies, it was incredibly influential in its time, not least during the Second World War, when the government needed planes. This, combined with the 1962 World Fair, cemented the city's role in advancing new technologies, enhanced again in 1978 when Bill Gates brought Microsoft to nearby Bellevue. The innovation wasn't restricted to technology though; art and music also flourished, particularly in the latter part of the century.

In the Nineties, Seattle turned the world's head with its music as Nirvana exploded onto the scene. Along with Pearl Jam and the record label Sub Pop, the grunge movement evolved through rock, punk and indie to ensure that teenagers all over the world would wear oversized jumpers and eyeliner. Albums such as Nirvana's *Nevermind* and Pearl Jam's *Ten* were huge and paved the way for today's alternative music tastes.

Art in general has been an important part of the city, lest we forget the celebrated Seattle Erotic Art Festival, something we attended purely as art critics. Thanks to the Seattle Art Museum, opened back in 1933, these creative traditions continue today.

The dot.com boom came to town in the Nineties – Seattle a hub for budding Internet entrepreneurs who pre-empted the actual financial rewards of online services with massive investment, only to see the bubble burst at the end of the decade. One company to survive and indeed prosper was Amazon.com, the bookseller now a profitable operation with its HQ consisting of three rather large buildings in Seattle.

Another big commercial addition to the city has been Starbucks, the first 'store' opened in the Seventies. By the Nineties, Starbucks were apparently building one a day, the success akin to McDonalds.

Talking of amazing cuisine, the proximity of Seattle and its Pacific coastline means fishing has also played a significant role in history. The Pike Place Market opened in 1907 and as well as fresh veg, fish quickly became a mainstay and remains so today. Around it a hub of businesses would gradually emerge, including the Pike Place Brewery next door in 1989.

Music, fish, beer, what more could you want? And all of it evolving in a remarkably brief 150 years to provide one of America's more vibrant and attractive cities.

The town today

Put on the map by a radio psychiatrist and a depressive grunge band front man, Seattle today keeps itself perky with some incredibly strong coffee and a rich vein of art and culture.

The fish market remains one of the must-see tourist stops with the market workers an attraction in their own right, flinging the day's catch around. The labours of local fishermen can be found in a host of good Seattle restaurants, beautifully fresh, and the chowder alone is worth a visit to one of the more low-key cafes.

That radio psychiatrist (*Frasier* from the multi-award winning sitcom for the uninitiated) promoted the popular image of the Space Needle in its credits, and consequently this is another popular tourist hangout. Panoramic views are always welcome, and it struts as proudly as John Holmes from the vista, so you can't miss it.

A keen sports town, the city boasts a Major League baseball side (Mariners), football team (Seahawks) and basketball outfit (Sonics), and tickets for all should be easily obtained.

But many come here for the music. Kurt Cobain and the Nineties grunge explosion have developed into something much more diverse in Seattle today. Gigs are ten a penny, with every musical representation on offer. Fliers stack up in every bar or coffee shop and wallpaper telephone poles. The local newspapers carry the listings.

Amazon.com and its success means books are important to people here today and prove an escape best served with coffee. Although Starbucks now inspires a sneer from locals, most will have a favourite independent coffee house, and you won't struggle to find one where, as with the music, all tastes are accounted for, every bean on offer.

Compared to somewhere like Portland, it's fair to say there's more of a corporate feel, but a liberal leaning remains and while locals might be viewed walking around in business attire, they'll have tattoos underneath. There's an underbelly, just as there is a conventional tourist ambience, making it a town with something for everyone.

Orientation

When we got to the airport car hire desk, tired and under prepared, we ended up with a Chrysler Cruiser convertible. This is definitely a camp motor, have no doubt, but also highly useless in a town where it regularly rains. Our advice: hire a car if you must, but don't get a convertible.

Without a car the options are buses or cabs. Buses are very well run, frequent and serve the entire terrain; stop off at a major station such as West Lake to get passes. Meanwhile the cabs are affordable while the pound is strong and in good supply should you want a more direct journey.

This is very much a neighbourhood town – there is a downtown area but it's tourist heavy and a bit pricier so try and get out and about. Residential areas are always broken up with a decent bar, and so are well worth exploring. Take Ballard, for example, north of Downtown, once remarkable only for its blue collar and residential persona. More recently it has added a host of top beer bars, and subsequently become a nightlife nucleus.

Fremont next door is a bit more middle class but equally endowed in the bar department. The U-District is dominated by the university and consequently has a student scene, but some of the best new bands play here, and it's a friendly night out. And up the road in Green Lake you have a couple of the most respected beer bars in town.

Georgetown is set on a main road, but the lively strip of bars includes a pizza place and is a gem for a night out. More conventional in its layout is Capitol Hill – buzzing with bars, it seems the busiest of the neighbourhoods and is also home to the gay scene.

Downtown is certainly not to be sniffed at, though, and has some good bars, not to mention the historic Pike Brewing Co. Brewpub in the Pike Market. Just up the road is Belltown, where a 'better class' of people try to recreate a Chelsea vibe.

There's plenty more: the Summit is a great find not far from Capitol Hill, while Prost, The Park and Sully's Snowgoose form a triumvirate of top boozers in Phinney.

As ever, our advice is buy a map and head to one of the neighbourhoods for the evening.

Accommodation

LUXURY

Grand Hyatt Seattle 721 Pine St., Seattle, WA 98101; **T** 206 774 1234
It's a Hyatt, so you should expect luxury, and as a result you'll pay through the nose, but if your trip to Seattle includes a non-beer fan who needs appeasing, we reckon this'll do the trick. $260 per night.

BUDGET

Green Tortoise Hostel 105 Pike St., Seattle, WA 98101; T 206 340 1222; www.greentortoise.net
A reasonable hostel (but not exactly super budget) well located in the Downtown area, invariably buzzing with global guests. Most rooms are for sharing, a four bed coming in at $29 per person.

Other stuff

The Space Needle   www.spaceneedle.com
Like any tourist attraction, expect a swarm of, well, tourists – but it does offer 360 degree spectacular views, 520 feet above the city. There's also a restaurant up here. Book well in advance. *Observation deck hours:* Sun-Thu 9am-11pm; Fri & Sat 9am-midnight

Seattle Aquarium

1483 Alaskan Way, Seattle, WA 98101; **T** 206 386 4300; www.seattleaquarium.org
Plenty of sea life on offer here, including a shark – alas not a great white – and a host of mammals. Adults $15 entry. *Opening hours:* 9:30am-7pm daily summer; 10am-5pm out of season

The Seattle beer scene

There's certainly a rich history of brewing in Seattle, with Seattle Malting and Brewing established way back in 1878, subsequently becoming the biggest industrial employer by 1914. In 1883, Andrew Hemrich opened the Bay View Brewery, more familiarly known as Rainer, and its legacy is still firmly in the hearts of most locals, particularly around its famous home in Georgetown – the building now used by Tully's Coffee for nine years.

Prohibition put a stop to all that, and it wasn't really until 1981 that local brewers re-established themselves in the city. It was in this year that Paul Shipman and Gordon Bowker opened Redhook Ales in Fremont, and it is their development that seems to have resuscitated the movement.

Among one of the early forerunners was Charles Finkel, an importer who brought great beer to the Seattle public's attention in the late Seventies. Charles would later open the Pike Brewing Company in 1989, following the success of Hales Ales, opened in 1983, and subsequently encouraging the opening of Maritime in 1990. All three are still important breweries today.

It seems ironic that the closure of such an iconic beer site in Rainer should coincide with the creation of the Washington State Brewers Guild, but in 1999 that's what happened. Since then, the Guild has been promoting its members' beers at various festivals throughout the year as well as the good work of its brewers.

These days, though, the majority of what you'll find is beer bars and because there's so much competition there is a rich diversity of venues, all very welcoming.

BREWERIES

Baron Brewing (1)

1605 South 93rd St., Building E, Unit L, Seattle, WA 98108

T 206 764 1213

www.baronbeer.com

This place is making some great beers, all German in style and most of them on offer at one of many bars around Seattle. The Baron Pils, for example, is a fine example of its breed, clear with a healthy, frothy head and as refreshing as the fall of the Berlin Wall. The Schwarzbier also delivers; smoky satisfaction balanced with a crisp, moderately bitter bite. The Hefe-Weisse is a move away from American interpretations and back towards the traditional style; the banana and chocolate aromas of the Uber-Weisse are richly rewarding. There are plenty of seasonal offerings as well; the Oktoberfest has a Batman POW, the Liberator Doppelbock Robin BLAM. All ingredients are imported, all brewing executed according to the Reinheitsgebot, and as a result this is not only a welcome addition to the brewing scene on the West Coast, but also ample evidence that a world-renowned style can be brewed successfully on foreign shores.

Brewery tours: by appointment only

Recommendation

The **Munich Helles Lager** *gets points for effort; this particular brew benefiting from a 10-12 week lagering process. Smooth and buttery, it has enough bitterness at the back to remind you that hops are involved, without intruding on the experience.*

Georgetown (2)

5840 Airport Way S., Unit 201, Seattle, WA 98108

T 206 766 8055

www.georgetownbeer.com

Highly recommended

A relative newcomer to the scene, the guys at Georgetown have kept things simple, offering three core beers and a seasonal. Manny's Pale is the flagship, making up 90% of sales, and the nod to Sierra Nevada's Pale is obvious but very capably executed. The citrus hit of the hop is just above the malt and at 5.5% is reasonably sessionable.

The Pilsner is also worthy, sweet but crisp and refreshing, and Choppers Red at 6.5% has a bit more punch. The seasonal Bob's Brown is a newer addition and perhaps it shows, but with all profits from the beer going to a cancer charity, try it for yourself.

The site is a must visit, not least because it's a brewery tour you can do before heading to the great bars lining the street opposite.

The team behind Georgetown are driven, focused and savvy; they've watched the market carefully over the last decade or so and have learned a great deal. They're also very friendly folk. Expect more from them in the future.

Opening hours: Mon-Fri, 10am-6pm; Sat, 9am-midnight; Sun, closed

Recommendation

Manny's Pale (5.5%)

The flagship for good reason. New but it's excellently done and could easily become a session beer for the craft crowd.

Pacific Rim Brewing Co. (3)

9832 14th Ave SW, Seattle, WA

www.pacificrimbrewing.com

Based in the White Centre part of Seattle, down south and not far from Burien, industrial surroundings make this a grey offering outside. Persevere and step inside where there's an impressive collection of tap handles hanging from the ceiling.

Elsewhere the commitment to beer is obvious; a direct fire kettle makes for an interesting addition to the brewery, which is producing a nice variety of beer. The Rat City IPA takes its name from local slang for the blue collar crowd and is a great example of a Pacific Northwest interpretation. The Driftwood Ale takes an American pale and gives it a stodgy Belgian feel. The brewers self distribute; beers can be found in bars around Seattle as well as on site. We hadn't been near the rim for some time but can recommend a taste of this one.

Opening hours: daily, 11am-11pm

Recommendation

Admiral ESB (7.5%)

Pacific Rim was set up by original Red Hook head brewer Charles McElevey, who makes a good fist of an ESB. Malty sweet, chewy, fruity and bitter, it has the lot and is a fair example of its breed.

BREWPUBS

Big Time (4)

4133 University Way NE., Seattle, WA 98105
T 206 545 4509
www.bigtimebrewery.com

Seattle's oldest brewpub can be found in the heart of the university district. Adding a bit of character to the standard setup, Big Time is more weathered than your average, the memorabilia on the wall reminiscent of the Berkeley set in California with exposed brick and woodwork and shuffleboard.

Subs and pizza slices hit the menu, very affordable and suitable cuisine for the locale, as is the crowd, which is clearly college, although possibly a bit older than other hangouts and certainly more discerning.

This we put down to the beer, which is very good. Indeed the Prime Time Pale Ale is a three times gold winner at the GABF. Its crisp bitterness and sweetness arrive in equal measure, making it a session beer that can easily be enjoyed the student way: in abundance.

Bhagwan's IPA Best is only 5% but doesn't lack any power in the citrus notes. A very good example of the style, the cask version is also a must if it's on. And talking of cask, it's a familiar friend here with plenty of experimentation throughout the year. A crucial beer stop on a Uni pub crawl.

Opening hours: Mon-Thu, 11.30am-12:30 am; Fri & Sat, 11.30am-1.30am

Recommendation

Coal Creek Porter (4.5%)
Another medal winner. Its incredible colour smacks of the local strong coffee and it doesn't disappoint on the palate, with its beautiful smoky flavour, lip-smacking chocolate-sweet front and bitter burnt moments at the end combining very nicely.

Elliott Bay Brewery Pub (5)

4720 California Ave. SW., Seattle, WA 98116
T 206 932 8695
www.elliottbaybrewing.com

The first and oldest of the two Elliott Bay sites, this one has more character and soul. The Elliot Bay Brewery staff are a noble lot, doing plenty to support the community and charitable causes, not least through the provision of tasty beer.

The Alembic Pale Ale is a great showcase for the Cascade hops, a useful alternative to Sierra Nevada; the Luna Weizen provides a welcome orange edge to an otherwise German offering and at 4.3% very sessionable.

Opening hours: Mon-Sat, 11am-midnight; Sun 11am-11pm

Recommendation

No Doubt Stout
Plenty of robust roasty qualities with a bit of sweet fruit on the side.

Elliott Bay Brewhouse & Pub (6)

255 SW 152nd St., Burien, Seattle, WA 98166
T 206 246 4211
www.elliottbaybrewing.com

Burien is a long way down and possibly best viewed on the way out of Seattle. A brand new venue, the sparkle and the size makes it an impressive place, but be warned, it sits on the end of a strip mall.

That said, while it may lack heritage it's still doing good business with the locals. This is no doubt partly due to the Elliott Bay beer and its reputation as award-winning stuff.

The regularly changing offerings here are interesting and with two cask beer engines it's clear the brewer is keen. The flagship is the Alembic Pale Ale, an interesting example of the style, more malty than its competitors and itself a gold winner at the GABF back in 2000. The Hop von Boorian is tasty, a hoppy offering with a Belgian yeast strain and plenty of citrus punch.

What is so impressive about this Elliott Bay set up is the commitment to the local scene. Doug Hindman is a brewer not afraid to put the local competition up against his own creations, and we say well done for that.

Opening hours: Mon-Sat, 11am-midnight; Sun, 11am-11pm

Recommendation

Highline IPA

Floral and malty in equal measure with a pleasant bitterness that isn't too overpowering.

Elysian (7)
542 1st Ave. S. Seattle, WA 98104
T 206 382 4498

Industrial chic sums up the design up here. Its impressive bar dominates proceedings in

Elysian (8)
1221 E. Pike St., Seattle, WA 98122
T 206 860 1920
www.elysianbrewing.com

The fact that brewer Dick Cantwell has been awarded Brewmaster of the Year in 1999, 2003 and 2004 gives an idea of how sound his skills really are, not to mention the countless trophies the beers have earned themselves. Dick was born in Germany but grew up in America and started his brewing career with the Seattle Brewing Co. In 1996, Dick then left his job at Pike Place Brewing Co. to set up the Elysian.

Business partners Joe Bisacca and Dave Buhler shared the vision of a brewpub, but one that was big enough to throw a decent party in. They selected an impressive building for its home in Capitol Hill, a site that remains one of the more imposing brewpubs on the West Coast. The 20-barrel brewing system got to work quickly once in place, and the good word of its beer spread successfully enough to spawn two more smaller sites in quick succession.

Since that time the team has brewed as many as 60 different types of beer, offering six standards and eight seasonals. Of them, the Wise Extra Special (5.9%) is efficiently carbonated, a beautiful deep and warm copper colour and finished with cascade hops to give it a little extra bite and character. The Perseus Porter is a creamy offering, all the smoke and bitter chocolate you'd hope for as well as a subtle citrus edge to keep it interesting. Meanwhile the Elysian Fields Pale proves the brewer has range, it's crisp, spark-

the centre of the room. Some fancy food offerings on the menu partner the always capable house beers. See the feature below for the Elysian on Pike Street.

Opening hours: daily, 11.30am-2am

Gordon Biersch (9)
600 Pine St., Seattle, WA, 98101
T 206 4054205
www.gordonbiersch.com

Opening hours: Sun-Thu, 11.30am-11pm; Fri & Sat, 11.30am-midnight

ling colour matched with a fresh grapefruit bitterness, and the Prometheus IPA, named after the fellow who stole fire from the gods to give to man, has four different hops to singe the taste buds.

Opening hours: Mon-Fri, 11.30am-2am; Sat & Sun, noon-2am

THE BEERS

Zephyrus Pilsner (4.7%)
This light, crisp effort is perfect on a blistering hot day. Spicy and malty, it's not without plenty of flavour as well as balance.

Elysian Fields Pale Ale (4.8%)
A great session beer, this has a bit of fruit and bite and crisp enough to refresh. The Simcoe hops are obvious but not to the point of over-bittering the beer. This is really tasty stuff.

Perseus Porter (5.4%)
With as much body as Pamela Anderson and then some, this beer has a sweet front and smoky end. The chocolate malts really do their job, and it's a great beer for a chilly, rainy day in Seattle.

The Wise ESB (5.9%)
A variety of malts, including ale, Munich, Crystal, Cara-hell and Belgian Special B might explain why this is deliciously... well malty. This fine dark ruby effort is a double gold winner at the GABF.

Immortal IPA (6.3%)
Plenty of complexity, with Pale, Munich, Crystal and Cara-hell malts, Chinook hops and finished with Amarillo and Centennial. This IPA is as refreshing as its lovely golden colour suggests.

Dragonstooth Stout (7.2%)
Recognised many times in competition, this stout has a tasty chocolate profile balanced with the Cascade and Centennial hops.

Hale's Ales (10)

4301 Leary Way NW, Seattle, WA 98107
T 206 706-1544
www.halesales.com
Highly recommended

Anyone who imports a red bus, sticks it in his brewery and turns it into a pub is alright by us. A bit eccentric, but alright. Mike Hale is definitely both and, having brewed in Seattle since 1983, he also makes decent beer.

The brewing arm of his business is set out the back of what used to be a hose manufacturing plant. As well as a bus, there's a 30-barrel, all steam-heated brewing system in full view from the pub.

The beer is very English in its persuasion. Indeed, Mike actually learned his craft at Gales Brewery in the UK, volunteering his services simply because of an interest and as a way to stay in the country.

"My wife was teaching there and I couldn't get a visa," says Mike. "So I walked in and asked if I could work and they said yes. It turned an interest into a passion and when I came back to the States I knew it was what I wanted to do."

He does it well, in particular the Mongoose IPA, which has much more of a malt profile than its American relations elsewhere on the West Coast. The Troll Porter is also interesting; again, much more subtle than others in this part of the world. Mike also spent some times with the Guinness crew, the influence clearly rubbing off on his stout.

The site is not exactly in Fremont but is worthy of a taxi ride. It is very near the Dish (4358 Leary Way), which serves a mean breakfast. And if you're here in April keep an eye out for the Moisture Festival with its neo-vaudeville and comic performers.
Opening hours: Mon-Thu, 11am-10pm; Fri, 11am-11pm; Sat, 9am-11pm; Sun, 9am-10pm
Recommendation
Red Menace Big Amber
A great example of the style; the caramel malt complementing the more citrus hops to give a warm winter fruit taste.

Maritime (11)

Jolly Roger Taproom, 1514 NW. Leary Way, Seattle, WA 98107
Highly recommended

Ahoy there matey (seriously) this is a local favourite, and while the brewery is small, the beers are genuinely loved in Seattle. Not least the Jolly Roger Christmas Ale which, as the name would suggest, is launched in the build up to Christmas – if you're here at that time then you must try it because the limited supply fast runs dry. The beer has such a buzz about it some bars keep it back until the summer when they'll throw festivals like 'Christmas in July' and crack it open again.

So why is it so special? Well, it's strong, very strong and as a result has a host of hilarious tales attached: 'I was in blah, blah, had a couple of Christmas Ales and the next thing I know I'm being woken up on a toilet...' And other such anecdotes. It also helps that it's very tasty, hence the problem of drinking more than one and losing part of the night. At 9% the alcohol is perfectly balanced with malt and spice; in fact it's utterly more-ish.

Situated on the edge of Ballard, the brewery was founded in 1990 by couple George and Jane Hancock. George resembles a salty seadog himself, and in the little tap room there's plenty of nautical reference. As well as the Christmas Ale the eclectic range includes the very solid Amber, Pilsner, ESB and Porter.

The bar is small but the staff is friendly and knowledgeable. The standard grub includes a German sausage selection, tasting all the better for the ambience.
Opening hours: Mon-Thu, 11am-11pm; Fri & Sat, 11am-midnight; Sun, 3pm-close
Brewery tours: If George is there and not busy he might take you around
Recommendation
Jolly Roger Christmas Ale (9%)
Did you really need to ask?

McMenamins (12)

Six Arms, 300 E. Pike St., Seattle, WA
T 206 223 1698
www.mcmenamins.com

A fairly low-key effort from the boys considering their pedigree in amazing sites, but it's just over the road from the Elysian and makes a nice change of scene.
Opening hours: Mon-Thu, 11:30am-1am; Fri & Sat, 11:30am-2am; Sun, 11:30am-midnight

Pike Brewing Company: innovators with a lot of bottle.

McMenamins (13)

Dad Watsons, 3601 Fremont Ave. N., Seattle, WA

T 206 632 6505

www.mcmenamins.com

Opening hours: Mon-Thu, 11:30am-1am; Fri & Sat, 11:30am-2am; Sun, 11:30am-midnight

---

Pike Brewing Company (14)

1415 1st Ave, Seattle, WA 98101

T 206 622 6044

www.pikebrewing.com

This is another piece of West Coast brewing history, with owner Charles Finkel the first man to import European beers into this part of the world. Obviously still frustrated by the lack of decent beer, Charles took his passion a step further when he and his wife Rose opened the Pike Pub and Brewing with back in 1989 and helped influence the trend of brewpubs and craft beer in Seattle.

This venue was subsequently sold, but Charles and Rose recently took it back on and are now brewing a lot of the beers for which it was once famous. The Pike Golden IPA is a good starting point; the citrus you'd hope for, the sweetness to make it interesting and the bitterness you've possibly come to love – watch yourself at 6.3% though. Naughty Nellies Ale comes in at 4.7% so is a bit more manageable; it's a bit lighter on the hop hit as well and quite a creamy offering that's well balanced.

And the Monk's Uncle proves the brewer has the range with all the spice of a Christmas pub balanced with a tropical fruit kick.

Opening hours: daily, 11am- closing varies

Recommendation

Kilt Lifter Scotch Ale (6.6%)

It's an interpretation of an interpretation but interesting because of it. At this strength you probably only need the one, but it's lighter than you might expect and the hops and yeast give it a fruitiness to offset too much peaty smoke.

Ram (15)

2650 University Village Plaza NE., Seattle, WA 98105

T 206 525 3565

The Ram brand is found across America in various states and while the venues match, the crowds obviously don't. In the U-District it's the younger crowd and with the sports facilities and big screen it's invariably 'jocks'. But you're here for the beers and while they're ok, they're not the best in Seattle. Of those we sampled and enjoyed, the Bighorn Maibock is worth a punt, and the porter Total Disorder picked up bronze at the GABF and is worth a try.

Opening hours: daily, 11am-1am

Recommendation

The **Monlake Pilsner** is cold and light, best served with sport and fries.

Rockbottom (16)

1333 Fifth Ave., Seattle, WA, 98101
T 206 623 3070
www.rockbottom.com
Opening hours: daily, 11am-close

Stix Billiards & Brewhouse (17)

1001 Fairview Ave. N., Seattle, WA
T 206 749 9088
www.stixbilliardsandbrew.com

More about shooting pool than beer, there are a few decent ales on the taps produced by a brewer who has been on the scene for a few years now.

Opening hours: daily, 3pm-2am
Recommendation
IPA (6.3%)
Has a touch of rye so it doesn't taste quite the same as its brothers in the north west. Give it a go.

Tangle Town Elysian Brewing Co. (18)

2106 N. 55th St. Seattle, WA 98103
T 206.547.5929

Much more of a neighbourhood offering for the Elysian crowd, this small bar is not far from Green Lake and offers a stack of great beers with a beautiful bar to boot.

Opening hours: Mon-Fri, 11.30am-2am; Sat & Sun, 10am-2am

BEER BARS

Ballard

Bad Albert's Tap & Grill (19)

5100 Ballard Ave. NW., Seattle, WA 98107
T 206 782 9623
www.badalberts.com

For those who don't know much about Cajun cuisine, let us tell you it's hot stuff. And we didn't taste better Cajun crawfish anywhere along the West Coast. So eat here and drink here, too, since this is an excellent little bar with a good Pacific Northwest representation and friendly staff and customers.

Opening hours: Mon, 11am-2am; Tue-Thu, 11am-2:30am; Fri, 11am-2am; Sat & Sun, 9am-2:30am

Barking Dog (20)

705 NW 70th St., Seattle, WA 98117
T 206 782 2974

Another classic neighbourhood hangout; modest bar, great beers, perfect crowd. There's a good selection of Belgians on in here as well as a strong selection of Pacific Northwest varieties.

Opening hours: Mon-Thu, 11am-10pm; Fri, 11am-11pm; Sat, 8:30am-11pm; Sun, 8:30am-10pm

Conor Byrne's (21)

5140 Ballard Ave. NW., Seattle, WA 98107
T 206 784 3640
www.conorbyrnepub.com

It's themed but it's OK. This place is Irish so you get the music, but its American Irish so you also get bluegrass and blues, and you get the craic, and you get simply good-natured American hospitality. Run by Irish Americans who love a bit of heritage but don't go too far, there's even a few decent West Coast craft beers next to the Guinness at the bar.

Opening hours: daily, 3pm-2am

King's Hardware (22)

5225 Ballard Ave. NW., Seattle, WA 98107
T 206 782 0027

Linda Derschang owns this gaff and has a bit of a reputation in Seattle as the queen of club land, owning a number of more hip joints. Here they celebrate meat; plenty of dead stuffed animals hang from the walls, so don't bring the veggies in. There are a few decent microbrews on and a decent friendly crowd to accompany them. So if you don't mind being stared at by dead animals then head on over.

Opening hours: Mon-Fri, 4pm-2am; Sat & Sun, noon-2am

Lock and Keel (23)

5144 Ballard Ave. NW., Seattle, WA 98107
T 206 781 8023

With its strong boating theme – a rowboat hangs from the ceiling – this bar is 'oar-some.' It's not a sparkly place; a bit rough around the edges but not in a contrived manner and the crowd are relaxed and friendly, as are the staff. They also smoke their own meat; the menu offers plenty of sturdy barbecue fare so again don't take the vegetarians.

Opening hours: Mon-Fri, 4pm-2am; Sat & Sun, 11.30am-2am

Old Town (24)

5233 Ballard Ave NW, Seattle, WA 98107
T 206 782 8323

Yet another useful beer hangout in this neighbourhood, with a firm commitment to the Pacific Northwest followed by other Americans and Belgians, too. The staff is informed and helpful, and the food is reasonable.

Opening hours: Mon, 11:30am-10pm; Tue-Thu, 11:30am-11pm; Fri & Sat, 11:30am-midnight; Sun, 11:30am-9pm

Reading Gaol (25)

418 Ballard Ave. NW. 65th, Seattle, WA 98117
T 206 783 3002

The Ballard of Reading Gaol. Do you get it? Well, we didn't but it's a reference to Oscar Wilde's famous poem. The staff is friendly, the food a mix of old favourites, with some surprisingly interesting selections, and the beer selection great with the 23 taps firing out some worthy local brews.

Opening hours: Mon-Fri, 3pm-1:45am; Sat & Sun, 1pm-1:45am

Capitol Hill

Bill's Off Broadway (26)

725 E. Pine St, Seattle, WA 98122
T 206 323 7200

We seemed to be of interest to a passing local with a rather alarming drug-induced lilt when we sat down in the pavement-side patio. The staff wasn't particularly welcoming either, and we wondered if we'd stormed into someone's front room uninvited. However, it's celebrated by others in this city for its pizza and beer so give it a go if you're hungry.

Opening hours: Mon-Thu, 11am-midnight; Fri, 11am-2am; Sat, noon-2am, Sun, 1pm-midnight

Hopvine (27)

507 15th Ave. E., Seattle, WA 98112
T 206 328 3120

A seriously solid neighbourhood bar serving fantastic sub sandwiches with a healthy feel and open mic easy listening music as entertainment. The Hopvine is part of a triumvirate that also includes the Fiddler's (see page 234) and the excellent Latona (see page 231). With all three there is a sense that the operators know exactly what to do with a neighbourhood hangout. Bright but not too shiny, the light wood in the Hopvine delivers an authentic feel and while the bar itself is quite small, it packs a mean punch with its beer offering, particularly strong on local favourites.

Opening hours: daily, 11.30am-midnight

Columbia City

Columbia City Ale House (30)
4914 Rainier Ave. S., Seattle, WA 98118
T 206 723 5123
www.seattlealehouses.com
This has an English pub feel, and with shepherds pie and Fuller's on the menu you might find the Seattle scene is better sampled elsewhere. But the beer selection is varied and carefully chosen to please different tastes, so if you're in the area it's worth checking out.
Opening hours: Sun-Thu, 11:30am-11pm; Fri & Sat, 11:30am-midnight

Downtown

Belltown Pub (31)
2322 1st Ave., Seattle, WA 98121
T 206 728 4311
There's more of a restaurant vibe to this one – a romantically lit red-brick venue with some booths for dining. Beers are a bit lacking and don't really match up to the wine and spirits selection, but there are one or two mainstream West Coast offerings on tap.
Opening hours: daily, 4pm-2am

Collins Pub (32)
526 2nd Ave., Seattle, WA 98104
T 206 623 1016
www.thecollinspub.com
One of the highlights in this part of town, Collins Pub is run by a man with a passion for good beer and food, and he offers a comprehensive beer list and some fresh, well-prepared pub grub. Collins Pub is in the business end of town so is busy after office hours, quieter at weekends, but the relaxed and family-friendly atmosphere makes it universally welcoming. As well as an appealing list of locals bottled and on draft, not to mention some useful Europeans, there's also a wide range of wines and a back bar stocked with good whisky. The capable bar staff is very friendly and can shake a decent cocktail, too.
Opening hours: daily, 11:30am-2am

Linda's Tavern (28)
707 E. Pine St., Seattle, WA 98122
T 206 325 1220
Another in the Derschang empire, this is a great low-key hangout and is perfect for a beer as much as a night of DJ-inspired music or cocktails. Check out the décor and the impressive buffalo head. We had the pleasure of meeting the eponymous Linda, who has a penchant for stuffed animals and meat, not to mention a decent beer. With a good outdoor area, a neighbourhood crowd and feel, and a cracking brunch offering at the weekend, this is another winner in the area.
Opening hours: daily, 4pm-2am

Stumbling Monk (29)
1635 E. Olive Way, Seattle, WA 98102
T 206 860 0916
Highly recommended
A great corner pub on the cusp of Capitol Hill, totally free from pretension.
It started as a speciality beer shop but the demand for somewhere to hang out became strong enough to convert the operation into a bar as well. Belgian beers are the order of the day here, with more than five on tap and a comprehensive bottle list. The atmosphere is quite low key, the clientele a very pleasant mix of neighbourhood folk. The owners and the staff are friendly and knowledgeable, not to mention keen activists in the Seattle beer scene. There's no food but you can eat your takeaway pizza here.
Opening hours: daily, 6pm-2am

Cyclops (33)

2421 1st Ave., Seattle, WA 98121

T 206 441 1677

www.cyclopsseattle.com

On the cusp of Belltown, this cool little bar has a diner feel to it with retro décor, black-and-white floor, chrome fixtures and vinyl fittings. It does seem to be trying a bit too hard, though, attempting an upmarket dive bar feel, but if you're looking for the savoury side of dive then this could be the place for you. There are plenty of beers and a good, healthy food menu, excellently prepared and presented.

Hours: Mon, 4pm-midnight; Tue-Fri, 4pm-2am; Sat, 9am-2am; Sun, 9am-midnight

Elephant & Castle (34)

1415 5th Ave., Seattle, WA 98101

T 206 624 9977

www.elephantcastle.com

An authentic English pub? Go to a neighbourhood bar, we say. Worse still, it's part of a chain, lacking charm and they say 'bang on' on the website. Flippin' heck!

Opening hours: Mon-Thu, 11:30am-midnight; Fri, 11:30am-2am; Sat, 8am-2am; Sun, 8am-midnight

Kells Irish Pub (35)

1916 Post Aly, Seattle, WA 98101

T 206 728 1916

If you're a fan of English theme pubs then maybe you'll enjoy this Irish one, too. The fact is the beer selection isn't great and with Pike's around the corner you might be better served getting a taste of American craft brewing history there instead.

Opening hours: daily, 11:30am-2am

Two Bells (36)

2313 4th Ave., Seattle, WA 98121

T 206 441 3050

The closest this part of town gets to a neighbourhood pub but not quite on the level of the bars out of town. Around seven beers are on tap and two more bells at the bar when we made it there.

Opening hours: Sun-Fri, 11am-2am; Sat, 1pm-2am

Downtown (North)

The Summit Public House (37)

601 Summit Ave. E., Ste 102, Seattle, WA 98102

T 206 324 7611

www.summitpublichouse.com

Free pool is always a good thing, but free pool plus good craft beer, with friendly staff well equipped to advise on choices, a cracking local crowd, an outside area and a 2am closing time – that's about as perfect as it gets.

The Summit sits at the end of a short row of businesses that includes a restaurant, cocktail bar and coffee shop, and seems to attract mature students judging by the look of some of them. Quite dark, almost divey, it is somewhere you can pop into day or night. Just a really good, laid back bar.

Opening hours: daily, 4pm-2am

Fremont

Brouwer's Café (38)

400 N. 35th St., Seattle, WA 98103

T 206 267 BIER

www.brouwerscafe.com

Highly recommended

Bunker-esque, this steel and wood building has a modern industrial chic feel, and the enormous bar at its centre is one of the more stunning you'll see in Seattle. The name and the Manneken Pis at the door is a clear indication of the Belgium skew, and the incredible list of beers – there are 50 taps and 100 bottles from which to choose – confirms that, with a healthy selection of American ales, too. Food is also very European – a welcome break from the standard American burgers elsewhere. This is a must visit beer bar.

Opening hours: daily, 11am-2am

Buckaroo (39)

4201 Fremont Ave. N., Seattle, WA 98103

T 206 634 3161

This is a biker bar, and one with an incredibly friendly atmosphere. We'd only been here five minutes before a number of people came and said hello. It's pure dive and a neighbourhood in its outlook –

Buckaroo: great name, great bar.

satisfactorily scruffy, the booths have been 'decorated' with various messages, some worth reading, others a bit more offensive, but most people seem to sit at the bar anyway. The black and white tiled floor features here as in other Seattle dive bars. There is a pool table and some interesting bric-a-brac. American craft beers litter the menu, making it an all-round top spot.

Opening hours: daily, 11am-2am

Nickerson Street (40)
318 Nickerson St., Seattle, WA 98109
T 206 284 8819

An interesting little building with an impressive bar. The owner is a fan of Hunter S. Thompson and there is a shrine in one corner to the journalist. Elsewhere the walls are adorned with historic pictures revealing the history of the area. More of an evening place, its furniture, carpet and slightly dingy atmosphere give it a middle of the road English pub feel. The food menu offers a reasonable selection, but more importantly the beer list is representative of the area with brews regularly rotated. There is a large outdoor area, and if you time it right you can see the bridge being raised.

Opening hours: daily, 11:30am-2am

Norm's Eatery and Ale House (41)
460 N. 36th St., Seattle, WA 98103
T 206 547 1417

Another solid addition to the vibrant Fremont scene, the burgers are a firm fave with the locals who pack the place at lunchtime. The beer selection is modest.

Opening hours: Mon-Wed, 11am-midnight; Thu & Fri, 11am-2am; Sat, 10am-2am; Sun, 10am-midnight

Pacific Inn (42)
3501 Stone Way N., Seattle, WA 98103
T 206 547 2967

You get an idea of how things used to be in these parts when you walk into the Pacific. It's a dive bar with a mainly male crowd, not unfriendly but certainly old school, and while the occasional youthful burst of noise breaks out at the weekend, it's best viewed during the day in its raw form. The beer is local; the selection a good one.

Opening hours: Mon-Fri, 11am-2am; Sat & Sun, noon-2am

Red Door (43)
3401 Evanston Ave. N., WA 98103
T 206 547 7521
www.reddoorseattle.com

Another impressive building, this retains a local feel and some quirky décor with an impressive wooden bar giving it a reasonably unique touch. Plenty of taps represent all the local favourites, and standard American pub fare is on the menu.

Opening hours: daily, 11am-2am

Triangle (44)
3507 Fremont, Seattle, WA 98103
T 206 632 0880

A bit divey, a bit moody, too, this is more of a hard liquor hang out – the beers proving a bit average. The shape of the building is a triangle. Very clever and it's opposite Norm's so tick it off as you pass through.

Opening hours: daily, 11.30am-2am

Georgetown

9lb Hammer (45)
6009 Airport Way S., Seattle, WA 98108
T 206 762 3373

Driving through and parking up in Georgetown you'd be forgiven for thinking you were in the wrong place – the urban wasteland peppered with graffitied derelict houses, the regular howl of overhead planes and honk of passing juggernauts. But persevere. This is one of the cooler parts of town, and the Georgetown bars are among the best around.

9lb Hammer is one of them. Scruffy décor, some Pacific Northwest beer and a cracking mixed crowd of punk, bikers, artists and occasionally pasty malnourished Brits, this one provides all you need for a top night out.

Opening hours: daily, 5pm-2am

Jules Maes Saloon (46)

5919 Airport Way S., Seattle, WA 98108
T 206 763 0570

Occasionally referred to as the oldest bar in Seattle (although the site has changed), this is another winner on the Georgetown strip. Weird décor and amazing onion rings are among the stand-out features on entering. Head out back and find the pool in a huge games room, leading to a gig room with red windows hosting everything from blues to techno. All are welcome to join the mixed, but arty, crowd enjoying the vibe. There's a number of great beers on the list, too.

Opening hours: daily, 3pm-2am

Georgetown bars come complete with flightpath.

Smartypants (47)

6017 Airport Way S, Seattle, WA 98108
T 206 762 4777

Yet another great bar on the Georgetown strip, red brick and industrial chic in feel, with an outside area at the back. A modest craft beer selection aside, the friendly but cool and arty crowd recommends the bar's solid selection of sarnies and salad. With a big theme around bikes, you'll be more than welcome if you park up on two wheels.

Hours: Mon-Fri, 11am-2am, Sat, 10am-2am; Sun, 10am-3pm

Green Lake

Duck Island Ale House (48)

7317 Aurora Ave. N., Seattle, WA 98103
T 206 783 3360

Part of the Green Lake set, this one is on the outskirts of the neighbourhood and sits on a main road (as in a motorway running through the town), a few doors down from Butch's Gun Shop. Don't let that put you off though, since it's serious about its beer. When we visited in the summer it was one of the few Seattle bars that could serve us the Maritime Jolly Roger, a rare and mind-blowing find.

Tap handles hang from the ceiling and are as ornate as those gracing the bar, which include the ever extravagant Belgian Lucifer. There are plenty of American crafts on offer, too. While the L-shaped bar is quite divey and the regulars who frequent it reasonably 'alternative' the mood seems friendly.

It's also a stone's throw from Beth's Diner, a legendary breakfast hangout that serves up omelettes 24 hours – a real favourite with Duck Island locals.

Opening hours: daily, 3pm-2am

Greenlake Bar and Grill (49)

7200 E. Green Lake Dr. N., Seattle, WA 98115
T 206 729 6179
www.greenlakebarandgrill.com

More of a restaurant than anything else but a nice spot for a bite to eat when you're checking out the surrounding area.

Opening hours: Mon-Fri, 11am-11:30pm; Sat & Sun, 9am-11:30pm (bar till 2am, Fri & Sat only)

Latona: look out for the game birds.

Latona (50)
6423 Latona Ave. NE., Seattle, WA 98115
T 206 525 2238

A perfect example of the Seattle neighbourhood bar, this venue has been here for more than 20 years. It has a laid back community feel with cracking staff, friendly locals, great organic food, regular events and of course fantastic beers. The outdoor area is modest, but if you're lucky you might bump into a couple of parrots.

Opening hours: Mon-Fri, 4:30pm-2am; Sat, 10am-2am; Sun, 10am-midnight

Lake City

Cooper's (51)
8065 Lake City Way NE., Seattle, WA 98115
T 206 522 2923
www.coopersalehouse.com

We'd heard it was like Cheers but no one shouted 'Norm' when we walked in. Still, we're not called Norm and were delighted to find the crowd as warm and receptive as you'd expect on a fictional sitcom. Otherwise it's a basic no-frills bar with the emphasis on the beers and service as well as a bit of sport. There are a host of local favourites on tap here, all served excellently. Head over on NFL game day, and it will be packed.

Opening hours: Mon-Fri, 3pm-2am; Sat & Sun, 1pm-midnight

Madison Park

The Attic (52)
4226 E. Madison St., Seattle, WA 98112
T 206 323 3131

A decent example of a neighbourhood bar with standard but tasty bar food, screens showing sport, dim lighting and plenty of wood. Welcoming if a little local, it offers a great selection of beer. There are around 20 taps, and the beers we sampled were good quality and well kept. With a few shops and restaurants in this area, tree-lined streets and a family residential demographic, it's a wonderfully laid back hangout. If you catch it in fine weather it's a great place to sit on the porch and take in the surroundings.

Opening hours: Mon-Wed, 11am-midnight; Thu & Fri, 11am-2am; Sat, 9am-2am; Sun, 9am-midnight

Roanoke (53)
2409 10th Ave. E., Seattle, WA 98102
T 206 324 5882

Decent divey bar with an English pub atmosphere. A bit more out of town than neighbourhood in its feel, but worth checking out.

Opening hours: Mon-Thu, 4pm-2am; Fri & Sat, noon-2am

Madrona

Madrona (54)
1138 34th Ave, Seattle, WA 98122-5139
T 206 323 7807

It's not difficult to see where this place gets its name – from the surrounding neighbourhood– and it's perfectly reflective of the laid-back scene. Kids are welcome, and there is a genuine community buzz about the place, with comfy sofas and TVs to view the sport at a leisurely pace. There are some good local beers here, making it the perfect place to spend a week night. Burgers are great here, too.

Opening hours: daily, 5pm-11pm

Phinney Ridge

74th Street Ale House   (55)

7401 Greenwood Ave. N., Seattle, WA 98103
T 206 784 2955
www.seattlealehouses.com

Phinney has a family vibe but some great bars with it. 74th Street is one of the older kids on the block and takes its cue from an English pub without losing its Northwest identity.

Pictures of British pubs adorn the walls for those missing home, and Fuller's London Pride makes it on to the tap selection. But it remains loyal to local brews, with the excellent Boundary Bay IPA on when we visited. It also has a strong reputation for food and very friendly staff.

Opening hours: daily, 11:30am-midnight

74th Street Ale House is double the fun.

The Park Pub   (56)

6114 Phinney Ave. N., Seattle
T 206 789-8187

Of all the bars in the area this one has the most going for it. More divey and American than the rest, it attracts a younger crowd. Scruffy chic décor includes a black and white tiled floor, eclectic furniture and boho local art on the weirdly blue walls. What's impressive is that this bar maintains an unpretentious vibe – there's a reasonably healthy feel to the menu as well and a small outdoor area in which to enjoy it. The beers are great, with local brews, some Californians, not to mention a trappist on tap during our visit. It even has free pool.

Opening hours: daily, 4pm-2am

The Park Pub: an indoor park with fine beers.

Prost!   (57)

7311 Greenwood Ave. N., Seattle, WA 98103
T 206 706 5430
www.prosttavern.net

Not far from 74th Street, this is one of the German set and owned by the team behind Die Bierstube and Feierebend. It's a local hangout, even offering its regulars membership to a club that can secure them a bar stool if they drink enough beer. As friendly as they are local, the patrons keep the atmosphere laid back, and with top staff thrown in this is a great stop on a mini Phinney crawl.

Opening hours: Mon-Thu, 4pm-2am; Fri-Sun, 3pm-2am.

Sully's Snow Goose Saloon   (58)

6119 Phinney Ave. N., Seattle, WA 98103
T 206 782 9231

The owner here, like the authors of this book, seems to know the value of a female customer and is said to have offered young ladies chocolate-covered strawberries in a bid to entice them in. It doesn't seem to have solved the problem as far as we can tell; this is still dominated by chaps who gave us a look mixed with gormless confusion and vague. Could just be us of course, but if you're not bothered by a frosty welcome this alpine-themed bar has a decent beer selection.

Opening hours: 4pm-2am

Queen Anne

Buckley's (59)
232 1st Ave W, Seattle, WA 98119
T 206 691-0232
www.buckleysseattle.com

Busy little bar with a few craft beers, it has a strong sports feel and some of the fizzy yellow stuff on the menu to prove it. Nice atmosphere though with some decent standard tucker and friendly staff, worth dropping into on game night for the atmosphere.

Opening hours: Mon-Fri, 11am-1am; Sat & Sun, 9am-1am

Hilltop Ale House is on top of a hill... fancy that.

South Lake Union

Hilltop Ale House (60)
2129 Queen Anne Ave N, Seattle, WA 98109
T 206 285-3877
www.seattlealehouses.com

This neighbourhood bar is from the crew behind the 74th Street Ale House. Expect more of the same then; a red-brick building, long bar and friendly staff with a vague English theme but strong Seattle sentiment and local brews like Boundary Bay as well as Europeans, and of course some decent tucker. In fact the food menu is really rather good, making this an excellent stop for lunch.

Opening hours: Mon-Wed & Sun, 11:30am-midnight; Thu-Sat, 11:30am-1am

Feierabend (62)
422 Yale Ave. N., Seattle, WA 98109
T 206 340 2528
www.feierabendseattle.com

Another of Chris Navarra's three German outlets, as with Prost (see page 232) and Die Bierstube this, too, has a great selection of German beers. Eighteen are on tap, most imported and all served with the correct glasswear; highlights including Dinkel Acker Dunkel, Franziskaner Weissbier, Paulaner Oktoberfest and Spaten Lager. As ever the German theme doesn't hinder a Seattle feel – even the *currywurst mit pomme frites* doesn't matter – it still maintains the vivre of a local run by a German beer fan.

Opening hours: daily, 11:30am-1am

Ravenna

Die Bierstube (61)
6106 Roosevelt Way NW., Seattle, WA 98115
T 206 527 7019
www.diebierstube.com

The theme might be German, but they've maintained a Seattle neighbourhood vibe and while there are some die-hard beer fans they are balanced by young professionals and college students to create a nice ambience. But they're all here for the beer, around 15 taps, including some of the local Baron brews, all served in authentic glassware and next to a decent menu of sausage. We weren't tempted by the cucumber-infused vodka though.

Opening hours: Mon-Thu, 4pm-2am; Fri-Sun, 2pm-2am

U-District

Blue Moon (63)
712 NE. 45th St., Seattle, WA 98105
T 206 545 9775

This one is rough and ready with a mix of college students and local soaks. Full of character to go with the characters, it gets rammed during a term-time weekend; beer fans swarming round the wonky wooden chairs and tables. Sawdust on the floor, books lining the walls, pool and grimy lavs – this has all the components that put 'dive' in 'dive bar'. It also has some decent beer and friendly bar staff, so give it a go.

Opening hours: daily, noon-2am

The Blue Moon puts the dive into dive bar.

College Inn Pub (64)

4006 University Way NE., Seattle, WA 98105
T 206 634 2307
www.collegeinnseattle.com
Highly recommended

The dingy basement venue has the feel of an English pub due to the décor and basic pub grub, but a distinctly American selection of craft beers. The throng of local youth means there's more to it than meets the eye – and it stands out as one of the most popular student bars. Twelve taps represent the best of West beer, and the staff is informed about ale. This is the pick of the bars in the area.

Opening hours: daily, 11am–2am

The Monkey (65)

5305 Roosevelt Way NE., Seattle, WA 98105
T 206 523 6457

No chimps in suits at the bar but plenty of students. It didn't seem overly 'frat boy' to us and was actually quite chilled and the beer selection is quite good, with a reasonable line up of the local Washington and Oregon brews. There are also live bands at the weekend, so it's a good place to catch some of the local talent enjoying some of the local beer.

Opening hours: daily, 5pm–2am

Wallingford

Blue Star Café (66)

4512 Stone Way N., Seattle, WA 98103
T 206 548 0345

If you, like us, enjoy some breakfast with your beer, then head over here for an omelet and sample one of 20 local brews on tap.

Hours: Mon–Thu, 7am–10pm; Fri, 7am–11pm; Sat, 8am–11pm; Sun, 8am–10pm

Murphy's (67)

1928 N 45th Street, Seattle, WA 98103-6805
T 206 634-2110
www.murphyseattle.com

True they have Guinness, there's some stuff that's Irish on the wall. And yes there's a fireplace that wouldn't look out of place in a Dublin boozer, but this bar also has 22 taps, most of which offer Pacific Northwest beer. Like the German and British theme pubs elsewhere in Seattle, this Irish offering seems to have held on to everything that's important in Seattle and, as a result, it's another worthy neighbourhood bar with a good atmosphere, nice enough food and above all great beer.

Opening hours: daily, noon–2am

Wedgewood

Fiddler's (68)

9219 35th Ave. NE., Seattle, WA 98115
T 206 525 0752

No, not an Irish theme bar, not as far as we could tell anyway, simply a decent bar with a fine choice of craft beers and pizza. Part of the Latona crowd and it shows; no nonsense on the décor but pleasing on the eye regard-less, great grub and above all an outstanding selection of beers. Another fantastic example of the neighbourhood bar.

Opening hours: daily, 11am–2am

West Seattle

Beveridge Place Pub (69)

6451 California Ave. SW., Seattle, WA 98136

T 206 932 9906

www.beveridgeplacepub.ca

We lost count of the number of beers on the bottle list, simply because we'd got stuck in to the beers on tap, but there must be around 100. There's an array of Americans –West Coast and East Coast – represented on draft, and bottled brews from Europe, and indeed throughout the world. There's also a good wine list, including some Pacific Northwest varieties. Food is ordered in from local restaurants, there's table football and a lovely back bar as well as a warm crowd.

Opening hours: Mon-Fri, 3pm-2am; Sat & Sun, 2pm-2am

Circa (70)

2605 California Ave. SW., Seattle, WA 98116

T 206 923 1102

Healthy selection of beer and also a good, healthy selection of food here. Indeed the wholesome options on the menu here are incredibly tasty and worthy, bringing a new perspective to beer and food matching.

Opening hours: Mon-Thu, 11am-midnight; Fri, 11am-1am; Sat, 9am-1am; Sun, 9am-midnight

BEER AND FOOD

McCormick & Schmick's (71)

1103 1st Ave., Seattle, WA 98101

T 206 623 5500

www.mccormickandschmicks.com

As a chain restaurant you'll find this seafood eatery replicated elsewhere, but if you're in the tourist mix then it's not a bad offering. A serious looking décor, dark mahogany wood and deep green carpets, make it feel more upmarket that it is, but it does offer a few local craft beers. A Brewmaster beer and food matching dinner is hosted every month so the staff is well-equipped to advise you on what to drink with your meal.

Opening hours: Mon-Thu, 11.30am-midnight; Fri & Sat 11.30am-2am; Sun 11.30am-11.30am

Mitchelli's (72)

84 Yesler Way, Seattle, WA 98104

T 206 623 3883

www.mitchellis.com

Decent Italian grub – beers are modest and vary; wines incredible. Worth a look at the draughts if you are passing and hungry.

Opening hours: Mon-Thu, 8am-10pm; Fri, 8am-4am; Sat, 9am-4am; Sun, 9am-10pm

Northlake Tavern (73)

660 NE. Northlake Way, Seattle, WA 98105

T 206 633-5317

Great value for money, offering big portions of tasty pizza and a range of Pacific Northwest beers on the menu. This is possibly why this pizza house is a big favourite with the local students. There's no natural light in this odd, dingy hangout, but it's not without charm; it seems very authentic if nothing else. A good place to start an evening.

Opening hours: Mon-Wed, 11am-11pm; Thu, 11am-midnight; Fri & Sat, 11am-1am; Sun, 1pm-11pm

Piecora (74)

1405 E. Madison St., Seattle, WA 98122

T 206 322-9411

www.piecoras.com

Quirky New York Style pizzeria with a decent selection of craft beers to go with a very tasty slice. Piecora is just across the road from the Elysian, not to mention the American Artificial Limb Co. where we understand things cost an arm and a leg.

Opening hours: Mon-Thu, 11.30am-11pm; Fri, 11.30am-midnight; Sat, noon-midnight; Sun, noon-10pm

Pick up a pizza at the Piecora pizzeria.

Pies & Pints   (75)

1215 NE. 65th St., Seattle, WA 98115
T 206 524 7082

The beers are the regulars, some of the best
from the West Coast, plus a couple of locals;
there's enough to keep the interest up. And
they serve pies – really good pies.

Opening hours: Sun-Wed, 4pm-midnight; Thu & Fri,
4pm-2am; Sat, noon-2am

Pyramid Brewery   (76)

1201 1st Ave. S., Seattle, WA 98134
T 206 682 3377
www.pyramidbrew.com

This is the headquarters of Pyramid
Brewery, but the beer and food matching
is so strong that we're putting them under
the 'Beer and Food' banner instead. It's an
impressive set up, conveniently located
opposite the Safeco Field stadium.

There's plenty of brewing history to be
admired; the roots of the brewery found in
Hart Brewing in Washington way back in
1984. One of the original founders, a Geordie
called George Hancock, is still involved
today. Various financial progressions since
that time have seen Pyramid rise, and it is
now up there with Sierra Nevada and Red
Hook as one of the biggest craft breweries in
the country – so if you're interested in how
the bigger players are keeping things 'craft'
then it's a great example.

With plenty of money at its disposal it
comes as no surprise that things are shiny
here. Polished and gleaming fixtures and
fittings come as standard, and the food is
equally impressive, with head chef Marcos
Villagren keen to match his creations
with the beer. There's a family feel to the
restaurant, livelier on game day obviously,
and it's a pleasant place to visit.

But what's the beer like? Well, with outlets all over the West Coast, you might already
know what to expect. There's certainly range
with Pyramid. Somewhere along the way
the brewery has become less fashionable
but in its time has been rewarded for its
excellence. The Hefe Weizen (5.2%) took a
gold medal at the 2004 GABF and is a subtle
variation on the theme; part of a three-Hefe
stable, it is backed up by the Amber and
Apricot. The Apricot Weizen (5.1%) has also
picked up a gold as a fruit beer at the 1994
GABF and, while it is as you'd expect up
front, there's a bit of a welcome sour kick at
the end. The Amber Weizen (5.1%) is the
milder of the three but good as a comparison.
Elsewhere the seasonals see the brewer
going after other styles; the Snow Cap Ale
(7%) an English strong ale for the winter, the
Curve Ball Kolsch (4.9%) for the summer.

Opening hours: Mon-Thu, 11am-10pm; Fri & Sat,
11am-11pm; Sun, 11am-9pm

Recommendation

The **Imperial IPA** *comes under the banner of the*
Brewmaster Reserve and, as is often the case, offers
a bit more than some of the staples on the menu.

Stellar Pizza & Ale   (77)

5513 Airport Way S., Seattle, WA 98108
www.stellarpizza.com
Highly recommended

The hand-tossed pizza is some of the best in
Seattle so if you are doing Georgetown we
recommend you start or finish a night out
here. It has a diner feel inside, pool and
pinball to keep you occupied and outside
seating by the main road if the weather is
fine. Laid-back and fun, there are plenty of
beers from which to choose.

Opening hours: Mon-Thu, 11am-midnight; Sat,
3pm-midnight; Sun, 3pm-11pm

Rest of Washington State

Diamond Knot B2 Brewery (1)

4602 Chennault Beach Rd., B2, Mukilteo, WA 98275

www.diamondknot.com

The first microbrewery in Mukilteo, the Diamond Knot revolution started in 1993 and has been going strong ever since – the marvellous beers spreading throughout the Puget Sound region.

The IPA (6.2%) these guys brew is a must-try beer with a golden glow and perfect balance of bitter grapefruit and sweet malts.

The Possession Porter (5.6%) is also worth a quaff, an almost spicy cinnamon quality to the chocolate warmth, backed up with some pine from the hops and an almost perfect appearance in its rich colours.

And the deep amber Brown Ale (5.6%) uses a London ale yeast strain to great effect, malts providing a sweet molasses edge, Willamette finishing hops reminding us it's an American creation.

This one's not for visiting though – see the Diamond Knot Brewery and Ale House (page 246) for details on how to enjoy the beer.

Recommendation
*It's no surprise that the **IPA** (6.2%) is so great when you discover how much care and attention goes into it. A complex four-malt blend includes two-row pale, crystal, carapils and Munich, and the hops prove equally interesting with Galena, Columbus, London Ale and then a dry hop with Columbus again. It really does deliver.*

Ellersick Brewing Co. (2)

5030 208th St., SW. Suit A, Lynnwood, WA 98036

T 425 672 7051

www.ellersickbrewing.com

It's on a business park a little out of town, but the feel of the place is still neighbourhood hangout and the beers are tasty. You'll find a Pilsner, Red, an interesting Blackberry, an IPA, Scotch and Golden as you'd expect. You can also find a high-profile party system on the website, which says a lot more about the entertaining gang here.

Opening hours: Tue-Thu, 1pm-8pm; Fri & Sat, 1pm-9pm

Recommendation
Holiday Spice
Full of plenty and makes a warm change from the standards.

Hood Canal Brewing (3)

26449 Bond Rd. NE., Kingston, WA 98346

www.hoodcanalbrewery.com

Opened in 1995, this brewery is not far from the rather unusual pseudo Norwegian-style fishing town of Breidablik. There's a seven-barrel system on display, and it produces around 10,000 barrels of good beer every year. The Special Ale shows off the floral hops with a bit of nut, the ESB is a decent session and the IPA is a good 'un. No tours required; you can see the brewing from the seating area.

Opening hours: daily, 12-8pm

Recommendation
Big Beef Oatmeal Stout (5%)
Big and indeed beefy.

Iron Horse Brewery (4)

1000 Prospect Ave., No.4, Ellensburg, WA 98926

T 509 933 3134

www.iron-horse-brewery.com

Founded in 2004, this is one of those 'lots on a business park' affairs, but the beer helps to keep the Ellensburg chin up. Fresh-faced owner Greg Partner offered six regulars at the time of visit: Rodeo Extra Pale Ale,

No horses needed to cart the beer today.

Loco-Motive Imperial Red Ale, Cream Ale, Brown Ale, India Pale Ale and Quilter's Irish Death (an imperial sweet stout), and all were palatable. But keep an eye out for the seasonals, which have always had the beer fans drooling. Some of the experiments tasted very good indeed.

Opening hours: Mon & Tue, 4pm-6pm; Wed-Sat, noon-6pm

Recommendation

Saison

This seasonal is s lighter than its Belgian forebears, it offers some citrus punch and is plenty yeasty – a good nod to the style.

Lazy Boy Brewing (5)

715 100th St., Suite A-1, Everett, WA 98208
T 425 423 7700
www.lazyboybrewing.com

It's only really a good idea to call yourself Lazy Boy Brewing if you can actually brew. Fortunately these guys can. The Hefeweizen (5.5%) is very good, strong on clove and bananas but refreshing with it, and the Belgian Strong (9.3%) is strong but well balanced.

Brewery tours: Sat, noon-5pm

Recommendation

IPA (6.5%)

As easy on the eye as Jessica Biel and almost as tasty. It's a feisty brew, the pale, Munich and crystal malts fronting up to Chinook, Cascade and Amarillo hops, weighing in at 75 IBUs.

Mac & Jack's Brewery (6)

17825 NE 65th St., Redmond, WA 98052
T 425 558 9697
www.macandjacks.com

Another brewery to emerge during the Nineties Washington spurt, Mac & Jack's

has been around since 1993 and is now a mainstay in the area; its beers are to be found in many bars, particularly in Seattle.

The unusually named African Ale is a favourite – an amber that is unpasteurised and unfiltered, with a creamy biscuit start matching a fruity, hoppy bite in the tail. The Blackcat Porter is particularly rewarding on a colder rainy day – plenty of roasty sweetness with a pleasant dry finish.

Opening hours: vary so call ahead

Recommendation

The **African Ale** *is a great beer but if you fancy a comparison of quality then try the* **IPA***, another very good effort with the hop profile you'd expect and a malty balance of power.*

Port Townsend Brewing Co. (7)

330 10th St., Port Townsend, WA
T 360 385 9967
www.porttownsendbrewing.com

Re-opened ten years ago, the name had previously held some historic ties to Washington brewing, established in 1905. Today it's simple enough with a tasting room attached and a host of styles, all a stone's throw from the Keystone/Whidbey Island Ferry.

Among the best are the Winter Ale (7.4%), a solid English ale, and the Strait Stout (5.8%), dark and nutty. The Bitter End Pale (6.3%) is not bad either, clear and golden with plenty of Cascade hop finish.

Opening hours: Mon-Thu, noon-7pm; Fri, 11am-9pm; Sat & Sun, noon-7pm

Recommendation

Barley wine (10.5%)

The alcohol doesn't dominate, the Galena hops offering decent balance to the sweetness.

BREWPUBS

Seattle outskirts

Issaquah Brewhouse (8)
35 Sunset Way, Issaquah, WA 98027
T 425 557 1911
www.rogue.com

Bought by Rogue in 2000, this Washington 'micro meeting hall' is the best in this area. Twenty-one taps include firm favourite Issaquah Bullfrog Ale, a silver medal-winning wheat beer at the GABF 2004, and a light and lemony offering. Elsewhere the Chamomellow is an interesting herbal brew with, as the name suggests, an infusion of chamomile, which took a gold in its category in the GABF 2003, or there is the Chipotle Ale, complete with jalapeno peppers. It's all great stuff and perfectly accompanied by a healthy seafood from a steam pot.

Recommendation
Frosty Frog (9%)
A winter warmer with raisins and molasses added to provide spiced rum-like flavours.

Red Hook Brewery & Forecasters Public House (9)
14300 NE. 145th St., Woodinville, WA 98072
www.redhook.com

Originally from Ballard and operating for more than 20 years, the brewery moved out to Woodinville in 1994 and now nestles in beautiful grounds just 20 miles outside the city. One of the fellows who opened it, Gordon Bowker, went on to become one of the founders of the original Starbucks, so it comes as no surprise that Redhook is a commercial success. It has also added a brewery over in New Hampshire.

The original aim was to mimic the Belgian offerings, but these days there's quite a mix of styles. The ESB (5.7%) stands out for starters, quite mild but well-balanced, and the IPA (6%) is standard fare that doesn't put a foot wrong. There's a restaurant here as well, making it a perfect Sunday jaunt should you fancy a trip out of the city.

Opening hours: varies so check website for details

Recommendation
The **Winterhook Ale** *(5.5%) has a lovely amber colour and despite its light carbonation is very smooth, with a nice hoppy finish. There's also something interesting in the fruit profile, slightly sour and spicy, like cherry.*

Peninsula West Region

Silver City Restaurant & Brewery (10)
2799 NW. Myhre Rd., Silverdale, WA 98383
T 360 698 5879
www.silvercitybrewery.com
Highly recommended

Despite its name, the beers at Silver City Restaurant & Brewery have won more golds in competition than silver or bronze medals, such is the quality of the ale. The Fat Scotch Ale (9.2%), Gold Mountain Pilsner and Imperial Stout (9.2%) have all been recognised in various competitions, which suggests that head brewer Don Spencer knows more about his onions than most French folk. A professional brewer for 11 years, Don has been committed to range from the outset and, thanks to his hands-on approach, maintains quality across the board.

The building itself is a modern brewpub on a commercial lot, so not exactly dripping in character, but neither is it offensive; a good solid home for the brewery. And there's not much else in town unless you're a weapons geek – the Trident nuclear submarines are in nearby Bangor, according to some raving lunatic who accosted us on the street. Still, there's enough on the food menu in the brewpub to line the stomach and ensure you stay put for a few more pints, which we strongly advise.

Recommendation
We didn't try anything we didn't enjoy but among the most recognised is the **Scotch***. A deep, dark red colour, it has an inviting warm plum nose and plenty going on with its caramel palate with dried fruits in the finish.*

Opening hours: Mon-Thu, 11am-10pm; Fri & Sat, 11am-11pm; Sun, 11am-9pm

The Water Street Brewing & Ale House keeps authenticity levels up.

Water Street Brewing & Ale House (11)

639 Water St., Port Townsend, WA 98368
T 360 379 6438
www.waterstreetbrewing.com

A beautiful building in the middle of quaint Port Townsend, this is another northern brewery with a big reputation, opened by five brewers and bar tenders from around the Pacific Northwest. As you'd expect, the beer is good, in particular the Queen Nina Imperial IPA (7.5%), which has taken a gold at the Beer World Cup.

The building itself is huge; to the back is a small beer garden with a stunning view of the Port Townsend bay, upstairs are two pool tables and table football. The food is also great and there's live music at weekends.

Opening hours: daily, from 11am
Recommendation
Phat Morning Wood (12%)
A great name but the IPA is the more adult choice.

Southern Region

Dick's Brewing Co. (12)

5945 Prather Rd., Centralia, WA 98631
T 360 736 7760
www.dicksbeer.com
Highly recommended

Once you get past the puerile nonsense around a name – a box of matches here boasts 'You can't beat Dick's meat' – it becomes apparent that this rather inauspicious turn off a Centralia through road leads to one of the best breweries on the West Coast.

For a start, before we get to the beer even, the meat is indeed unbeatable. The sausage deli offers great variety with the addition of a smokehouse out back. Meat is hunted fresh or reared locally and butchered on site, so it's about as organic as it can get, tasty enough to tempt the most stubborn of veggies.

But you're here for the beer, or should be. On the list you'll find around 20 ales, covering a full range that includes the IPA you've come to love and some Belgians. The best

bet is to try a range: the Imperial Stout (7.3%) offers warmth and spice, the Grand Cru strong Belgian is a yeasty and fruity smacker using native strains, the Barley Wine (10%) has all the ripe raisin goodness you'd hope for. There's even a line of hand-made sodas, made with the same attention to detail: Dick's Root Beer, Champagne Cola and Orange Soda.

Opening times: Mon-Wed, 9.30pm-5pm; Thu & Fri, 9.30am-9pm; Sat, 9.30am-5pm

Recommendation

Dick's Lava Rock Porter (7%)
Really is one of the best examples on the West Coast – so much caramel and malty sweetness it could be a Mars Bar when it hits the front of the mouth, but let it work its way back and enjoy the extra bite.

Engine House No. 9 (13)

611 N. Pine St., Tacoma, WA 98406
T 253 272 3435
www.ehouse9.com

We were told this part of Tacoma is where the action's at, and it's a cool little spot, although it seemed a little more edgy than the fun times of somewhere like Bellingham or the Seattle neighbourhoods. Still, the beer in this 1907 fire station is quite tasty with a choice of eight brews, three of them cask conditioned. The staff is friendly, and the food hearty.

Opening hours: Mon-Thu, 11.30am-midnight; Fri & Sat, 11.30am-2am; Sun, 9.30am-midnight

Recommendation

The **Fire Engine Red** (5.7%) is sweet and dry.

Fish Brewing Company/ Fish Tale Brew Pub (14)

515 Jefferson St, SE, Olympia
T 360 943 6480
www.fishbrewing.com

This is one of the state's biggest producers, although to look at the brewery from the outside, it might not seem that way. Plenty of noise and activity on a daily basis give the game away. The brewpub across the road is standard inside but offers food that is very appetizing and fresh and excellent beer – well worth staying a night in Olympia for. The Organic Amber (5.5%) is certified by the Washington State Department of Agriculture and blends pale, Munich and crystal malts to good effect, mixing it up with Hallertauer hops for a bit of zest. The organic theme continues through the IPA (6.5%) and Wild Salmon Organic Pale (5.5%) to good effect and in the outstanding Detonator Doppel-bock (8%) is fantastically full bodied. On top of that the Old Woody English-style ale picked up a gold at the 2006 GABF to the delight of talented brewer Jennifer Gridley.

Opening hours: Mon-Sat, 11am-midnight; Sun, noon-10am

Recommendation

The barrel-aged **Monkfish Belgian Triple** *(9%) is highly regarded for its balance. Failing that the* **Leviathan Barleywine Ale** *(8%) is superb, all the sweet front and bitter length you could hope for.*

Grey Parrot Brewing Co. (15)
1504 Pacific Ave. N., Long Beach, WA 98631
T 360 642 8556

It was a bit of a mission finding this one, which essentially resembles a mobile home. We didn't stay long as the beer wasn't great, although with the scale of the operation (it must be one of the smallest breweries in the country) it can't be easy to do great things. The menu looked good though so if you're in the area pop in for the novelty alone.

Opening hours: call ahead

Harmon Brewing (16)
1938 Pacific Ave, Tacoma, WA
T 253 383 2739
www.harmonbrewing.com

A brewpub with a skiing theme and around ten reasonable beers, including a standard Blonde Ale session at 3.8% and an award-winning Puget Sound Porter (5.6%) and Brown's Point ESB (5.6%).

Opening hours: Mon-Thu, 11am-11pm; Fri, 11am-midnight; Sat, 8am-midnight; Sun, 8am-9.30pm

Recommendation
Point Defiance IPA (5.6%)
A great American IPA, with 12lbs of Amarillo added after the fermentation to ensure a bitter mouth.

Hazel Dell Brewpub (17)
8513 NE. Highway 99, Vancouver, WA 98665
T 360 576 0996

Opened in 1993, this one has stood the test of time. It has quite a range on the beer menu with an equally big selection of grub.

Opening hours: Mon-Thu, 11.30am-11pm; Fri & Sat, 11am-1am; Sun, 11am-midnight

Recommendation
Red Zone (5.6%)
English-style bitter, with pale, Munich and Crystal malt as well as Perle Hops to offer plenty of hearty body and then some Cascade to give it that all-American edge.

McMenamins on the Columbia (18)
1801 SE. Columbia River Dr., Vancouver, WA 98661
T 360 699 1521
www.mcmenamins.com

Smashing views of the river and an open brewery that can be seen as you grab your pints.

Opening hours: Mon-Wed, 11am-midnight; Thu-Sat, 11am-1am; Sun, 11am-midnight

Powerhouse Restaurant & Brewery (19)
454 E. Main, Puyallup, WA 98372
T 253 845 1370
www.powerhousebrewpub.com

From the team that brought you Tacoma's Enginehouse Number 9 (see backpage) comes this brewpub, in a small converted power station. The building is a basic offering but interesting thanks to its 1907 birthday. The beer is made with plenty of love – a standard menu but the 4 Alarm Stout and Roasted Porter are sound examples.

Opening hours: daily, 11am-close

Recommendation
Powerhouse IPA (5.7%)
Plenty of bitterness, but a balanced, good example.

Salmon Creek Brewing Co. (20)
108 W. Evergreen St., Vancouver, WA 98660
T 360 993 1827
www.salmoncreekbrewpub.com

This brewpub is well worth the trip thanks to its lovely location. The pub itself is standard enough but offers a welcoming staff, warm crowd and hearty brewpub menu. The beer is pale, red and dark as you'd expect, with the addition of Brother Larry's Belgian, and all very capably brewed: the Sweet Stout and Thunderbolt Porter standing out.

Opening hours: Mon-Thu, 11am-9pm; Fri & Sat, 11am-10pm

Recommendation
Brother Larry's Belgian (9%)
Cinnamon spiciness and plenty of warmth.

Speedway Brewing Co. (21)
1225 Ruddell Rd. SE., Suite F, Lacey, WA 98503
T 360 493 1616
www.speedwaybrewing.com

A barbeque and beer operation, with a Texan feel, hot links, brisket and ribs. There is a solid range of beer but not quite up to the standards of others, so go if you're hungry, not necessarily thirsty.

Opening hours: Mon, closed; Tue-Thu, 11am-8pm; Fri, 11am-10pm, Sat, noon-10pm; Sun, 12-6pm

Recommendation
Hopwheels IPA (7.3%)
Best of the bunch.

Walking Man Brewing (22)

240 SW. Frist St., Stevenson, WA
T 509 427 5520
www.walkingmanbrewing.com
Highly recommended

While we're not entirely sure the waitress appreciated our dry wit and subsequently seemed a bit off with us, the food and beer here is outstanding. It's a lovely setting too; Stevenson is a tiny town by the stunning Columbia River Gorge.

The beer is great too, the Barefoot Brown (5.3%) a rich caramel colour but balanced and medium in body with enough veg on the hops to balance; the Black Cherry Stout (7.2%) a beautiful dark ruby colour sweet enough to appeal up front but sour enough to stop it leaving the mouth furry. The Walking Stick Stout (7.2%) is a sweet one but a fantastic match with the lovely spring rolls, and the spicy fresh Flip-Flop Pilsner (5.7%) proves the brewers have range.

Opening hours: Mon & Tue, closed; Wed-Fri, 4pm-9pm; Sat, 3pm-9pm; Sun, 3pm-8pm

Recommendation
Jaywalker Russian Imperial Stout (12.7%)
Simply marvellous and a worthy winner of the GABF gold in 2005. Stunning colour, awesome roast and fantastic alcohol warmth.

Eastern Region

Atomic Ale Brewhouse (23)

1015 Lee Blvd., Richland, WA 99352
T 509 946 5465

Rather resembles a drive-through hamburger joint but offers reasonable pizza from a wood fire oven and a few beers to sample if you're passing.

Opening hours: Mon-Thu, 11am-10pm; Fri & Sat, 11am-11pm; Sun, closed

Recommendation
The **Oatmeal Stout** ticked the boxes.

Ice Harbour Brewing Co. (24)

206 N. Benton St., Kennewick, WA 99336
T 509 582 5340
www.iceharbor.com

Beer and pizza is usually one of the classic combinations of the American brewing scene.

Not here. The pizza at Ice Harbour tastes like it came from a freezer and was zapped in a microwave. The freezer might well have doubled as a toilet and the microwave was possibly broken so they held it over a naked flame. The beer is alright and the building looks interesting enough from the outside, but some bloke stared at us the entire time we were in there. And the pizza was bad.

Opening hours: Mon-Wed, 11am-9pm; Thu, 11am-10pm; Fri & Sat, 11am-11pm; Sun, noon-6pm

Recommendation
The **Pale Ale** is quite strong at 6% but good, herbal and has a nice touch of fruit.

Laht Neppur Brewing (25)

444 Preston Ave., Hway. 12, Waitsburg, WA 99361
T 509 337 6261
www.lahtneppur.com

A small bar area attached to a basic brewery, but this place is about the beer. If the crowd at the bar is anything to go by, it delivers.

Opening hours: Mon-Thu, noon-8pm; Fri & Sat, noon-10pm; Sun, noon-6pm

Recommendation
Mr Ken's Winter Warmer (7%)
Seems to keep the locals hot, with flavours ranging from Christmas cake to orange blossom.

Skye Book & Brew (26)

148 E. Main St., Dayton, WA 99328
T 509 382 4677
www.skyebookandbrew.com

Beers and books, eh? Well why not, they seem to sit so well with coffee and, if you're trying to brew something interesting, not to mention offering some substantial sarnies, then we say more power to you. The beer is average, but the place has a great feel – a nice little venue to hang out in.

Opening hours: Mon, 4pm-8pm; Tue-Thu, 11am-2pm, 4pm-8pm; Fri, 11am-2pm, 4pm-10pm; Sat, 11am-10pm; Sun, closed

Recommendation
Cougar Canyon Amber (5.6%)
About the best in a modest selection.

Snipes Mountain Brewery & Restaurant (27)

905 Yakmia Valley Hwy., Sunnyside, WA 98944
T 509 837 2739
www.snipesmountain.com

With an address like this you'd expect something a bit more picturesque. But it's off a highway, so no surprises really. It's the best in the area, but there's not a lot else

around it, so you get a modern faux-chalet style building with shiny fixtures and fittings, a banquet room and a lack of character.

Don't judge a book, though, since the beer has won a number of awards. The Sunnyside Pale Ale (4.6%) is perfectly bitter and the Porter (4.2%) suitably robust. The Roza Reserve (9.2%) is a very strong ale but drinkable and the Hefeweizen (4.3%) covers the range. You'll pass this place on your way to the hops so give it a go.

Opening hours: Sun-Thu, 10am-10pm; Fri & Sat, 11am-11pm

Recommendation
The **Maibock** (6.5%) *a seasonal but if it's on then sample it - plenty of depth and whisky warmth.*

Snoqualmie Falls (28)

8032 Falls Ave., Snoqualmie, WA 98065
T 425 831 2357
www.fallsbrew.com

Opened in 1997, this is a stone's throw from the stunning 260ft waterfall and offers beer to match the views. The PGA Amber (4%) is an easy-drinking session beer. The Haystack Hef (5.3%) has a citrus, spicy finish thanks to German Tettnanger hops but is also very approachable, and the Copperhead Pale (5.3%) is medium bodied, light and crisp. Naturally the IPA stands out, the Wildcat as it has been named is about is feisty as a leather-clad Michelle Pfeifer and at 6.6% possibly one to book a hotel for. If you fancy something a little less alcoholic then they make their own root beer, serve their own coffee and even make their own soaps. We wouldn't recommend you consume the soap though, no matter how drunk you are and even if you have run out of toothpaste.

All the food is natural and sourced locally, so while the menu has a standard brewpub feel it's well worth munching on. While the venue itself is quite unassuming it's a worthy addition to the guide.

Opening hours: Mon-Fri, 11am-11pm; Sat & Sun, 11am-10pm

Recommendation
Steam Train Porter (5%)
As it says on the tin, mellow and malty and has a smoky quality to rival the Seattle cafes.

Whitstran Brewing Company (29)

1427 Wine Country Rd, Prosser, WA 99350

T 509 786 3883

It's another lot on a business park, isolated, generic, really nothing to it. But if you pass, you should definitely pop in; the beers are exceptional. This is very much wine country, so it's refreshing to see a craft brewery keeping the good fight going and the roasty Heavy Water Stout (5.6%) and crisp Eleventh Hour Pale (5.6%) are examples of perfect range. Should the company ever open a brewpub in the nearby town of Prosser it's sure to do well.

Opening hours: vary so call ahead

Recommendation

Friars Penance (10%)

Probably one that should be enjoyed in the safety of a hotel room, but do take one away. It's a lavish beer, rich and malty with enough bitterness to keep it interesting. A great showcase for the talents of the team.

Winthrop Brewing Co. (30)

155 Riverside Ave., Winthrop, WA 98862

T 509 996 3183

www.webspinnings.com/winthrop

A quirky little brewpub in a quaint little Wild West town. There's a smashing beer garden and the beers themselves seem suitably considered. Coming off an eight-barrel system, they've been brewing here since 1993 and there's quite a range. Each of the beers on tap is pulled from fairly odd wood carved handles.

Opening hours: vary so call ahead

Recommendation

Tomb Stone Barley Wine (10%)

Will knock you on your arse, but it's worth the whack.

Northern Region

Anacortes Brewery/Rockfish Grill (31)

320 Commercial Ave., Anacortes, WA 98221

T 360 588 1720

www.anacortesrockfish.com

A local's description of Anacortes: 'every day is like a Monday, every night a Sunday', so don't expect too much excitement. This brewpub is possibly the best stop in town; while not quite the best of the northern brewpubs, it is worth checking out if you're passing. It offers good locally sourced food plus pizza, and the beers are OK too – the standard range with some more unusual additions, and certainly a capable offering.

Opening hours: daily, 11.30am-close

Recommendation

Aviator Doppelbock (8.4%)

Great amber colour, and the hop is high enough to give it a punch.

Birdsview Brewing Co. (32)

38306 St. Route 20, Concrete, WA 98237

T 360 826 3406

www.birdsviewbrewingco.com

Heading in a bit to Concrete, you'll find this cabin brewpub and deli in the shadow of the rural local hills and looking over Skagit River Valley. There's a great community feel to the place with some hearty sandwiches and reasonable beer to quench the thirst after a decent hike.

Opening hours: Tue-Thu, noon-9pm; Fri & Sat, noon-10pm; Sun, noon-8pm

Recommendation

Pail Ale (6%)

Sorts a thirst, bit of toffee on the nose but surprisingly fruity on the palate and quite strong.

Boundary Bay Brewery (33)

1107 Railroad Ave., Bellingham, WA 98225

T 360 647 5593

www.bbaybrewery.com

Highly recommended

We love Bellingham. It's a little quaint, 'nice' even, but sometimes that's good. And there's plenty going on at night with it being a college town 'n' all. More importantly, it's home to Boundary Bay, possibly one of the best brewpubs on the West Coast.

Founded in 1995, the brewers here are more in the groove than Madonna. The commitment to craft is unfaltering, the theme simply a commitment to classic styles. So you'll find an Amber, Dry Irish Stout, Bellingham Blonde and Best Bitter ESB. But the Amber is richer and fruitier than Elton, the Irish would make a Dubliner turn from Guinness and the Blonde is better than Marilyn.

And on the seasonal list you're guaranteed a raft of excellent beers; the Imperial IPA appreciated nationally for its aggressive fresh hop, the Harvest Ale a fine blend of dark crystal, Carastan and Munich malts. There's a cask tapped every Thursday, they even have beer bread for Lord's sake.

And it doesn't stop there. The food menu is superb, fresh and inventive, encouraging hectic trade. The venue bustles on a Saturday evening, live afternoon music occasionally handing over to DJs, and the atmosphere is relaxed and friendly. Everything about it feels authentic – the fact that it houses itself in a 1922 warehouse undoubtedly helps, but there's more to it than that, trust us.

Opening hours: daily, 11am

Recommendation

Galena Single Hop Pale Ale (5%)

While we like to choose a staple where possible, here we feel it necessary to give a shout out to this one which we tried at the Oregon Beer Festival. You should also try the IPA; it's what everyone on the West Coast is talking about.

Diamond Knot Brewery & Alehouse (33)

621 Front St., Mukilteo, WA 98275

T 425 355 4488

www.diamondknot.com

Highly recommended

We must have been in here for about 20 minutes before 'Johnny Vegas', a Port Townsend ferryman, offered us a place to stay the night. Being British we naturally regarded the gesture with a level of cynicism and, fearing we'd be somehow chopped up and a feature in his wife's stew, said yes then promptly disappeared. The fact is, he was simply a generous and friendly local and a perfect example of what this bar offers. Sawdust on the floor, burgers in baskets and perfectly shabby in its décor, this place is free from pretensions. It's all about the beer

and the company and both are great, particularly the beer, with Diamond Knot commanding a strong reputation around the state. Creations have been emerging here since 1994, and it was due to their success that the main brewing facility has now been relocated, but they continue to produce very good stuff here.

Big or 'over-the-hop' beers are the order of the day, so make sure you find somewhere near to rest a head that could well be pounding the day after. If it's on, have a go at the Industrial IPA (8.2%). They've left the hops in the keg during conditioning, giving it a stunning aroma and plenty of bitterness – it really gives the SoCal boys a run for their money, and with five different malts it maintains a bit of balance.

The food is good and includes a Stonegrill serving. Don't touch the stone, that's what you cook the meat on and it's hot. A quirky touch in an otherwise no-nonsense gaff that we can't speak highly enough of, and close enough to the ferry to provide the perfect end to a journey.

Opening hours: Mon-Thu, 11am-1am; Fri & Sat, 11am-2am

Recommendation

If the **Ho Ho** *is on, either Christmas or Christmas in July, then give it a whirl, otherwise the* **Possession Porter** *is a great quaff to accompany a hearty steak and the mist off the water.*

The Diamond Knot Brewery & Alehouse is one of the best examples of Washington's beer scene.

Eagle Brewing Co./Riley's Pizza (35)

625 4th St., Mukilteo, WA 98275
T 425 348 8088

It's tough to be in a town with a Diamond Knot on the waterfront, and this venue, set slightly back from the water, was never likely to take first place. But it's a very good second bet and provides an adequate change of scene if you're in town overnight, particularly if you fancy a pizza.

Opening hours: Mon-Thu, 11am-9pm; Fri, 11am-10pm; Sat, noon-10pm; Sun, 4pm-9 pm

Recommendation
The **IPA** *isn't bad, sits nicely with the pizza.*

Gallaghers' Where You Brew (35)

120 5th Ave. S., Edmonds, WA 98020
T 425 776 4209
www.whereubrew.com

A basic place with a community feel but it's a brew-on-site concept, so if you fancy having a go at making your own then factor in a two-week stay around the area. This isn't such a bad idea as the town is by a ferry port and a very pretty place to plonk yourself.

Opening hours: Mon, closed; Tue-Fri, 2pm-8pm; Sat, 10am-5 pm; Sun, appointment only

La Conner Brewing Co. (36)

117 S. 1st Ave., La Conner, WA 98257
T 360 466 1415

An award-winning brewpub in a small resort town with woodfire pizza and a family feel. Yards from the harbour, this is a good spot to enjoy a few beers with wheat, pilsner, pale, brown, ESB and porter all represented to good effect.

Opening hours: Sun-Thu, 11:30am-10pm; Fri & Sat, 11:30am-11pm

Recommendation
The **Doppelbock** *(6.3%) here is very good. As is the clam chowder.*

North Fork Brewery (38)

6186 Mount Baker Hwy., Deming, WA 98244
T 360 599 2337
www.northforkbrewery.com

A welcome stop if you're in the area for skiing, or indeed eagle watching apparently. This cosy little small-batch operation seems to take a lead from English ales and, while its beers are not among the best in this part of the country, they are fair efforts. There is also a beer shrine and wedding minister on site should the beauty of the area send you doolally and into proposal mode.

Opening hours: Mon-Fri, 3pm-10pm; Sat & Sun, noon-11pm

Recommendation
*The bestseller is still an **IPA** (5.9%) does the job, but the **Belgian Hefeweizen** is also interesting, packed with more fruit than a camp greengrocer.*

Sailfish Bar and Grill/ Twin Rivers Brewing (38)

104 N. Lewis St., Monroe, WA 98272
T 360 794 4056

More of a restaurant than brewpub and the food and beer reflect this somewhat – food good, beer less so.

Opening hours: Tue-Sat, 5pm-10pm

Recommendation
*The **Kolsh** is the best on offer here.*

San Juan Brewing Co./ Front Street Ale House (40)

One Front St., Friday Harbour, WA 98250
T 360 378 2337
www.sanjuanbrewing.com

The trip around this area is breathtaking and needs plenty of time to take it all in. Here is the perfect place to take a break and enjoy a tasty beer at the same time.

Try the Red – it is good to see a beer living up to a billing of malt and fruit – and the Russian Imperial has the warmth and roasty qualities you want with a bit of hop as well. There's some interesting variety on the food menu, too.

Opening hours: Sun, 11am-9pm; Mon-Thu, 11am-10pm; Fri & Sat, 11am-11pm

Recommendation
*The **Erik the Red Ale** (7.3%) gets top marks.*

Scuttlebutt Brewing Co. (41)

1524 W. Marine View Dr., Everett, WA 98201
T 425 257 9316
(*Brewery:* 3310 Cedar Ave., Everett, WA 98201
T 425 257 9316)
www.scuttlebuttbrewing.com

A corrugated iron building gives this one more rugged authenticity than some other polished brewpubs, but the maritime theme inside was a bit Popeye for our liking. Even so, there's a good selection of beers well brewed here; the IPA and Porter stand out, the latter particularly well balanced. Even the Amber here stands up, evidence that the brewer knows what he's doing. With a mixed and friendly crowd with efficient, and indeed attractive, waitresses, there is certainly nothing to complain about.

Opening hours: Mon-Thu, 11.30am-8pm; Fri & Sat, 11.30am-9pm; Sun, closed

Recommendation
*It's a seasonal but if the **Winter Weizen** (7.4%) on then it's the choice offering – biscuity, bready quality to balance out a pine zing and rich malt.*

Skagit River Brewery (42)

404 S. 3rd St., Mount Vernon, WA 98273
T 360 336 2884
www.skagitbrew.com

A quaint little brewpub set just off the railway line, smacking of authenticity with its friendly community feel and wooden shack approach. James Brown was playing when we walked, nay slid and shuffled, through the door. That alone would be enough for us, but there's also hearty pub fare including a pucker shepherd's pie, and some interesting beers. The Highwater Porter scored highly – lovely colour and enough bitterness to give it length – and the Trumpeter Stout (10%) is a weighty proposal.

Recommendation
*The **Sculler's IPA** (6.8%) not only showcases the style, it will leave you skulled if you have too many.*

Scuttlebutt Brewing Co. produces a fine range of beers.

Cross the tracks for great beer at Skagit River Brewery.

BEER BARS

The 4th Ave Alehouse (43)
210 E. 4th Ave., Olympia, WA 98501
T 360 786 144
www.the4thave.com
A great beer bar in Olympia with some great beers to match, a full food menu and live music. It's a bit more divey than the other offerings in town and more authentic because of it.
Opening hours: seasonal, call ahead

Alehouse Pub (44)
2122 Mildred St. W., Tacoma, WA 98466
T 206 565 9367
www.alehousepub.com
There's a vast array of taps here, more than 50 in fact, and while that's not always wise, the beers we tried were quite clean and tasty. Alongside the ale is plenty of burger fare and pizza, with sport on the eye from every possible part of the bar and a decent shuffleboard table.
Opening hours: daily, 11am-2am

Archer Alehouse (45)
1212 10th St., Bellingham, WA 98225
T 360 647 7002
Get out and about in Bellingham if you can, it's a college town with a lively young scene and lots of pretty people. This one has a few decent beers on the taps as well as darts; a good neighbourhood hangout.
Opening hours: Mon-Thu, 3pm-11pm; Fri & Sat, 11.30am-midnight; Sun 11.30am-9pm

The Eastside (46)
410 E. 4th Ave., Olympia, WA 98501
T 360 357 9985
www.theeastsideclub.com
Another Olympia site with great beers as well as pool and ping pong. There's food and the long Sunday hours make it a perfect stop if your in town for a long weekend.
Opening hours: Mon-Fri, noon-2am; Sat & Sun 3pm-2am

Green Lantern (47)
1606 E. Isaacs Ave., Walla Walla, WA 99362
T 509 525 6303
There was a brewpub in this town when we visited, but the beer was average and the group of horribly drunk and brash idiots in

the corner put us off. Better then to head here if you're in town; it attracts a young college crowd but one that encouraged us back to a house party and to dance around a fire and then the hop fields in our underpants. If you're with a wine fan it's worth a trip out and this bar offers a reminder of all the best West Coast offerings.

Opening hours: daily, 11am-2am

McMenamins Spar Cafe (48)
114 4th Ave. E., Olympia, WA 98501
T 360 357 6444
www.mcmenamins.com

The Spar Café is a cool-looking art deco–style building, with a few pool tables inside. Certainly ticks the McMenamins's boxes.

Opening hours: Sun-Thu, 7am-midnight; Fri & Sat, 7am-1am

Meconi's (49)
709 Pacific Ave., Tacoma, WA 98402
T 253 383 3388
www.tacomapub.com

Subs, soups, pizza and burgers and, of course, beer. Plenty of it and some of the best from the Pacific Northwest. There's also a wine list and cocktails for those who don't like their beer. Weirdos we mean.

Pumphouse (50)
11802 NE. 8th St., Bellevue, WA 98005
T 425 455 4110
www.pumphousebellevue.com

Serving the area since 1978, the Pumphouse is strongly committed to local craft beers. This is more of a hamburger and sports joint than anything but there's still a bit of character and with the friendly staff has a welcoming feel.

Opening hours: Mon-Sat, 9am-midnight; Sun, 9am-9pm

Sirens (51)
823 Water St., Port Townsend, WA 98368
T 360 379 1100

Once you get past the strange set-up in the building – it's like walking into a block of flats – you'll realise why we've listed this.

An atmospheric bar, cosy, funky and alternative, with a pool room and healthy craft beer selection. The real prize, however, is the balcony which looks out across the bay. One of the best views from a bar in Washington.

Opening hours: vary, call ahead

OTHER BEER DESTINATIONS

American Hop Museum (52)
22 S. 'B' St., Toppenish, WA, 98948
T 509 865 4677
www.americanhopmuseum.org

Depending on what you want to see, bear in mind that September is the harvest and into October brewers come up for selection so things are insanely busy at this time. If you want to learn more, though, then this is a great place to do so.

Opening hours: May 1-September 30, Wed-Sat, 10am-4pm; Sun, 11am-4pm

Hopunion (53)
203 Division St., Yakima, WA 98902
T 1 800 952 4873
www.hopunion.com

No, it's not an association set up by the ex of a Beatles' bass man; the Hopunion happens to be one of the most significant businesses on the West Coast beer scene.

Hops are a key ingredient in American beer, for many the soul of their brews, but keeping up the supply is a tough challenge, and its one for which Hopunion takes responsibility. Based in the Yakima Valley in Washington and run by Ralph and Ralph – owner Ralph Olson and sales director Ralph Woodall (pictured below) – the Hopunion

provides hops, leaf hops, hop pellets, hop extracts and hop oil to (they estimate) around 99% of craft brewers on the West Coast. With around 1,500 customers – Deschutes, Sierra Nevada and Full Sail to name just a few – essentially, any beer you try could well include a Hopunion ingredient.

Obviously hops have been grown in America for many years now – no matter how bland their brews, the big-boy brewers use them in their beers – but the role of this company in the craft-brewing revolution has grown as the scene itself has expanded. It was an existing business in the Seventies but has changed hands over the years and was finally bought by Ralph in 2000.

The Yakima Valley itself offers some of the most fertile earth in the world, with a desert heat coupled with a water supply from river irrigation. As a result, around 75% of all American hops grow here. It's a lot of land, and Hopunion has to employ an army of people when it comes to harvesting the crop. In the quieter times, research is the name of the game and the team also runs a hop brew

school, now in its fifth year. It's because of this devotion that the two Ralphs are essentially encyclopedic on the subject.

"There are basically two types of hops," says Ralph Woodall. "Aroma hops are typified by low alpha acids, higher levels of beta acids, and an oil profile associated with good aroma. These hops would generally be used as a finishing or conditioning hop. And Bitter hops have a much higher level of alpha acids than beta acids.

"Among the most popular for American brewers is Cascade. After that Willamette is big, as are Tettnanger and Crystal. We have more than 50 varieties growing here but are also importing the likes of Kent Golding, Target, Challenger and Czech Saaz.

"Around 60% of what we do is pellets, much more convenient for storage and moving, but we do around 40% whole as well."

If you're interested in learning more and visiting then trips can be organised on special occasions, although you must call in advance and might find more joy at the nearby Hop Museum.

SEATTLE

Discovery Park

Puget Sound

Green Lake

Woodland Park

Market St

Emerson St

34th Av

Magnolia Blvd

Gilman Av

Nickerson St

3rd Av

Westlake Av

Lake Union

Aurora Av

Queen Anne Av

Elliott Av

Mercer St

Denny Way

Volunteer Park

Aloha St

Broadway

Madison St

Union St

Cherry St

Yesler Way

Jackson St

Washington Park

Lake Washington Blvd

Madison St

Evergreen Point Floating Bridge

Union Bay

Portage Bay

Eastlake Av

Boyer Av

24th Av

L a k e W a s h i n g t o n

Warren Magnuson Park

Sandpoint Way

75th St

65th Av

55th St

Montlake Blvd

Roosevelt Way

15th Av

25th Av

35th Av

80th St

85th St

Greenwood Av

Aurora Av

65th St

8th Av

15th Av

24th Av

32nd Av

Seaview Av

3rd Av

Leary Way

50th St

45th St

40th St

34th St

45th St

Martin Luther King Jr Way

Lakeside Av

Alaskan Way Viaduct

1st Av

4th Av

15th Av

24th Av

Airport Way

99

Spokane St

Jefferson Park

Beacon Av

Genesee St

Orcas St

Graham St

Othello St

Seward Park Av

Renton Av

Rainier Av

Beacon Av

Martin Luther King Jr Way

Lake Washington Blvd

Admiral Way

Volunteer Park

Beach Drive

California Av

35th Av

Delridge Way

Alaska St

16th Av

35th Av

9th Av

Roxbury St

Westcrest Park

Burien Frwy

W Marginal Way

E Marginal Way

Marginal Way

Duwamish

509

99

N

1km
1 miles

3 miles

Brewery
Brewpub
Beer bar
Beer and food

Las Vegas

BRIGHT LIGHTS, 'ping ping' and lots and lots of money – that kind of sums up Las Vegas. There's the money spent by hotel owners on absurd life-size replicas of the Seven Wonders of the World, and then the money spent on the casino tables, where punters gamble small fortunes in the hope of a lucky break. There's money spent on ladies who won't be there in the morning and, increasingly, money spent on decent beer. Vegas isn't the most illustrious of microbrewing cities, but alcohol marries well with celebration or commiseration – both of which are in abundance here – so beer has certainly found a welcome home.

History

Obviously, Las Vegas didn't start out as a bright-lights city. After all, it's at the largely inhospitable and sweaty foot of Death Valley – a highly unlikely location to draw tourists if you're in the business of town planning. There is water in Vegas, though, which is what attracted Mexicans to the area in 1829. A trading party en route to Los Angeles was travelling on the so-called 'journey of death' when an intrepid young scout called Rafael Rivera discovered a plush oasis with vegetation and water. The weary travellers soon forgot about their arduous journey and named the location Las Vegas, from the Spanish for 'The Meadows'. Explorers like naming things.

Some 13 years later, Captain John 'The Pathfinder' Fremont put Las Vegas on the map, quite literally. Once he had recorded it on paper, Las Vegas became a popular stop-off for traders. Slowly, the area developed into a small town, hitting an economic peak in the late 1800s as mining combined with the arrival of the railroads. Las Vegas was the ideal choice for settlers embracing the move West, and in 1905 it received city status.

During the early days of economic boom, gambling was a popular pastime. A nationwide ban at the turn of the twentieth century hit Nevada hard, but in the Thirties gambling enjoyed a legal comeback. The mining industry had failed and America was in the midst of the Great Depression, but the Hoover Dam offered some hope of recovery. After the Second World War, Vegas hit the big time when hotels and casinos made their mark in the desert.

Bootlegger 'Bugsy' Siegel is credited with realising the Las Vegas dream – building the Flamingo Hotel on what is now the famous Strip. Unfortunately, Siegel hadn't thought through the costs, and he was murdered over a financial debacle. But the Flamingo flourished and inspired more development, particularly in the Sixties when business tycoon Howard Hughes pumped millions into the city. Hughes had been living in a room at the Sands Hotel so long that he was asked to leave. Instead, he bought the Sands. Together with the reforms in gaming legislation, Hughes' love affair helped Vegas become what it is today.

A modern city

Gambling is king in the modern Vegas, and its crown is gaudy. The place is a veritable feast of spending that seems rather like a cash point in reverse. Gaming machines litter every casino floor and many other obscure parts of town, including the airport. Their electronic chime is invariably accompanied by a cursing groan – rarely by a winning 'whoop' of joy. Either way, just as the dawn bird squawk punishes a hungover ear, so too do the tuneless anthems persist.

Left: The façade of the New York New York hotel

Elsewhere on the casino floors the tables are surrounded by high rollers and mug punters. The turn of a card can make or break your evening, but it's not all about the transfer of money to the hotel cash vault. Alongside the gaming floors there are shows with rare white tigers and beautiful dancing girls. Every night, some of the world's best art meets face to face with some of the worst. And every conceivable form of international cuisine gets a representation.

With more than 500,000 permanent residents and another 5,000 heading there each month, Vegas is also one of America's fastest growing cities. It's a constant scene of development. Cranes are a mainstay, and the Strip is progressing at such a rate that part of it is no longer in the Las Vegas city limits. But it's the amazing number of visitors who add to the Vegas hustle and bustle. In 2006, around 40 million people visited Vegas – a few on business, too, with more than 20,000 conventions held here in the same year. And at only $55 for a marriage license, and no need for a blood test, some will have undoubtedly decided to tie the knot.

Absurd as it is exciting, there can be few places on Earth that rival Vegas for glitz and glamour. If you come here with cash in your pocket, you can't fail to have an experience worth talking about in the pub back home.

Finding your feet

First things first, it's hot. Hot enough to burn the soul of Elvis, according to the King's famous song. And dry, so very dry – but then it *is* the desert. That said, it can also be brisk at certain times of the year. Las Vegas winters at the same time as the UK, and while the locals might be wearing Arctic snow gear, to us hardier types it feels like a warm spring climate. But bear in mind that the evenings can get chilly, and check out the weather reports before you fly out.

You should be flying to Las Vegas McCarran International Airport. The bright lights of the Strip aren't too far away, but you can't walk there. Not because it's too far away, but rather that the Americans like their cars too much. If you haven't hired one, it's probably easiest to join the queue for the taxi rank. Alternatively, there's a good bus service to the main hotels, even servicing the outskirts and Downtown.

The Strip is drowning in cabs. They can't stop on the roadside, though, so you'll have to book one in advance or pick one up from a casino. If you're away from the Strip, and lucky, your hotel might operate a bus service with drivers working for tips. As well as the taxis, there's a train service running from one end of the Strip to the other. It's a deceptively long way from end to end, so this option is worth considering if you are planning to take your chances at the Sahara and MGM on the same night.

Vegas won't be shouting about its public transport system, though. There are 16 bus and/or charter firms in the city, with 31 routes throughout the Las Vegas metropolitan area. However, you'll do well to catch one as most of the traffic away from the Strip speeds relentlessly along dual carriageways. If you're in Vegas for a short stay, it might be better to plonk yourself on the Strip and simply take it all in from there. Any more than a week and it's probably worth picking up a hire car. Then you'll be able to visit some of the more residential areas and sample a decent beer.

Other stuff

Getting hitched Drink enough strong beer and marriage might seem like a good idea. Vegas is well equipped for this purpose, with more than 30 registered chapels charging as little as $99 for the service. A visit to the Clark County Marriage License Bureau is required. It's open 8am to midnight every day. You can even opt for a themed service, with Elvis or Star Trek costumes available to make the wedding photos truly special.

Chopper ride From around $200 you can charter a helicopter ride from Vegas to the Grand Canyon. You'll fly over Lake Mead and the Hoover Dam and then plunge down into the Canyon itself. If you're unsure about flying, we recommend trying it on an empty stomach. Although this isn't cheap, at least you get something for your money, which is more than can be said for the gaming tables.

Hoover Dam At 726 feet in height, the Hoover Dam is an enormous structure and definitely worth the 30-mile drive from the city centre. Parking is $5 and a discovery tour with hardhat $11.

Lake Mead and Valley of Fire State Park If you're in Vegas for long enough, these two spots offer a welcome break from the 'beauty' of the Strip. The Valley of Fire State Park is particularly stunning at sunset, and Lake Mead offers cruises with a spot of lunch. Head out on your own or take a guided tour if you're still in the mood for spending money. Either way, both provide an excellent opportunity to take in the breathtaking 'big country' of Nevada.

Accommodation

Your choice of hotel will obviously depend on your budget. If you've money to burn, then you might as well stay in one of the top-end themed hotels along the Strip. While the price and quality may vary, all of them offer a true taste of Vegas.

Downtown is considerably cheaper in all respects, and it also has a hotel scene of its own with the Golden Gate – the first hotel/casino combo built in Vegas. However, the journey to the Strip on a busy Saturday can take up to half an hour. So if you're looking for the silver-screen version of Las Vegas, you're better off sticking closer to the Strip.

The Bellagio 3600 Las Vegas Blvd. S., Las Vegas, NV 89109; **T** 702 693 7111; **www.bellagio.com**
This is the hotel featured at the end of *Ocean's 11*, with a stallion water display of more than 1,000 fountains ejaculating every half hour. The Bellagio remains one of the more upmarket options. Rooms from $199.

The Venetian 3355 Las Vegas Blvd. S., Las Vegas, NV 89109; **T** 702 796 1110; **www.thevenetian.com**
There's a canal in the hotel. That's right... *in the hotel*. It's as if the interior designers decided on the most challenging and expensive feature possible, realised it was absurd, then did it anyway. Rooms from $179.

New York New York 3790 Las Vegas Blvd. S., Las Vegas, NV 89109; **T** 866 815 4365; **www.nynyhotelcasino.com**
This hotel has a bit more history and is marginally cheaper than its newer rivals but remains in a prime location. With a roller coaster speeding around the façade, which happens to be a replica of the Manhattan skyline, a night at this hotel is appropriately bizarre and great value for money for a hotel on the Strip. Rooms from $90.

ALTERNATIVE ABODES

There are plenty of more affordable options off the Strip, including the familiar Best Western. In fact, there are three of them in Vegas, but the nearest to the Strip is the Mardi Gras. Having personally taken advantage of the hospitality, we'd like to recommend a stay during the Elvis impersonator weekend (some of them are actually bald). Truly mesmerising stuff.

Best Western Mardi Gras 3500 Paradise Rd., Las Vegas, NV 89109; **T** 702 735 2182; **www.bestwestern.com**
Basic but at this price you can't complain. Just 10 minutes from the Strip in the courtesy minibus, with the driver working for tips. Rooms from $55.

Main Street 200 N. Main St., Las Vegas, NV 89101; **T** 800 713 8933; **www.mainstreetcasino.com**
Cheaper than the motels off the Strip, at least this establishment tries to give you a little of the Vegas experience you'd get from one of the themed hotels on the Strip. Rooms from $40.

Beer scene

The most esteemed beer writer in Las Vegas, Bob Barnes, is a native and has seen the fan base for good beer develop in recent years.

"Up until the Nineties, Las Vegas was a beer desert," says Bob. "Today, there's a healthy smattering of brewpubs, pubs with substantial beer lists, restaurants pairing great beer with epicurean excellence and mega-resorts offering mega-beer lists. It's become a bit of a beer oasis.

"It all began in 1993 when Vegas' first brewpub, Holy Cow, opened on the north end of the Strip. Others followed, with roughly one new brewery opening each year until the turn of the century. Holy Cow has since relocated and changed its name to Big Dog's Brewing Company. Seven more brewpubs have appeared, along with two brewhouses.

"Collectively, Vegas brewpubs have garnered over 20 GABF and WBC medals. In addition to the brewpubs, pubs with quality selection abound, the foremost of which is Freakin' Frog, with an astounding 500 brews available. Rosemary's Restaurant, voted by locals as the number one Las Vegas gourmet restaurant year after year, and ranked fourth in the *Celebrator Beer News* poll of best beer restaurants in North America, has one of the finest beer lists of any local restaurant and hosts beer-themed dinners quarterly."

Blimey! So even before you flick through the listings, it's safe to say there's beer in the Vegas valley. Even better, you can usually pick up your ale for free.

"What's better than drinking great beer?" asks Bob. "Drinking it for free, that's what, and in Las Vegas, if you're inclined to gamble, your drinks are free."

You can get your hands on a beer 24 hours a day. It never stops – not even on the Sabbath. Never. Stops. So pace yourself.

Big Dog beer sampler

system visible from the bar. There's something for everyone here, from Kolsch and IPA to wheat and stout. While the ubiquitous games machines and sports screens are present, they don't seem quite so intrusive when Big Dog's beer is this good.

If you enjoy them here, you can also sample the ales at Big Dog's Bar and Grill at 1511 N. Nellis Blvd. and Big Dog's Café and Casino at 6390 W. Sahara Ave.

Opening hours: 24 hours, 7 days a week at all three locations

Recommendation
Red Hydrant Ale (5.3%)
A fine brew with rich caramel malts and a hint of English hops. The beer picked up the English Brown Ale Gold Medal at the 2006 World Beer Cup.

BREWERIES

Big Dog's Brewery (1)
Big Dog's Draft House, 4543 N. Rancho, Las Vegas, NV 89101
T 702 645 1404
www.bigdogsbrews.com

The Draft House is one of three Big Dog's Brewery sites and is a great neighbourhood hangout, with decent American chow and some reasonable beers on offer. While it's a bit of a drive from the Strip, the Draft House offers a taste of real Las Vegas – the sort of place the locals choose – so it's a fair bet you'll enjoy the visit. It's also the house, or kennel, for Big Dog's 15 hand-crafted, award-winning beers brewed from a 15-barrel

Gordon Biersch (2)
3987 Paradise Rd., Las Vegas, NV 89109
T 702 312 5247
www.gordonbiersch.com

Gordon Biersch has a brewing facility near town, and its beers can be enjoyed in one of the nearby restaurants. One Gordon Biersch venue is much the same as another, but this one proves very popular with locals. The laid-back atmosphere is best enjoyed on a Sunday with some live jazz. A welcome distraction from the mayhem on the nearby

to the *Reinheitsgebot* – a welcome change to the Euro-import bottles found on most casino floors. The bar at Planet Hollywood also boasts some branded gear, including a Sin City 'I Have Sinned' thong. And very comfortable it is, too. If you decide you're a fan, you can sup the beers in various bars through Treasure Island, The Mirage and Mandalay Bay hotels.

Opening hours: Sun-Thu, 10am-midnight; Fri & Sat, 10am-1am or later

Recommendation

Sin City Amber (5.7%)

A full-bodied Oktoberfest-style beer with plenty of malt character and imported German Hallertauer hops. Deceptively strong.

Strip, the beers are all up to an agreeably refreshing standard and can be enjoyed with tasty fare from the kitchen. If you enjoy free-style trumpet and finger clicking with your beer, this place is worth a visit (*see above*).

Opening hours: Sun-Thu, 11am-midnight; Fri & Sat, 11am-1am

Recommendation

If you've checked out a Gordon Biersch before you'll know what to expect. Here, the **Winter Bock** *(7.5%) seems very refreshing with a nice balance of caramel and dark fruit.*

Sin City Brewing Co. (3)

Planet Hollywood Hotel, 3667 Las Vegas Blvd. S., Las Vegas, NV 89109
www.sincitybeer.com

Rich Johnson's Sin City Beer is brewed out of the Gordon Biersch facility. It's available from a number of Vegas locations, including the branded bar at Planet Hollywood (formerly the Aladdin). If you're looking for a distraction from gambling, the modest venue is in the Miracle Mile shopping mall, where the lighting of the painted skyscape tricks you into thinking it's dusk 24 hours a day – fairly disconcerting if you've just taken a 13-hour flight. An advocate of German lagers, Johnson has four beers on tap. All are refreshing and brewed with strict adherence

BREWPUBS

Chicago Brewing Company (4)

2201 S. Fort Apache Rd, Las Vegas, NV 89117
T 702 254 333
www.chicagobrewingcolv.com

Head brewer Kyle Cormier is widely regarded as the best beer man in town, and he deserves the recognition. His award-winning beers also end up at the Four Queens Casino in Fremont Street. Despite the name, this place doesn't have a full-scale replica of the Sears Tower in the car park, and the only wind you're likely to suffer might be generated from the Daikon sprouts in the tasty Asian Ahi salad. Rather, this

venue is in the red-brick traditions of America's brewpubs. The place is set on two floors complete with multiple screens for sport and pinging machines. It has five beers on tap: a Kolsch, pale ale, amber ale, stout and seasonal – say something appreciative in Flemish should the seasonal be the Belgian. This place is at Sahara and Fort Apache (actually on Fort Apache just north of Sahara) about 10 miles west of the Strip. A designated driver would be cheaper than a taxi, but as you pass Rosemary's Restaurant on the way back, you have an obvious reward on offer.

Opening hours: 24 hours, 7 days a week

Recommendation

Old Town Brown (4.6%)

The long cellaring on this award-winning beer gives the desired effect. This German-style brown ale is well rounded with a nice chocolate character.

Ellis Island Casino and Brewery (5)
4178 Koval Lane, Las Vegas, NV 89109
T 702 733 8901

If you find yourself here in the morning, make sure you enjoy the breakfast. For less than three bucks you can get the special. And if you order during those familiar breakfast hours of 11pm–6am, you'll get it half price and can have the eggs with biscuits and home-made gravy. And if you're really desperate, why not try the baby back ribs or steak for less than $10. Sit back and enjoy on the brewery patio or accompanied by the dulcet tones of the laser karaoke. This place also has some beers. While they're not

up to the standard of some of the other brewpubs, they wash down the tucker admirably.

Opening hours: casino rules apply

Recommendation

The **Oktoberfest** *is the best bet, but digest your breakfast before taking on a sample tray.*

Main Street Station (6)
200 N. Main, Las Vegas, NV 89101
T 702 387 1896
www.mainstreetcasino.com

One of the best hotels in the less salubrious Downtown area, the Main Street Station has a Victorian theme, complete with lamps that once graced the streets of eighteenth century Brussels. We can't tell whether or not this will float your boat, but the hotel does have the only Downtown casino brewpub and it's set just off the gaming floor.

The sparkling brewing system is set a level above the standard open plan American restaurant, with a tasty selection of pub grub to accompany some equally tasty beers. Creator Matt Marino is a keen innovator who offers up mainstays that include a porter and pale. He's not afraid to

offer something a bit different, too, and most of it is well worth a try. This place is a casino, so turn up when you like, but there's a Graveyard Special from midnight–7am, when 16oz beers are available for just $1.

Opening hours: casino rules apply

Recommendation

Royal Red (4.5%)
By American standards, this lager is slightly lighter on the hop sensation, nicely attenuated with a malt edge. It's a useful session beer to accompany the generous American platters.

BEER BARS

Freakin' Frog (7)
4700 Maryland Pkwy., Las Vegas, NV 89119
T 702 597 9702
www.freakinfrog.com

At last count, this place was pushing more than 1,000 beers. Some say that's too many, but owner Adam Carmer is doing nothing if he's not promoting beer. He's particularly supportive of the native brews, so we say 'Yeehah!' and other such American things. With a mix that includes Belgium's Triple Karmeliet or Scotland's Traquair Jacobite, and most things American in between, Carmer's range is so eclectic that it's unlikely to be matched anywhere on the West Coast. Freakin' Frog is only a short taxi ride from the Strip, situated on Maryland Parkway near Harmon, right behind Moose McGillicuddy's. With a lively university crowd on its doorstep, and live music, this venue marries a range of great beers with a genuine local Vegas feel.

Opening hours: 11am–late

Recommendation
With 1,000 beers available, God help you if you can't find one that you like. Just allow plenty of time to make your choice.

Steiner's Pub (8)
8410 W. Cheyenne, Las Vegas, NV 89129
T 702 395 8777
www.steinerspub.com

This Nevada-style pub houses 24 taps and more than 60 bottled beers, including native microbrews. With fried oyster and fried

The dark and divey Freakin' Frog

shrimp sandwiches, salmon fillet, ribs and steak all on the menu, it's well worth a look.

Opening hours: 24 hours, 7 days a week

Recommendation
Any of the American microbrews available.

CASINO BARS

Bellagio's Petrossian Bar (9)
3600 Las Vegas Blvd. S., Las Vegas, NV 89109
T 702 693 7111
www.bellagio.com

The Bellagio is not just a casino with an absurdly large fountain out front, around which smug movie stars gather at the end of light-hearted crime-caper films, it's also a casino with a beer conscience. The bar staff may pride themselves on their vodka cocktails, but the range of beers is equally impressive, with a varied list including

Chimay Red, Spaten Franziskaner and Lindemans Framboise. You'll also find the likes of Sierra Nevada and Anchor Steam.

Opening hours: 24 hours, 7 days a week

Recommendation
Get your chops round a bottle of **Firestone Double Barrel** *(5%) if you can. Cracking stuff.*

MGM Grand's Zuri and Centrifuge (10)
3799 Las Vegas Blvd. S., Las Vegas, NV 89109
T 702 891 1111
www.mgmgrand.com

One of the best things about Zuri is that it's right by the entrance, so you can spend some of your money on beer before you blow most of it on the gaming tables. You can also toast your success on the way out if Lady Luck has smiled down on you. Either way, Zuri's commitment to variety is commendable, with Young's Double Chocolate Stout among other unusual varieties on the menu. If you can make It to Centrifuge Bar, you'll find more of the Firestone Double Barrel as well as New Belgian's Skinny Dip on draft. Both accompany 'progressive beats' and 'freestyle dance performances', so don't forget your dancing shoes.

Opening hours: 24 hours, 7 days a week

Recommendation
Anything American followed by something European.

Mandalay Bay (11)
3950 Las Vegas Blvd. S., Las Vegas, NV 89119
T 702 632 7777
www.mandalaybay.com

The Burger Bar (see page 263) is the nugget at Mandalay Bay. Elsewhere, The Lounge serves a useful selection of European beers including Samuel Smith Pale Ale, with the same choice in the 3950 Restaurant. Here they are matched with fine seafood – no doubt flown in on the cheap like everything else in this city. Sierra Nevada Pale Ale is served throughout the hotel.

Opening hours: casino rules apply

Recommendation
Enjoy a steak and a **Chimay Blue** *(9%) in the 3950 Restaurant.*

New York New York (12)
3790 Las Vegas Blvd. S., Las Vegas, NV 89109
T 866 815 4365
www.nynyhotelcasino.com

A couple of venues with modest selections, the best being the ESPN Zone – a sports bar with a few American taps, including Sierra Nevada, Widmer Blonde and Pyramid Hefe.

Opening hours: casino rules apply

Recommendation
Sierra Nevada Pale Ale *(5.6%)*
Works well with the 'football'. Someone should tell the locals that the 'football' works better with a round ball and less padding.

ENGLISH/IRISH BARS

There are few more surreal sights than a traditional English/Irish boozer in the middle of the desert, and with all that's on offer in Las Vegas it would be a surprising choice for the Brits and Irish to consider. But there's something of everything in this city. If you're tempted by the Hofbräuhaus then there's no reason to dismiss the homegrown pubs on offer. There are a few excellent examples from which to choose.

Crown & Anchor (13)

1350 E. Tropicana Ave., Las Vegas, NV89122
T 702 0739 8676
www.crownandanchorlv.com

This place shows a proper commitment to beer and offers a wide selection of European beers, with some familiar faces in the form of Old Speckled Hen and Abbot. With 30 taps and 50 bottles, the Crown & Anchor has a lively atmosphere and fish and chips and curry on the menu. And it's only two miles from the Strip, so it's not too far if you're after a night of homegrown entertainment.

Recommendation
Try the British ales if you're here. They won't be the same, but it's interesting to compare.

McMullan's Irish Pub (14)

4650 W. Tropicana, Las Vegas, NV 89103
T 702 247 7000
www.mcmullansirishpub.com

This Irish offering is on the way to Rosemary's, so pop in if you're feeling homesick. But an authentic Irish experience in Vegas? A frosty look from the bar indicated that there's more craic in a pair of builder's jeans. The usual fare is on offer, including Guinness, Bass and Stella, but the standard Sierra Nevada and Anchor Steam pumps are also on show.

Opening hours: 24 hours, 7 days a week

Recommendation
If you fancy an Irish night the Guinness is fine. With plenty of live music through the week, you'll no doubt fancy a jig after it. Quite why, though...

BEER AND FOOD

Burger Bar (11)

Mandalay Bay Hotel, 3930 Las Vegas Blvd. S., Las Vegas, NV 89119
T 702 632 9364
www.fleurdelyssf.com

If you like good beer and burgers, this place has nailed them both. Set in the Strip's Mandalay Bay hotel, in a shopping mall well away from the hustle and bustle of the gaming floors, this diner-style bar and restaurant offers a great selection of around 20 American microbrews to accompany a Kobe or Colorado lamb burger, grilled lobster, sautéed fois gras or shaved truffles. A worthy distraction from the gambling and a much better use of your money.

Opening hours: Mon-Thu, 10.30am-11pm; Fri & Sat, 10am-1am; Sun, 10am-11pm

Recommendation
With the hop hit of American beers, it's probably best to go for a light pale depending on what's on offer. Match it with the Kobe burger. It's a bit pricey, but you might as well splash out – it is called the Burger Bar after all.

Café Heidelberg (15)

610 E. Sahara, Las Vegas
T 702 731 5310
www.usmenuguide.com/cafeheidelberg.html

Café Heidelberg has been around for 40 years. As a winner of the *Las Vegas Review-Journal* best ethnic restaurant in 2002 and 2005, it's unlikely to disappoint... if you're looking for German food and a German beer that is. Here you can enjoy a fine array of imported darks and lagers, not to mention the 10 or more Weissbiers or Öffnung.

Recommendation
Order a Bavarian Jaegerschnitzel sautéed in mushroom and onion wine sauce to accompany your **Hirsch Bavarian Doppelbock**.

Hofbräuhaus (16)

4510 Paradise Road, Las Vegas, NV 89169
T 702 853 2337
www.HofbrauhausLasVegas.com

Step into the Vegas Hofbräuhaus and you'll instantly be transported to historic Münich. Listen to the 'oompah' band and gaze at busty dirndl-clad barmaids clutching a handful of steins. Now wake up! You're dribbling down that nice new Hawaiian shirt. You're still in Vegas, but we'll forgive you for being sucked in. Hofbräuhaus is a cut above the usual themed venues. The beer is incredibly fresh for a start, imported from the Fatherland under the watchful eye of its keepers. The staff are kitted out in authentic clobber, the band members are genuine Germans and the sausages are bigger than anything Dirk Diggler might be packing. No expense has been spared in this remarkable venue and while it's a bit of an oddity to find a German beer hall in the middle of the desert, the incarnation of the Hofbräuhaus is well worth the taxi ride from the Strip.

Opening hours: Sun-Thu, 11am-11pm; Fri & Sat, 11am-midnight

Recommendation

Hofbräu Dunkel (5.5%)

The original Hofbräu brew and archetypal Bavarian quaff. Refreshing, spicy and a perfect accompaniment to a tasty Wurstplatte.

Rosemary's (17)

8125 W. Sahara, Las Vegas, NV 89117
T 702 869 2251
www.rosemarysrestaurant.com

Rosemary's isn't the cheapest option, but it has a healthy list of European beers and the food is truly outstanding. The menus are changed daily so it helps that the staff are well versed in the ways of beer as well as wine and are more than capable of advising on a match that best suits your palate. Drinks co-ordinator Michael Shelter has a preference for Belgian beers but matches some strong American microbrews. With a sincere devotion to branded glassware, and a listing as the best gourmet restaurant in town for the last five years, this is a jewel in the Vegas crown. Located on Sahara, just east of Cimmaron, it's best enjoyed on the way back from a trip to the Chicago Brewery.

Opening hours: reservations are taken from 7.30pm daily; essential to phone in advance.

Recommendation

If you fancy matching an American microbrew then the floral nose and clean finish of the North Coast Brewing Co. **Pranqster** *complements the crispy skin striped bass.*

Take a trip down The Strip

Alaska

By James 'Dr Fermento' Roberts

PEOPLE ARE LURED TO ALASKA for a variety of reasons. From coastline to mountain to glacier, stunning landscapes provide endless eye candy for people who want a real wilderness experience. Oh, and there's plenty of beer, too.

History

The expeditions of Russian explorer Vitus Bearing put Alaska firmly on the map. After a number of rollicking voyages to the Arctic, the Russians finally set foot on what's now Alaska's mainland in 1741. In 1867, America bought Alaska from Russia for a paltry $7.2 million – roughly 1.9 cents an acre. Not a bad price considering the gold fever that gripped Alaska in the late 1880s. It was then that Alaska's beer history really got rolling as breweries popped up to keep the miners well lubricated.

In 1959, Alaska became America's 49th state, and it really hit the jackpot with the discovery of crude oil in 1968. The oil industry pumps millions of dollars into the state's coffers, providing lucrative jobs for the inhabitants and giving them plenty of well-earned dollars to spend on a pint or two.

Today

Alaska is vast. Even getting to Alaska from Washington – the closest US state – is an adventure itself. Separated by a little country called Canada, it is nearly 2,500 miles between Seattle and Anchorage by road.

The three main regions of Alaska are Southeast Alaska (also known as the Alaska Panhandle), South Central and the Interior. Southeast Alaska is surrounded entirely by water on the west and jagged, towering mountains to the east. If beer is the primary reason for a visit to Alaska, South Central is the best place to start since most of Alaska's frothy beer culture is located here. It also happens to be the most accessible and visited part of the state. Things flatten out considerably in Alaska's vast Interior. Fairbanks is the largest city here and boasts the state's second biggest brewery as well as a number of great watering holes in which to slake the thirst on hot summer days.

Accommodation

It's vital to plan accommodation in Alaska. In the summer, most of the hotels, motels and bed-and-breakfast accommodation are jammed to capacity. Making arrangements in advance can mean the difference between a hot shower and comfortable bed, or enduring more spartan conditions much farther away. In the winter, it's especially important to call ahead for reservations because some places simply close up during the months when there aren't enough visitors to support them staying open.

Beer scene

Alaska's beer scene is as varied as the huge state that surrounds it. Alaskans are very fond of Belgian ale, so many of the breweries and brewpubs produce one or two Belgian styles. The countrymen's love of big, robust and hoppy beers is also evident.

Winter is the best time to experience local brewing. The Great Alaska Beer and Barley Wine Festival takes place in January every year and showcases some of Alaska's heady, formidable beer. Virtually every brewery and brewpub produces dark winter ales and a barley wine each year, and some produce multiple batches. Ageing beer in wood is another hallmark of ale in Alaska.

Left: one of Alaska's magnificent glaciers

Juneau

The city of Juneau is pressed up against the mountains within Southeast Alaska's spectacular Inside Passage. In 1880, a couple of prospectors (Joe Juneau and Dick Harris) found gold in what is now downtown Juneau. Since then, more gold has been hauled out of Juneau than anywhere else in the world. Although Anchorage is the geographical and population centre of the state, Juneau is the capital. Tourism and fishing drive the local economy, but Juneau is also home to the state's biggest brewery.

BREWERY

Alaskan Brewing Company (1)
5429 Shaune Dr., Juneau, AK 99801
T 907 780 5866
www.alaskanbeer.com

Co-founders Geoff and Marci Larson came to Alaska to live the dream of the ultimate wilderness experience and ended up owning the state's biggest, most prolific and influential brewery. The flagship line (in addition to the Amber and Pale) includes an ESB, a stout and an IPA. Seasonal specialty beers include Alaskan Summer Ale (a Kölsch), Alaskan Winter Ale (often seasoned with hand-picked spruce tips), Alaskan Big Nugget Barley Wine and the incredibly famous Alaskan Smoked Porter – the single most award-winning beer in the history of the Great American Beer Festival. This viscous, oily-black, smoky beer is best enjoyed with rich foods or as a nightcap around a crackling fire. Early vintages are now collector's items.

Tour hours: daily, 11am-5pm, May-Sept; Thu-Sun, 11am-5pm, Oct-April

Recommendation
Alaskan Big Nugget Barley Wine (10.4%)
is conditioned 360 feet deep inside the historic AJ Mine. It's only produced once a year, and might not be easy to get hold of, but if you're at the brewery, ask for it. You can also take a tour of the AJ Mine/Gastineau Mill in Thane, just to the south of Juneau.

BEER BARS

Alaskan Hotel and Bar (2)
167 S. Franklin St., Juneau, AK 99801
T 1 800 327 9347
www.thealaskanhotel.com

Experience a little bit of history and a warm welcome from the locals (*below*) at the historic Alaskan Bar. Here you can sample some of the aforementioned Alaskan Brewing Company beers and a fine line of Belgian and pseudo-Belgian ales that will keep the most discriminating drinker happy.

Opening hours: daily, 11am-close

The Hangar (3)
2 Marine Way #106, Juneau, AK 99801
T 907 586 5018
www.hangaronthewharf.com

The Hangar is located downtown right on the water. Alaskan Brewing Company's beers are featured along with other notable Pacific Northwest selections. An excellent bottle selection rounds out the mix to bring the total to 100 beer choices. Reasonably-priced pub grub is standard beer soak-up fare, but the main menu includes fresh local seafood.

Opening hours: Mon-Fri, 11am-1am; Sat 11am-3am; Sun 11am-1am

The Imperial Billiard and Bar (4)
241 Front St., Juneau, AK 99801
T 907 586 1960

The Imperial Billiard and Bar is worthy of a visit if you want to step foot in the oldest continuously operating bar in Alaska. Quite simply, it's a nice quiet place to enjoy a good pint.

Opening hours: daily, 11am-close

The Island Pub (5)
1102 2nd St., Douglas, AK 99824
T 907 364 1595
www.theislandpub.com

If you want to escape the hustle and bustle of Juneau, hop across the Gastineau Channel in Douglas (by car or local transportation) to the Island Pub. The tap line is a broad mix of local selections, smatterings of Pacific Northwest craft beers and mainstream national names. You can enjoy a decent pizza here, too.

Opening hours: daily, 11.30am-close

The Red Dog Saloon (6)
278 S. Franklin St., Juneau, AK 99801
T 907 463 3658

Originally located further uphill on Franklin Street, the Red Dog Saloon used to be one of the most authentic Alaskan bars, but greedy ownership relocated the establishment to intercept tourist traffic closer to the ferry terminals. At first glance, it might fit a visitor's paradigm of turn-of-the century Alaska, but gone is the true local flavour of the real thing.

Haines

North of Juneau at the tip of Southeast Alaska is the city of Haines – an important mining district at the turn of the twentieth century. The Dalton Trail started here, and ambitious miners used this route to cross the Chilkat Mountains and access the rich gold fields of the Yukon. Haines is home to the annual Great Alaska Craft Beer and Homebrew Competition that takes place on Memorial Day every year.

BREWERY

Haines Brewing Company (7)
108 White Fang Way, Haines, AK 99827
T 907 776 3828

Haines Brewing Company is a small outfit that produces world-class beer. The 3.5-barrel brewhouse produces just over 300 barrels of beer a year. Most of the sales come from growlers as residents stock up their remote cabins and homesteads.

Brewmaster Paul Wheeler produces a deep line of specialty products, but the flagship beers you're most likely to encounter during a visit include Dalton Trail Ale, IPA, Eldred Rock Red, Lookout Stout, Black Fang and Spruce Tip Ale.

Black Fang is a deeply potent Imperial stout. Virtually opaque, it hints of roast barley, chocolate and a characteristic fruity character, with a balancing hop element and a 9% alcohol bite. Its body and light vanilla notes that swirl around the edges are more reminiscent of a robust porter.

If the seasonal lineup includes it, Wheeler's Big Hammer Barley Wine is a local favourite. This big, fruity barley wine is a regular at the Great Alaskan Beer and Barley Wine Festival in Anchorage.

Brewery tours: call ahead

Recommendation
Locally harvested spruce tips add a spicy touch to **Captain Cook's Spruce Tip Ale**, *a slightly hazy, orange-amber brew with rich earthy and pine notes. The spruce emerges more in the aroma and mid-to-end parts of the taste.*

BEER BAR

The Fogcutter Bar (8)
188 Main St., Haines, AK 99827
T 907 776 2555

Visit the Fogcutter Bar for a good dose of local flavour. Haines Brewing Company beers feature alongside favourites from Alaskan Brewing Company and other Alaskan craft beers. The place is spread out and affords billiards, sports TV and a laid-back atmosphere that might be a welcome break from the more touristy destinations that dot the Southeast landscape.

Opening hours: daily, 11am-close

Skagway

Skagway is a formidable 359 'around-the-corner-and-through-one-country (Canada)' driving miles from Haines, but only 14 water miles away. So it's easy to jump on the Alaska State Ferry System for a day trip. The town started out as a tent city supporting the gold frenzy. Today, it's a haven for tourists as the cruise ships dock here at the northern terminus of the cruise route. A truly memorable experience is an excursion on the White Pass and Yukon Route Railway, following the original 40-mile White Pass access route toward Lake Bennett where miners would disembark, hastily construct rafts and float their goods down the Yukon River into Dawson, the gateway to the gold fields.

BREWERY

Skagway Brewing Company (9)
3rd and Broadway, Skagway, AK 99840

Skagway Brewing Company is a small outfit that only operates in the summer, if it operates at all. Wander by and you might get lucky. The beer is spotty but makes for a curious pint if you're one of those people that just has to try everything local.

BEER BAR

The Red Onion Saloon (10)
205 Broadway, Skagway, AK 99840
T 907 983 2414
www.redonion1898.com

The main drinking hole in Skagway is the notorious Red Onion Saloon on 2nd and Broadway. Formerly a bordello, this entirely authentic, restored establishment provides a real glimpse into the spicier past. Upstairs, the tight-quarters tour can be amusing after a few beers. Tourists keep the Onion lively during its summer-only months, but locals frequent the bar to people watch and enjoy a respectable tap line (mostly Alaskan Brewing Company) and decent bottle selection of beers from around the world.

Opening hours: 10.30am-late, mid April-mid Oct

Fairbanks

Fairbanks is a big, historic city in the heart of Alaska's Interior. Its origins lie in the sketchy transportation infrastructure that followed gold throughout the state. Even today, Fairbanks is the state's crossroad connecting the Alaska, Parks, Dalton, Elliott and Steese Highways that radiate out in all directions from the Interior.

There's enough to do around Fairbanks to stay a few days, especially for the adventurous who don't mind a little travel to some outlying areas. Eight miles out of town is the popular Alyeska Pipeline Visitor Center. Visitors can get up close to the massive oil vein that extends 800 miles from north to south in the state.

Touristy sternwheeler rides and other riverboat tours will enable exploration of the region's twisted and breattakingly scenic waterways. Alaskaland (Airport Way and Peger Road) is a glitzy theme park that was built to host the 1967 Centennial Exposition, but probably has a little bit of something for everyone, especially those with limited time up north. It's only open during the summer months, though.

BREWERY

Silver Gulch Brewing Company and Brewpub (11)

The Fox Roadhouse, 2195 Old Steese Hwy., Fox, AK 99708

T 907 452 2739

www.silvergulch.com

Situated in the small community of Fox, just 11 miles outside Fairbanks, Silver Gulch Brewing Company is the second biggest brewery in Alaska. In the Eighties, president and brewmaster Glenn Brady started the restoration work on the historic Fox Roadhouse (*right*) – his grandmother's turn-of-the century roadhouse. Today, the restaurant is in full swing with an extensive menu, varied tap line and good bottle selection.

The brewery produces a strong lager line with fairly mainstream, but high quality, beers. The water used to make the beer comes from a local spring that taps deep into the mountains. Copper Creek Amber Ale, Fairbanks Lager and Pick Axe Porter make up the flagship line. Seasonal beers include the heady, bright Grand Reserve. This sweet, viscous, Eisbock-like beer is more of a slow-sipping desert beer than a quaffer, but alas, the beer is no longer in production and only comes out on special occasions.

Another interesting line is the Old 55, which originated from the long-defunct Bird Creek Brewery. Silver Gulch's version is not as hoppy as the original, but it must be commended that Glenn Brady resurrected a beer with so much influence in the state. Bird Creek Anchorage Ale and Bird Creek Denali Ale pay homage to the small brewery with a lot of might but little staying power during the defining days of Alaskan craft beer.

Brewery tours: Fri, 5pm-7pm

BEER BARS

The Chena Pump House   (12)
796 Chena Pump Rd., Fairbanks, AK
T 907 479 8452
www.pumphouse.com
The Chena Pump House is a national historic monument that was originally designed to pump water to the Chena Ridge where extensive mining took place at the turn of the century. The pumping station was reconstructed in 1978 and furnished with a notable restaurant and adjoining pub that features Alaska and Pacific Northwest beers, among others. Fresh salmon and aged steaks feature on the menu and the restaurant and pub are open year-round.
Opening hours: daily, 10am-11pm summer; 10am-midnight winter

Pike's Landing Restaurant and Pub (13)
1850 Hoselton Dr., Fairbanks, AK 99709
T 907 456 4500
www.pikeslodge.com
Pike's Landing Restaurant and Pub provides a mix of outstanding food, an awesome tap line and a reasonably decent selection of bottled beers. Just outside the Fairbanks International Airport, this is a convenient location if your itinerary includes air travel in and out of the city. The legendary Sunday Brunch at Pike's Landing is extremely popular and requires reservations a day in advance.

The adjoining Pike's Waterfront Lodge will satisfy even the most discriminating sleepers. It's more expensive than other venues, but well worth it if you want to be pampered. Outdoor cabins can also be secured for the night, but again, reservations are essential.
Opening hours: Mon-Fri, 11am-10pm; Sat, 10am-11pm; Sun, 10am-10pm

Talkeetna

The name *Talkeetna* reflects native dialect meaning 'where the rivers meet'; the Talkeetna, Susitna and Chulitna rivers converge outside this historic town. The rugged Talkeetna mountain range to the east is forbidding to all but the most robust explorers, but provides a beautiful, scenic backdrop to a grass-roots town that's the anchor point for hearty individuals who live remotely within its proximity. There are only around 500 year-round residents in Talkeetna, but you wouldn't know it during the height of McKinley climbing season. Primary climbing access takes place via ski-plane from the Talkeetna airstrip to the Kahiltna Glacier on the mountain's south side.

BEER BAR

The West Rib Pub and Grill   (14)
PO Box 906, Main St., Talkeetna, AK 99676
T 907 733 3663
www.westribpub.info
The West Rib Pub and Grill is a popular watering hole located behind the town's small general store. The bar offers a good, cold pint of mostly local Alaskan beers and a smattering of more popular national and international brands, accompanied by reasonably priced burgers, sandwiches, seasonal fresh fish and a good selection of pub-grub appetisers when just a little taste is in order.
Opening hours: daily in summer, noon-midnight
Recommendation
The West Rib features a signature beer made exclusively for the establishment by Glacier Brewhouse in Anchorage. **Ice Axe Ale** *(9%) is a formidable light ale that's been responsible for many missed climbing departures out of Talkeetna.*

Matanuska Valley

Forty-two miles north of Anchorage on the Parks Highway is the city of Wasilla – the epicentre of the Matanuska/Susitna Valley. Palmer lies east of Wasilla and a few miles down the road from each of these cities is the intersection of the Parks and Glenn highways. The region is commonly known as 'The Valley' and encompasses a flat area between the Chugach Mountains to the east and the Knik Arm of Cook Inlet to the west.

The Valley is dotted with lakes and fishing and water sports lure thousands from nearby Anchorage. A myriad of rivers lace in and out of the wet lake region and world class salmon and trout fishing, combined with easy access, makes this part of the state a sporting paradise. The Independence Mine State Historic Park lies just out of Palmer on the Fishook-Willow Road. The mine sits just below Hatcher's Pass and a semi-improved dirt road crosses the pass from the Palmer side and empties out on the Wasilla side just north of Willow. It makes for a great, scenic ride with a stop at the mine's interpretative sites.

BREWERY

The Great Bear Brewing Company (15)
238 N. Boundary St., Wasilla, AK 99654
T 907 373 4782
www.greatbearbrewing.com

In the Valley, the hub of good beer is the Great Bear Brewing Company in Wasilla. It's open 11am-midnight and offers decent pub grub and reasonably priced meals to complement the broad mix of hand-crafted ales on tap. The flagship line includes Settler's Bay Hefeweizen, Great Bear Gold, Archangel Amber, Black Beary Ale, Old Town Brown and Pioneer Peak Porter to name a few. More interesting is the occasional lineup of bigger, headier beers including the Valley Trash Blonde Ale (8.4%), Big Su Strong Ale (8.3%) and Three Bruins Tripel (varies).

Local music livens the place on occasion, and numerous special events include beer tastings, beer dinners and festivals.
Opening hours: daily, 11am-midnight
Recommendation
The incredible **Arskigger** *(13%) is a Scotch ale with ample peated malt flavours, a nice vanilla contingent and big caramel malt. Overall a sweetish ale, there is a slight balancing bitterness in the background.*

BEER BARS

The Mugshot Saloon (16)
251 W. Parks Hwy., Wasilla, AK 99654
T 907 376 161

The Mugshot Saloon is a down-to-earth, pseudo-biker saloon with billiards, 10 beers on tap and a good selection of bottle stock that's kept very cold. Tall, frothy mugs of Alaskan Amber are popular.

Schwabenhof (17)
Mile 6.5, Palmer-Wasilla Hwy., Wasilla, AK 99687
T 907 357 2739

Schwabenhof is billed as a German restaurant and bier garden, but there's no real restaurant and the German food is limited to brauts, krauts and pretzels. That said, Schwabenhof is one of the most charming places in which to enjoy a beer. Perched atop a hill overlooking the rolling valley landscape, local hand-hewn wood makes the interior light and warm. The beer is served in appropriate glassware and the mood is authentically German with a singing bartender accompanied by a German lady on the accordion. Expect to find Franziskaner and Spaten beers, and Aventinus, alongside some Alaskan microbrews and a couple of Belgian Lambics.
Opening hours: daily, 11am-close

Anchorage

Anchorage lies tucked away in a sweeping arc of the Chugach Range to the east and the Turnagain and Knik Arms of Cook Inlet to the west.

Anchorage is as modern as most other American cities. Stores and supermarkets abound, fine dining and entertainment are always close at hand and there are some unique oddities that even the most hardcore tourist will marvel at. Anchorage has a museum, public library and zoo. A modern airport, train depot and bus system move people around with grace and efficiency.

There are more breweries and brewpubs in Anchorage than anywhere else in Alaska, so you're never far from a good pint. Many breweries and brewpubs have come and gone since the craft beer wave crested in the late Eighties. In a sort of Darwinian 'survival of the fittest', what remains are excellent establishments with Gibraltar-solid ales and lagers. Some beer-loving visitors never get to see more than what Anchorage has to offer, but it's often enough because the variety can be daunting and sampling every local offering takes some real strategy.

BREWERIES

Celestial Meads (18)
700 W. 41st Ave., Unit H, Anchorage, AK 99508
T 907 250 8362
www.celestialmeads.com

Celestial Meads is the visionary passion of homebrewer Mike Kiker, who has devoted his early retirement years to infusing Alaska with the mystical, alluring, high-gravity substance known as mead. Celestial Meads features purely authentic meads that boast long fermentation times and a worldly lineup of honeys in the manufacture that keep the beverages forever interesting.

Brewery tours: Fri, 5.15pm-8pm, call ahead

Midnight Sun Brewing Company (19)
7329 Arctic Blvd
T 907 344 1179
www.midnightsunbrewing.com

Midnight Sun Brewing Company is the heart of brewing in Alaska. It's not the biggest Alaskan brewery but it has the biggest Alaskan attitude. Established in 1995 by Mark Staples and Barb Miller, Midnight Sun continues to amaze and amuse with cutting-edge brewing techniques and some very unusual beers. Local artist Dan Miller creates each of Midnight Sun's label masterpieces.

Flagship ales include Kodiak Nut Brown Ale, Old Whiskers Hefeweizen, Sockeye Red IPA, Arctic Rhino Coffee Porter and Oosik Amber Ale. Midnight Sun also dabbles with Belgian-style ales. Epluche-Culotte ('Panty Peeler') is a tripel with a knee-knocking 9% alcohol and dry, fruity, spicy and earthy notes. Bitter Curacao orange peel and coriander lend an almost witbier airiness to the brew, but it's a tripel through and through. La Maitresse du Moine ('The Monk's Mistress') is a Belgian-style dark, strong ale at 9%.

Celestial Meads – not beer but a tasty drop

It's a full, complex dark beer with hints of raisins, figs and plums.

On June 6, 2006, Midnight Sun brewed a Belgian-style Golden Strong Ale named Fallen Angel (6-6-6). The beer elicited a cult-like following – the batch sold out in the first two days of its release. The success of Fallen Angel spawned the 2007 series of Seven Deadly Sins beers: Greed (a Belgian-style single ale), Envy (an Imperial pilsner), Gluttony (a triple IPA), Sloth (a Belgian-style Imperial stout), Wrath (a Belgian-style double IPA), Pride (a Belgian-style strong pale ale) and Lust (a Belgian-style dark strong ale).

Midnight Sun also releases a cask-conditioned ale every month at one of two venues (Café Amsterdam and Subzero Microlounge). All of its Belgian style ales are either cask or bottle conditioned – a practice that not too many American breweries are espousing at this point in time.

Brewery tours: Fri, 5pm-7pm

Recommendation

Arctic Devil Barleywine (10%) *is a multiple award-winning beer that sweeps competitions wherever it appears. Each year's version is slightly different because the beer comes from various ageing mediums including all types of oak, back-blending across a number of kegs and other iterations that keep Arctic Devil forever interesting.*

BREWPUBS

Glacier Brewhouse (20)
737 W. 5th Ave., Ste 110, Anchorage, AK 99501
T 907 274 2739
www.glacierbrewhouse.com

Glacier Brewhouse offers top-notch beers to complement the fine-dining menu. You can get a good Hefeweizen, amber ale, Porter and Stout, but brewer Kevin Burton ensures these mainstays are surrounded by specialty beers with a distinct English character. Glacier's speciality is oak-aged beers and barley wine. Watch for Burton's Jim Beam

Oak Aged selections – they're truly unique and make fabulous pairings with many of the great menu items.

Glacier Brewhouse arguably produces more barley wines than any other brewery in the world. Every year in December, this armada of knee-knocking fermented giants is featured in the Brewhouse's Twelve Days of Barley Wine Celebration. Each day, between two and three different selections are featured, many of which are oak-aged versions that come from American, French and even Ukrainian virgin and used oak barrels.

Opening hours: Mon, 11am-9.30pm; Tue-Thu, 11am-10pm; Fri & Sat 11am-11pm; Sun, noon-9.30pm

Kevin Burton in the Glacier Brewhouse

Moose's Tooth Pub and Pizzeria   (21)

3300 Old Seward Hwy., Anchorage, AK
T 907 258 2537
www.moosestooth.net

This eclectic venue is part of an expanding chain which includes an offsite brewery that services the pizzeria, Bear Tooth Theaterpub and the adjoining Bear Tooth Grill in the Spenard district. At full capacity, more than 14 beers are available between the three establishments. Noteworthy are the Prince William Porter and Pipeline Stout – two dark ales that are true to style and refreshing if you're just chasing suds. The Bear Tooth Brown Ale is another award-winning selection. The speciality Darth Delirium is a Belgian-style stout with rich chocolate overtones and a dense mix of dark beer flavours.

Opening hours: Mon, 11am-11pm; Tue-Thu, 11am-midnight; Fri & Sat 11am-1am; Sun, noon-11pm

Recommendation

Moose's Tooth Fairweather IPA (6.1%) *shows many faces from intensely balanced to green and grassy, but is always spot-on delicious.*

The Snow Goose Restaurant and Sleeping Lady Brewing Company   (22)

717 W, 3rd Ave., Anchorage, AK, 99501
T 907 277 7727
www.alaskabeers.com

'The Goose' was born in 1996 when home-brewer and beer fanatic Gary Klopfer (*below, front*) wanted to extend his talents. The brewery affords a range of ales from light to dark and many seasonal and one-off varieties. The Susitna Hefeweizen is replete with a soft creamy texture and loads of banana-bubblegum notes. When in season, the Old Gander Barley Wine is a good pick if you're into the bigger stuff, and has won awards at the Great American Beer Festival and the World Beer Cup.

Opening hours: daily, 11am-11pm

BEER BARS

Bernie's Bungalow Lounge (23)

626 D Street, Anchorage, AK 99501
T 907 276 8909
www.berniesbungalowlounge.com

Bernie's offers the Anchorage alternative to drinking beer at home. This place has gone through various incarnations – a restaurant, deli, among other venues – before Bernie turned it into a hip, vogue drinking establishment in which to enjoy a decent drink in comfortable surroundings.

Opening hours: daily, noon-2am

Café Amsterdam (24)

530 E. Benson Blvd., Anchorage, AK 99503
T 907 274 074
www.cafe-amsterdam.com

If you want a quiet pint of nothing but top-shelf beer, Café Amsterdam (*right and below*) is the place to be. The bar's reach-in cooler is stocked with the newest, most original and quirkiest beers from around the globe, and the servers' have an intimate knowledge about the products they offer. If ale is your passion, this is the place to strike up a lively conversation about the elixir of the Gods.

Opening hours: Tue-Sat, 7am-3pm, 5pm-9pm

Chilkoot Charlie's (25)

1071 W. 25th Ave., Anchorage, AK 99503
T 907 279 1692
www.koots.com

Service with a smile at Humpy's

Chilkoot Charlie's represents the rowdier element of Anchorage nightlife – the type of venue common in the city's early days. Established in 1970, and inspired by local radio and author personality Ruben Gaines, Chilkoot Charlie's is undoubtedly Anchorage's party headquarters. 'Koot's', as it's affectionately known, was listed in *Playboy* magazine as the Number 1 Bar in America in 2000. Once you're past the long queue, Koot's boasts one of the biggest music venues in town, with three stages, three dance floors and 10 bars. A respectable tap line and great bottle selection will slake your thirst as you elbow around and explore the venue.

Opening hours: daily, 10.30am-late

Humpy's Great Alaskan Alehouse (26)

610 W. 6th Ave., Anchorage, AK 99501
T 907 276 BEER
www.humpys.com

Humpy's Great Alaskan Alehouse is the place to go for local beer. The 55-tap draught line features as much local beer from surrounding brewpubs and breweries as can be obtained on a constant basis. Owner/proprietor Billy Opinksy has a real passion for beer and spends his time ferreting out what's new locally, across America and also in the international arena. Although mass-produced American lagers also feature here, this assures that even the most stalwart mainstream drinkers will have something to enjoy while they visit with their more discerning peers.

Humpy's is always packed during meal times and especially on rowdy evenings at the weekend when people go to see and be seen. The crowd is slightly younger, the music is always hot and Humpy's is always filled to capacity with standing room only. The prospect of getting a table (no reservations) is remote – once the evening sets in, people are often there for the long haul and table turnover is minimal.

Opening hours: daily, 11am-2am

Midnight Sun Brewing Company tasting at Humpy's

McGinley's Pub (27)

645 G St., Suite 101, Anchorage, AK 99501
T 907 279 1782
www.mcginleyspub.com

McGinley's is an Irish bar that hauls in fermented gems from the English countryside. It also offers a decent menu of food, none of which is fried, and lively conversation that comes in part from the overflow from Humpy's when it's jammed to capacity.

Opening hours: Sun-Thu, 11am-midnight; Fri & Sat 11am-2.30am

Mo's O'Brady's Burger and Brew (28)

1501 Huffman Rd., Ste. 190, Anchorage, AK 99515
T 907 338 1080

Mo's boasts a uniquely Irish theme both in beer and cuisine. The original O'Brady's Burger and Brew and proprietor Maurice McDonald were neighborhood fixtures on Anchorage's east side until the building lease expired and 'Mo' was forced to relocate to the current site on the south side of town. Most of Mo's clientele faithfully 'relocated' too, and remain loyal patrons today. A humble but aspiring tap line offers predominantly Euro-imports and a good smattering of local and national craft beers.

SubZero Microlounge (29)

612 F Street, Anchorage, AK 99501
T 907 276 BEER
www.subzeromicrolounge.com

SubZero was born when Humpy's proprietors Billy Opinsky and Jim Maurer decided to add an upscale 'Belgian bar' with Belgian ales, carefully selected local beers and top-shelf martinis in a truly new wave setting. The windows, sharp, stainless steel fittings and fixtures and muted lighting create an almost mysterious glow, making SubZero much more intimate than Humpy's next door.

The short tap line features only the best, and only the finest Belgian ales are found within the reach-in cooler. A limited menu is available if you get hungry between pints. Quality beer tastings and beer dinners, custom designed by Opinsky and his executive chef Tim Farley, are held here on occasion, though generally private.

Opening hours: Mon-Sat, 4.30pm-close

Tap Root Café (30)

1330 Huffman Rd., Anchorage, AK 99515
T 907 345 0292
www.taprootcafe.com

Small, organically led café on the south side of town offering a growing tap line and featuring local beer and local music. Although not tied at the hip, owner Rebecca Mohlman works with Pamela Hatzis (the owner of Anchorage's premier beer speciality store La Bodega in the midtown University Mall) to bring in highly specialised beers. Good, wholesome food is available, and acoustic music is the norm on most nights.

Opening hours: Mon, 9am-3pm; Tue-Sat 9am-10pm

The Whale's Tail @ The Hotel Captain Cook (31)

4th and K Streets, Anchorage, AK
T 907 276 6000

Within the Hotel Captain Cook is the Whale's Tail, which features a decent tap line and limited bottle selection. It's nicely appointed and typically quiet. Wine and beer tastings are often offered for hotel guests and outside patrons. The Whale's Tail is not particularly noteworthy from a beer perspective but provides recourse if you're staying at the hotel and don't want to stray too far off the beaten track.

Opening hours: daily, 11am-close

Belgian beers at SubZero Microlounge

Kenai Peninsula

The Seward Highway from Anchorage to Seward and the Sterling Highway, which splits off 90 miles from Anchorage, are two of the state's most scenic routes. Seward, Soldotna, Kenai and Homer are the major population epicentres in this sporting playground, where you can fish in one of the hundreds of lakes and streams or hunt wild game to exhaustion. Boating, canoeing and all other forms of water sports are common in the summer and winter sports take over when the cold freezes the lakes and snow blankets the area. Like the Matanuska Valley, the palate for really good beer is still emerging in this area, but three breweries show their local colours and are worthy of a visit.

BREWERIES

Homer Brewing Company (32)
1411 Lake Shore Dr., Homer, AK 99603
T 907 235 3626

Despite its small size, the Homer Brewing Company is an institution. Locals drain the fermenters into growlers and five-gallon Cornelius kegs for draught service at home. There is little left over. Whenever

an errant keg or two shows up in Anchorage, it is downed with abandon. Only high-quality ingredients are used to produce squeaky-clean beers, including the flagship Old Inlet Pale Ale, Broken Birch Bitter, Red Knot Scottish Ale, China Poot Porter and Odyssey Oatmeal Stout. Speciality and seasonals include King and Winge ESB, Old Gnarly Barleywine, a Russian imperial stout and the winter-spiced Celestiale.

Brewery tours: daily, noon-3pm

Kassik's Kenai River Brew Stop (33)
47160 Spruce Haven St., Kenai, AK 99611
T 907 7776 4055
www.kassikskenaibrewstop.com

Kassik's Kenai River Brew Stop is hard to find. The address may indicate Kenai, but the brewery is closer to the small town of Nikiski farther west. Eight fairly standard beers compose the flagship line, and a few seasonal and speciality beers round out the mix. Look for Beaver Tail Blonde, Gold Nugget Hefeweizen (a summer seasonal), Pale Moon Ale, Otter Creek Amber, Caribou Kilt (a strong Scotch ale), Morning Wood IPA (English style), Roughneck (Oatmeal) Stout and Holiday Nut Brown (spiced seasonal). Growler sales are robust at the brewery. The beers are draught only and feature in a handful of beer bars.

Opening hours: Mon-Fri, noon-7pm; Sat, 10am-7pm; Sun, noon-6pm; closed Mon winter
Recommendation
Kassik's Moose Point Porter (5.2%) *is a surprisingly authentic dry-sided English-style Porter with dense, rich, dark malt notes, swirling caramel notes, perfectly balanced hop profile and a clean, well-rounded finish.*

Kenai River Brewing Company (34)
241 N. Aspen St., Ste 100, Soldotna, AK 99669
T 907 262 BEER
www.kenairiverbrewing.com

The Kenai River Brewing Company (KRBC) started out as the hobby of Doug Hogue and Wendell Dutcher but became a commercial enterprise in 2006. The small brewery soon established a loyal following. Look for Resurrection Summer Ale (seasonal),

The folks at Homer Brewing Company

Honeymoon Hefe, Pillars Pale Ale, Sunken Island IPA, Pot Hole Porter and Russian River Razz at the brewery and at the more discriminating restaurants and watering holes around the Peninsula.
Opening hours: Mon–Sat, noon–7pm; Sun, noon–5pm
Recommendation
Skilak Scottish Ale (4.9%) *is a well-rounded, malt rich, balanced, somewhat darker beer with some light peated notes, somewhat aggressive roast character and a rounded, smooth, sweetish finish.*

BEER BARS

Alice's Champagne Palace (35)
195 E. Pioneer Ave, Homer, AK 99603
T 907 235 7650

Alice's Champagne Palace has been going since 1980. Something about the place seems to draw people inside on any night. Eight taps and decent bottle stock provide good beer from around the world. The menu offers limited pub-grub.
Opening hours: daily, until late

Back Door Lounge and Sports Bar (36)
47 Spur View Dr., Kenai, AK 99611
T 907 283 3241

The Back Door is a sports bar, but the joint commands more respect because it is appointed more like a turn-of-the-century saloon. There are moose heads on the wall, dark wooden bars and walls, and friendly, attentive staff. A bunch of sports memorabilia, free hors d'oeuvres and a full-service menu from the adjoining Louie's Restaurant complement Kassik's Kenai Brew Stop beers, a limited craft ale selection and a decent bottled offering.

The Crossing (37)
44789 Sterling Hwy., Soldotna, AK 99669
T 907 262 1906
www.thecrossingrestaurant.net

The Crossing faces the Kenai River, and it's nice to enjoy a drink and look out over the lazily flowing water below as occasional boats drift past. The restaurant bar features six taps including a Belgian import. The Crossing serves locally produced beer from both Kassiks Kenai Brew Stop and the Kenai River Brewing Company. The usual craft beer suspects and a few light lagers round out the list. The place is popular and reservations are strongly recommended (and essential in summer).
Opening hours: Tue–Thu, 11.30am–9pm; Fri & Sat, 11.30am–10pm

Down East Saloon (38)
59909 East End Rd., Homer, AK 99603
T 907 235 6002

Karen Berger and Steve McCasland of Homer Brewing Company recommended the Down East Saloon, a couple of miles out of town on the East End Road, as a worthy stopping point. Although there are only a couple of Homer Brewing beers on tap, there are other good reasons to visit. The bar has the most extensive tap line in town and the music is always good. There's no real food, so get your carbs in before you head out.
Opening hours: daily

Hooligan's Lodge and Saloon (39)
44715 Sterling Hwy., Soldotna, AK 99669
T 907 262 9388
www.hooliganslodge.com

Hooligan's Lodge and Saloon is a local hang-out on summer evenings and especially at the weekend. Shuffleboard, big-screen TVs and pool tables keep the place hopping when local bands aren't spicing things up. There's generally some kind of music event every night during the summer and fall.

Opening hours: daily

Kenai Landing (Sockeyes) Restaurant (40)

Kenai Landing Waterfront Resort, 2101 Bowpicker Lane, Kenai, AK 99611
T 907 335 2500
www.kenailanding.com

The Kenai Landing Restaurant is a beautiful resort on the Kalifornski Beach Road. It's only open between May and September, during the huge salmon runs. As a destination for beer, there's just a couple of taps and an okay bottled selection. Some Alaskans find the entire spectacle a little bit touristy, but there's a good feel about the place so worth a visit.

Opening hours: daily, 10am-close

Mykel's Restaurant and Lounge (41)

35041 Kenai Spur Hwy., Soldotna, AK 99669
T 907 262 4353
www.mykels.com

Part of The Soldotna Inn, Mykel's restaurant is where the beer is – like many other fine-dining establishments, it's starting to figure out that beer has a place on the dinner table as well as wine. The bar has six taps of local brews which can be enjoyed in a cosy, non-smoking area. The relaxed atmosphere and welcoming staff are another breath of fresh air after a long day exploring, fishing or hiking on the Peninsula.

Opening hours: Sun-Thu, 11am-9pm; Fri & Sat, 11am-10pm

The Salty Dawg Saloon (42)

4380 Homer Spit Road, Homer, AK
T 907 235 6718
www.saltydawgsaloon.com

Situated on the sandy strip that bisects Kachemak Bay, the 100-year-old Salty Dawg Saloon is a ramshackle log-cabin/lighthouse. Homer Brewing Company beers are featured along with the a choice of craft beers, some international selections and the usual offerings from the big domestic giants.

Billiards, darts and good music shake the place, especially on the weekends and in the summer. An essential stop off if you end up in Homer.

Opening hours: summer only, call ahead

Seward Windsong Lodge (43)

Herman Leirer/Exit Glacier Rd., Seward, AK
T 907 224 7116
www.sewardwindsong.com

The world-class Seward Windsong Lodge features incredible vistas, exploring opportunities, food and a healthy 16-tap affair offering local beers and a few examples from around the Pacific Northwest. The secluded lodge offers easy access to the launching point into fjords, wildlife sighting, hiking

and deep-water fishing opportunities. The Goliath Lounge is where you'll find the fermented goods, and there's no crap on tap.

Opening hours: daily, 5pm-midnight

The Upper Deck (44)

Kenai Airport, 427 N. Willow St., Kenai, AK 99611
T 907 283 2277

If your itinerary involves air travel to or from Kenai airport, it's worth a visit to the Upper Deck. This quiet bar has two taps featuring Kassik's Kenai Brew Stop Beers and a well-rounded bottle selection. While the views of the runway are rather uninspiring, it's fun to cast your eyes over the truly Alaskan décor. And the prices are reasonable, too.

Opening hours: daily, 10am-late

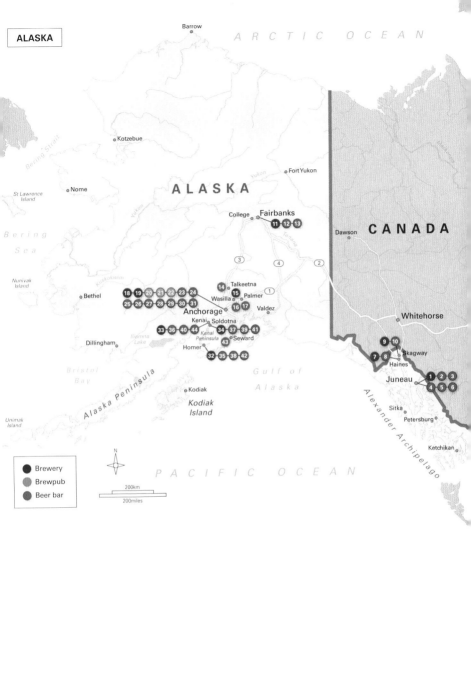

ALASKA

Hawaii

By Tom Dalldorf

History

Some 2200 miles southwest of continental United States, the Hawaiian Islands are a chain of various sized outcroppings (actually the tops of a massive submerged mountain range), with Oahu one of the smallest and the 'Big Island' of Hawaii by far the largest island. Arrayed from northwest to southeast and spanning several hundred miles, they have been known collectively as the State of Hawaii since 1959.

The 'Sandwich Islands' was the name bestowed on the territory by Captain James Cook when he discovered them in 1778 – the name in honour of his patron John Montagu, 4th Earl of Sandwich. Cook was later dispatched by some angry locals and may or may not have been the main course at a feast to celebrate the English departure. Such unpleasantness has long been forgotten and the modern traveller can expect a much warmer reception.

Between 1810 and 1893 Hawaii existed as a kingdom in its own right until the Americans and Europeans got involved. By 1898 it had become a US territory – although it would self govern until it became a state in 1959.

For centuries the key economic drivers of sandalwood and whaling kept things going but over the last 50 years the biggest trend has become tourism. This influx of West Coast holidaymakers has left some areas looking like American holiday camps.

The statehood has, however, brought some changes that some may regard as positive, among them education, and in 1978 the Office of Hawaiian Affairs was set up to promote Hawaiian culture. Hawaiian also remains the national language next to English, but these nods to heritage haven't calmed the debate that continues to rage over the original takeover of the Islands.

Left: North Shore surfing

Today

There are some vestiges of 'old Hawaii' left in the island chain. But not many. Visit the island of Molokai to see old Hawaii devoid of mega resorts and urban density. Today, downtown Honolulu on the island of Oahu has more of a 'little LA' look to it, with towering high-rise hotels and buildings chock-a-block along the once famed Waikiki beach. If you think you can spot the historic Royal Hawaiian Hotel from the main drag, think again. This 1920s-era masterpiece is now obscured by other hotels and resorts. But from the beach at Waikiki, in front of the famed pink palace, you still have a clear view to the landmark Diamond Head.

That said, there is still an undeniable amount of beauty, interest and fun on the Islands. Visit Pearl Harbor or the pineapple plantation on Oahu, take a horseback ride at Kualoa Ranch on the Winward Coast or see the Iolani Palace in Honolulu. North Shore's Haleiwa is a great surf town and Waimea Bay offers world class action.

Surfing, of course, is not a new pastime – Captain Cook's records note the first viewing of the sport on the Islands, and it continues to make waves today with the biggest swell hitting the north shores between November and March.

The climate is warm all year round; up to 90°F in the summer months of April to November, with around 80°F high and 65°F low between December and March.

Getting there

As a main entry point, look for flights from the US to Honolulu International Airport (HNL) on Oahu. This is Hawaii's main airport and more than 20 major domestic carriers and 16 international carriers fly this way. There are also direct flights from the mainland to

285

Hiking on Haleakala Crater, Maui

Maui, Kauai and Hawaii's Big Island, but most times you need to connect through Oahu.

Beer

The beer scene in the Hawaiian Islands has changed a bit over recent years as well. This time, indisputably, for the better. Visitors to the islands in the Seventies and Eighties could expect light industrial lager from the major US brewers with Steinlager from New Zealand taking the place of the otherwise ubiquitous Heineken as the 'premium' beer on offer. And everything was served in a frozen glass. A tropical paradise devoid of good beer? Egad!

The good beer evolution in America has manifested itself on the islands in several ways. The old Primo Brewery (light lager) is gone and in its place are several small craft breweries and brewpubs, offering more flavourful and assertive ales and lagers for thirsty locals and parched tourists alike. There are a few pubs, taverns and hotel bars making an effort to include good beer along

with the fine wine and requisite cocktails on offer. A few speciality retailers and grocery stores are also making strides in their beer selections for off sale.

The frozen glass is still with us, thanks to tourists who insist on beer at its coldest, so be sure to request a room-temperature glass if you care to actually smell and taste your lovely libation.

Visitors seeking the tropical Polynesian experience tend to visit just one or two of Hawaii's islands as inter-island travel requires an extra airfare or time-intensive ferry passage. We'll examine the beery landscape from the garden island Kauai in the northwest to the Big Island of Hawaii in the southeast in our quest for the best beer opportunities in Hawaii.

Kauai

The Garden Isle gets its name as a result of the significant amount of rainfall it receives every year. Indeed, the top of Mount Wai'ale'ale is reputed to be the wettest spot on earth with an average rainfall of some 460in (1,170cm). The lush tropical landscape and waterfalls are a delight to visit, with a good beer a godsend after a damp day of exploration. Some of the most beautiful terrain is located to the north along the Na Pali coastline – part of the Na Pali Coast State Park, a vast tract of rain forests, forbidding cliffs and expansive beaches covering 6,175 acres. The northern coast is so rugged that you cannot get to the western side of the island from here.

The port city of Lihue on the southeast part of the island is the second largest city and home of the only microbrewery on Kauai.

In the southwest is the town of Waimea, located at the mouth of the Waimea River, which carved its way through the interior of Kauai over the millennia, creating the Waimea Canyon (known as the Grand Canyon of the Pacific). Parts of the landscape will be familiar to viewers of the movies *South Pacific, Raiders of the Lost Ark* and *Jurassic Park*. And Elvis rocked the beach near Waimea in *Blue Hawaii* some years ago.

BREWERY

Keoki Brewing Co. (1)
2976 Aukele Street, Lihue, HI, 96766
T 808 245 8884
www.keokibrewing.com

The Keoki Brewing Company is in an industrial area of Lihue and was founded in 1998 with a mission to produce fresh, locally produced beer. The brewery has settled on two beers to sustain the company's fortunes: Keoki Gold Golden Ale and Keoki Sunset Amber Ale. The Keoki Gold is a serviceable blond ale and Keoki Sunset a flavourful amber with a touch more hops. Both are available on draught and in bottles at local retail outlets around Kauai and throughout the islands.

Opening hours: call ahead for visits
Recommendation
Keoki Sunset
With two-row malts as well as Carapils, White Wheat, Caramel Vienne and hops of Simcoe for bittering and Vanguard for flavour, it's the better of the pair.

BREWPUB

Waimea Brewing Co. (2)
9400 Kaumuali`i Highway, Waimea, HI, 96796
T 808 338 9733
www.waimeabrewing.com

The Waimea Brewing Company is in an open and spacious old school plantation-style building with wraparound porches that allow the visitor to have the best seat in the house no matter what the time of day or direction of the pervasive trade winds. The beers are assertively hopped and subject to the whims and vicissitudes of the brewer – exactly what you would want and expect from a brewpub. Good food and friendly service in an inviting setting make this a compelling destination. Cottages are available so stay overnight and watch the sunset from the world's westernmost brewpub.

Opening hours: Sun-Thu, 11am-9pm; Fri & Sat, 11am-11pm
Recommendation
Captain Cook's Original IPA *(6%) will be welcomed by the unrepentant hophead.*

BEER AND FOOD

Kalypso's Beach House (3)
5-5190 Kuhio Avenue, Hanalei, HI, 96714
T 808 828 1435

Locals recommend Kalypso's Beach House for its decent beer selection and good food. Hanalei Bay is gorgeous with vibrant green cliffs and waterfalls cascading into the bay. Winter surfing here is amazing.

Opening hours: daily, 11am-10pm

The Wine Garden (4)
4495 Puhi Rd, Lihue, HI 96766
T 808 245 5766

The Wine Garden store sells an excellent selection of beer despite the name – owner Collette Savage stocks the best beer choice on Kauai. Offerings range from bottles from classic mainland micros such as Sierra Nevada and Rogue to international treasures including Chimays and Lindemans Lambics, sure to excite the beer-savvy tourist.

Opening hours: seasonal, check in advance

Kalua pig is roasted for a traditional Hawaiian *luau*

287

Oahu

The smallest of the main islands has the largest population. Honolulu – Hawaii's largest city, its state capital and the main deepwater marine port for the state – is located on Oahu. The island's best known features include Waikiki Beach, Pearl Harbor, Diamond Head, the 'living aquarium' of Hanauma Bay, and the rugged surfing bonanza of the North Shore. It is no surprise that Hawaii's most populous region has the most evolved beer scene.

Local beers in Honolulu include Bruddah's Cream Ale, Bumucha Stout, Ehu Ale, S-Team California Common Beer and Skipper's Hefe-Weizen, a true Bavarian-style beer.

As the largest city in the island chain, Honolulu has myriad pubs, taverns and hotel bars with beer selections running from cold or very cold to well-stocked bottle choices and well-maintained and inspired draught selections.

At multi-taps it's always a good idea to inquire which are the freshest kegs. Some places, known for a massive collection of taps, are slow to rotate beers.

Left: a hula dancer is silhouetted against the sunset

BREWPUBS

Gordon Biersch (5)
1 Aloha Tower Market Place, Honolulu, HI, 96813
T 808 599 4877

Brewpub pioneers Gordon Biersch moved in early and established a brewery restaurant on the water at the Aloha Towers near Honolulu's busy International Airport. Sitting on the deck you can also see air traffic from Hickam Air Force Base and are not far from the legendary Pearl Harbor Naval Base. The food and service at Gordon Biersch are well above average and the beers can be too, depending on the spirit in the brewhouse.

Opening hours: Sun-Thu, 10am-midnight; Fri & Sat, 10am-1am

Recommendation
Seasonal offerings can be more interesting with the German-style **Hefeweizen** (5.4%) *and* **Blond Bock** (7%) *getting the nod at various times of the year.*

Kona Brewing Co. – Koko Marina (6)
7192 Kalanianaole Highway, Honolulu, HI, 96825
T 808 394 5662
www.konabrewingco.com

The Kona Brewing Co. pub restaurant at the Koko Marina is part of the Kona Brewing Company on the Big Island. Consequently, its beers are always in pristine shape and among the most characterful produced on the islands.

Opening hours: daily

Recommendation
Dark beer lovers will want to try the **Pipeline Porter** (5.4%) *made with Kona coffee. Rich and roasty.*

BEER BARS

Bar 35 (7)
35 N. Hotel St., Honolulu, HI, 96817
T 808 537 3535

Hip and happening, with a dark interior and beers from all around the world.

Opening hours: Mon-Sat, 4pm-2am

Duke's Canoe Club Waikiki (8)

The Outrigger Waikiki Hotel, 2335 Kalakaua Ave, Honolulu, Oahu, HI 96815
T 808 922 2268

For a classic Waikiki experience, sit at the outdoor bar at Duke's Canoe Club Waikiki. It has a small draught list (but features Kona beers), a good bottle selection and great people-watching. It is truly amazing what visitors will wear to a beach when they are safely out of their own habitat.

Opening hours: daily

LuLu's Surf Club (9)

2586 Kalakaua Ave, Waikiki, HI, 96815
T 808 926 5222

Another venue with a stunning view, this time of the Diamond Head Crater and Waikiki Beach.

Opening hours: daily, 7am-4am

BEER AND FOOD

Brew Moon Restaurant and Microbrewery (10)

1200 Ala Moana Blvd, Honolulu, HI, 96814
T (808) 593 0088
www.brewmoon.com

A stylish eatery in the Ward Centre shopping centre with an extensive menu from pupus (small bites) to heavier entrées.

Opening hours: Sun-Thu, 11am-11pm; Fri & Sat, 11am-2am

Recommendation
The beers are on the lighter side but be sure to check out the **Black Hole Lager** *German-style Schwarz bier that took a Gold Medal at the 2002 World Beer Cup competition.*

Buzz's Original Steak House (11)

413 Kawailoa Rd, Kailua, HI, 96734
T 808 261 4661
www.buzzssteakhouse.com

Surf and turf is the order of the day here, specifically Kiawe grilled steak. Apparently Clinton has dined here.

Opening hours: daily 11am-3pm, 5pm-9pm

Jameson's by the Sea (12)

62-540 Kamehameha Hwy, Haleiwa, HI, 96712
T 808 637 6272
www.jamesonshawaii.com

A decked open-air dining area proves the perfect place to enjoy fresh seafood and ocean views.

Opening hours: Mon-Fri, 11am-9:30pm; Sat & Sun, 9am-9:30pm

Murphy's Bar & Grill (13)

2 Merchant Street, Honolulu, HI, 96813
T 808 531 0422

Smart and friendly venue popular with locals, tourists and sports fans. The food is standard pub grub.

Opening hours: daily, 11:30am-2:30pm, 5pm-10pm

Ryan's Grill at Ward Centre (14)

1200 Ala Moana Blvd., Honolulu, HI, 96814
T 808 591 9132

Family-friendly restaurant, excellent for beers, appetisers and some decent pupu.

Opening hours: Mon-Sat, 11:15am-2am; Sun, 10:30am-2am

Sam Choy's Big Aloha Brewery (15)

580 N. Nimitz Highway, Honolulu, HI, 96817
T 808 545 7979
www.samchoy.com

This is a vast warehouse-sized enterprise offering large portions of excellent food, great service and yet another brewing programme that can and does produce some excellent beers. Stick to the local fish, char siu (Chinese barbecue), baby back ribs, or Sam's special fried poke (flash-fried tuna).

Opening hours: daily, 10.30am-10pm

Yard House (16)

226 Lewers St, Honolulu, HI, 96815
T 808 923-9273
www.yardhouse.com

It's a Yard House so you'll know what you're getting but it does showcase a number of West Coast beers. Worth checking out if you're struggling elsewhere.

Opening hours: daily, 11am-1am

Maui

Maui is the second largest of the Hawaiian islands, made up of two volcanoes attached by an isthmus. The old whaling town of Lahaina offers plenty of restaurants and pubs as well as many tourist attractions. Three smaller islands, Lanai, Kahoolawe and Molokai (famed for its leper colony), complete the Maui group. Christian missionaries were a part of the westernisation of Maui in the early eighteenth century, bringing new world contributions of hygiene and written language and eradicating disapproved-of customs such as dancing the hula and not wearing clothes.

Maui has some stunning scenery and spectacular resorts. The more adventurous might consider going on a bike tour, perhaps even cycling down the Haleakala volcano. Riding up it is not recommended.

BREWERY

Maui Brewing Co. (17)
910 Honoapiilani Highway #55, Lahaina, Maui, HI, 96761
T 877 MAUI-BREW
Brewpub: Kahana Gateway Center, Honoapiilani Highway, Lahaina, HI, 96761
T 808 669 3474
www.mauibrewingco.com

After your strenuous outdoor activities, grab a pint at the Maui Brewing Company brewpub in Lahaina. This very popular restaurant also brews its own beer and has some ales you wouldn't expect to find in the tropics. In addition to the Bikini Blonde Lager and Maui Pale Ale, check out the Big Swell IPA (also available in cans) which is assertively hopped and delicious – one not to be missed by hopheads. A variety of other Maui beer including a Belgian Abbey Ale, Mana Belgian Wheat, Double Overhead IPA, Dunkel Weizen and Mai Bock can be found at various times of the year.

Not far from this brewpub is the company's microbrewery and canning facility. Maui Brewing beers are available in pubs and hotel bars around the island and also throughout the Hawaiian Island chain.

Brewpub opening hours: daily, 11:30am-12:30am
Brewery/tasting room: call for information
Recommendation
The **CoCoNut PorTeR** *(their caps)* **(5.7%)** *is simply wonderful and speaks of indigenous ingredients (also available in cans).*

Hawaii (Big Island)

The Island of Hawaii has the highest number of active volcanoes in the island chain. The Big Island gets its name from its 4,000 square miles of land mass – it is larger than all the other islands combined – yet it has less than half the population of Honolulu.

The county seat is Hilo on the windward side, set amid lush tropical rainforests and macadamia plantations. On the leeward side is the town of Kailua Kona, the population centre of the more arid and rocky volcanic region dotted with luxury resorts and snorkelling beaches. Looming between them are the twin volcanic mountains of Mauna Loa and Kilauea as well as the extinct volcano Mauna Kea – these make up the Hawaii Volcanoes National Park. Mauna Kea would be the tallest mountain in the world if measured from its base at the bottom of the ocean. The southern tip of the island is an active volcanic lava flow and is the southernmost part of US territory.

BREWERIES

Kona Brewing Company   (18)
75-5629 Kuakini Highway, Kailua Kona, HI, 96740
T 808 334 1133
www.konabrewingco.com

Kona Brewing Company has been around since 1994, providing fresh Kona beer to its own pub next to the brewery and to a satellite pub in Honolulu. Kona beer can also be found throughout the islands and increasingly in bottles in the US where it is produced in Portland, Oregon.

At the pub expect to find up to a dozen different brews at any one time. Bottles include the flagship Longboard Island Lager, a slightly hoppy Pilsener; Fire Rock Pale Ale, a crisp, citrus, copper-coloured pale ale; Big Wave Golden Ale, a blond ale with nice balance; the rich and roasty Pipeline Porter made with 100% Kona coffee; and the limited release Wailua Wheat. The restaurants feature signature gourmet oven-baked pizza, great salads and fresh fish. Live local music makes Kona a beer-lover's destination of choice.

Brewery tours: Mon-Fri, 10:30am & 3pm

Opening hours: Sun-Thu, 11am-10pm; Fri & Sat, 11am-11pm

Recommendation

The **Wailua Wheat** (5.4%) *is a light, crisp ale brewed with tropical passion fruit.*

Mehana Brewing Company (19)

275 East Kawili Street, Hilo, HI, 96720

T 808 934 8211

www.mehana.com

Situated in an old canning and bottling facility, Mehana's beers can be found around the Big Island and at pubs and retailers throughout the Islands. Beers include Hawaii Lager, smooth with lots of body; Mauna Kea Pale Ale, a northwest-style pale and Humpback Blue Beer, an oddly named Hawaiian-style Kölsch.

Opening hours: call ahead

Recommendations

The **Volcano Red Ale**, *a full-bodied amber;* **Roy's Private Reserve Beer** (4.9%), *a milder version of the amber with a slightly nutty flavour.*

BEER AND FOOD

Huggo's On The Rocks (20)

75-5828 Kahakai Road, Kailua-Kona, HI 96740

T 808 329 1493

www.huggos.com

A bit of tiki tiki by the beach, served with a little light Hawaiian grub.

Opening hours: Mon-Sun, from 11.30am

Jameson's by the Sea (21)

77-6452 Ali'i Drive, Kailua-Kona, HI, 96740

T 808 329 3195

www.jamesonshawaii.com

Great sea views, decent tucker and Kona beers.

Opening hours: Mon-Fri, 11am-9pm

LuLu's (22)

75-5819 Ali'i Drive, Kailua Kona, HI, 96740-1311

T 808 331 2633

www.lulushawaii.com

'Dancing' is even listed in the opening hours, which is quite a special thing. More of the same from Lulu's: snack-style food, beer and views, with plenty of fun by night.

Opening hours: restaurant 11am-10pm, bar 11am-1:30am; dancing Thu, 9pm-1:30am; Fri & Sat, 10pm-1:30am.

Huggo's On The Rocks – a bit of tiki tiki by the beach

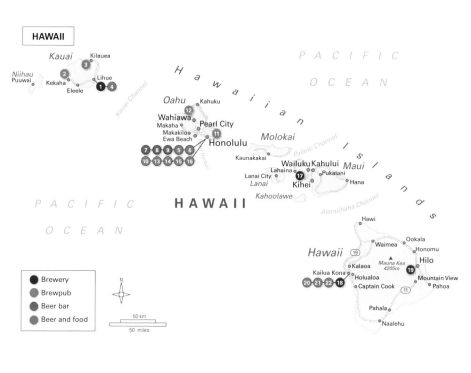

HAWAII

Kauai
Niihau
Puuwai
Kekaha
Eleele
Kilauea
Lihue

Oahu
Kahuku
Wahiawa
Makaha
Makakilo
Ewa Beach
Pearl City
Honolulu

PACIFIC OCEAN

Hawaiian Islands

Molokai
Kaunakakai

Lanai
Lanai City
Lahaina
Wailuku Kahului
Maui
Pukalani
Kihei
Hana

Kahoolawe

PACIFIC OCEAN

HAWAII

Hawi
Waimea
Ookala
Honomu
Hawaii
Kalaoa
Mauna Kea 4205m
Hilo
Kailua Kona
Holualoa
Mountain View
Captain Cook
Pahoa
Pahala
Naalehu

● Brewery
● Brewpub
● Beer bar
● Beer and food

N

50 km
50 miles

The best places to ...

Enjoy the view

Belmont Brewing Company, *Long Beach, California, page 85*
Elliot Glacier Public House, *Oregon, page 184*
Full Sail, *Hood River, Oregon, page 185*
Pelican Pub & Brewery, *Pacific City, Oregon, page 187*
San Juan Brewing Company, *Washington, page 248*
Sirens, *Port Townsend, Washington, page 181*

Go surfing

Beach Chalet, *San Francisco, California, page 110*
Half Moon Bay Brewing, *California, page 98*
Liars Club, *San Diego, California, page 68*
Pizza Port, *San Clemente, California, page 76*
Red Bar & Restaurant, *Santa Cruz, California, page 99*

Match beer & food

Bar Crudo, *San Francisco, California, page 115*
Bouchon, *Santa Barbara, California, page 175*
Higgins, *Portland, Oregon, page 174*
The Linkery, *San Diego, California, page 71*
Rosemary's, *Las Vegas, page 257*
Thirsty Bear, *San Francisco, California, page 111*

Gorge on beer & pizza

Laurelhurst, *Portland, Oregon, page 176*
Laurelwood, *Portland, Oregon, page 164*
Pizza Port, *California, page 64*
Russian River, *Santa Rosa, page 142-143*
Stellar, *Seattle, Washington, page 236*

Grab a beer & sandwich

Belmont Station, *Portland, Oregon, page 172*
The Bier Stein, *Eugene, Oregon, page 195*
Hollingshead's Deli, *Orange, California, page 77*

Pix Patisserie, *Portland, Oregon, page 179*
Stuffed Sandwich, *Los Angeles, California, page 86*

Drink in a brewpub

21st Amendment, *San Francisco, California, page 110*
Boundary Bay, *Washington, page 245*
Diamond Knot, *Washington, page 246*
Elysian, *Washington, page 222*
Magnolia, *San Francisco, California, page 111*

Enjoy a beer in wine country

Firestone Walker, *San Luis Obispo, California, page 94*
Golden Valley, *McMinnville, Oregon, page 188*
Lagunitas, *Petaluma, California, page 128*
The Original Spike's, *San Luis Obispo, California, page 93*

Experience a dive vibe

Basement Pub, *Portland, Oregon, page 172*
Blue Moon, *Seattle, Washington, page 233*
Buckaroo, *Seattle, Washington, page 228*
Clinton Street Pub, *Portland, Oregon, page 173*
Goat Hill Tavern, *Costa Mesa, California, page 77*
Hamiltons' Tavern, *San Diego, California, page 67*
Liars Club, *San Diego, California, page 68*
Lucky 13, *San Francisco, California, page 114*
Sam Bonds Garage, *Eugene, Oregon, page 197*
Toronado, *San Francisco, California, page 114*

Try Belgian beers

Brouwer's, *Seattle, Washington, page 228*
Higgins, *Portland, Oregon page 175*
Lucky Baldwins, *Pasadena, California, page 85*
O'Brien's, *Santa Monica, California, page 69*
Stumbling Monk, *Seattle, Washington, page 227*

left Enjoy a beer in a brewery: Sierra Nevada Brewing Company, Chico, California (*see page 130*)

Drink extreme beer

AleSmith Brewing, *San Diego, California, page 55*
Lost Abbey, *San Marcos, California, page 60*
Rogue Brewing, *Newport, Oregon, page 190–191*
Russian River Brewing, *Santa Rosa, California, page 142*
Stone Brewing, *Escondido, California, page 56*

Enjoy a beer in a brewery

Alpine Brewing, *Alpine, California, page 55*
Island Brewing, *Carpinteria, California, page 90*
Lost Abbey, *San Marcos, California, page 60*
Sierra Nevada Brewing Company, *Chico, California, page 130*
Stone Brewing, *Escondido, California, page 56*

Drink alfresco

Anderson Valley, *Boonville, California, page 126*
Beach Chalet, *San Francisco, California, page 110*

Edgefield McMenamins, *Troutdale, Oregon, page 184*
Naja's Place, *Redondo Beach, California, page 77*
Walking Man, *Stevenson, Washington, page 243*

Take a date

The 3rd Stop, *Los Angeles, California, page 88*
Bouchon, *Santa Barbara, California, page 98*
Novo, *San Luis Obispo, California, page 99*
Standing Stone, *Ashland, Oregon, page 200*

Drink in memorable surroundings

Acropolis *(adults only), Portland, Oregon, page 171*
Apotheke, *Portland, Oregon, page 171*
Cameron's English Pub, *Half Moon Bay, California, page 94*
Maiden Publick House, *Big Sur, California, page 97*
Wanker's Corner Saloon, *Wilsonville, Oregon, page 188*

Drink in memorable surroundings: Maiden Publik House, Big Sur, California (*see page 97*)

American beer stores in the US

If you've been on the road all day and discover the motel's pay-per-view channels are hotwired for free access – all night long – you might decide the option of a few take-out beers is more appealing. Equally, having read this book, you should probably conclude that turning up to a friend's for dinner with a six pack that doesn't challenge the taste buds is a proper faux pas.

Don't fear though, since much of the West Coast has embraced the craft revolution and due to this you can find at least one or two of the more widely distributed American craft beers in many liquor stores, markets and even gas stations.

If you're looking to buy in for the evening then the local and brewery will sell you a take-home selection, but if you're hoping for more diversity then get yourself online and try and locate the nearest Whole Foods, www.wholefoodsmarket.com, where there's usually an eclectic mix. Beverages & More! is another with plenty of locations, www.bevmo.com.

Also, keep an eye out for one of the many sandwich stores listed in our book – these provide the most amazing ranges of beers. Belmont Station is among them and there's a reminder below, but if you're in a particular town check the local sources listed.

Elsewhere you might want to run in to one of the stores listed below if you see them:

California

City Beer Store
1168 Folsom Street, San Francisco, CA 94103
T 415 503 1033

Mesa Liquor & Wine Co.
4919 Convoy Street, San Diego, CA 92111
T 619 279-5292

Pine Cove Bottle Shop
29th & E, Sacramento, CA 95814
T 916 447-4070

Ray's Liquor
207 Walnut St., Chico, CA 95928
T 530 343-3249

Wally's Liquors
2107 Westwood Blvd., Los Angeles, CA 90025
T 310 475-0606   www.wallywine.com

Las Vegas

Lee's Discount Liquor
3480 E. Flamingo Road, Las Vegas, NV 89121
T 702 458-5700

Oregon

Belmont Station
4500 SE Stark St. Portland, OR 97215
T 503 232 8538

Washington

Bottleworks
1710 North 45th, Suite number 3, Seattle WA 98103
T 206 633 BIER

American beer in the UK

If you're after a sample of some of the West Coast beers when you're back at home in the UK, then the most likely breeds you'll stumble across are Anchor Steam and Sierra Nevada Pale Ale. These beers are growing in popularity in the UK and as a result can be found in some of the better bars and pubs across the country, at the occasional market and in selected supermarkets.

If you're in the trade there are also a few specialist importers bringing them in and in this section we've put together a few details on who to contact and where to go.

There are a host of other American craft beers on sale at some of these venues, Brooklyn and Goose Island also being quite fashionable. But they're from New York and Chicago respectively and this is a West Coast title. So, while these are splendid brews, you'll have to wait until our yet-to-be-commissioned East and Central guides to learn more about them.

We've listed the draught establishments when it comes to pubs and obviously supermarkets etc will stock the bottles. As with everything we list, these are subject to change so please contact the distributors if you seek confirmation.

Pubs

Anchor Steam
Distributed by James Clay. **www.beersolutions.co.uk**

LONDON
All Star Lanes, *Bayswater and Holborn, London*

NORTH
Devonshire Cat, *49 Wellington Street, Sheffield*
Fly in the Loaf, *35A Hardman Street, Liverpool*
Reform, *12-14 Merrion Street, Leeds*
Trof, *2A Landcross Road, Manchester*

SCOTLAND
Anderson, *Union Street, Fortrose, nr. Inverness*
Republic Bier Halle, *9 Gordon Street, Glasgow*

Sierra Nevada Pale Ale
Distributed by Vertical Drinks. **www.verticaldrinks.com**

LONDON
Devonshire Arms, *37 Marloes Road, Kensington*
The Green Man, *36 Riding House Street, Fitzrovia*
Micro Bar, *14 Lavender Hill*
The Rake, *14 Winchester Walk, Borough Market*
White Horse, *1-3 Parsons Green*

WEST
Coltson Yard, *Colston Street, Bristol*

MIDLANDS
Flores, *14 King Street, Leicester*

NORTH
Alberts Bar, *49-51 Parliament Street, Harrogate*
The Cornerhouse, *70 Oxford Street, Manchester*
North Bar, *24 New Briggate, Leeds*
Pivo, *Patrick Pool, York*
Thomas Rigby's, *23-25 Dale Street, Liverpool*
Trof, *2A Landcross Road, Manchester*

Supermarkets & Stores

Harvey Nicholls
House of Fraser wine departments
Peckham and Rye, *Glasgow and Edinburgh*
Sainsbury's
Selfridges
Tesco
Utobeer, *Borough Market*
Waitrose

Online

Ale Cellar	wwwalecellar.com
Beer Here	www.beerhere.co.uk
BeerRitz	www.beerritz.co.uk
Beers of Europe	www.beersofeurope.co.uk
Onlyfinebeer	www.onlyfinebeer.co.uk
The Beer Shop	www.pitfieldbeershop.co.uk
Utobeer	www.utobeer.co.uk

Index of beers

General index and venues

Acknowledgements and bibliography

Bibliography

We used many reference materials during our research. Some of the most helpful books were *Ambitious Brew* by Maureen Ogle (a great history of American beer); *Beer Blast* by Philip Van Munching; *Travels with Barley : A Journey Through Beer Culture in America* by Ken Wells; *Fugitives and Refugees* by Chuck Palahniuk; *Life, Liberty and the Pursuit of Happiness: Social History of the United States of America in Documents* by Joan Chandler; *The Growth of The American Republic*, by Samuel Eliot Morison, Henry Steele Commager and William E. Leuchtenburg and *The Free and The Unfree, A New History of the United States* by Peter N. Carroll and David W. Noble.

We also found **beeradvocate.com**, **beermapping.com** and **ratebeer.com** to be invaluable resources as well as *Celebrator Beer News*, *Northwest Brewing News* and, don't tell anyone, **Wikipedia.com**. We also called upon many newspaper and online sources – far too many to list.

Ben and Tom's Acknowledgements

Alas, space and time doesn't allow for an exhaustive list of everyone who came to the aid of two clueless, booze-addled limey buffoons but we'd like to raise a special glass to those who did.

The first casualty of this pesky tome has been our livers, swiftly followed by our collective memory. So, sincere apologies if we've not mentioned you by name but you know who you are.

First of all, Ben and Tom are enormously grateful to all the marvellous folk who make up the West coast's craft beer community. Without their infectious enthusiasm, assistance and advice, we simply couldn't have written this book. So don't blame us, blame the following (in no particular order): Bob Barnes in Las Vegas for steering us through the bright lights and jet-lag; the terrific Dave McLean, Shaun O'Sullivan, Ron Silberstein, Allan Paul, the Fulgonis and all at the San Francisco Brewers Guild for going beyond the call of duty and gently wiping the dribble from our weary chins; Fritz Maytag for great beer and meteorological enlightenment; all the Double IPA worshippers at the Bistro in Hayward for loosening our limp grip on reality; Chris Crabb for being brilliant in every way; Tom Nickel and the San Diego Brewers Guild; Greg Koch; Tomme Arthur; Tom McCormick; Lisa Morrison; Fred Eckhardt; Adam Lambert and Jack Joyce for their generosity and insight into the "real" Portland; the Oregon Brewers Guild; Matt Marino; David Meisels (sorry pal – we owe you a pint); Adin Wener for lending us his stash of mags; the inspirational Ken Grossman; Alec Moss (you still haven't sent us the "other" swimwear shots); Renee Rank and the McMenamin Brothers; the Brewers Association; Don Barkley; Vinnie Cilurzo; Don Younger; Paul Wright; Ralph and Ralph at Hop Union; David Farnworth; Mark Jilg; Jay Porter; Rick Smets; Matt Brynildson; Alastair Hook for introducing us to the joys of American beer; the legend that is Michael Jackson for broadening beer drinking horizons; the erudite endeavours of Glenn Scoggins and Bruce Paton; Thomas Dalldorf and James 'Dr Fermento' Roberts whose hard work and terrific words saved our British bacon and are really, really very much appreciated; and every brewer, bartender, bar owner, beer writer and dedicated beer-loving elbow-bender that we were fortunate enough to meet on our travels.

Beyond the world of beer, Ben & Tom would like to give a big thank you to the following: Susan, Alex and Katie Karras; Katie Francis @ Virgin (other airlines are available); Steve Atkinson of KGTV 10 News; the law enforcement communities of California, Oregon and Washington for their kind clemency; any motorist we happened to offend/injure; all the boys at "Lube It USA" in Eugene (wonderful, wonderful men ...each and every one); Russell Brand & Matt Morgan for making us laugh. A lot; all the helpful tourist boards; the Marine Corps of San Clemente (you boys were THIS close to waking up with a crowd around you); Chrysler for making the world's campest car; Maker's Mark for providing inspirational respite from the beer; an obscure strain of Shingles for not hurting too much and, lest we forget (and we won't), the jazz-scatting, back-seat burrito-munching (no eggs), ale-quaffing companion that was Glenn Payne – thanks for all your help buddy.

We owe an enormous thanks to Maureen & Leo, Heidi (the bar dream lives on!), Matthias, Andrea & Steve, Leopold & Max, Madelyn & Dana and Sophie & Henrietta (the finest pair of asses on the West Coast) – all for being utterly brilliant, and massively generous in letting us stay for so long – it was great fun and we're hugely thankful.

We'd also like to give a thrusting "poke" to all the Facebookers who joined our group. Don't just read this in the shop, take it up to the counter and buy it. Please. And a massive pat on the back to Dale, Ione, Leon and Simon at CAMRA for their patience, hard work and forgiveness.

Ben's Acknowledgements

A colossal thanks goes to all the following: Mum for all her love, proofing skills, emergency financial assistance and understanding during what were some rather daft and difficult times; my morale-boosting brother Barnaby whose unrelenting support and knack of making things seem much better really did make things much better; Dad for all his advice and encouragement; Tom and Hattie Deards – truly amazing friends who also put on a lovely spread; and Terry and Monkey for their invaluable editorial input and late night chats.

Thanks must also go to the following friends: Dallat and Sonya; Eddie and Zoe; James and Diane; Tom Innes; Deards' brother; QPR FC; all who play for the mighty Nottsborough FC and, nearly last but very much not least, Tom for being a hilarious and hard-working buddy and travel companion. Finally, I am especially grateful to the wonderful Lovely Lisa for all her encouragement and kindness.

Tom's Acknowledgements

A special thanks to Claire who suffered more than anyone during this process. Without your love and patience I couldn't have done it, you've been amazing throughout and I promise we'll get our lives back now it's over.

A massive thanks to Mum and Dad as well – for continuing support both financially and emotionally. I wouldn't even be a writer without your help. And brother and sister, Edward and Ellen – you'll see more of me in the pub now it's done.

Family friends Nuala and Joe, Joan and Colin and many more. All of Claire's family as well, thanks for the fantastic support, and Claire's friends – she really does have a boyfriend. Mr Clarke and Heather, who witnessed some of the hardship, and other pals who formed my warped humour: Steve, Seamus, Ben, Liam, Alex, Waitey, Tait, Bickley, Rob, Chorne and Collins, Siobhan and NCTJ-ers; the Dudley massive; Justin and all at Alchemy Media who made it possible to take time off; the John Brown Publishing crowd; and Richard Knight and Andy Lines for my start in journalism.

And, of course, co-author Ben – despite the occasional moan it was an adventure and I laughed a lot. At you. Thanks for getting me involved.

CONTRIBUTORS

TOM DALLDORF is editor and publisher of the *Celebrator Beer News*, a national publication based in the San Francisco Bay Area. He was a wine merchant and wine judge from 1979–1989 before seeing the light that true beer can bring to a life. He has travelled extensively in the beer capitals of the world tasting beer, writing about it and photographing his experiences. You can find out more about the *Celebrator* at **celebrator.com**.

Dr. FERMENTO is the alter ego of *Anchorage Press* and *Celebrator Beer News* beer columnist James Roberts. In July of 2007, he surpassed his 10th year and 500th weekly column with the Press and his fourth year with the Celebrator. His singular writing objective is "To make people thirsty for good beer." He lives and drinks in Alaska.

Books for Beer lovers

CAMRA Books, the publishing arm of the Campaign for Real Ale, is the leading publisher of books on beer and pubs. Key titles include:

300 Beers To Try Before You Die!

ROGER PROTZ

300 beers from around the world, handpicked by award-winning journalist, author and broadcaster Roger Protz to try before you die! A comprehensive portfolio of top beers from the smallest microbreweries in the United States to family-run British breweries and the world's largest brands. This book is indispensable for both beer novices and aficionados.

£14.99   ISBN 978 1 85249 213 7

Good Beer Guide

Editor: ROGER PROTZ

The *Good Beer Guide* is the only guide you will need to find the right pint, in the right place, every time. It's the original and the best independent guide to around 4,500 pubs and more than 600 breweries throughout the UK. In 2002 it was named as one of the *Guardian* newspapers books of the year and the *Sun* newspaper rated the 2004 edition in the top 20 books of all time! This annual publication is a comprehensive and informative guide to the best real ale pubs in the UK, researched and written exclusively by CAMRA members and fully updated every year.

£14.99   ISBN 978 1 85249 231 1

CAMRA's London Pub Walks

BOB STEEL

A practical pocket-sized guide enabling you to explore the English capital, whilst never being far away from a decent pint. It includes 30 walks around more than 180 pubs serving fine real ale, from the heart of the City and bustling West End to majestic riverside routes and the leafy Wimbledon Common, with each pub selected for its high-quality real ale, its location and its superb architectural heritage. The walks feature more pubs than any other London pub-walk guide.

£8.99   ISBN 978 1 85249 216 8

Good Beer Guide Prague & The Czech Republic

EVAN RAIL

This fully updated and expanded version of a collectible classic is the first new edition to be published by CAMRA for 10 years! It is the definitive guide for visitors to the Czech Republic and compulsory reading for fans of great beer, featuring more than 100 Czech breweries, 400 different beers and over 100 great places to try them. It includes listings of brewery-hotels and regional attractions for planning complete vacations outside of the capital, sections on historical background, how to get there and what to expect, as well as detailed descriptions of the 12 most common Czech beer styles.

£12.99   ISBN 978 1 85249 233 5

Good Beer Guide Germany

STEVE THOMAS

The first ever comprehensive region-by-region guide to Germany's brewers, beer and outlets. Includes more than 1,200 breweries, 1,000 brewery taps and bars and more than 7,200 different beers. Complete with useful travel information on how to get there, informative essays on German beer and brewing plus beer festival listings.

£16.99   ISBN 978 1 85249 219 9

Good Beer Guide Belgium

TIM WEBB

Now in its 5th edition and in full colour, this book has developed a cult following among committed beer lovers and beer tourists. It is the definitive, totally independent guide to understanding and finding the best of Belgian beer and an essential companion for any beer drinker visiting Belgium or seeking out Belgian beer in Britain. Includes details of the 120 breweries and over 800 beers in regular production, as well as 500 of the best hand-picked cafes in Belgium.

£12.99   ISBN 978 1 85249 210 6

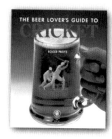

Beer Lover's Guide to Cricket
ROGER PROTZ

There are many books about cricket and many on beer, but this is the first book to bring the two subjects together. Leading beer writer and cricket enthusiast Roger Protz has visited the major grounds of all the First Class counties and gives in-depth profiles of them – their history, museums, and memorabilia, plus listings of the best real ale pubs to visit within easy reach of each ground and details of the cask ales available. This fully illustrated book also features individual sections on the birth of the modern game of cricket and the history of each featured ground, making it an essential purchase for any cricket fan.

£16.99   ISBN 978 1 85249 227 4

Beer, Bed & Breakfast
SUSAN NOWAK AND JILL ADAM

A unique and comprehensive guide to more than 500 of the UK's real ale pubs that also offer great accommodation, from tiny inns with a couple of rooms upstairs to luxury gastro-pubs with country-house style bedrooms. All entries include contact details, type and extent of accommodation, beers served, meal types and times, and an easy-to-understand price guide to help plan your budget. This year, why not stay somewhere with a comfortable bed, a decent breakfast and a well-kept pint of beer, providing a home from home wherever you are in the country.

£14.99   ISBN 978 1 85249 230 4

The Book of Beer Knowledge
JEFF EVANS

A unique collection of entertaining trivia and essential wisdom, this is the perfect gift for beer lovers everywhere. Fully revised and updated it includes more than 200 entries covering everything from the fictional 'celebrity landlords' of soap pubs to the harsh facts detailing the world's biggest brewers; from bizarre beer names to the serious subject of fermentation.

£9.99   ISBN 978 1 85249 198 7

An Appetite For Ale

FIONA BECKETT/WILL BECKETT

A beer and food revolution is under way in Britain and award-winning food writer Fiona Beckett and her publican son, Will, have joined forces to write the first cookbook to explore this exciting new food phenomenon that celebrates beer as a culinary tour de force. This collection of more than 100 simple and approachable recipes has been specially created to show the versatility and fantastic flavour that ale has to offer. With sections on Snacks, Spreads and Dips, Soups, Pasta and Risotto, Seafood, Chicken and other Birds, Meat Feasts, Spicy Foods, Bread and Cheese and Sweet Treats it provides countless ideas for using beer from around the world. With an open mind, a bottle opener and a well-stocked larder, this exciting book will allow you to enjoy real food, real ale and real flavour.

£16.99   ISBN 978 1 85249 234 2

Fuzzy Logic

TOM WAINE

A completely dispensable collection of intriguing nonsense devised or overheard in the pub, compiled and created by regular pub goer Tom Waine. Whether you experience a light-bulb moment while downing a swift half or think you have discovered the meaning of life while imbibing your favourite session beer, this book is packed full of smart ideas, fully-formed theories, unanswered questions – and sheer rubbish. Fuzzy Logic could well leave you entertained, amused and educated for longer than it takes to down a pint.

£9.99   ISBN 978 1 85249 232 8

BOOKS

Order these and other CAMRA books online at
www.camra.org.uk/books,
ask at your local bookstore, or contact:
CAMRA, 230 Hatfield Road, St Albans, AL1 4LW.
Telephone 01727 867201

It takes all sorts to Campaign for Real Ale

CAMRA, the Campaign for Real Ale, is an independent not-for-profit, volunteer-led consumer group. We actively campaign for full pints and more flexible licensing hours, as well as protecting the 'local' pub and lobbying government to champion pub-goers' rights.

CAMRA has 89,000 members from all ages and backgrounds, brought together by a common belief in the issues that CAMRA deals with and their love of good quality British beer. For just £20 a year, that's less than a pint a month, you can join CAMRA and enjoy the following benefits:

A monthly colour newspaper informing you about beer and pub news and detailing events and beer festivals around the country.

Free or reduced entry to over 140 national, regional and local beer festivals.

Money off many of our publications including the *Good Beer Guide* and the *Good Bottled Beer Guide*.

Access to a members-only section of our national website, **www.camra.org.uk** which gives up-to-the-minute news stories and includes a special offer section with regular features saving money on beer and trips away.

The opportunity to campaign to save pubs under threat of closure, for pubs to be open when people want to drink and a reduction in beer duty that will help Britain's brewing industry survive.

Log onto **www.camra.org.uk** for up-to-date CAMRA membership prices and information

CAMPAIGN
FOR
REAL ALE

Do you feel passionately about your pint? Then why not join CAMRA

Just fill in the application form (or a photocopy of it) and the Direct Debit form on the next page to receive three months' membership FREE!*

If you wish to join but do not want to pay by Direct Debit, fill in the application form below and send a cheque, payable to CAMRA to: CAMRA, 230 Hatfield Road, St Albans, Hertfordshire, AL1 4LW. Please note that non Direct Debit payments will incur a £2 surcharge. Figures are given below.

Current rate	Direct Debit	Non DD
☐ Single Membership (UK & EU)	£20	£22
☐ Concessionary Membership (under 26 or 60 and over)	£11	£13
☐ Joint membership	£25	£27
☐ Concessionary Joint membership	£14	£16

Life membership information is available on request.

Title _____ Surname _____ Forename(s) _____

Address _____

_____ Post Code _____

Date of Birth _____ E-mail address _____

Signature _____

Partner's details if required

Title _____ Surname _____ Forename(s) _____

Date of Birth _____ E-mail address _____

CAMRA will occasionally send you e-mails related to your membership. We will also allow your local branch access to your e-mail if you would like to opt-out of contact from your local branch please tick here ☐ (at no point will your details be released to a third party)

Find out more about CAMRA at **www.camra.org.uk**

*Three months free is only available the first time a member pays by DD.

CAMPAIGN FOR REAL ALE

Instruction to your Bank or Building Society to pay by Direct Debit

DIRECT Debit

Please fill in the form and send to: Campaign for Real Ale Ltd. 230 Hatfield Road, St. Albans, Herts. AL1 4LW

Name and full postal address of your Bank or Building Society

To The Manager	Bank or Building Society

Address

Postcode

Name (s) of Account Holder (s)

Bank or Building Society account number

Branch Sort Code

Reference Number

Banks and Building Societies may not accept Direct Debit Instructions for some types of account

Originator's Identification Number

9	2	6	1	2	9

FOR CAMRA OFFICIAL USE ONLY
This is not part of the instruction to your **Bank or Building Society**

Membership Number

Name

Postcode

Instruction to your Bank or Building Society

Please pay CAMRA Direct Debits from the account detailed on this Instruction subject to the safeguards assured by the Direct Debit Guarantee. I understand that this instruction may remain with CAMRA and, if so, will be passed electronically to my Bank/Building Society

Signature(s)

Date

✂ detached and retained this section

DIRECT Debit

This Guarantee should be detached and retained by the payer.

The Direct Debit Guarantee

- This Guarantee is offered by all Banks and Building Societies that take part in the Direct Debit Scheme. The efficiency and security of the Scheme is monitored and protected by your own Bank or Building Society.

- If the amounts to be paid or the payment dates change CAMRA will notify you 10 working days in advance of your account being debited or as otherwise agreed.

- If an error is made by CAMRA or your Bank or Building Society, you are guaranteed a full and immediate refund from your branch of the amount paid.

- You can cancel a Direct Debit at any time by writing to your Bank or Building Society. Please also send a copy of your letter to us.